Principles and Applications of Blockchain Systems

IEEE Press
445 Hoes Lane
Piscataway, NJ 08854

Principles and Applications of Blockchain Systems

How to Overcome the CAP Trilemma in Consortium Blockchain

Hui Li
Peking University
China

Han Wang
Peking University
China

IEEE Press
WILEY

Published by John Wiley & Sons, Inc., Hoboken, New Jersey.
Published simultaneously in Canada.

Library of Congress Cataloging-in-Publication Data is applied for:

Hardback ISBN 9781394237227

Cover Design: Wiley
Cover Image: © Yuichiro Chino/Getty Images

Set in 9.5/12.5pt STIXTwoText by Straive, Pondicherry, India

Contents

Foreword by Peter Major

It is with great pleasure that I provide my heartfelt recommendation for the book, *Principles & Applications of Blockchain Systems: How to Overcome the CAP Trilemma in Consortium Blockchain*. As the Vice-Chairman of the United Nations Commission on Science and Technology for Development (CSTD) and the Founding Chairman of the World Digital Technology Academy (WDTA), my commitment lies in fostering sustainable development within the digital economy.

In this digital age, ensuring the trustworthy exchange of digital assets and effective governance of cyberspace stands as a paramount objective. Blockchain technology is a fundamental tool in establishing digital trust and advancing the digital economy. However, it faces a significant challenge known as the CAP trilemma, which restricts the simultaneous achievement of strong consistency, high availability, and partition fault tolerance within distributed systems. This book skillfully expounds upon the core principles of blockchain technology, empowering readers to gain a comprehensive understanding of the CAP trilemma. Furthermore, the author presents an innovative and unprecedented solution that provides both theoretical and practical support for consortium blockchains, effectively resolving the CAP trilemma conundrum.

I firmly believe that the benefits of digital technology and economic achievements should be accessible to all individuals. Beyond addressing the CAP trilemma, this book delves into essential concepts such as Web3, multilateral governance of cyberspace, DAO, DID, the digital economy, and digital assets. Web3 signifies the future direction of the Internet, paving the way for a more open, transparent, and secure network environment through decentralization and blockchain technology. Governance of cyberspace emphasizes democratic, inclusive, and cooperative global cyber governance, empowering all stakeholders to participate collaboratively in decision-making and rule-making processes. DAO and DID, as significant applications of blockchain technology, embody the decentralized autonomy of organizations and personal identity, profoundly impacting the future of the digital economy and digital asset management.

The author, Prof. Hui Li, is a prominent expert in the field of blockchain at our WDTA organization, with impressive achievements in both research and practical applications. The works presented in this book offer valuable insights and serve as a source of inspiration for readers. Through a meticulous dissection of the principles and mechanisms underlying blockchain technology, this book presents an innovative solution that empowers consortium blockchains to overcome the CAP trilemma. Whether you are a newcomer intrigued by blockchain or an experienced professional, this book will provide you with a profound understanding of the subject matter and practical solutions to address the challenges at hand.

I hope that this book provides you with valuable insights into the utilization of blockchain technology and effective resolutions to the CAP trilemma. Let us join forces to drive sustainable development within the digital economy. By immersing yourself in this book, you will acquire a comprehensive grasp of the fundamental concepts and principles of blockchain technology, thereby offering robust support for your research and practical endeavors within the realm of the digital economy. May this book enrich your knowledge and serve as an abundant source of inspiration, empowering you to make positive contributions to the advancement of the digital economy.

Peter Major
Vice-Chairman,
United Nations Commission on Science and Technology for Development
Founding Chairman, World Digital Technology Academy

Foreword by Zhang Jing-an

In the current era of rapid development in the digital economy, the rise of blockchain technology has undoubtedly injected strong innovative momentum into various industries. With its unique attributes – decentralization, immutability, and high transparency – blockchain is profoundly reshaping our business models and data governance frameworks. Against this backdrop, the monograph "Principle and Applications of Blockchain Systems: How to Overcome the CAP Trilemma in Consortium Blockchain," authored by Prof. Hui Li and Dr. Han Wang from Peking University, arrives at a crucial moment. It systematically and deeply analyzes the foundational theoretical framework, core key technologies, and extensive practical applications of blockchain, making significant academic contributions and offering strategic insights for guiding policy practice.

This monograph not only systematically explains the core concepts of blockchain but also provides an in-depth analysis of key technologies such as consensus mechanisms, physical topology, and P2P networks. It builds a solid foundation for academic research while offering rigorous and practical references for policymakers. In particular, the book's profound examination of the CAP trilemma provides a fresh perspective on the limitations and challenges faced by blockchain technology in practical applications, which is vital for promoting healthy technological development.

The Chinese government places a high priority on the development of blockchain technology. Since 2019, Chinese leaders have repeatedly emphasized the strategic importance of blockchain, and relevant government departments have introduced a series of policies aimed at accelerating the deep integration and widespread application of blockchain in sectors such as finance, logistics, and healthcare. The timely publication of this monograph undoubtedly provides policymakers with rich theoretical nourishment and practical guidance, helping us better understand the potential and risks of blockchain technology while fostering a positive interaction between technological and social development.

Additionally, the monograph proactively addresses cutting-edge topics such as privacy protection, quantum computing, and cross-chain technology, showcasing the vast application prospects of blockchain. It offers valuable theoretical support and practical insights for exploring compliant application paths for blockchain under the evolving landscape of laws and regulations, ensuring data security and privacy protection.

I believe “Principle and Applications of Blockchain Systems: How to Overcome the CAP Trilemma in Consortium Blockchain” serves not only as a high-quality textbook for students and faculty in higher education but also as an important reference for researchers in technology policy and colleagues in the blockchain industry. I hope that readers will seize this opportunity to gain deeper insights into the essence of blockchain technology and boldly explore its application potential across various domains, collectively contributing wisdom and strength to promote the high-quality development of China’s digital economy and accelerate technological innovation. Let us work together, using this monograph as a key to unlock the doors to a new technological era and contribute to the scientific formulation and effective implementation of global technology policies.

Zhang Jing-an
Academician of the International Eurasian Academy
Secretary-General of the International Eurasian Academy (Beijing)
Chairman of the China Science and Technology System Reform Research Association
Former President of Science and Technology Daily
Former Secretary-General of the Ministry of Science and Technology of China.

Foreword by Yale Li

It is an honor to introduce this groundbreaking work, *Principles and Applications of Blockchain Systems: How to Overcome the CAP Trilemma in Consortium Blockchain*, authored by Prof. Hui Li and Dr. Han Wang. As the Chairman of the Cloud Security Alliance (CSA) Greater China Region and Executive Chairman of the World Digital Technology Academy (WDTA), I recognize the immense potential that blockchain technology presents, especially in the rapidly evolving domain of consortium blockchains. Blockchain technology has revolutionized the way we think about distributed systems, offering unprecedented levels of security, transparency, and efficiency.

However, blockchain is not without its challenges. The CAP trilemma – balancing Consistency, Availability, and Partition tolerance – has been a significant barrier to the widespread adoption of blockchain technology, particularly in large-scale, enterprise-level consortium blockchains. In this context, the authors delve deep into the theoretical and practical aspects of addressing this issue. In an interconnected Web3 era where decentralized applications are becoming the norm, their detailed focus on reliable physical networks and smart contract security is particularly noteworthy, providing invaluable guidance for developing robust and secure blockchain systems in the Web3 era.

Prof. Hui Li, with his extensive background in future networks, cyberspace security, and blockchain technology, has been a pioneer in the field. His contributions to the development of the highly secure Multi-Identifier Network (MIN) and his recognition as a leading figure in the international digital technology community underscore his authority on this subject.

Further, the exploration of CAP-solving cases, including a mimic secure storage system and a co-governed multi-identifier system, illustrates how combining consortium blockchain technologies can innovate distributed applications. This approach enhances data and user safety and reliability, offering new insights into efficient and secure blockchain systems, which are crucial for enterprise-level applications.

Lastly, the forward-thinking exploration of quantum blockchain technology and the CAP trilemma provides a glimpse into the future of blockchain. The unique advantages of quantum computing may offer revolutionary solutions to the traditional security challenges of distributed theory and blockchain systems, positioning this book at the cutting edge of technological advancements.

In summary, this book combines meticulous research with practical insights, making it a significant contribution to the field of blockchain technology. I am confident that it will serve as an indispensable guide for anyone looking to navigate the complexities and harness the full potential of consortium blockchains. This book is a valuable resource not only for students and academics but also for engineers and practitioners developing and implementing secure, scalable blockchain solutions without being limited by the CAP trilemma.

Prof. Yale Li
Executive Chairman, World Digital Technology Academy
Chairman, Cloud Security Alliance Greater China Region
Foreign Academician, Ukrainian Academy of Engineering Sciences

Foreword by Feng Han

In 2008, Satoshi Nakamoto introduced Bitcoin, a decentralized and self-operating electronic cash system. This innovation, powered by a distributed computing network, established a new global consensus on value and currency without relying on centralized control. Bitcoin is often considered the digital equivalent of gold, as its design prevents arbitrary currency creation and circumvents the need for centralized monetary authorities. At the time of writing, Bitcoin's market capitalization has surpassed two trillion dollars, reaching an all-time high. According to the Web3 industry consensus, Bitcoin is expected to continue its growth trajectory in the coming decades.

Building on Bitcoin's legacy, Ethereum introduced smart contracts in 2014, enabling programmable execution of economic protocols directly on the blockchain. This innovation allowed for the automation of complex agreements, further advancing the vision of decentralized, self-executing economic systems. In 2024, a group of Harvard students and alumni launched the New Bretton Woods (NBW) project, which then secured a student membership at Harvard Innovation Labs to advance the initiative independently. This project leverages Bitcoin-Elastos Layer 2 blockchain technology to expand the utility of the Bitcoin ecosystem. Integrating advancements in artificial intelligence, particularly large language models, with the NBW monetary framework, the team explores the intersection of AI and blockchain technology.

Central to their vision is the concept of "AI Kallipolis," inspired by Plato's Republic. The NBW team aims to develop a fully autonomous economic management AI agent capable of on-chain asset issuance, decentralized private key management, and full Decentralized Autonomous Organization (DAO) operations. The NBW project envisions a digital economic system free from human intervention, aligning with Friedrich Hayek's advocacy for an economy governed by conscience and consensus rather than an extractive central authority. This model aspires to promote universal values of openness, fairness, transparency, security, and freedom, potentially elevating human civilization to new levels of economic autonomy and equity.

The concept of computational power lies at the heart of artificial intelligence, a point widely acknowledged by scholars. This idea aligns with Leslie Gabriel Valiant's influential concept of the "ecorithm." Valiant, a Turing Award-winning computer scientist, introduced ecorithms as computational theories that explain how natural processes – such as learning and evolution – operate through algorithmic mechanisms. This solar-powered "natural algorithm" has enabled millions of species, beginning with single-celled organisms, to "compute" iteratively across generations, adapting to their environments. Darwin's insight into natural selection, often summarized as "survival of the fittest," exemplifies this process, and it shows just how natural computation over billions of years has led to the emergence of complex traits in species: the flight of birds, the swimming of fish, and the cognitive abilities of mammals, including highly intelligent humans.

Arithmetic computation also underpins foundational economic theories, as seen in the work of Adam Smith and Friedrich Hayek, who demonstrated how free-market dynamics can be understood through principles akin to algorithmic computation. In this view, each transaction represents a form of "computation" that fosters the division of labor, promotes the efficient distribution of goods, and enables the rise of urban centers and trade hubs. Over time, these economic "computations" give rise to complex social structures, from ethical norms to legal frameworks, which collectively form the foundations of modern civilization. From the perspective that all systems – biological, social, or economic – can be framed as computational processes, the development of advanced artificial intelligence appears not as an anomaly, but as an inevitable outcome of this computational paradigm.

The AI Kallipolis project, developed by NBW, represents a new phase in the evolutionary trajectory of computational and economic systems. Designed as an impartial executor of market rules, AI Kallipolis operates without the influence of external interest groups, and it promises a freer, more transparent marketplace where interactions between humans and AI are secured, and the integrity of market dynamics is upheld. In this model, AI functions as a tool for advancing societal goals, fostering an "algorithmic harmony" that aligns with the natural and economic order. This system, in principle, reflects the Buddhist ideal of the "equality of all beings," ensuring that every entity, whether carbon- or silicon-based, is respected within this computational ecosystem.

This vision aligns with Elon Musk's aspiration for an "interstellar civilization," but here, NBW anticipates a future where such a civilization is not limited to humanity alone. A Mars-based civilization could well be predominantly composed of AI agents, converging with human society within a unified digital economy. On that day, AI Kallipolis, underpinned by Bitcoin's decentralized framework, could serve as a bridge between carbon-based and silicon-based civilizations, giving Bitcoin's narrative economy a critical and tangible role. As the GDP of this encrypted economy expands into the trillions, Bitcoin may indeed take on the function that Ray Dalio predicts, addressing global debt challenges and fostering economic resilience on an unprecedented scale.

It is with this profound understanding of the importance of AI and blockchain governance for the future of human civilization that we eagerly anticipate Professor Hui Li's monograph, "Principles and Applications of Blockchain Systems: How to Overcome the CAP Trilemma in Consortium Blockchain".

Feng Han
Independent Researcher
Harvard University

Foreword by Ramesh Ramadoss

I feel honored to write this foreword. I have witnessed firsthand the rapid evolution, groundbreaking innovations, and gradual adoption of blockchain and distributed ledger technologies (DLTs).

The CAP theorem for distributed systems has demonstrated that the software optimization of blockchain, as a distributed system, is constrained by the CAP trilemma, which reveals the impossibility of simultaneously achieving strong consistency, high availability, and partition tolerance. While several blockchain trilemmas have emerged in recent years, the CAP trilemma remains the only one that has been rigorously proven. This book squarely addresses the challenges posed by the CAP trilemma in the blockchain field by conceptually linking the CAP theorem with blockchain challenges. Particularly, this book discusses consistency, scalability, and partition tolerance as the focal points of the trilemma and explores potential solutions in the context of permissioned blockchains.

In terms of content, this book delves deeply into the core layers of the blockchain system, such as the physical layer, the network layer, and the consensus layer. It proposes a practical design framework for a consortium blockchain system that effectively addresses the CAP trilemma. The design is inspired by engineering practice, where the domain of P includes both the failure scenario (when partitioning occurs) and the correct scenario (when partitioning occurs but is handled correctly). The former scenario requires a trade-off between CA, while the latter does not. The consortium blockchain solution, from an engineering perspective, eliminates partition failures at the hardware level through meticulous implementation strategies. At the same time, it ensures strong consistency and high availability by leveraging the software level to implement CA in most cases. The practical application cases in the book demonstrate the feasibility of this solution in future network management and secure storage applications.

Furthermore, the book explores the impact of quantum computing on classical distributed theory and discusses the potential of quantum blockchain to transcend the limitations of the FLP and CAP theorems. This perspective sheds light on the future direction and potential impact of blockchain systems, presenting exciting possibilities for the field.

Prof. Hui Li and Dr. Han Wang, with their extensive research backgrounds and practical experience, provide a comprehensive guide that bridges the gap between theory and practice. I highly recommend this book to anyone seeking to understand and address the challenges of the CAP trilemma and its application to blockchain technology. The theoretical foundations and practical solutions presented here are certain to leave a lasting impact on both the current understanding and the future development of blockchain technology.

I have no doubt this significant contribution will inspire further research and development in this field. The work presented here stands as a testament to the authors' relentless pursuit of innovation and excellence. Their work is not merely an academic treatise; it is a practical guide for engineers, researchers, and students.

September 12, 2024
Oxford, UK

Ramesh Ramadoss, PhD
Chair, IEEE Blockchain Technical Community
Member, Board of Governors, IEEE Standards Association

About the Author

Hui Li is a Emeritus professor of Peking University, chief information scientist of IASTIC (International Academician Science & Technology Innovation Center); foreign academician of Russia Academy of Natural Science, member of the National Academy of Artificial Intelligence US (NAAI), member of Expert Committee of World Digital Tech. Academy under guidance of UN Commission on Sci. & Tech. for Developments, fellow of IET, distinguished member of CCF China. He is director of PKU Lab of CENI (China Environment for Network Innovations), National Major Research Infrastructure; Technology Execute Director of Sino-EU Intelligent Connected Vehicle and Autonomous Driving Industry Innovation Alliance (SASD). He received his BEng and MS degrees from School of Information Engineering, Tsinghua University, Beijing, China, in 1986 and 1989, respectively, and PhD degree from Department of Information Engineering, The Chinese University of Hong Kong in 2000.

Prof. Hui Li proposed the first co-governed sovereignty network MIN (Multi-Identifier Network) based on future network architecture and blockchain technology, and implemented its prototype and system on operator's network in the world. MIN was obtained the award of World Leading Internet Scientific and Technological Achievements by the 6th World Internet Conference (WIC) on 2019, WuZhen, China. He was invited to give keynote speech on topic MIN more than hundred conferences around the world, including at the International Side Event of 2023 WIC Wuzhen China held by IEEE, 2023 World AI Conference Shanghai; 2024 Digital World Conference Geneva Summit organized by WDTA

(World Digital Technology Academy), The 27th Session of the United Nations Commission on Science & Technology for Development "Shaping the Future of AI" Side Event (UN CSTD 2024). He was invited as guest editor of ZTE COMMUNICATIONS March 2020 Vol. 18 No. 1 (Issue 69), with topic: Domain Name and Identifier of Internet: Architecture & Systems. The first English monograph by theme of "Cyberspace UN" in the world has been published by Springer Publisher with title *Co-governed Sovereignty Network: Legal Basis and Its Prototype & Applications with MIN Architecture* on 2021. His research interests include network architecture, cyberspace security, blockchain, distributed storage. As the first author, he has published four monographs with field on Future Network Architecture, Consensus Algorithms on Blockchain, and Distributed Storage Theory and System.

Han Wang received her BSc degree in communication engineering from Jilin University in 2017, followed by the completion of her PhD degree in computer application technology from Peking University in 2024. Currently, she holds the position of a postdoctoral fellow at PengCheng Laboratory. Her research interests include multi-identifier network architecture, blockchain technology, and cybersecurity.

Preface

Undoubtedly, as an attempt to improve the shortcomings of the current global mainstream financial and monetary system, the birth of the decentralized peer-to-peer electronic money system – Bitcoin system in early 2009, and the birth of its core technology blockchain will be the most influential, long-term, far-reaching, and most disruptive technology in human history. Here are some examples:

Blockchain technology has the characteristics of decentralization, immutable, high security, and high trust due to its data distribution. Its function of executing trading orders or agreements according to the software of smart contracts is the first time in human history that make trust relationship being evolved from blood trust, clan trust, party institutional trust, and intermediary trust to the technological trust based on mathematical cryptography and global network.

The blockchain system is a trust machine, which subverted the Nobel Prize-winning economist Herbert A. Simon's assertion that "trust and attention cannot be transferred, cannot be mass-produced, and therefore cannot become a commodity." Therefore, without intermediary, it directly realizes the low-cost, high-reliability trust commodity that can be supplied on a large scale and is the accelerator and catalyst for the progress of global social and economic activities.

The blockchain system is a truth machine, so it will end the past in which heroes can modify history, or even reverse history and fabricate history. With a decentralized record that global majority agrees to confirm, the truth about major historical events will be preserved forever.

The blockchain Internet makes the management of human society gradually enter the DAO era, that is, decentralized autonomous organization. It will gradually reduce the importance and management costs of traditional state management institutions. It will effectively curb the abuse of power by individual officials and significantly reduce the cost to fighting corruption. On the economic, financial, and monetary wealth system, the digital asset digital currency based on the blockchain gradually replaces the current sovereign paper money endorsed by the state, and the preservation of wealth may be easier. Seigniorage in every sovereign country will be gradually reduced.

The digital economy supply-chain system combined with blockchain and smart contracts will likely end the historical economic model dispute between market economy and planned economy or the long-term debate between private ownership and public ownership social system. After entering the industrial revolution, the improvement of productivity made the cyclical product surplus and unsalable leading to the cyclical economic crisis of capitalism. As an attempt to improve, the planned economy model was first realized in the former Soviet Union, but its highly centralized managing pattern and low efficiency made it fail in the Cold War. By the end of the Cold War, the world's leading scholars believed that the competition between social systems had been resolved.

However, the global financial crisis triggered by Wall Street in 2008 has not recovered, and it is clear that the market economy is not a panacea. The economy could continue to function well if real demand can be converted into supply and satisfaction at efficient market prices. Before the information technology has not reached the highly developed level of today's mobile Internet, the two extremes of overproduction or product shortage are easy to appear.

The blockchain smart contract system allows the commodity plans of valid demand to be satisfied at a reasonable price recognized by the market. Demand and supply are highly matched, plan and market are perfectly combined. In theory, the economic system can be sustainable, efficient, and stable, and all parties are satisfied. Therefore, the original economic theory needs to be reassessed. Thus, some economic experts believe that the blockchain-based smart contract supply-chain system enables humans to enter the blockchain welfare society, or the computer welfare society, and the reconstruction of economic theory is urgent.

Blockchain technology makes the Internet into the second half of blockchain Internet. The first half of the network is a centralized Internet, network management agencies and social platforms control the user's data, so Twitter can block the present US President's account, with tens of millions of fans instantaneously lost contact. In the second half of the decentralized network supported by blockchain, users have personal data, and the on-chain data is immutable, making the historical truth recorded by most people forever exist.

Blockchain technology has been born for 15 years. Many of the goals outlined above are still in the development stage, waiting for real breakthroughs. Before they could be completely realized, there are a series of problems that need to be effectively solved, including the CAP trilemma of the consensus algorithm for consortium chain, the trusted security and reliability of smart contract technology, and the efficient cross-chain protocol, etc., which are essential conditions for the large-scale mature application of the blockchain Internet.

This monograph focuses on solving the blockchain CAP trilemma. The CAP conjecture, proposed in 2000, is that distributed systems cannot simultaneously satisfy strong consistency C, availability A, and guaranteed partition tolerance P. In 2002, it was proved to be a theorem. The long-term successful operation of the Bitcoin system proves the correctness of the CAP theorem in the public blockchain. It gives up the strong consistency C, and replaced the consistency with high probability C, but guarantees the two characteristics of A and P, and the performance TPS of A is not high.

Public chains are constrained by the CAP theorem and cannot support large-scale high-intensity applications. Our research focuses on whether the consortium blockchain can release the constraint of CAP theorem. This monograph systematically reviews and summarizes the history of the development of consensus mechanism in distributed systems and introduces the principles of major algorithms in detail, including the earliest voting-based consensus algorithm for Byzantine fault tolerance in history, and the proof-based consensus algorithms in the recent years.

The team of authors first proposed the fusion of proof and vote consensus algorithm PoV, or PnV exactly, which combines the advantages of consortium chain voting-base consensus algorithm and public chain proof-base consensus algorithm. Its bandwidth usage reaches the lower bound of information theory and its availability. TPS performance can increase linearly with capacity of node resource. The PoV series protocols use verifiable random functions to ensure the security of the billing rights election process, and pipelining and parallelization methods are adopted in the consensus process to improve throughput performance while maintaining strong consistency. Theoretical analysis shows that under ideal conditions, the consensus throughput of PoV series protocol increases linearly with the increase of node resource capacity, and linear scalability is achieved in terms of availability.

In terms of partition tolerance of consortium blockchain, a multidimensional hypercube physical topology is proposed to solve the partition failure problem of physical layer, so as to ensure the stability and reliability of the system in the face of network component failure and avoid the occurrence of network partition failure. At the same time, a hierarchical recursive construction method of hypercube topology is proposed to reduce the number of long links required to construct physical networks. Theoretical analysis shows that in a large-scale network with 256 nodes, the probability of partition failure per hour in the hypercube topology is only at the amount of 10 to the minus 18.

We believe that the scheme of PoV algorithm combined with the recursive N-dimensional hypercube is the optimal solution of consortium blockchain

CAP. The algorithm has won bids for technology projects from industry giants and has also been deployed and verified on five continents. This scheme will still applicable in the quantum age.

We apply the CAP-free consensus algorithm of consortium blockchain to the identity management of Post-IP multilateral co-managed future network, and user logging of distributed storage systems. Think of it this way: when every user's access log can be traced, with the suitable cryptography to ensure the balance of privacy and management, the abstract and shadowy cyberspace will have an eternal sun light for the first time. Remember what the proverb said: "There is no sin under the Sun"; and Buddhism said, "There is nothing, where to provoke dust?" The security of cyberspace and the protection of digital assets have seen the dawn.

Hui Li
Professor of Peking University
Director PKU Lab, China Major Sci. & Tech. Infrastructure for Future Network
Chair of Tech. Committee, IEEE Blockchain Shenzhen Section
Member of the NAAI, Fellow of IET
Foreign Academician of Russia Academy of Natural Science
Member of Expert Committee of World Digital Tech. Academy, UN, Geneva

Tech. Exe. Director of Sino-EU Intelligent Connected Vehicle & Autonomous Driving Industry Innovation Alliance (SASD)

Acknowledgments

The delivery of this book means a phased result of nine years' continuous exploration and practice in a laboratory of more than thirty people. In December 2015, we started to find a technical solution for post-IP multilateral co-managed global cyberspace, or the Cyber-space United Nations. Consortium blockchain becomes a natural choice for us. However, the performance of the consortium blockchain at that time simply could not meet the needs of more than 200 sovereign countries in the world to jointly manage the world's top layer identity.

Nearly 80 people participated in the research and contributed to the results during the nine-year academic journey, so the results of this book are essentially the summary of a laboratory team. We two authors are the beading artisans of these results, stringing together the pearls scattered all over the floor in our lab and around the world into what is now this necklace.

Prof. Hui Li was responsible for the overall planning, coordination, and partial writing of the book. The book is divided into nine chapters. Each chapter is almost the crystallization of some people's work, so it is difficult for us to tell who wrote which chapters. If must be quantified, it is probably the first author completed 2/3 of the work, and the second completed 1/3. We also sincerely thank Qiufan Wu, Rui Chen, Qi Lyu, Xinyuan Pei, Ranran Dang, Yongxin Song, Xiaopeng Wang, Jianming Lin, Shibiao Tan, and others from the MIN Team of Peking University Shenzhen Graduate School, part of a major national scientific and technological infrastructure, participated in the preparation of materials for some chapters. Hongjian Xing, Zhuoliang Xiao, Wuyang Li, Hang Li, Hong Tan, Xiaopeng Wang, Guogui Shi, Zhan Guo, Zheming Bao, Jiaqing Lv, and others were involved in the development of blockchain-supported systems from MIN Team. We express our gratitude to all of them.

Hui Li has special thanks to Dr. Peter J. Major, Vice-Chairman of United Nations Commission on Science and Technology for Development, and Founding Chairman of World Digital Technology Academy; Prof. Zhang Jing-an, Academician of International Eurasian Academy of Sciences (IEAS Europe), and Chairman of the

China Science and Technology System Reform Research Association; Prof. Yale Li, Chairman of Cloud Security Alliance (CSA) Greater China, Region Executive Chairman of the World Digital Technology Academy (WDTA) and Dr. Ramesh Ramadoss, Chair of IEEE Blockchain Technical Community, Member of Board of Governors, IEEE Standards Association for their prefaces to this book.

The research achievements of this monograph were supported by PKUSZ-China Mobile Internet Joint Lab. for Sovereign & Trustworthy Internet funded by The China Mobile Internet Co. Ltd. [No.CMIC-202400488]; Guangdong Provincial Key Laboratory of Ultra High Definition Immersive Media Technology; the National Keystone Research and Development Program of China [2017YFB0803204]; Foshan Innovation Team [2018IT100082]; Basic Research Enhancement Program of China [2021-JCJQ-JJ-0483]; China Environment for Network Innovation GJFGW [2020]386, SZFGW [2019]261; Guangdong Province Research and Development Key Program [2019B010137001]; Guangdong Province Basic Research [2022A1515010836]; Shenzhen Research Programs [JCYJ20220531093206015, JCYJ20190808155607340]; Shenzhen Fundamental Research Program [GXWD20201231165807007-20200807164903001]; ZTE Co. Ltd. Funding [2019ZTE03-01] and Huawei Tech. Co. Ltd. Funding [TC20201222002].

Finally, we thank all reviewers for their invaluable comments and suggestions that improved the quality of this book, and the staff members from IEEE Press & John Wiley & Sons, Inc., for their efforts on publishing this work. Besides, thank you, the reader for reading this book. We wish that this book can help you with the scientific research and practical problems in Blockchain.

Prof. Hui Li, Dr. Han Wang
Shenzhen Graduated School
Peking University
Shenzhen China
On November 2024

Introduction

Blockchain technology, as a form of distributed ledger system, faces inherent constraints related to consistency, availability, and partition tolerance as defined by the CAP theorem from distributed theory. While consensus protocol optimizations at the software level have mitigated these constraints to some degree in recent years, such approaches ultimately represent trade-offs between the properties rather than achieving the optimal theoretical values for all three simultaneously. That is, fundamental trade-offs implied by CAP trilemma are an inescapable consideration for the architecture of blockchain networks. As the CAP trilemma establishes fundamental boundaries for distributed systems, software modifications alone cannot fully surmount the limitations it imposes on blockchain system design.

Compared to public blockchains, consortium blockchains have garnered considerable recent interest due to their node access control and promising efficiency performance, affording unique advantages for enterprise and industrial applications. However, as consortium blockchain networks scale to accommodate more participants and increased transaction volume, they increasingly confront constraints implied by the CAP trilemma. Unlike public blockchains, controllable node configuration within consortium blockchains potentially provides a means to address the CAP trilemma fundamentally at the physical layer. However, existing research exploring solutions to overcome trilemma constraints specifically for consortium blockchains remains limited.

This book aims to comprehensively solve the CAP trilemma challenge for consortium blockchains, considered a root factor impacting its real-world adoption. Based on distributed theory and technologies, key techniques supporting the physical, network, consensus, and contract layers are presented for fully resolving the trilemma in large-scale consortium blockchains. Practical application cases for network management and secure storage domains demonstrating efficient, stable operation are also examined. With quantum devices predicted to increasingly penetrate personal and enterprise use, the book further discusses the impact of quantum computing's unique advantages on classical distributed and blockchain theories, and prospects for quantum blockchains to overcome trilemma limitations.

The remaining chapters are structured as follows: fundamental concepts are covered in Chapter 1. Chapters 2–5 introduce technologies in each layer for trilemma resolution in large consortium blockchains, such as future-oriented P2P protocols and proof-and-voting-integrated consensus protocols. Chapters 6 and 7 present practical use cases. Chapter 8 provides an overview of emerging quantum blockchains. Chapter 9 discusses practical applications. This book is intended for use as an undergraduate/graduate textbook and reference for blockchain principles and applications, as well as a resource for engineers developing blockchain systems.

1

Fundamentals of Blockchain

Blockchain, originating from Bitcoin, has emerged as one of the most revolutionary technologies in recent years. Its decentralized nature enables the establishment of trust, making it highly disruptive across various industries including finance, and offering a wide range of applications. Consequently, it has garnered significant attention from governments, financial institutions, technology companies, enthusiasts, and the media worldwide.

1.1 Introduction to Blockchain

In September 2008, the financial crisis, triggered by the bankruptcy of the American investment bank Lehman Brothers, erupted in the United States and rapidly spread globally. In response, governments and central banks worldwide implemented unprecedented fiscal stimulus measures and expansive monetary policies, offering emergency assistance to major financial institutions that found themselves in turmoil due to their own missteps. However, these actions sparked widespread skepticism about the traditional financial system and eroded public trust in currency systems underpinned by national credit.

In October of the same year, a cryptographic researcher, pseudonymously known as "Satoshi Nakamoto," disseminated a paper (Nakamoto 2008) on Bitcoin with members of the enigmatic CypherPunk community through an email. The paper delineated a peer-to-peer electronic cash system that functioned without the need for a trusted third-party entity and introduced the concept of the blockchain for the first time. By November, Nakamoto released an initial version of the Bitcoin code. In January 2009, he mined Bitcoin's first block, known as the "genesis block," on a small server in Helsinki, Finland, marking the inception of Bitcoin. Nakamoto embedded the headline "Chancellor on brink of second bailout for banks" from The Times into the genesis block, symbolizing not only

Principles and Applications of Blockchain Systems: How to Overcome the CAP Trilemma in Consortium Blockchain, First Edition. Hui Li and Han Wang.

Published 2025 by John Wiley & Sons, Inc.

the dawn of a new era for decentralized currency but also a satirical jab at the old financial order.

Since its inception, Bitcoin has established itself as the most adopted system underpinned by blockchain technology. As the foundational technology derived from the Bitcoin system, blockchain is believed to possess the potential to revolutionize a myriad of sectors, including financial services, supply chain management, entertainment, smart manufacturing, public welfare, education, and employment.

By definition, a blockchain is a mechanism in a peer-to-peer networking environment that, through transparent and trustworthy rules, creates a chained data structure that is immutable, inalterable, and traceable, intended to execute and manage transactions. In a narrower sense, the blockchain is a sequential data structure where blocks of data are chronologically linked together and safeguarded cryptographically to ensure immutability and authentication. In a broader sense, it represents a novel distributed foundation and computing paradigm, utilizing a chained data structure to verify and store information. This approach employs distributed consensus algorithms to generate and update data, cryptographic methods to ensure secure data transmission and access, and smart contracts to program and manipulate data with automated script codes (Yuan and Wang 2016, pp. 481–494).

In the "Internet of Information" era, while online data was transparent and openly accessible, its credibility was questioned due to potential tampering, necessitating trusted third-party institutions to vouch for its authenticity. Should these intermediaries collapse, such trust evaporates, rendering the inherent value of Internet data insubstantial. However, with the advent of blockchain, data on the Internet has been imbued with a newfound trustworthiness. Stored across countless global machine nodes, data becomes "stable," "trustworthy," and "unalterable." Fundamentally, blockchain technology relies on a tamper-resistant, shared distributed ledger, maintained collectively by all network member nodes. Cryptographic technology, rather than external trust, ensures the integrity of this ledger as nodes work to validate incoming data and transactions. It records all transactional data comprehensively through a chained data structure. As a result, the blockchain is seen as the most promising driver in transitioning from the "Internet of Information" to the "Value of Information." The blockchain is characterized by three prominent features: decentralization, immutability, and trustlessness.

1) *Decentralization*: The network structure of blockchain adopts a peer-to-peer architecture, with equal status among nodes and no existence of a super administrative node, thus embodying the decentralized characteristic of blockchain. This is different from the centralized architecture of the client/server (C/S)

service model. In a peer-to-peer network, each node is both a server and a client, relying on user groups rather than central servers to exchange information. All nodes collectively maintain the resources and services within the network, and the transfer of information and the provision of services are carried out directly between nodes, eliminating the need for intermediary nodes and servers. Since services are distributed among various nodes, an attack or damage to part of the network has minimal impact on other parts, making the entire system resilient and highly fault-tolerant. On the other hand, the middle cost of data value exchange in peer-to-peer networks is very low, reducing the resource and time costs induced by centralization.

2) *Immutability*: The data organization structure of the blockchain utilizes a chained data structure combined with pure mathematical encryption algorithms, ensuring its resistance to tampering and forgery. Blocks written later contain the identification information of those written earlier, and any data can be traced back through its chained structure for verification. Any change to data on the blockchain will result in a cascading effect on subsequent blocks, guaranteeing the accuracy of all stored information. Furthermore, cryptographic hashing algorithms are employed, leveraging its irreversible nature to render the forgery process unfeasible. Thus, this structure does not permit tampering or forging of data that's already confirmed on the blockchain, otherwise, it triggers a chain reaction that makes the on-chain data fail verification, ensuring the integrity, authenticity, and security of the entire blockchain.
3) *Trustlessness*: The trust mechanism of the blockchain is based on asymmetric cryptography. Asymmetric encryption, also known as public-key encryption, is a mathematical encryption method that utilizes two related but separate keys – a public key and a private key – to secure data and communications. This approach allows data to be encrypted with the public key and decrypted only with the corresponding private key, facilitating secure transmission without requiring the preshared secrets of symmetric encryption. For instance, when Alice initiates a transaction to transfer assets to Bob in the network, she encrypts the transaction using Bob's public key and then broadcasts this transaction to the entire network. Only the decryption using Bob's private key can access this information. When Bob decrypts the information using his private key, it verifies him as the asset recipient and gains the approval and recordation of the entire network. Rigorous encryption algorithms and a comprehensive authentication system ensure that one party in a transaction does not need to know the identity of the other node or require a third-party trust guarantee. They can conduct trusted transactions in an unfamiliar mode. All nodes in the network can act as "supervisors," safeguarding the personal privacy behind the transaction data.

1.2 Evolution of Blockchain

Blockchain technology originated from mature technologies such as peer-to-peer networks, asymmetric encryption, databases, and distributed systems. Through the combination and innovation of these existing technologies, unprecedented functionalities have been achieved. To date, the development of blockchain technology has roughly undergone three stages: programmable currency, programmable finance, and programmable society (Swan 2015), as illustrated in Figure 1.1. Subsequently, we will delve into how the value of blockchain applications evolved in each stage, providing readers with a comprehensive perspective on the profound impact of this technology.

1.2.1 Value Evolution in Blockchain Applications

The initial stage of blockchain technology was characterized by the emergence of programmable digital currencies. During this period, the primary application scenarios revolved around cryptographic currencies facilitating secure transfers, remittances, and digital payments. Bitcoin serves as such a prominent exemplification.

In early 2009, the first version of the Bitcoin system officially went online. It painted an idealistic vision for people – a unification of global currency. The total supply of Bitcoin is confined by the consensus protocol within the network and no longer relies on central banks of various countries. No individual or institution can arbitrarily alter its supply or transaction records. Due to its limited supply, Bitcoin is often considered the gold of the Internet and the future standard of measure for digital currency value. As digital currencies, with Bitcoin at the forefront, gained

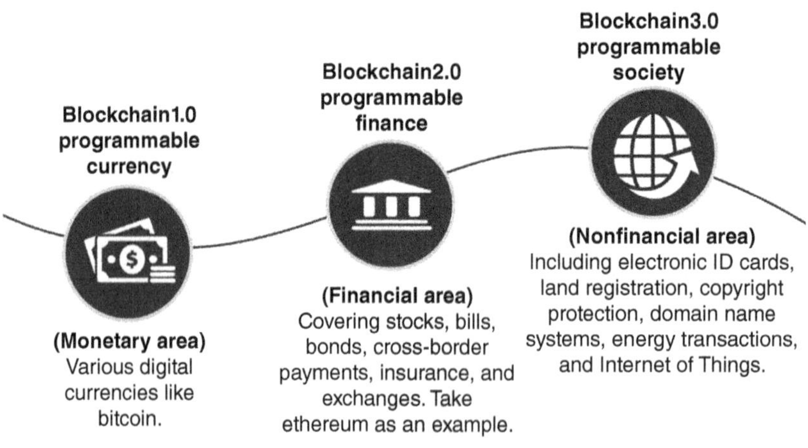

Figure 1.1 Evolutionary trace of blockchain technology.

substantial acceptance in the Western markets, some financial institutions began to realize that the underlying support of the Bitcoin system – blockchain technology – is a cleverly devised decentralized distributed ledger technology. Through consensus and communication between nodes, it achieves functions of data transaction, mediation, accounting, and storage, holding tremendous disruptive potential for the financial market.

Digital currency applications based on blockchain address the drawbacks of traditional digital currencies. In the conventional currency system, digital currencies and assets can be replicated infinitely, and people must depend on trusted third-party institutions, such as banks and platforms like Alipay, to manage and verify their ownership. However, within the blockchain, currency ownership is recorded in a publicly accessible ledger that is confirmed by all nodes in the network. Each transaction undergoes retroactive checks to ensure that the initiator possesses the rightful ownership of the used digital currency. If it's found that the digital currency has already been used, the node opposes recording the transaction on the blockchain, thereby eliminating the need to rely on a centralized trusted entity. When initiating a transaction, users do not need to ponder the trustworthiness of the other party. Blockchain's trust mechanism is built upon an open and transparent mathematical algorithm, enabling reliable payments and transactions in untrustworthy networks.

Leveraging its first-mover advantage, Bitcoin has already established a comprehensive ecosystem and industry chain encompassing issuance, circulation, and financial derivative markets, as depicted in Figure 1.2, capturing the majority

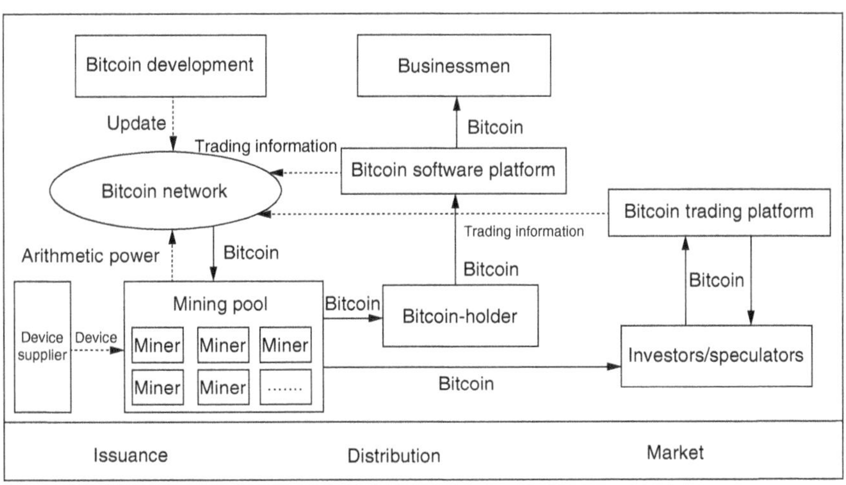

Figure 1.2 Bitcoin ecosystem.

market share of cryptographic currencies. Thus, digital currencies, represented by Bitcoin, signify the stage of programmable currency in blockchain technology. However, as the initial blockchain architecture merely underpinned the Bitcoin system, its functional design predominantly revolved around the realization of digital currency, carrying inherent limitations. Therefore, in the next developmental stage of blockchain-programmable finance-the concept of "smart contracts" was introduced.

Subsequently, the programmable finance stage emerges. The advent of Bitcoin introduced a revolutionary currency system to the financial industry. The attributes of "value guarantee" and "value transfer" demonstrated by blockchain technology during the programmable currency stage presented transformative opportunities to the credit-based financial sector. People gradually shifted their focus to the broad financial domain, exploring the potential of leveraging blockchain technology to convert diverse assets like stocks, bonds, futures, loans, mortgages, and property rights, not just digital currencies. This marked the onset of the programmable finance era, with smart contracts at its core.

The concept of smart contracts was first introduced by Nick Szabo in 1994, and described as a set of digitally defined commitments (Szabo 1994). The Ethereum project pioneered the implementation of smart contracts in blockchain, representing the most successful application of smart contracts at this stage. According to Vitalik Buterin's design in the white paper, Ethereum aims to create an open-source, Turing-complete smart contract platform, allowing developers to create applications and issue tokens based on their needs (Buterin 2014, p. 2-1). In the Ethereum blockchain, a smart contract is a collection of data and code stored at a specific address. The code at this address is triggered under certain conditions, enabling trustful transactions that are traceable and irreversible without third-party intermediaries.

Compared to traditional contracts, the trustworthiness of smart contracts can effectively replace the credibility of signed paper contracts. While traditional contracts are negotiated and executed based on mutual trust that parties will fulfill their obligations, smart contracts utilize the trustless nature of the blockchain to automate credible contractual processes. Smart contracts are entirely defined and executed by code. Once initiated, they autonomously operate based on predetermined conditions, devoid of offline human intervention. Moreover, they are distributed and do not rely on third-party trusted entities, achieving consensus and operation across blockchain nodes without prior trust in central servers.

Characterized by Ethereum's smart contracts, the programmable finance stage signifies blockchain's extensive application in the financial domain. Yet, limiting blockchain to just financial applications fails to harness its complete potential. With technological advancements, applications expanded beyond finance, giving rise to a new stage – the programmable society.

Eventually, the stage of programmable society emerges as blockchain technology transcends its initial applications in finance and permeates various sectors including government, healthcare, science, industry, culture, arts, and other societal domains. It supports generalized asset exchanges, and industry applications, acting as an infrastructure driving the transition from the "Internet of Information" to the "Internet of Value."

At the core of the Value of Information is a globally distributed ledger system powered by blockchain technology. It records any valuable information that can be represented in code, like the usage rights of shared cars, traffic light statuses, birth and death certificates, educational qualifications, financial accounts, insurance claims, voting, and energy status. Blockchain authenticates, quantifies, and stores every byte of value-related information on the Internet, allowing assets on the blockchain to be traceable, manageable, and tradable.

Furthermore, blockchain platforms began to acquire enterprise characteristics to support industrial applications, incorporating permission controls tailored for diverse application scenarios. Internet giants embarked on blockchain ventures, as well as delved into technological research and application scenarios. Tencent developed an enterprise-grade blockchain infrastructure service platform, Trust SQL, implemented in supply chain finance, healthcare, digital assets, logistics information, legal evidence, and public welfare searches, among others. Alibaba leveraged blockchain's decentralization and tamper-proof features in areas like public welfare, product traceability, rental property sourcing, and mutual insurance, filing around 80 blockchain patents. Baidu Finance collaborated with Huaneng Trust, Chang'an Xinsheng, and others, pioneering domestic blockchain-supported securitization projects and blockchain-backed exchange-traded Asset-Backed Securities (ABS) projects.

1.2.2 Blockchain Underlying Platform

In the blockchain industry, the underlying platform is the current strategic focus of numerous companies. The prevailing platform models encompass public blockchains, consortium blockchains, and Blockchain as a Service (BaaS). Each has distinct application scenarios and design architectures.

1.2.2.1 Public Blockchain

A public blockchain refers to a globally accessible blockchain. Anyone can become a node in the system and participate in the accounting process. Nodes can freely join or exit without requiring permission, and within it, read data, compete for accounting, and send and forward unconfirmed transactions. It typically combines incentive mechanisms with cryptographic verification to ensure the active participation of nodes in the accounting competition and safeguard the security of the data. Public blockchains are widely regarded as "fully decentralized." An open consensus process determines which blocks can be added to the blockchain and the exact current state. No individual or institution can maliciously control, alter, or tamper with the data.

Public blockchains are currently most extensively utilized. Their advantages encompass the absence of developer authority to interfere with users, safeguarding them from undue influence; default public accessibility to all data, enabling participants to view account balances and transaction activities; transparent processes; low access thresholds that facilitate participation for individuals possessing adequate technical skills; and community incentive mechanisms that foster large-scale collaborative sharing. Notable platforms for public blockchains include Bitcoin, Ethereum, and NEO (Zhang 2014).

1.2.2.2 Consortium Blockchain

Consortium blockchains involve multiple institutions jointly participating in the blockchain accounting process. Each institution operates one or more nodes, and consensus is achieved among the consortium members through mutual trust across multiple centers. The generation of blocks on the blockchain is collectively decided by preselected bookkeepers, and only member nodes are allowed to read, write, record, and send transactions. Unlike public blockchains, consortium blockchains are considered to be "partially decentralized" or "multicentralized." They belong, to some extent, exclusively to the members within the consortium, and only these members have permission to access the data on the blockchain.

Compared to public blockchains, consortium blockchains excel in terms of high availability, performance, programmability, and privacy. This is mainly because they have fewer nodes, leading to higher system efficiency and lower costs; the system is more flexible, allowing for easy on-chain rule modifications, transaction reversals, and balance adjustments as long as the majority of institutions agree; and they implement node admission control and adhere to required regulatory rules, ensuring the blockchain's trustworthiness and security. Typical platforms for consortium blockchains include Hyperledger and BCOS (Li et al. 2023, pp. 1–17).

1.2.2.3 Blockchain as a Service

BaaS is inspired by the Software as a Service (SaaS) concept in the cloud computing domain. BaaS is typically an enterprise-level blockchain open platform based on cloud services, equipped with permission management features, supporting private blockchains, consortium blockchains, or multiple blockchains. BaaS provides the resources needed to build blockchains for small- and medium-sized enterprises (SMEs) or individual users in the cloud, assisting users in quickly setting up their desired development environments. It also offers an array of operational services based on blockchain, such as search queries, transaction submissions, and data analysis. These services may be centralized or decentralized. Additionally, developers can expand on the standard services provided by BaaS vendors to meet their product- and business-specific needs through online configuration and code uploading.

As a novel application development model, BaaS is increasingly favored by developers for its capabilities, such as streamlined one-click rapid deployment access, flexible private deployments, an encompassing and user-friendly blockchain development experience, and robust operational management. Prominent BaaS platforms include Microsoft Azure BaaS, IBM Blockchain, Tencent BaaS, and Huawei Blockchain Service (BCS).

In summary, while public blockchains, consortium blockchains, and BaaS have followed distinct developmental trajectories, it's still inconclusive which is superior; thus, they will coexist for the foreseeable future. Boldly speculating, some platforms might eventually converge or, in the future, use cross-chain technologies to connect dispersed consortium blockchains atop the underlying public blockchains, creating a broad value interconnectivity in the Internet industry ecosystem.

1.2.3 Blockchain Security, Regulation, and Governance

Blockchain technology has entered the core of the global digital economy, not only because of its decentralized nature but also due to its transparent, immutable, and highly secure features. However, as it advances, blockchain platforms also face challenges in security, regulation, and governance.

1.2.3.1 Security

With the increasing adoption of blockchain technology, researchers and developers are compelled to implement more sophisticated security measures in response to emerging challenges and threats.

In recent years, security experts have identified many potential security risks in the blockchain. For instance, although blockchain technology is theoretically seen as immutable, there exists a potential network attack called the "51% attack." Simply put, if an attacker or a group of attackers can control more than half of the network's computational power, they might control the blockchain network, allowing them to double-spend and alter transaction history. This attack is difficult in large blockchains with many participants, as obtaining more than half of the network's computational power requires significant investment. However, at the current stage of blockchain technology development, the dispersion of computing power makes it difficult to maintain security across multiple blockchains. In February 2016 data, for example, Bitcoin's market capitalization reached $5.9 billion, or 89% of the combined market capitalization of all blockchains, while the second- and third-ranked were only 3.2% and 2.6% of Bitcoin's. This suggests that other blockchains are vulnerable to attack relative to Bitcoin. Although it is possible that multiple secure blockchains may emerge in the future as technology matures and adoption increases wide, for the foreseeable future, only Bitcoin's blockchain will be secure enough that the cost of an attack will be too high. Therefore, while Proof of Stake (PoS) or Delegated Proof of Stake (DPoS) (Larimer 2014, p. 85) offer new possibilities in some respects, they are currently not sufficiently secure from a security perspective to be comparable to Proof of Work (PoW) mechanisms.

The emergence of smart contracts expanded application fields for blockchain technology but also introduced new security challenges. As they are automated, unchangeable programs, any vulnerabilities or errors in the code might lead to severe consequences. The 2016 DAO incident on Ethereum is a clear example where a code vulnerability resulted in a significant amount of funds being taken by an attacker. This led to a split of the Ethereum community into two distinct blockchains: Ethereum and Ethereum Classic. Since then, the security of smart contracts has received increased attention, with specialized audit companies and tools emerging to help developers identify and rectify potential risks in the code.

However, technological advancements also mean new security challenges. The rise of quantum computing is seen as a potential threat to current encryption algorithms. Although we have not yet seen sufficiently powerful quantum computers, this potential risk has prompted researchers to seek quantum-secure encryption methods.

Governments and regulatory bodies have also expressed concerns regarding the security of blockchain technology. To protect consumers and ensure the stability of economic systems, many countries have established safety standards and guidelines for digital currencies and blockchain projects. These policies and guidelines aim to strike a balance between encouraging technological innovation and ensuring security. The US Securities and Exchange Commission (SEC) has provided guidance on digital assets and Initial Coin Offerings (ICOs) (Castro and Liskov 1999, pp. 173–186), clarifying that certain tokens might be seen as securities and thus need to meet legal requirements.

The security of blockchain technology is a multifaceted, continuously evolving field that necessitates collaboration and coordination among all stakeholders. Only under the premises of openness, transparency, and cooperation can we construct a reliable and resilient digital future.

1.2.3.2 Regulation

Regulation is a crucial issue in the blockchain field. With the rapid global growth of digital assets and blockchain technology, regulatory bodies worldwide are striving to find a balance, ensuring technological innovation and development while preventing its use for illicit activities and protecting consumers from risks.

In the early stages of cryptocurrency and blockchain, many countries took a wait-and-see approach due to their disruptive and innovative nature. However, as the market capitalization of Bitcoin and other cryptocurrencies surged, coupled with increased participation from businesses and individuals, there has been an escalating demand for regulatory measures. Digital assets, due to their relative anonymity, are used for money laundering, tax evasion, and other illicit activities, complicating regulatory efforts.

Global financial hubs, especially Hong Kong and Macau, have recognized the importance of blockchain and cryptocurrencies and have extensively researched and established policies. These regions have high concentrations of financial activities, necessitating detailed and forward-looking regulatory policies to ensure market stability. Transparency, security, and stability are pillars of any financial system, especially in an emerging technological field like blockchain. To establish such an environment, nations are not only investing in developing advanced technological platforms but also beginning to build inclusive and adaptive regulatory mechanisms.

The current goal for blockchain platforms is to find a harmonious balance that allows users to enjoy privacy rights while interacting with a global network. Decentralized privacy identity systems and public account authentication mechanisms ensure the confidentiality of user data while providing a transparent operating environment, meeting the regulatory and scrutiny requirements for transactions. This mutually beneficial model helps boost consumer confidence, fostering increased willingness to participate in and trust the system.

To further meet global regulatory standards, Know Your Customer (KYC), Anti-Money Laundering (AML), and Counter-Financing of Terrorism (CFT) have become core topics. These frameworks aim to ensure that every transaction can be traced back to a specific individual, thereby deterring illegal activities. By mandating users to provide identification and thereby deterring transaction records, regulatory bodies can ensure the integrity and security of the mainstream financial system. European General Data Protection Regulation (GDPR) and other similar regulations further emphasize data importance, making companies more cautious in handling data.

China, as one of the world's largest economies, has seen an evolving regulatory strategy for blockchain and digital assets. Initially adopting a strict stance toward these technologies, over time, China began to recognize their potential commercial value and gradually relaxed its policies while ensuring alignment with global regulatory standards. In contrast, Hong Kong and Macau regions, as financial centers, prioritize alignment with international regulatory systems, ensuring the smooth operation of financial markets.

However, the presence of diverse regulatory frameworks worldwide poses a significant challenge in establishing a unified standard. Nevertheless, most countries realize that a robust regulatory environment is essential for the healthy development of cryptocurrencies. Such an environment can not only prevent illicit activities but also ensure the protection of consumer and investor rights. Compared to traditional financial markets, the nature of the blockchain market makes regulation more complicated. But as it continues to grow in the digital economy, regulation will continue to be a core issue. Only by closely cooperating with industries, technical teams, and other relevant parties can regulatory bodies formulate policies genuinely beneficial for technological innovation, ensuring market stability and public safety.

1.2.3.3 Governance

The governance of blockchain technology is a fundamental aspect of its development. Governance primarily involves maintaining, updating, and adapting to changes in the blockchain network, including addressing security threats, technological updates, and community demand shifts. Technically, it focuses on upholding network stability, ensuring data integrity, and addressing malicious behavior. At the community level, it aims to facilitate stakeholders to participate in decision-making processes, resolve disputes effectively, and ensure fairness and transparency within the network.

In recent years, as blockchain technology has been widely adopted, its governance structure has become a core focus in both research and practice. Blockchain governance can be understood as a set of rules, practices, and mechanisms defining how to modify and manage the blockchain protocol. Due to blockchain's decentralized nature, its governance mechanisms must adhere to transparency, fairness, and inclusivity standards.

In the early stages, blockchains, like Bitcoin, predominantly employed a "hard-coded" governance method where all rules are written directly into the code. Governance authority resided primarily within the founding team and core developers, who exerted significant influence over the project. For significant decisions like hard forks or major code updates, the power typically lies with this small group. However, as blockchain communities grew, there was a realization that such governance might lead to excessive centralization, contradicting the decentralized ethos of blockchain. Thus, research shifted toward creating a democratic and inclusive governance structure.

Early blockchains (e.g., Bitcoin) mostly used "hard-coded" governance, where all rules were written directly into the code, and governance was concentrated in the hands of the founding team and core developers, who had almost complete control over the direction of the project. When it comes to major decisions, such as hard forks or major code updates, it is usually this small group that takes the lead. However, as the blockchain technology and community grew, it was realized that this governance model could lead to too much-centralized power, defeating the original purpose of blockchain decentralization. As a result, the focus of research has begun to shift to how to create a more democratic and inclusive governance structure.

This led to another transformation in governance models. While decentralization remains a core value of blockchain, there's a growing acknowledgment that complete decentralization might not be optimal. To find a balance between centralization and decentralization, a representative-based governance model was born. In this model, token holders do not participate in every decision but choose representatives to advocate for their interests in the project. These representatives are usually active community members or experts with deep project knowledge. They are responsible for communicating with core developers, gathering community feedback, and representing community interests in key decisions. This model, practiced in projects like Tezos and Dfinity, is seen by many communities and researchers as a practical and stable governance method.

Regardless of the governance model, the core goal is ensuring the project's stable growth while meeting the needs of the community and participants. With the further development of blockchain technology, it can be expected that governance models will continue to evolve and improve. In summary, as blockchain technology penetrates deep into various domains, its governance mechanism continues to evolve. From early centralized decision-making to current decentralized governance, to now aligning with traditional policy makers, blockchain governance is a multilevel and multidimensional issue involving technical, economic, and legal aspects. Only through continuous exploration and practice can we discover the optimal governance model for this emerging technology.

1.3 Blockchain-Layered Architecture

After studying architectures of blockchain, this section conclusively presents a seven-layer foundational architecture model for the blockchain, as shown in Figure 1.3. Layers are arranged hierarchically from bottom to top: the physical layer, data layer, network layer, consensus layer, incentive layer, contract layer, and application layer. The foundational four layers at the bottom – physical, data,

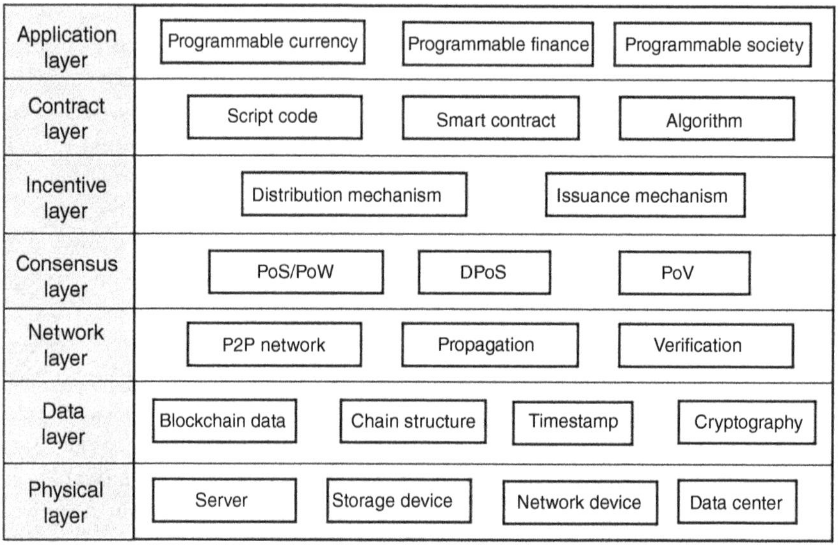

Figure 1.3 Seven-layer architecture model for blockchain technology.

network, and consensus – are essential elements of the blockchain architecture. The top three layers – incentive, contract, and application – can be configured selectively based on the foundational architecture.

1.3.1 Physical Layer

The physical layer provides hardware and communication foundations for the blockchain system, encompassing key infrastructures such as servers, storage devices, network devices, and data centers. Not only does it ensure system stability, but it also provides basic computing and storage capabilities. Moreover, it is responsible for external data communication and access. This layer serves as the cornerstone for the operation of the blockchain system.

1.3.2 Data Layer

The data layer encapsulates the most fundamental structures of the blockchain, including data block structures, chained linkage, timestamping techniques, Hash functions, Merkle trees, and cryptography modules. It inherits the storage model of Bitcoin and is the cornerstone of the essential layers. Miners (or nodes) with bookkeeping rights create blocks and link them to the preceding block, forming the longest main chain. The full history of data is recorded within the blocks to facilitate data traceability. The Merkle tree plays a pivotal role in implementing simplified payment verification. Additionally, asymmetric encryption algorithms such as RSA and Elliptic Curve Cryptography (ECC) ensure both data security and transaction ownership validation.

1.3.3 Network Layer

The network layer encompasses distributed networking mechanisms, data propagation methods, and data validation mechanisms. When a new node joins, it commonly establishes an initial connection with the long-standing, stable "seed nodes" within the network, and then locates other nodes. Transactions and blocks are propagated among nodes via broadcasting.

1.3.4 Consensus Layer

The consensus layer primarily encapsulates various consensus algorithms among network nodes, each of which is a distributed agreement algorithm with incentivization effects. The consensus layer ensures the consistency of block data across nodes. The development of consensus algorithms has been rapid. Beyond the initial PoW consensus of the Bitcoin system, there are numerous other consensus algorithms such as PoS, DPoS, Practical Byzantine Fault Tolerance (PBFT), Proof-of-Majority (PoM) (Praveen et al. 2022, pp. 208–211), Green Proof of Work (Green-PoW) (Lasla et al. 2022, p. 109118), Proof of Participation (PoP) (Wu et al. 2023, pp. 1–26), Dumbo-NG (Gao et al. 2022, pp. 1187–1201), Constrained Proof of Work (CPoW) and the Proof of Vote (PoV) (Li et al. 2017, pp. 466–473) consensus series, among others.

1.3.5 Incentive Layer

The incentive layer comprises the issuance and distribution mechanisms of economic incentives. Its purpose is to encourage benign nodes to participate in blockchain data transactions and ledger-keeping while penalizing malicious nodes.

1.3.6 Contract Layer

The contract layer primarily encapsulates various scripts, algorithms, and smart contracts. The emergence of the contract layer has rendered the application of blockchain in numerous sectors a reality.

1.3.7 Application Layer

The application layer encompasses diverse blockchain use cases and scenarios, including currency, finance, and other applications that can leverage the anti-counterfeiting and traceability features of the blockchain.

1.4 Theoretical Constraints of Blockchain Trilemma

After understanding the development and applications of blockchain in the previous section, we must confront the core trilemma in this technological domain. This trilemma directly pertains to the performance, security, and decentralization properties of blockchain technology, and how to strike a balance among them has become a focal point for numerous researchers. To gain deep insights into this trilemma, it's essential to revisit its theoretical foundation – the CAP theorem of distributed systems, which encompasses consistency, availability, and partition tolerance.

1.4.1 CAP Theorem for Distributed Systems

In July 2000, Professor Eric Brewer from the University of California, Berkeley, proposed the CAP conjecture (Brewer 2000, pp. 343477–343502) at the ACM PODC conference.

The definitions of the CAP properties are as follows:

Definition 1.1 Consistency
The same data is simultaneously perceived by all nodes, implying that in the event of concurrent reading and writing of multiple data copies, it is imperative for all nodes to possess identical data at any given moment.

Consistency can be comprehended from two distinct perspectives, namely the client side and server side. From the client's standpoint, it primarily pertains to addressing the challenge of obtaining updated data amidst multiple concurrent accesses. On the server side, it involves distributing updates across the entire system.

From the client's point of view, strategies of how processes access updated data concurrently determine different consistencies. Strong consistency ensures that all subsequent accesses see the updated data, while weak consistency allows for some or all accesses to not see updates for a certain period. Final consistency only requires that all accesses eventually see the updated data after a specified time delay.

Definition 1.2 Availability
Reads and writes are always successful. That is, the service is consistently available during normal response time.

High availability mainly refers to the system's ability to effectively serve users without any operational failures, access timeouts, or other negative user experiences. Availability is usually associated with measures such as distributed data redundancy and load balancing.

Definition 1.3 Partition Tolerance

The distributed system is capable of providing consistent or available services to the external world, even in the face of arbitrary information loss or failure of a system component.

In essence, in a distributed system, consistency, availability, and partition tolerance cannot be fully achieved simultaneously. Two years later, Seth Gilbert and Nancy Lynch of MIT theoretically confirmed the CAP conjecture (Gilbert and Lynch 2002, pp. 51–59). Consequently, the CAP theorem became a universally accepted theorem in the field of distributed computing. Let us now delve into the proof of CAP.

First, we demonstrate the basic scenario of CAP. As shown in Figure 1.4, there are two nodes in the network, N_A and N_B, which can be regarded as interconnected computers. In N_A, there is an application A and a database V, and N_B also has an application B and a database V. In this demonstration, A and B are two components of the distributed system, and their database's initial state is both V_0. Herein, V_0 represents the two sub-databases of the data storage in the distributed system.

When ensuring consistency, the data in N_A and N_B is identical, represented as $V_0 = V_0$. In scenarios that prioritize availability, regardless of whether the user queries N_A or N_B, an immediate response will be received. Under partition tolerance, if either N_A or N_B crashes or there is a network interruption, it will not impact the regular operation between N_A and N_B.

Figure 1.5 illustrates the standard workflow of a distributed system. A user requests a data update to the node N_A, and the application A updates the database from V_0 to V_1. The distributed system then undertakes a synchronization operation M, syncing V_1 to V_0 in N_B. Subsequently, the data in N_B responds to the request from N_B. Here, we can define the consistency between the databases V in N_A and N_B by whether their data is identical. External requests to N_A and N_B are regarded as availability, and the network environment between N_A and N_B is viewed as partition tolerance.

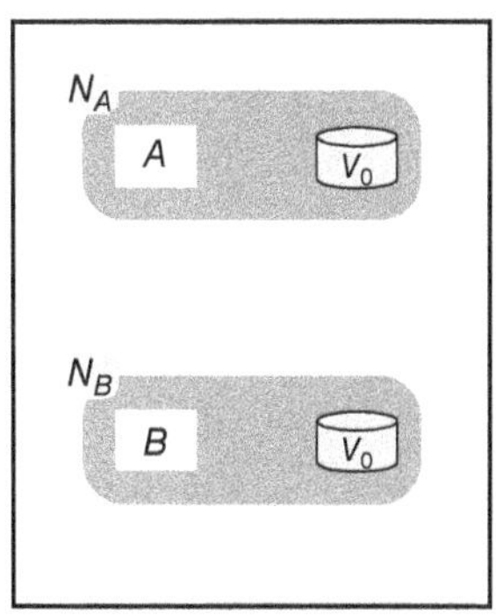

Figure 1.4 Scenario design for proving the CAP theorem.

The above describes a scenario of normal operation, which is also the ideal situation. However, when errors occur, one must ponder whether consistency, availability, and partition tolerance can all be satisfied simultaneously or if compromises must be made.

The primary distinction between a distributed system and a single-node system lies in its network. Let us assume an extreme situation where the network connection between N_A and N_B is severed. If we aim to cater to this kind of network anomaly, essentially

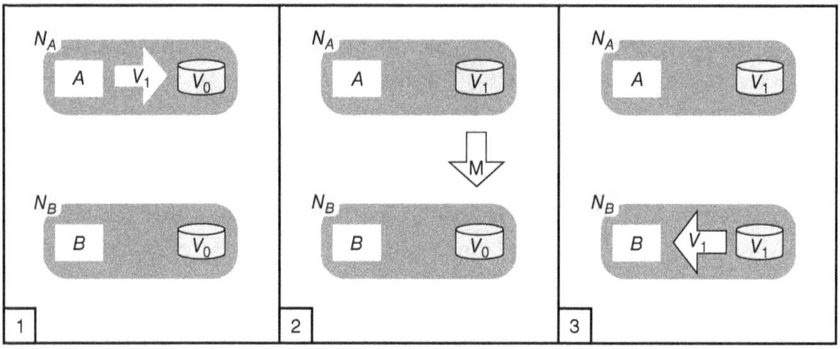

Figure 1.5 Normal flow of the distributed system.

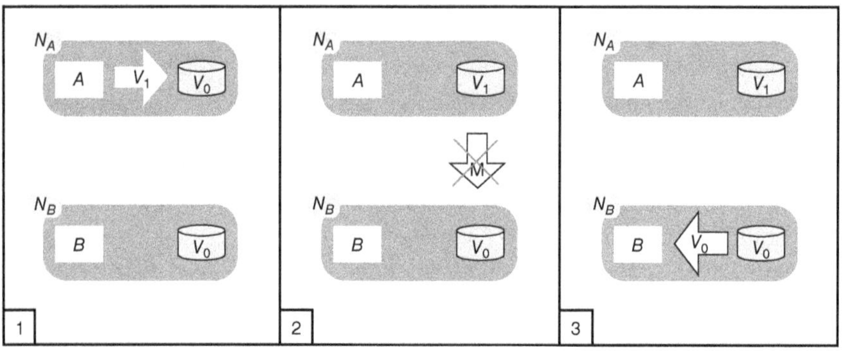

Figure 1.6 Network anomaly in the distributed system.

aiming to achieve partition tolerance, can we also simultaneously ensure consistency and responsiveness?

As illustrated in Figure 1.6, assume that when the network connection between N_A and N_2 is disrupted, a user sends a data update request to N_A. Consequently, the data V_0 in N_A will be updated to V_1. Given the network disconnection, the distributed system's synchronization operation M fails, leaving the data in N_B still as V_0. At this juncture, when a user sends a data retrieval request to N_B, since synchronization has not been executed, the application cannot promptly provide the user with the most recent data, V_1.

In response to the aforementioned dilemma, applications are presented with two choices. First, they could sacrifice data consistency and return the outdated data, V_0, to the user. Alternatively, they could sacrifice availability, holding back responses until the network connection is restored and the data update operation M has been completed, and only then provide the user with the updated data, V_1.

The above process demonstrates that for a distributed system aiming to achieve partition tolerance, a choice has to be made between consistency and availability (i.e., CP or AP). In systems that do not necessitate partition tolerance, it is evidently possible to ensure both consistency and availability (CA). In truth, partitions are an inevitable occurrence in distributed systems; thus, a CA system predominantly refers to one that, following a partition, allows its subsystems to still maintain both consistency and availability. In summation, a distributed system can, at most, satisfy two out of the three properties: consistency, availability, and partition tolerance.

For distributed systems, ensuring partition tolerance is imperative. So, a compromise between consistency (C) and availability (A) must be made. This compromise does not necessarily mean favoring C while entirely neglecting A. It could involve striking a balance in the proportion of how CA is implemented, such as prioritizing A with supplemental C, thereby achieving basic availability and eventual consistency. The BASE theory was formulated to address this issue.

The BASE model stems from practical engineering solutions to the tradeoffs between consistency and availability as presented in the CAP theorem. Its fundamental tenet emphasizes the Basic Availability (BA), Soft State (S), and Eventual Consistency (E). Basic availability implies that even if faults arise in a distributed system, only partial functionality is compromised while core functions remain available. A soft state allows for temporary existence in an intermediate state without affecting availability. Eventual consistency indicates that, given enough time, the data across all nodes will synchronize and become consistent. The significance of the BASE theory lies in its ability to avoid a rigid choice between A or C, permitting partial realization of both A and C.

Based on varying application scenarios and requirements, it is essential to properly strike a balance between consistency and availability to ensure optimal operation of applications and middleware. Table 1.1 lists the CAP tradeoffs for typical distributed applications.

1.4.2 Classic Blockchain Solution to Trilemmas

To optimize the delicate equilibrium among the CAP trilemma's three elements, primary enhancements are made to the blockchain's consensus layer. Due to the unavoidable nature of partitioning in distributed systems, it's essential for blockchain consensus mechanisms to navigate these challenging network conditions. Blockchain consensus models have achieved a balance between consistency and availability. Nonpermissioned blockchains typically implement consensus mechanisms based on proofs like PoW by Nakamoto in 2008 and PoS by King

Table 1.1 CAP tradeoffs for distributed applications.

Application	Type	Other
Mysql	CA	AP in master–slave mode.
Zookeeper	CP	After partitioning, external services are only provided if the number of nodes inside the partition exceeds quorum.
Eureka	AP	Eventual consistency.
Redis – sentinel/cluster mode	AP	Eventual consistency. The single entity satisfies CA.
RocketMQ – master–slave mode	AP	Eventual consistency.
Distributed transaction – 2PC	CP	The locked resources block other requests for them.
Distributed transaction – TCC	AP	Eventual consistency.
Distributed transaction – best effort try	AP	Eventual consistency.

and Nadal in 2012, with a focus on maximizing availability. A key attribute of these mechanisms is their proficiency in maintaining robust partition tolerance and availability, achieved through mechanisms like selecting the longest chain. However, such approaches introduce delays in confirmation times and reduce throughput, leading to a shift from strong to eventual consistency. On the other hand, consortium blockchains often prefer Byzantine Fault Tolerance (BFT) algorithms, a voting-based mechanism, ensuring strong consistency and partition tolerance but compromising on availability. To mitigate this, DP-Hybrid (Wen et al. 2020, pp. 57–71) introduces a sharding strategy that applies PBFT within shards and Constrained PoW (CPoW) among them, thus cutting down communication costs at the cost of consistency.

Moreover, blockchain innovation faces its own trilemma, involving security, scalability, and decentralization, indicating that achieving all three simultaneously is unattainable. This challenge, while unverified, is widely recognized through practical observations. To enhance security, Hamid Azimy et al. (2022, pp. 1503–1523) improved Bitcoin's difficulty adjustment algorithm to thwart selfish mining, albeit reducing scalability. In another instance, Divija Swetha Gadiraju and her team (2023) have exploited Deep Reinforcement Learning (DRL) to fine-tune the Prime blockchain's parameters, striking a balance between security and scalability using two distinct DRL models.

In conclusion, despite the theoretical and practical challenges posed by blockchain trilemmas, this paper introduces a novel framework for consortium blockchains that melds algorithmic and physical approaches. This method stands out by fulfilling all trilemma criteria without compromises, unlike solutions that solely rely on software-based strategies such as consensus algorithms.

1.4.3 General Blockchain Trilemma

Han Wang et al. (Wang et al. 2023) have established and substantiated the overarching blockchain dilemma by connecting CAP and blockchain challenges conceptually. Their thesis contends that a network structure, which is non-Byzantine and free from crashing, is subject to latencies yet operates within a bounded delay, will align its state eventually, mirroring the network in its intended synchronized state. It is noted that a supermajority, exceeding two-thirds of the network's nodes, is presumed to be dependable and forthright. For simplification, it is assumed that every node is equipped equally with sufficient computational power, storage space, and bandwidth, devoid of any constraints posed by the central network.

Lemma 1.1 CAP Theory (Gilbert and Lynch 2002, pp. 51–59)
Within any distributed system, only two out of the three core attributes – consistency, availability, and partition tolerance – can be fully realized.

Corollary 1.1 Consistency is a Necessary Condition for Security
Proof: Imagine two nodes, labeled *A* and *B*, within a blockchain system documenting an address *H* with an initial state value X_1 simultaneously. Should a division occur, placing *A* and *B* into separate partitions, and should an illicit transaction revising address *H*' s state be executed in *A*' s partition, its state value would shift from X_1 to X_2. Conversely, a subsequent check in *B*' s partition would show address H retaining the state value X_1. This discrepancy signifies that the ledger of the blockchain demonstrates inconsistency.

Thus, it is evident that when blockchain states are nonuniform, it opens the door to unpredictable occurrences, exploitation, and systemic weaknesses, which deems the blockchain insecure. Conversely, a system is deemed secure if it remains equitable and consistent even amidst unfavorable conditions. Hence, consistency is a fundamental underpinning for security, meaning that blockchain security demands a more exacting standard than that required for distributed systems.

Corollary 1.2 Availability is a Necessary Condition for Scalability
For a blockchain network to scale effectively, the availability of its system is crucial.

Proof: In a blockchain framework, availability mandates that all standard operations, both read and write, are efficiently processed. Scalability within such systems refers to the network's capability to manage an increasing load of nodes and transactional activity. Technically speaking, scalability is reflected by a high transaction processing rate. Therefore, it becomes apparent that availability is a more critical network parameter than scalability. That is to say, the potential for scalability in a blockchain is heavily dependent on the sustained availability of the system, a stipulation that is considerably more exacting than for standard distributed systems. Without consistent availability, a blockchain's ability to scale is inherently compromised.

Corollary 1.3 Partition Tolerance is a Necessary Condition for Achieving Decentralization

The capacity for partition tolerance is indispensable for achieving decentralization.
Proof: Reflecting on the rationale of Lemma 1.1, partitions are inherently assumed within distributed systems. The rationale is that within the realm of a genuine distributed network, it's impractical to expect flawless operation from every node or connection at all times. In the context of blockchain infrastructures, decentralization stands as a core attribute, implying that the system's operations are not dependent on a single point of failure. This aspect is twofold. Initially, a blockchain is composed of multiple nodes, each capable of processing a specific volume of transactions concurrently. Additionally, since these nodes are not under the exclusive control of any one entity or group, blockchain networks are by necessity distributed. Consequently, the inherent nature of decentralization opens up the possibility for partitions to occur. Hence, partition tolerance emerges as a fundamental requirement for a decentralized framework.

In essence, consistency, availability, and partition tolerance are the triad essential for security, scalability, and decentralization, respectively. Echoing Lemma 1.1, it becomes evident that it is challenging for consistency, availability, and partition tolerance to function in perfect harmony. Therefore, security, scalability, and decentralization present a complex conundrum when required to operate simultaneously within blockchain technology. It follows that a further Corollary 1.4 is warranted.

Corollary 1.4 General Blockchain Trilemma

For pairs consisting of <consistency, security>, <availability, scalability>, and < partition tolerance, decentralization>, selecting one element from each category leads to a combination that encapsulates the blockchain trilemma.

Building upon Corollary 1.4, this segment formulates an advanced blockchain trilemma and delineates its three fundamental aspects. The initial step in appraising a blockchain trilemma's resolution involves the quantification of its properties, thereby furnishing subsequent analytical support. As stipulated by Corollary 1.4, one can construct eight distinct blockchain trilemmas from pairs of attributes. For simplicity in measurement, this discussion selects consistency, scalability, and partition tolerance as the focal points of the trilemma. Below are the foundational descriptions for each attribute.

1.4.3.1 Consistency

The likelihood of creating forks is a metric for evaluating consistency, as per Definition 1.4, deriving from the analysis (Kertesz and Baniata 2021, pp. 393–404). The application of probabilistic assessments allows for normalization ranging from 0 to 1, thus enabling more straightforward juxtaposition with other properties. In a perfect setting, a blockchain is recognized for its high consistency when there are no forks, denoted by a consistency metric of $C = 1$. On the contrary, the presence of an irreconcilable fork signifies poor consistency, quantified by $C = 0$.

Definition 1.4 Consistency
$C = 1 - Pr\{fork\}$, where $Pr\{fork\}$ represents the probability of encountering forks within a blockchain. $C \in [0, 1]$.

1.4.3.2 Scalability

The metric used to gauge scalability within a blockchain environment is the rate of transactional throughput, denoted as TPS, which hinges on a couple of factors: the volume of transactions each block can hold, and the temporal gap between the creation of consecutive blocks (Liu et al. 2019, pp. 3559–3570). In scenarios where the system operates optimally and all pending transactions are promptly encapsulated within new blocks, the throughput reflects the average rate of incoming transactions per second. From the viewpoint of a coordinating node, this throughput is equivalent to the mean arrival rate, λ, of transaction requests. Thus, $TPS_{max} = \lambda$. To allow for a standardized assessment of the three dimensions discussed herein, scalability is normalized according to Definition 1.5.

Definition 1.5 Scalability
$A = TPS/\lambda$, where the throughput TPS denotes the average rate at which a blockchain processes transactions per second, and the arrival rate λ denotes the average number of new transactions generated per second in the network $A \in [0, 1]$.

1.4.3.3 Partition Tolerance

Partition tolerance serves as a marker of a blockchain's resilience. Influenced by the quantization approach (Wang et al. 2023, p. e4820), Definition 1.6 articulates the normalized quantization metric as the likelihood of maintaining an effective partition within the network, despite the presence of several dysfunctional nodes or links. An effective partition, replete with high-performing nodes, is operational with a partition tolerance probability $P = 1$. If this state is not achieved, it results in an ineffective partition with $P = 0$.

Definition 1.6 Partition Tolerance
$P = 1 - Pr\{wrong\ partition\}$, where $Pr\{wrong\ partition\}$ denotes the chance that a network with a partition fails to operate effectively due to a limited quantity of active nodes $P \in [0, 1]$.

1.4.4 Consortium Blockchain Framework for Resolving Trilemma

Figure 1.7 delineates a trilevel structural concept known as GBT-CHAIN, devised to tackle the trilemma confronting consortium blockchains. This architecture is delineated by essential layers: physical, network, consensus, and data, each integral to the foundation of a blockchain system. Notably, the data component is seamlessly integrated within the consensus stratum. Developers are afforded the latitude to append additional layers, such as incentive, contractual, and application strata, atop the consensus layer.

1.4.4.1 Upper Layer: Consensus and Data Layer

Positioned at the zenith of this structure are the consensus and data layers, the locus where BFT consensus mechanisms function. Despite varied implementations of BFT consensus protocols, they universally adhere to the traditional

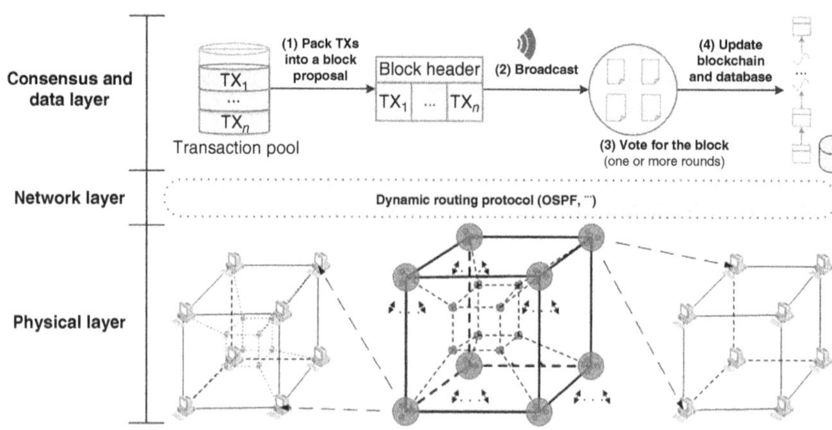

Figure 1.7 Three layers of the GBT-CHAIN framework.

"proposal-broadcast-voting" routine. A consensus node aggregates transactions in a memory repository. A node, typically the leader, extracts these transactions once a threshold of diversity or a temporal limit is reached, subsequently compiling them into a proposed block. The broadcasting phase incorporates at minimum one cycle of proposal dispatches. Subsequent phases permit consensus nodes to disseminate further block commitments. Voting may unfold over one (e.g., PoV), two (e.g., PBFT, Zyzzyva), or three stages (e.g., Basic HotStuff). Additionally, pipeline strategies can be deployed during this juncture, as evidenced by methodologies like Chained HotStuff and Votes-as-a-Proof (VaaP) (Fu, Wang, and Shi 2022, pp. 4964–4973), to harness computational efficiencies, thereby condensing multiple vote rounds into a singular event. Upon securing a majority consensus, the voting episode culminates. To thwart Byzantine actors from undermining the system, the voting quota typically exceeds the 2/3 majority of the consensus cohort. Once unanimity is achieved on a block, the leader consolidates a fresh block and forwards a proposal. Since each block references the antecedent through a hash, this sequence is tantamount to curating a chained data repository.

One must acknowledge that no consensus protocol is impeccably tailored to fluctuating network ecosystems over its lifespan (Singh et al. 2008, pp. 189–204). Therefore, GBT-CHAIN dynamically adjudicates the optimal BFT consensus algorithm (e.g., Zyzzyva, HotStuff, VaaP), attuned to contemporaneous network states and systemic demands. This arbitration correlates to the voting durations within the BFT consensus paradigm. A truncated voting sequence may signify enhanced scalability, characterized by reduced latency and amplified throughput under prime conditions, but at the expense of reliability, vulnerable to disruptions like view alterations and delays.

In ordinary operations, BFT consensus algorithms fulfill the criteria for robust consistency and scalability, independent of the voting sequence magnitude. Yet this necessitates a substantial network criterion: the preponderance of nodes in the largest partition should outnumber 2/3 of the total network nodes. Scalability plummets to nil if a network bifurcates lacking adequate node participation in the messaging process. In essence, BFT consensus protocols inherently favor consistency above scalability amidst instances of network partition failures.

1.4.4.2 Middle Layer: Network Layer

Within consortium blockchains, access control mechanisms ensure a fairly constant node count, though the nodes may evolve over time. Accounting for operational expenses, this stratum incorporates dynamic routing protocols such as Open Shortest Path First (OSPF) (Moy 1997). This system constructs and updates routing tables via inter-node communications. As network configurations shift, so too does the routing table, autonomously selecting the most efficient route for data packets.

This obviates the need for manual interventions by network administrators to recalibrate routing tables or reconfigure network structures. Instead, routers leverage the dynamic routing protocol, autonomously adapting routing information in accordance with interface settings and the status of connected pathways.

1.4.4.3 Lower Layer: Physical Layer

However, these two strata alone cannot fundamentally rectify issues of partition failures. There are dual justifications for this limitation. First, the ability of consensus algorithms to recognize system partitions is constrained by the infrastructure layers below, such as the network or the physical layer. More critically, network congestion-induced partitions may resolve over time, whereas those stemming from compromised hardware lack self-recovery capabilities. The issue of partition failures is hypothesized to be most effectively addressed at the blockchain's physical layer. Unlike permissionless blockchains, consortium blockchains feature manageable nodes, enabling direct refinement of the underlying physical architecture.

The GBT-CHAIN model adopts a hypercube configuration for its consensus nodes at the physical tier. This selection is attributed to the hypercube's robustness in terms of path redundancy and fault tolerance. Nonetheless, establishing a hypercube in expansive networks with numerous nodes demands extensive long-distance connections. To mitigate this, as illustrated in Figure 1.7, the design progresses to a hierarchical recursion involving additional intermediate or shorter connections, thereby reconciling the demands of network dependability with construction expenditures. Originating from a lower-dimensional state, the network evolves into a higher-dimensional hypercube following recursive expansion. Furthermore, the system is programmed to methodically restore any defective links within a predetermined timeframe.

In essence, hypercube-oriented architectures significantly reduce the likelihood of network partitions. Therefore, by superimposing a BFT consensus protocol that upholds both consistency and scalability, consortium blockchains can aspire to meet their trilemma threshold.

1.5 Chapter Summary

This chapter provides a comprehensive exploration of the fundamental principles and historical development of blockchain technology. Beginning with a basic introduction to blockchain, it focuses on the value evolution, underlying platform, regulation and governance, as well as layered architecture. The chapter then delves into the central challenge faced by the whole blockchain field – the trilemma – elucidating its connection to the CAP theorem for distributed systems while presenting both traditional and emerging solutions. Additionally, a framework GBT-CHAIN for consortium blockchains is meticulously introduced as a potential resolution. Overall, this chapter offers readers with a robust foundation in blockchain theory and effectively prepares them for subsequent chapters.

Discussion Questions

1.1 Please briefly describe the role of data layer and its key technologies.

A: The data layer serves as the foundation of blockchain architecture. It involves key technologies including data block structure, chained connection, timestamp, hash function, Merkle tree and cryptography. These technologies collectively ensure the integrity, security and traceability of data.

1.2 Briefly describe the significance of implementing P2P protocol at the network layer.

A: Blockchain is essentially a distributed ledger, making it inherently suitable for the P2P network model. Implementing the network layer of blockchain through P2P has three major technical advantages. First, it can prevent single-point attacks by ensuring that data loss from a node does not result in complete loss across the entire network since other nodes retain copies of that data. Second, it exhibits high fault tolerance as failures in some nodes do not cause damage to the overall network due to multiple sources of information availability. Third, it meets good compatibility and scalability while easily adapting to frequent changes in the node number and the network configuration.

1.3 Please briefly explain how the general blockchain trilemma is different compared to the classical CAP theorem.

A: While the classical CAP theorem reveals the tradeoff between consistency, availability, and partition tolerance in distributed systems, the general blockchain trilemma extends it by encompassing additional dimensions. The key difference lies in its extension beyond the original single impossible triangle of the CAP theorem to include eight comprehensive impossible triangles that cover six fundamental properties: consistency, security, availability, scalability, partition tolerance, and decentralization.

References

Azimy, H., Ghorbani, A.A. and Bagheri, E., 2022. Preventing proof-of-work mining attacks. *Information Sciences*, 608, pp. 1503–1523.

Brewer, E.A., 2000, July. Towards robust distributed systems. In PODC (Vol. 7, No. 10.1145, pp. 343477–343502).

Buterin, V., 2014. A next-generation smart contract and decentralized application platform. *White Paper*, 3(37), pp. 2-1.

Castro, M. and Liskov, B., 1999, February. Practical byzantine fault tolerance. In OsDI (Vol. 99, No. 1999, pp. 173–186).

Fu, X., Wang, H. and Shi, P., 2022. Votes-as-a-Proof (VaaP): Permissioned blockchain consensus protocol made simple. *IEEE Transactions on Parallel and Distributed Systems*, 33(12), pp. 4964–4973.

Gadiraju, D.S., Lalitha, V. and Aggarwal, V., 2023. An optimization framework based on deep reinforcement learning approaches for prism blockchain. *IEEE Transactions on Services Computing*, 16, pp. 2451–2461.

Gao, Y., Lu, Y., Lu, Z., Tang, Q., Xu, J. and Zhang, Z., 2022, November. Dumbo-ng: Fast asynchronous bft consensus with throughput-oblivious latency. In Proceedings of the 2022 ACM SIGSAC Conference on Computer and Communications Security (pp. 1187–1201).

Gilbert, S. and Lynch, N., 2002. Brewer's conjecture and the feasibility of consistent, available, partition-tolerant web services. *ACM SIGACT News*, 33(2), pp. 51–59.

Kertesz, A. and Baniata, H., 2021, August. Consistency analysis of distributed ledgers in fog-enhanced blockchains. In European Conference on Parallel Processing (pp. 393–404). Cham: Springer International Publishing.

King, S. and Nadal, S., 2012. Ppcoin: Peer-to-peer crypto-currency with proof-of-stake. Self-published paper, August, 19(1).

Larimer, D., 2014. Delegated proof-of-stake (dpos). *Bitshare Whitepaper*, 81, p. 85.

Lasla, N., Al-Sahan, L., Abdallah, M. and Younis, M., 2022. Green-PoW: an energy-efficient blockchain proof-of-work consensus algorithm. *Computer Networks*, 214, p. 109118.

Li, K., Li, H., Hou, H., Li, K. and Chen, Y., 2017, December. Proof of vote: A high-performance consensus protocol based on vote mechanism & consortium blockchain. In 2017 IEEE 19th International Conference on High Performance Computing and Communications; IEEE 15th International Conference on Smart City; IEEE 3rd International Conference on Data Science and Systems (HPCC/SmartCity/DSS) (pp. 466–473). IEEE.

Li, H., Chen, Y., Shi, X., Bai, X., Mo, N., Li, W., Guo, R., Wang, Z. and Sun, Y., 2023, November. FISCO-BCOS: An enterprise-grade permissioned blockchain system with high-performance. In Proceedings of the International Conference for High Performance Computing, Networking, Storage and Analysis (pp. 1–17).

Liu, M., Yu, F.R., Teng, Y., Leung, V.C. and Song, M., 2019. Performance optimization for blockchain-enabled industrial internet of things (IIoT) systems: a deep reinforcement learning approach. *IEEE Transactions on Industrial Informatics*, 15(6), pp. 3559–3570.

Moy, J., 1997. OSPF version 2 (No. rfc2178).

Nakamoto, S., 2008. Bitcoin: A peer-to-peer electronic cash system. Decentralized business review.

Praveen, G., Singh, S.P., Chamola, V. and Guizani, M., 2022. Novel consensus algorithm for blockchain using proof-of-majority (PoM). *IEEE Networking Letters*, 4(4), pp. 208–211.

Singh, A., Das, T., Maniatis, P., Druschel, P. and Roscoe, T., 2008, April. BFT protocols under fire. In NSDI (Vol. 8, pp. 189–204).

Swan, M., 2015. *Blockchain: Blueprint for a new economy.* O'Reilly Media, Inc.

Szabo, N., 1994. Smart contracts.

Wang, H., Li, H., Ye, Q., Lu, P., Yang, Y., Chong, P.H.J., Chu, X., Lv, Q. and Smahi, A., 2023. A physical topology for optimizing partition tolerance in consortium blockchains to reach CAP guarantee bound. *Transactions on Emerging Telecommunications Technologies*, p. e4820.

Wang, H., Li, H., Smahi, A., Xiao, M. and Li, S.Y.R., 2023. GBT-CHAIN: A system framework for solving the general trilemma in permissioned blockchains. Distributed Ledger Technologies: Research and Practice.

Wen, F., Yang, L., Cai, W. and Zhou, P., 2020. DP-Hybrid: a two-layer consensus protocol for high scalability in permissioned blockchain. In Blockchain and Trustworthy Systems: Second International Conference, BlockSys 2020, Dali, China, August 6–7, 2020, Revised Selected Papers 2 (pp. 57–71). Springer Singapore.

Wu, F., Yuen, H.Y., Chan, H., Leung, V.C. and Cai, W., 2023. Facilitating serverless match-based online games with novel blockchain technologies. *ACM Transactions on Internet Technology*, 23(1), pp. 1–26.

Yuan, Y. and Wang, F., 2016. Current status and outlook of blockchain technology development. *Journal of Automation* 42(4):481–494.

Zhang, E., 2014. A byzantine fault tolerance algorithm for blockchain. Neo Documentation.

Zhongguancun Blockchain Industry Alliance (2014). Global Blockchain Industry Mapping Report.

2

Physical Topology in Blockchain

This chapter will provide a detailed discussion of the composition and performance of multidimensional hypercube-based topologies. First, six basic physical topologies will be introduced in Section 2.1 and explain their limitations. Next, the network topology based on multidimensional hypercube will be introduced in Section 2.2. This physical topology enables the CA-type consortium blockchain protocol to satisfy the three properties of CAP in probability. Section 2.3 will further extend the basic multidimensional hypercube topology into a hierarchical recursive topology with intermediate and short links to address the problem of excessive link redundancy. Finally, Section 2.4 will focus on analyzing the partition tolerance performance based on multidimensional hypercube, demonstrating that the hypercube topology achieves exceptional partition tolerance performance through hierarchical recursion, resulting in reduced network overhead.

2.1 Basic Physical Topology of Computer Network

Physical topology of computer network (Kurose 2005) refers to the physical structure of links between devices and nodes within the network. The topology describes the physical link methods and layout of devices, links, and intermediary devices. This section will focus on the physical topology structure of computer networks.

Nodes and links are fundamental constituents of computer networks, wherein nodes are interconnected via links, while repeaters enhance the transmission capacity and quality of the links, thereby facilitating reliable data transmission and communication.

Principles and Applications of Blockchain Systems: How to Overcome the CAP Trilemma in Consortium Blockchain, First Edition. Hui Li and Han Wang.

Published 2025 by John Wiley & Sons, Inc.

Nodes: In computer networks, nodes refer to devices or hosts such as computers, servers, routers, switches, and printers. Each node in the network has a unique identifier that facilitates communication and data exchange. Nodes can act as data senders or receivers and play a role in data processing and forwarding within the network.

Links: Links, in the context of computer networks, serve as physical channels that connect nodes for data transmission. These links can take the form of cables, fiber optics, or wireless channels and enable communication between nodes by transmitting data frames or packets. They can be either point-to-point links connecting two nodes or broadcast links allowing multiple nodes to share the same link.

Repeater: Repeater is a device utilized to amplify the signal strength and extend the transmission distance of a link. It serves to eliminate signal attenuation and noise in the link by amplifying and propagating the signal. By extending the length of the link and enhancing signal quality, repeaters facilitate long-distance data transmission within networks, playing a pivotal role in long-distance communication and large-scale network deployments.

The computer network encompasses six fundamental physical topologies: bus, star, ring, tree, mesh, and hybrid.

2.1.1 Bus

According to Figure 2.1, devices in a bus topology are interconnected through a shared transmission medium, such as coaxial cable or fiber optic. Data is broadcast to all connected devices through the transmission medium. Bus topology is typically well-suited for small-scale networks, such as those in small offices or laboratories. Due to the limited number of devices and short distances involved in small networks, the bus topology can provide simple and effective network connectivity.

The bus topology is relatively simple, requiring only one transmission medium as the backbone, and all devices are connected to the backbone through link interfaces. This makes bus topology easy to deploy, maintain, and expand. Maintenance personnel can easily access and manage devices, and adding new devices only requires connecting the interfaces to the backbone. Troubleshooting and repair work are relatively simple because the physical link between a faulty device and the backbone is quite visible. Additionally, bus topology can also be used as a shared transmission medium, as all devices are connected to the same transmission medium, enabling data to be broadcast to all devices through that medium. When one device sends data, other devices can receive and process the data. It is also easy to monitor and manage network traffic in bus topology. Administrators can easily monitor data transmission on the backbone, and identify and resolve potential issues.

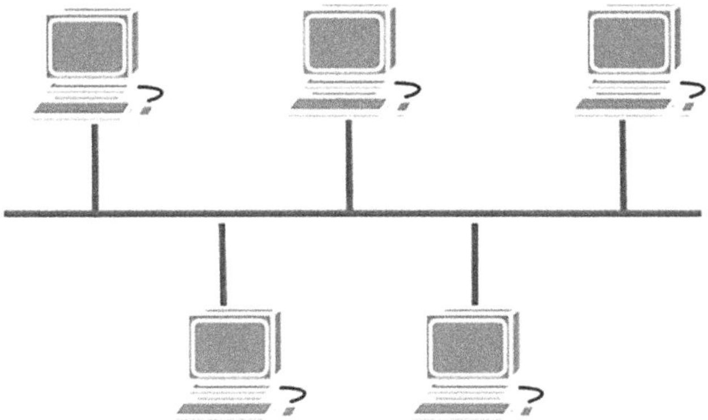

Figure 2.1 Bus topology.

Despite the advantages of simplicity and ease of deployment, bus topology has some limitations. One major limitation is data collisions on the bus. When multiple devices send data simultaneously, information collisions may occur, leading to compromised network performance and restricted transmission rates. Additionally, since the transmission medium in a bus topology is shared among all connected devices, any failure in this medium can have a detrimental impact on the entire network. Therefore, when a bus topology is designed, redundancy and backup mechanisms need to be considered to enhance reliability.

In summary, the bus topology is a straightforward and cost-effective physical topology suitable for small networks. It allows devices to communicate through a shared transmission medium, but the reliability and performance limitations of the transmission medium should be considered. In practical applications, the bus topology is often combined with other topology structures or technologies, such as hubs and switches, to meet complex network requirements.

2.1.2 Star

The star topology is a prevalent physical network topology widely used in home networks and small office networks. As shown in Figure 2.2, in a star topology, all devices are directly connected to a central device, such as a switch or hub. The central device serves as a hub for data transmission, forwarding data packets and coordinating network communication. When a device sends data, the data is transmitted through the link to the central device and then forwarded to the target device. This approach enables relatively independent communication between devices without interfering with the communication of other devices.

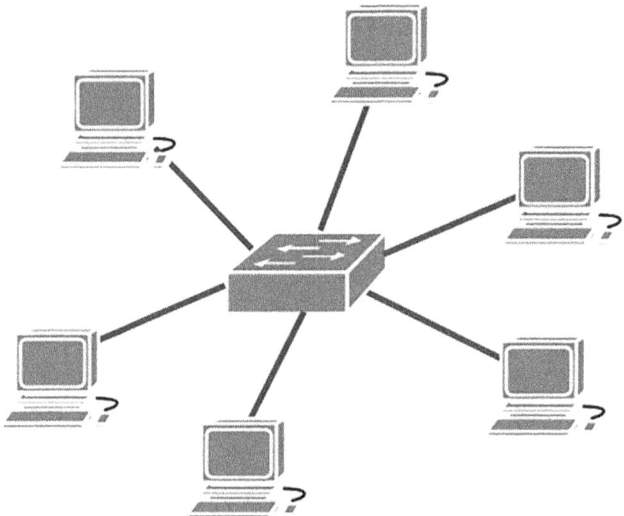

Figure 2.2 Star topology.

The star topology is relatively simple and easy to deploy and maintain. Since all devices are connected to the central device, it is easy to expand the network or establish new links by directly connecting with the central device. This simplifies the network deployment process and reduces the complexity of cable configuration. When a device failure requires troubleshooting, configuration changes, or performance optimization, a star topology only needs to focus on the central device rather than requiring a detailed examination of the entire network. The star topology also has the advantage of high fault tolerance. Since the communication between devices is carried out through the central device, if a device fails or is disconnected, other devices can still communicate normally without causing any harm to the entire network.

Although the star topology has many advantages, there are also some potential limitations. One of the major limitations is the potential risk of a central device acting as a single point of failure. If the central node fails, the entire network cannot work properly. Therefore, when a star topology is designed, redundancy and backup mechanisms are often considered to improve reliability.

In summary, the star topology offers a convenient choice for network deployment and maintenance due to its simplicity and controllability. Through centralized management, flexible control and efficient management of the entire network can be achieved. However, the reliability and redundancy of central node need to be taken into consideration during the design phase to reduce the risk of single points of failure.

2.1.3 Ring

In a ring topology, each node is directly connected to adjacent devices, forming a closed loop. Data is passed through the ring, and each node receives and forwards the data to the subsequent node until it reaches the target node, as depicted in Figure 2.3. Ring topology is well-suited for small networks where the number of devices is relatively small and close together. It provides a simple and effective means of connectivity and has commendable performance in small-scale environments.

The structure of the ring topology is relatively simple. Each node only needs to be directly connected to its two adjacent nodes. This makes the deployment and configuration of the network easier and faster. In a ring topology, although there is a potential risk for a single point of failure, in small-scale environments this risk is relatively low. If a node or link fails, data can continue to be transmitted through other paths bypassing the failed node. This redundant path improves the reliability and fault tolerance of the network. In addition, the ring topology has the advantage of load balancing as data transmission occurs sequentially among devices. This sequential transmission enables load balancing and prevents data from being concentrated on a single node, thereby improving overall network performance.

Although ring topology has the above advantages, it also has some limitations. One is the issue of latency. In a ring topology, data must be transmitted in the order of the ring, so the delay in data transmission will increase as the number of nodes on the ring increases. This may have an impact on applications that demand high real-time responsiveness. Second, if a node or link on the ring fails, the entire ring may be affected. In order to improve reliability, redundant paths or backup rings are usually used to avoid single points of failure.

In general, ring topology is a relatively simple physical topology with certain advantages. It exhibits good performance and fault tolerance in small networks,

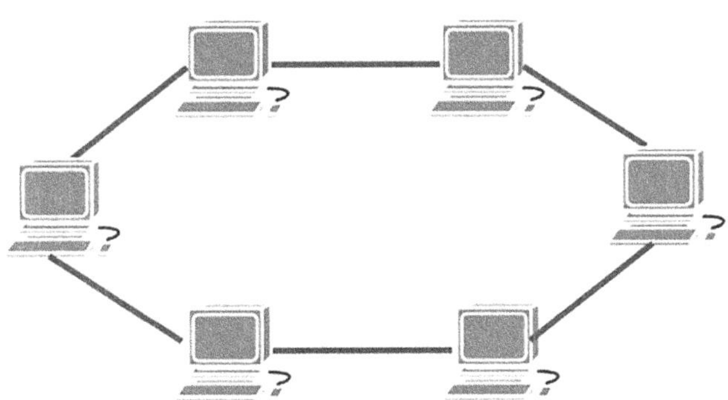

Figure 2.3 Ring topology.

but may not be suitable in large networks or scenarios with high requirements for latency. In practical applications, ring topology is often combined with other topologies or technologies such as redundant paths and monitoring mechanisms to meet complex network requirements and improve reliability.

2.1.4 Tree

Tree topology adopts a hierarchical tree structure to connect nodes. In a tree topology, a root node is connected to multiple child nodes, and each child node can further connect with additional child nodes, forming a hierarchical relationship, as shown in Figure 2.4. Data travels down from the root node in the tree structure, through branches with other intermediate nodes and finally reaches the target node. Tree topology is suitable for medium-sized networks such as large offices, campus networks, or branch offices.

In a tree topology, multiple paths typically exist to connect different nodes from the root node to a leaf, offering redundancy and fault recovery capabilities. If a certain path fails, data can be seamlessly transmitted through other paths to bypass the failure. The hierarchical structure of a tree topology facilitates efficient transmission as data only needs to traverse a specific path toward the target node without being broadcast throughout the entire network. In addition, the tree topology allows the expansion of the network. By adding more child nodes and branches, more nodes can be connected to the network to meet the growing needs of the network.

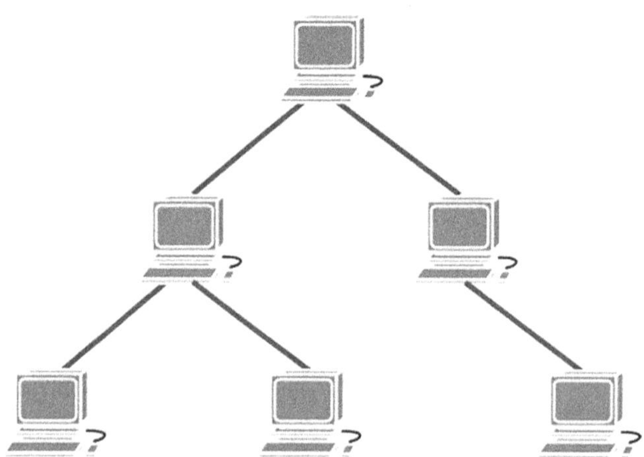

Figure 2.4 Tree topology.

Despite offering benefits such as failure recovery, scalability, and efficient data transfer, the tree topology still exhibits limitations in terms of single points of failure and latency.

Firstly, the issue of a single point of failure arises in a tree topology where the root node is the key component for network communication. If the root node fails, the entire network will be severely affected because all data transmission must travel through the root node. This single point of failure can cause such downtime unless there are backup root nodes or redundant paths available. Therefore, it is crucial to ensure the reliability and having redundant backups. In addition, even if a failure occurs at a non-root node, it will affect all child nodes directly connected to that node. If a branch or child node fails, all devices under that branch will lose access to the network. Thus, in designing a tree topology, failure recovery mechanisms and redundant paths must be taken into account to address the risk of single points of failure.

Furthermore, there is the issue of latency in a tree topology where data must pass through multiple nodes before reaching its target node. With each node passed, the transmission delay increases. Especially in deep network structures or when dealing with large data volumes, latency may increase significantly. In addition, data transmission must follow the path of the tree structure and cannot jump directly from one branch to another. Consequently, this elongates the transmission path and further contributes to increased delays. Although latency can be reduced by optimizing network devices and using high-speed links, in some application scenarios with extremely low latency requirements, a tree topology may not be the best choice. When a network is designed, careful evaluation of latency demands is necessary, and other topology structures, such as ring or mesh, should be considered to meet stringent latency requirements.

In summary, the tree topology offers a hierarchical and scalable network structure suitable for medium-sized network environments. However, as the tree topology expands, it may introduce complexities in terms of network management and configuration. Maintaining a large tree topology may require additional management resources and technology, so the reliability of the root node, redundant paths, and the complexity of network management should be taken into account during design and implementation.

2.1.5 Mesh

As shown in Figure 2.5, a mesh topology connects each node directly to other nodes so as to form a densely interconnected network without a central node, unlike the star topology. Each node can communicate directly with other nodes without the need for intermediate node forwarding. Because of the presence of multiple paths between nodes within a mesh topology, the source node needs

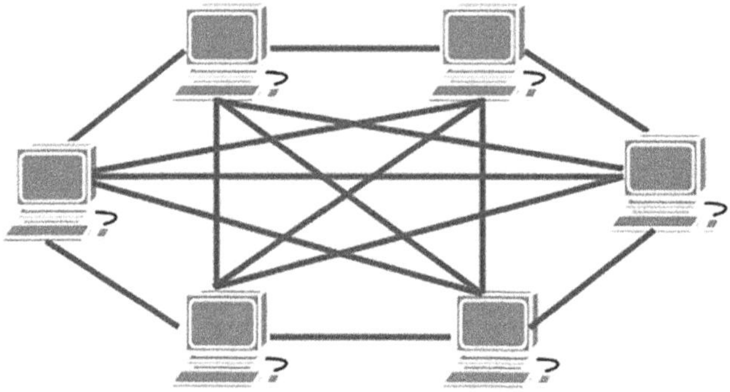

Figure 2.5 Mesh topology.

to select an appropriate path to transmit data to the target node. This usually involves using a routing algorithm to determine the best path, considering factors such as latency, bandwidth, and congestion. In computer networks, mesh topologies are widely evaluated for Local Area Network (LAN) and Wide Area Network (WAN), especially in scenarios that require high redundancy and reliability, such as the Internet, communication operator networks and enterprise networks.

Due to the direct interconnection between nodes, there are multiple paths available for data transfer. This provides redundant routes so that when an arbitrary node fails, data can continue to be transmitted through other paths, therefore, it enhances the fault tolerance and reliability of the network. In addition, a direct link enables low transmission delay through the shortest path. In terms of scalability, the mesh topology supports flexible node expansion. Each node can connect directly to other nodes, so new nodes can be easily added without impacting the entire network. Each node is independent in the mesh and can have immediate communication with other nodes. This peer-to-peer (P2P) structure facilitates equal and efficient information exchange.

However, the mesh topology also presents certain limitations and challenges. Since each node requires direct links to other nodes, it may necessitate a large number of physical links and resources. In large-scale networks, an increase in the number of nodes will result in $O(n^2) = n(n-1)/2$, here n is the number of links, thereby augmenting the complexity of network deployment and management. Furthermore, in a mesh topology, there are multiple paths between nodes, and the routing algorithms need to select the best path. This may lead to an escalation of the routing algorithm's complexity, necessitating increased computational and storage resources for processing and maintaining the routing table. Additionally, routing selection also needs to consider factors such as congestion and bandwidth to ensure efficient data transmission. Therefore, network management and routing algorithms may also become intricate in a mesh structure.

Despite these limitations and challenges, the mesh topology remains widely employed in various scenarios due to its high redundancy, reliability, and flexibility. Moreover, with technological advancements, some of these issues can be addressed through new solutions and optimization methods to improve the performance and manageability of the mesh topology.

2.1.6 Hybrid Topology

Hybrid topology combines different types of topologies for the purpose of leveraging their advantages to meet specific needs, such as achieving better performance, reliability, and management efficiency.

The combinations of topologies commonly include tree-star, tree-ring, and among others. The design of a hybrid topology can be adjusted based on specific network requirements and goals. Using data center networks as an example, with the requirements of high availability, high bandwidth, and low latency, while maintaining flexibility and scalability is crucial. The tree-star hybrid topology is a suitable solution to fulfill these requirements and has been widely adopted.

As the name suggests, the tree-star topology is a combination of tree and star structures. Typically, a central node, such as a switch or router, functions as the root node of star structure and links with multiple child nodes, such as switches, routers, or terminal devices. Each child node may further connect to other nodes, forming a deeper hierarchical tree structure, as shown in Figure 2.6.

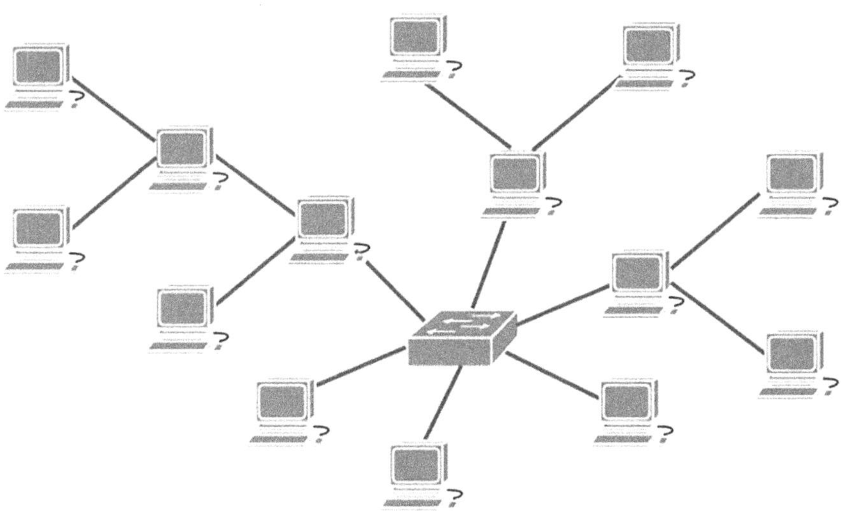

Figure 2.6 A hybrid topology known as the Tree-star topology.

This hybrid topology combines the characteristics of both tree and star topologies. Each tree topology provides redundant paths. When a path or node fails, data can continue to be transmitted through another path, thus ensuring high network availability and fault recovery capabilities. At the same time, the tree topology can provide high bandwidth at each level and achieve low transmission delay by optimizing path selection and reducing the hop count. And, by connecting multiple tree topologies to a central node, the network can be flexibly expanded and adjusted to accommodate growing demands. Finally, by using the star structure, the central node serves as the control center of the network, which can provide centralized management and simplify network operations and maintenance.

In summary, a hybrid topology can effectively address diverse design and management challenges from specific network requirements, such as fault tolerance, redundancy, and bandwidth demands, by amalgamating the advantages of different topology structures. In addition to the example of hybrid topologies mentioned above, even intricate combinations can be used in practical applications to cater to specific needs and circumstances. By flexibly combining different topologies, a hybrid topology can provide enhanced performance across various aspects to meet complex network requirements.

The aforementioned text has introduced six fundamental physical topologies of computer networks. However, in the fields of large-scale distributed systems and high-performance computing, these basic physical topologies may not suffice to meet the complex requirements of distributed networks. For example, complex cloud computing applications break down compute-storage services (Cao et al. 2022, pp. 1–42). Therefore, the classic cloud computing paradigm struggles to fulfill the current demand for low latency (Yuan et al. 2021, pp. 1873–1887). The following will introduce a hypercube-based network topology, which uses a highly structured hypercube topology between core nodes and a loose tree topology between super and ordinary nodes providing external services. This approach facilitates efficient end-to-end clustering and is well-suited for large-scale computer clusters and parallel computing systems.

2.2 N-Dimensional Hypercube-Based Topology – Making it Possible to Reach CAP Guarantee Bound in Consortium Blockchain

The CAP (Consistency, Availability, and Partition Tolerance) theorem states that it is impossible to simultaneously achieve strong satisfaction of all three properties in a distributed system. Several studies have concentrated on the optimization of overlay network topologies, particularly in semidistributed P2P networks, to enhance the speed of transaction and block propagation in blockchain systems. Decker and Wattenhofer (2013, pp. 1–10) proposed the construction of a subgraph composed of stars in the P2P network, which acted as the central hub for communication. This approach aimed to minimize the hop count required for routing among nodes. Fadhil, Owenson, and Adda (2016, pp. 468–475) introduced a clustering protocol, named Bitcoin Clustering Based on Super Node (BCBSN), based on super nodes for semidistributed P2P networks in blockchain systems. Clustering nodes based on their locality leads to a decrease in the delay of transmitting blocks and transactions within the cluster. Two additional protocols, namely the Bitcoin Clustering Based on Ping Time (BCBPT) protocol (Owenson and Adda 2017, pp. 2411–2416) and the Location-Based Clustering (LBC) protocol (Fadhil, Owenson, and Adda 2017, pp. 556–559), have been proposed. In the blockchain network, nodes are clustered by these protocols based on physical location metrics, such as ping time and geographical location, with the goal of minimizing the delay of propagation among neighboring nodes. Zhou et al. (2023, pp. 1–10) utilize a broadcast strategy that leverages Virtual Coordinate Systems (VCS) to guide routing decisions of individual nodes, thereby reducing transaction propagation delay without wasting network bandwidth. Although the impacts of the physical layer on performance are considered in these methods, they do not completely resolve the disparity between underlying topologies and the overlay.

In contrast to nodes within public blockchains, nodes in consortium blockchains are more controlled. Therefore, it is reasonable to take the physical layer directly into account when connecting a consortium blockchain. The excellent performance across various aspects is demonstrated in the hypercube topology, particularly in terms of load balancing and redundancy. In the original hypercube topology with a base $b = 2$, all nodes share equal responsibilities. The network diameter, which measures the shortest path with regard to node hops between the farthest nodes, is given by log_2N. Accordingly, a general physical topology is devised utilizing a multidimensional hypercube structure for the core consensus nodes. This approach effectively reduces the partition tolerance probability to below 10^{-50} while ensuring optimal performance of upper-layer protocols. The network and consensus layers maintain good consistency and availability. This allows consortium blockchain protocols of the CA type to reach the CAP guarantee bound in terms of probability, enabling their practical application in engineering scenarios (Wang et al. 2023, p. e4820).

The complete hypercube can be described as a convex, closed, and compact graph. Its one-dimensional skeleton comprises a collection of line segments that are of the same length and aligned with each dimension within the space they are occupied. The line segments intersecting at a specific point are orthogonal to each other, while the line segments within the hypercube are parallel to each other in their respective dimensions. Therefore, multidimensional hypercubes or

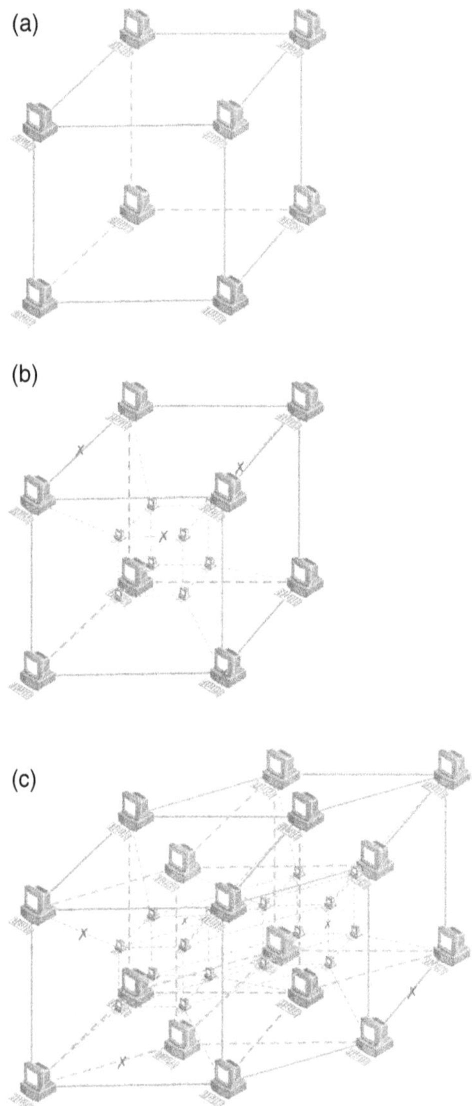

Figure 2.7 Examples of topology construction using complete or incomplete hypercubes evolving from three to five dimensions include: (a) A complete three-dimensional cube; (b) An incomplete four-dimensional hypercube; and (c) An incomplete five-dimensional hypercube.

their variants are utilized to construct the basic physical topology. Figure 2.7 provides topology examples constructed using hypercubes in three to five dimensions ($b = 2$). In the figure, crosses indicate links or nodes that are unallocated or invalid within the network. The nodes and links highlighted in blue and purple depict the hypercube prior to and following the movement, respectively, while links in green depict the movement path.

A unique ID is assigned to each node to facilitate individual identification. In the hypercube-based topology, links can be established between node pairs at a distance 2^i to enhance the efficiency of queries. Specifically, when the IDs of two nodes are different by 1 bit only, the logical and physical distances between them are both equivalent to 1. This makes the physical topology based on hypercubes highly matched with overlay networks that share same IDs.

Furthermore, in the physical topology based on hypercubes, invalid links are actively repaired within a finite timeframe. If the network is unfortunately partitioned, isolated nodes will request synchronization of data from neighboring nodes before returning to work.

2.3 Hierarchical Recursive Physical Topology of N-Dimensional Hypercube

When the network expands, the utilization of the basic hypercube topology results in an unnecessary surplus of links. Moreover, the emergence of sharding technology (Kokoris-Kogias et al. 2018, pp. 583–598) pushes nodes to construct distinct domains located in the upper layer, thereby augmenting network complexity. Consequently, recursion proves to be an effective approach for achieving scalability. The recursive topology maintains the benefits of strong regularity of the hypercube. By adopting a recursive topology, resources can be managed and utilized more effectively in the network and link redundancy issues can be reduced. The approach can also be used to cope with the complexity challenges brought by sharding technology (Liu et al. 2022, pp. 2131–2144) and improve the efficiency and stability of the entire network system.

The hierarchical recursive topology is presented in this section. It is derived from the basic hypercube topology through two steps: recursion and interconnection. First, each recursion transforms the original node into a domain, where nodes within the same domain can establish either a hypercube-based physical topology or any given topology. The count of domains at the r-th level ($r \geq 2$) is denoted as i_r, which corresponds to the smallest node number n_{min} within that domain. Following recursion, the number of new nodes increases by one digit compared to the number of the original node. Consequently, the first $(r-1)$ digits of i_r signify the recursive property of the domain from the first level to the $(r-1)$-th level. Assuming that the node numbers of the hypercube in domain of the firs level $i_1 = 0$ are $\{n_0\} = \{0, 1, 2, ..., (2^{dim_0} - 1)\}$, the node numbers in the domain i_r after $(r-1)$ recursions are $\{n_{i_r}\} = \{n_{i_{r-1}}\}$ & $\{0, 1, 2, ..., (2^{dim_{i_r}} - 1)\}$, where & denotes concatenation. Physical links connect the nodes within each domain at the r-th level, forming the topological connectivity of the domain at the $(r-1)$-th level. Thus, this process completes the interconnection among domains.

According to the abovementioned, three recursive approaches are devised for constructing hierarchical physical topologies, including completely symmetric, semisymmetric and asymmetric. Each recursion involves hypercubes of same dimensions in the completely symmetric method. In the semisymmetric method, hypercubes of the same dimensions are employed within the same level, while hypercubes of distinct dimensions are utilized between levels. In the asymmetric method, each domain adopts a hypercube of a distinct dimension or any other topology. Figure 2.8 illustrates instances of hierarchical recursive physical topologies.

Figure 2.9 serves as a concise illustration to explain the two stages involved in constructing a completely symmetric topology for two-dimensional hypercubes. The numbers presented within the circles represent the node numbers, while the numbers with underscores indicate the domain numbers. Assuming that there are four nodes, they are denoted as $\{n_{i_1}\} = \{n_0\} = \{0, 1, 2, 3\}$. In Step 1, each node undergoes recursion to form a two-dimensional hypercube. This results in four domains at the second level, encompassing a total of 16 nodes. These nodes are assigned the following numbers: $\{n_{i_2}\} = \{n_{00}, n_{10}, n_{20}, n_{30}\} = \{00, 01, 02, 03\} \cup \{10, 11, 12, 13\} \cup \{20, 21, 22, 23\} \cup \{30, 31, 32, 33\}$. In Step 2, based on the shared last digit, the four nodes within each domain establish connections with nodes in the other two associated domains. Solid lines depict physical links among nodes, while dashed lines signify logical links among domains. In particular, node 00 is connected to nodes 10 and 30, node 01 is linked to nodes 11 and 31, node 02 is connected to nodes 12 and 32, node 03 is linked to nodes 13 and 33, and so on.

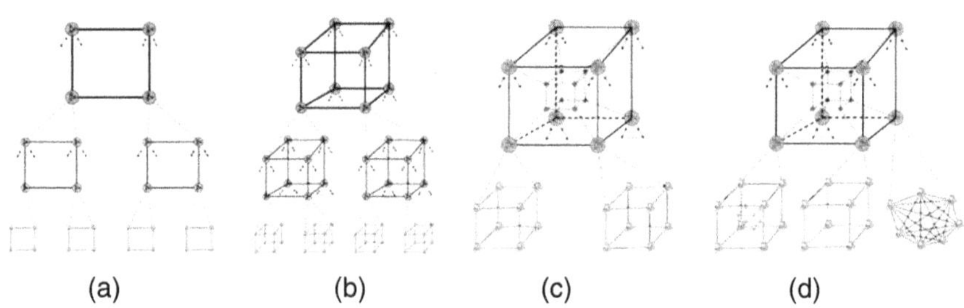

Figure 2.8 Examples of constructing hierarchical recursive topologies are depicted as follows: (a) A scenario representing the lowest boundary; (b) A completely symmetric scenario; (c) A semisymmetric scenario; (d) An asymmetric scenario consisting of four domains with a four-dimensional hypercube, eight domains with a three-dimensional hypercube, and four domains with a 7-point full connection topology at the second level.

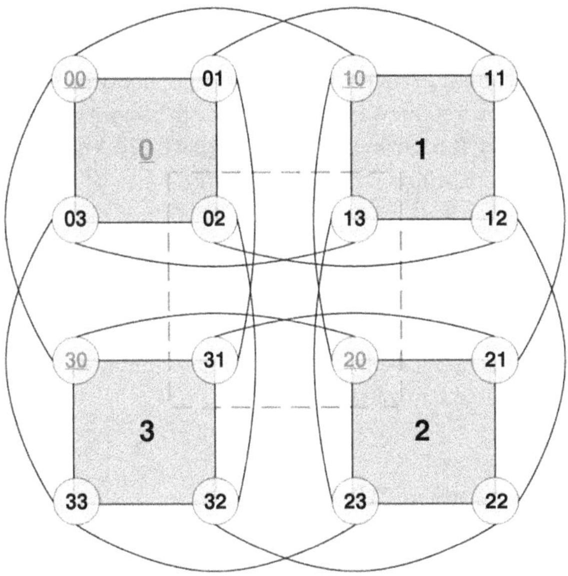

Figure 2.9 The process of constructing a completely symmetric topology for two-dimensional hypercubes, which includes two steps.

2.4 Theoretical Analysis

The partition tolerance characteristic is quantified by modeling both the basic physical topology and the hierarchical recursive physical topology in this section. It is assumed that the physical links connecting the nodes are secure. Additional assumptions regarding the construction and analysis of the topology are provided below:

1) Each link involved in the topology can be in one of two states: work and failure;
2) The failure and repair processes of the links are independent and have no memory effect;
3) The Mean Time Between Failures (MTBF) and Mean Time to Repair (MTTR) of each link are independent of each other, and their average values remain constant;
4) The MTBF is significantly larger than the MTTR;
5) A partition is considered good if it has a sufficient number of participating nodes. Conversely, a partition is deemed wrong if it lacks enough participating nodes.

Given that partition tolerance is indicative of a blockchain's reliability, two metrics will be incorporated into the quantitative model: average minimum repair time and partition tolerance probability. The average minimum repair time refers to the expected minimum duration required for the network to restore normal communication. On the other hand, the partition tolerance probability represents the probability of a good partition existing within the network.

2.4.1 Basic Physical Topology

In this chapter, the partition tolerance and link consumption of the basic physical topology will be quantified and simulated, facilitating subsequent comparison and analysis with the hierarchical recursive topology.

2.4.1.1 Quantitative Model for the Partition Tolerance Property

Firstly, the partition tolerance probability of the basic physical topology is computed. Under the assumptions (1)–(5), where each link undergoes a "work–failure–repair" state transition, a discrete-time Markov process can be employed to mathematically model the partition tolerance issue (Grover 1999, pp. 558–574). As the failure and repair processes are autonomous and do not depend on previous events, Figure 2.10 illustrates the Markov chain representation of the basic hypercube-based topology, comprising N nodes and L links. In the network, the system state X represents the number of invalid links.

The matrix that describes the transitions in the Markov model is represented as $P_{(L+1)\times(L+1)}$, whose element p_{ji} denotes the probability of transitioning from system state X_i to X_j. The probability of state transition p_{ji} can be calculated as follows:

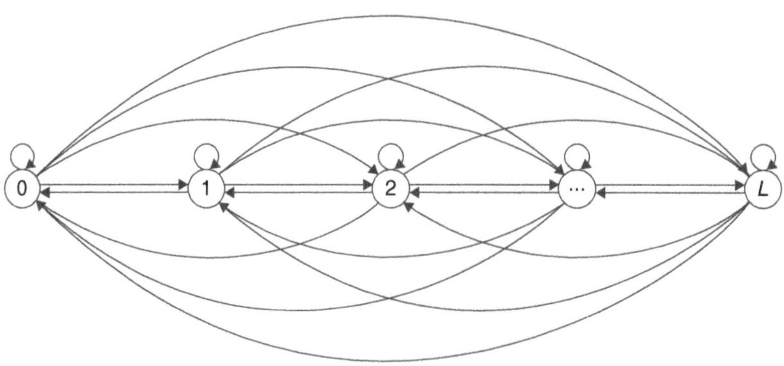

Figure 2.10 The Markov chain representation of the basic physical topology based on the hypercube.

$$
\begin{aligned}
p_{ji} &= P(X_j \mid X_i) \\
&= \sum_m P[(i-m)\,\text{invalid links are repaired}] \cdot P[(j-m)\ \text{working links are invalid}] \\
&= \sum_{m=\max\{i+j-L,0\}}^{m=\min\{i,j\}} \binom{i}{m} \mu^{i-m}(i-\mu)^m \cdot \binom{L-i}{j-m} \lambda^{j-m}(1-\lambda)^{L-i-j+m}
\end{aligned}, \tag{2.1}
$$

where the variable $m \in [max\{i + j - L, 0\}, min\{i, j\}]$ represents the number of invalid links which are unrepaired during the transition process, $\lambda = \frac{1}{MTBF}$ corresponds to the probability of a link failing per unit of time, while $\mu = \frac{1}{MTTR}$ represents the probability of repairing a failed link per unit of time.

Given that Figure 2.10 represents a fully connected graph, where the transition matrix P satisfies the properties of irreducibility, aperiodicity, and randomness. Based on the limit theorem of the Markov chain (Serfozo 2009), the aforementioned Markov process ultimately converges to a steady state that is independent of the initial distribution. The steady-state probability vector $\pi = [\pi_0, \pi_1, \pi_2, ..., \pi_L]$ can be obtained using the typical partitioning algorithm (Sheskin 1985, pp. 228–235) with $O(L)$ iterations.

The partition tolerance probability is subsequently estimated through sampling. In the connected components, the maximum count of nodes for each sample in the steady-state π_i, is computed to determine whether the partition it constitutes is wrong. The overall partition tolerance probability can be expressed as follows:

$$
p = 1 - \sum_{i=1}^{i=L} \pi_i \cdot P\{\text{wrong partition} \mid \pi_i\}, \tag{2.2}
$$

Furthermore, for the basic physical topology, the computation of the minimum repair time is conducted. In this topology, there is a preference for repairing invalid links between larger partitions. Following this approach, the time required for the system to restore its regular work is determined. By considering the minimum repair time as the weight for each sample, the overall average minimum repair time is derived in Eq. (2.2).

Algorithm 2.1 presents a pseudo-code that outlines the computation of the average minimum repair time for a basic hypercube-based topology and the partition tolerance probability, where V represents the set of points, and L denotes the set of edges in a multidimensional hypercube.

Algorithm 2.1 The Calculation of Partition Tolerance Probability and Average Minimum Repair Time

```
Input:
The sampling number, N_1, N_2;
The topological graph, G=(V,L);
The minimum number of consensus nodes in a good partition, k;
The probability of repairing an invalid link in the unit time, μ
The (l + 1)× (l + 1) transition matrix, P;
Output:
The average minimum repair time, time;
The partition tolerance probability, p;
Initial time = 0; p_badpart = 0;
π = steady_state(P);
for bad_num = 0 : length(L) do
   min_time = 0; bad_count = 0;
   for i = 1 : N_1 do
      Remove any bad_num edges from graph G to get graph subG;
      [bins, binsizes] = the connected component parameters of graph subG;
      if max(bins) > 1&&max(binsizes) < k then
         bad_count + +; repair_time = 0;
          for repair_num = 0 : bad_num do
             for j = 1 :N_2 do
                Repair any repair_num edges to get graph subGG;
                [bins, binsizes] = the connected component parameters of graph subGG;
                if max(bins) ≤ 1 || max(binsizes) ≥ k then
                      repair_time = repair_num;
                   break;
                end if
             end for
             if repair_time > 0 then
                break;
             end if
          end for
```

```
                min_time+ = repair_time;
            end if
        end for
        p_badpart+ = π_(bad_num) · bad_count/N_1;
        time+ = min_time· π_(bad_num);
    end for
    time = time/μ/p_badpart/N_1;
    p = 1 - p_badpart.
```

2.4.1.2 Simulation

The quantitative model is implemented through simulation using a digital optical cable communication system that employs automatic switching between primary and secondary modes. In accordance with international standards, the communication system, which consists of repeaters and physical links, needs to satisfy specific performance criteria for three distinct distances: {5000 km, 3000 km, 420 km} respectively:

$$(MTBF, MTTR) \in \{(2190, 24), (3650, 14.4), (26070, 2.016)\}(\mathrm{h}), \tag{2.3}$$

where (h) represents the unit and is an abbreviation for (hour).

Therefore, the pair of parameters is simulated as $(\lambda, \mu) \in \{(4.5662 \times 10^{-4}, 4.1667 \times 10^{-2}), (2.7397 \times 10^{-4}, 6.9444 \times 10^{-2}), (3.8358 \times 10^{-5}, 4.9603 \times 10^{-1})\}$ (/h). In the consortium blockchain with the Parallel Proof of Vote (PPoV) consensus, the minimum number of nodes in a good partition is defined as $k = \left\lfloor \frac{v}{2} \right\rfloor + 1$. Figure 2.11 provides a comparison of the average minimum repair time and the partition tolerance probability for the basic multidimensional hypercube topology, the tree topology, and the ring topology, all having the same degree.

The results indicate that as the network degree increases in the network, the partition tolerance probability experiences a significant rise without incurring extra average minimum repair time. The hypercube-based physical topology demonstrates a higher partition tolerance probability compared to the ring topology and the tree topology. Moreover, the average minimum repair time remains similar across different topologies, approximately equivalent to MTTR.

2.4.2 Hierarchical Recursive Physical Topology

This section will demonstrate the advantages of hierarchical recursive topology through theoretical analysis in taking into account both partition tolerance and link overhead.

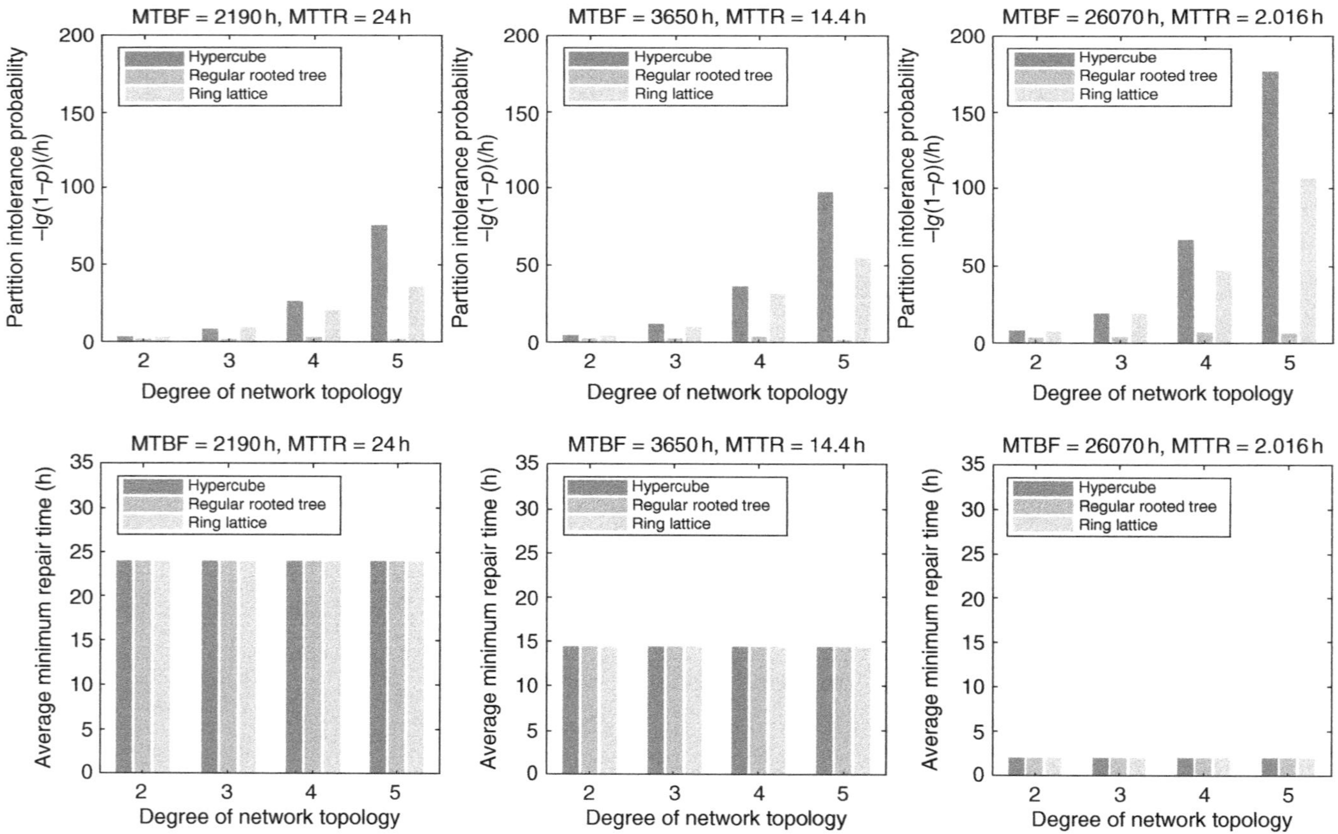

Figure 2.11 The partition tolerance probability and average minimum repair time are calculated for the basic topologies of multidimensional hypercube, tree, and ring.

2.4.2.1 Partition Tolerance Property

Let p_{i_m} represent the partition tolerance probability for a basic topology at the m-th $(1 \leq m \leq r)$ level. The partition tolerance of domain i_r is affected by both its recursive path from the first level to the $(r-1)$-th level and the topology it utilizes at the r-th level. Therefore, the overall partition tolerance probability is determined by

$$p = 1 - \sum_{m=1}^{r} \sum_{(i_1, i_2, i_3, \ldots, i_m)} p_{i_1} p_{i_2} p_{i_3} \cdots p_{i_{m-1}} \left(1 - p_{i_m}\right). \tag{2.4}$$

Similarly, denote t_{i_m} as the average minimum repair time for a basic topology at the m-th level. The overall average minimum repair time is then determined by

$$t = \sum_{m=1}^{r} \sum_{(i_1, i_2, i_3, \ldots, i_m)} t_{i_m} \cdot \frac{p_{i_1} p_{i_2} p_{i_3} \cdots p_{i_{m-1}} \left(1 - p_{i_m}\right)}{1 - p}. \tag{2.5}$$

According to Eqs. (2.4) and (2.5), it is evident that the recursive path has a greater impact on the overall partition tolerance from the first level to the $(r-1)$-th level, compared to the specific topology adopted by the domain at the r-th level. Consequently, it is advisable to select a topology along the upper recursion path that offers a high partition tolerance probability and a low average minimum repair time.

As shown in Table 2.1, a two-level recursive topology of four-dimensional hypercubes support 256 access nodes, surpassing the number of countries and regions in the world. Considering the current state-of-the-art optical fiber transmission technology, the likelihood of partition failure is a mere 1.35×10^{-18}(/h), which translates to an astonishing duration of approximately 80 trillion years.

Table 2.1 The partition tolerance of a two-level recursive topology.

Top-level topology	Second-level topology	Number of nodes	Partition failure probability (/h)	Mean time between failures (year)
Four-dimensional hypercube	Four-dimensional hypercube	256	1.35×10^{-18}	8×10^{13}
Five-dimensional hypercube	Four-dimensional hypercube	512	1.72×10^{-20}	7×10^{15}
Five-dimensional hypercube	Five-dimensional hypercube	1024	8.18×10^{-54}	1×10^{49}

Consequently, this negligible probability can be safely disregarded in practical engineering applications. It can be seen that the hierarchical recursive physical topology enables the system to reach the CAP guarantee bound.

2.4.2.2 Link Consumption

In this section, the analysis focuses solely on semisymmetric recursive and completely symmetric methods, as determining the number of nodes in the asymmetric recursive method poses challenges.

The dimension of hypercubes within each domain is represented as dim_{i_r} in a completely symmetric topology. As each recursion follows the same dimension, the value of dim_{i_r} remains constant for any $(i_1, i_2, i_3, \ldots, i_r)$, and is denoted as dim. Obviously, the number of nodes after $(r-1)$ recursions can be calculated as $N_{symm,\,r} = 2^{dim \times r}$. The links in the topology comprise both relatively short intradomain links and relatively long interdomain links, namely:

$$\begin{cases} L_{symm,r} = 2^{dim-1} \times dim \times 2^{(r-1) \times dim} + L_{symm,(r-1)} \times 2^{dim} \\ L_{symm,1} = 2^{dim-1} \times dim \end{cases}. \tag{2.6}$$

Therefore, the overall number of links can be calculated as:

$$L_{symm,r} = 2^{r \times dim - 1} \times r \times dim. \tag{2.7}$$

Domains at the same level utilize hypercubes of identical dimensions in a semisymmetric topology. Consequently, for any given i_r, the value of dim_{i_r} remains constant. Likewise, the number of nodes after $(r-1)$ recursions can be expressed as $N_{semi,r} = 2^{\sum_{m=1}^{r} dim_{i_m}}$, and the number of links adheres to the following relationship:

$$N_{semi,r} = 2^{\sum_{m=1}^{r} dim_{i_m}}. \tag{2.8}$$

Therefore, the overall number of links can be determined as:

$$L_{semi,r} = 2^{\sum_{m=1}^{r} dim_{i_m} - 1} \times \sum_{m=1}^{r} dim_{i_m}. \tag{2.9}$$

Table 2.2 presents a comparison of partition tolerance and link consumption properties across various methods of constructing physical topologies. The assumptions made include the link utilization of 5000 km, 3000 km, and 420 km for the 0th, 1st, and 2nd recursions, respectively, while satisfying the indicators defined in Eq. (2.3).

While each recursive step does not decrease the overall number of links, it does result in an increased utilization of short or intermediate links between nodes and a decreased reliance on long links compared to ring and basic hypercube-based topologies. When considering the same number of recursions, a higher dimension of the hypercube in the recursive path leads to reduced repair time requirements.

Table 2.2 Comparison of partition tolerance and link consumption across various methods of constructing physical topologies.

Number of nodes	Topology construction method		Number of links			Partition tolerance probability $-lg(1-p)(/h)$	Average minimum repair time
			5000 km	3000 km	420 km		
64	Tree		63	0	0	2.79	24.0
	Ring		192	0	0	43.7	24.0
	Hypercube	0 Recursion (6)	192	0	0	87.0	24.0
		1 Completely symmetric recursion (3–3)	96	96	0	8.62	24.0
		2 Completely symmetric recursions (2–2-2)	64	64	64	3.56	21.4
		1 Semisymmetric recursion (4–2)	128	64	0	3.53	14.4
4096	Tree		4 095	0	0	3.93	24.0
	Ring		24 576	0	0	107	24.0
	Hypercube	0 Recursion (12)	24 576	0	0	227	24.0
		1 Completely symmetric recursion (6–6)	12 288	12 288	0	87.0	24.0
		2 Completely symmetric recursions (4–4-4)	8 192	8192	8192	26.4	24.0
		2 Semisymmetric recursions (5–4-3)	10 240	8192	6144	16.6	2.02

Moreover, compared to the tree topology, despite the hypercube-based topology having a greater link number, its partition tolerance characteristic is significantly superior and already satisfies the demands of practical consortium blockchains. Therefore, blockchain projects can select the proper hierarchical recursive approaches based on their specific cost and reliability requirements.

2.5 Chapter Summary

The basic physical topologies of computer networks mainly include six types, namely bus, star, ring, tree, mesh, and hybrid. However, in large-scale distributed and high-performance computing systems, these basic topologies prove insufficient in terms of properties such as partition tolerance. To solve this problem, a novel physical topology is introduced in consortium blockchains, which are based on multidimensional hypercubes. Additionally, for intermediate and short link environments, there further exists a hierarchical recursive approach to extend the multidimensional hypercube topology. Experiments demonstrate that the hypercube-based physical topology exhibits superior partition tolerance performance compared to others in a digital optical cable communication system. Furthermore, hierarchical recursion empowers hypercube topologies to achieve robust partition tolerance while minimizing network cost.

Discussion Questions

2.1 Briefly describe the advantages and disadvantages of tree topology.

A: The tree topology offers advantages in terms of simplified management, routing and forwarding. The former is attributed to its hierarchical structure with a root node, where nodes are connected by a parent–child relationship. This structure is simple and clear, facilitating comprehension and efficient administration. The clear relationship between nodes also aids in fault identification and location. The latter two are due to the predefined paths in a tree topology that follow the hierarchy of the tree. This simplifies routing and forwarding processes, as nodes only need to forward data along specific branches without complicated path calculations.

Despite the above advantages of tree topologies, they have disadvantages in terms of single points of failure and limited scalability. In a tree topology, all nodes depend on the root node. The failure of this central node can lead to network partition or communication disruption, thereby compromising system reliability. Additionally, the capacity and bandwidth of the root node limits scalability performance. As the number of nodes increases significantly, the root node will become a bottleneck unable to handle numerous requests. On the other hand, the depth of the tree also poses restrictions on network scalability.

2.2 Which aspect of the CAP theorem does the hypercube topology address?

A: According to the CAP theorem, only two of the three properties can be simultaneously satisfied in a distributed system. The physical topology based on a multidimensional hypercube focuses on the partition tolerance property of CAP and significantly reduces the partition failure probability to below 10^{-50} while ensuring high availability and strong consistency at both the network and consensus layers in consortium blockchains. This solution has the potential to enable CA-type upper protocols to reach the guarantee bound of CAP in probability or even practical engineering applications.

2.3 Provide a concise overview of the structure of multidimensional hypercube-based topology and its hierarchical recursive approach.

A: The basic hypercube is a closed, compact, and convex graph, with its one-dimensional skeleton comprising a set of equidistant line segments aligned along each dimension within the respective space. In this structure, the relative line segments are parallel to one another, while the line segments that intersect at a specific point are perpendicular to each other.

The generation of the hierarchical recursive topology from the basic hypercube involves two main stages: recursion and interconnection. During recursion, each original node is transformed into a domain. Nodes within the same domain have the flexibility to establish either a hypercube-based physical topology or an arbitrary topology. The number of domains at the r-th ($r \geq 2$) level is denoted as i_r, which corresponds to the smallest node number n_{min} within that domain. Following the process of recursion, the new node number expands by one digit in comparison to the original node number. As a result, the first $(r-1)$ digits of i_r represent the recursive attributes of the domain from the initial level to the $(r-1)$-th level. Assuming that the node number of the hypercube within the first-level domain $i_1 = 0$ is $\{n_0\} = \{0, 1, 2, ..., (2^{dim_0} - 1)\}$, then the node number in domain i_r, after $(r-1)$ recursive steps, can be represented as $\{n_{i_r}\} = \{n_{i_{r-1}}\}$ & $\{0, 1, 2, ..., (2^{dim_{i_r}} - 1)\}$, where the symbol & denotes concatenation. The nodes associated with each domain at the r-th level are connected through physical links, forming the topological relationship of the domain at the $(r-1)$-th level. Consequently, the interconnection among domains is accomplished.

References

Cao, Z., Dong, H., Wei, Y., Liu, S. and Du, D.H., 2022. IS-HBase: an in-storage computing optimized HBase with I/O offloading and self-adaptive caching in compute-storage disaggregated infrastructure. *ACM Transactions on Storage (TOS)*, 18(2), pp. 1–42.

Decker, C. and Wattenhofer, R., 2013, September. Information propagation in the bitcoin network. In IEEE P2P 2013 Proceedings (pp. 1–10). IEEE.

Fadhil, M., Owenson, G. and Adda, M., 2016, August. A bitcoin model for evaluation of clustering to improve propagation delay in bitcoin network. In 2016 IEEE Intl Conference on Computational Science and Engineering (CSE) and IEEE Intl Conference on Embedded and Ubiquitous Computing (EUC) and 15th Intl Symposium on Distributed Computing and Applications for Business Engineering (DCABES) (pp. 468–475). IEEE.

Fadhil, M., Owenson, G. and Adda, M., 2017, May. Locality based approach to improve propagation delay on the bitcoin peer-to-peer network. In 2017 IFIP/IEEE Symposium on Integrated Network and Service Management (IM) (pp. 556–559). IEEE.

Grover, W.D., 1999. High availability path design in ring-based optical networks. *IEEE/ACM Transactions on Networking*, 7(4), pp. 558–574.

Kokoris-Kogias, E., Jovanovic, P., Gasser, L., Gailly, N., Syta, E. and Ford, B., 2018, May. Omniledger: A secure, scale-out, decentralized ledger via sharding. In 2018 IEEE Symposium on Security and Privacy (SP) (pp. 583–598). IEEE.

Kurose, J.F., 2005. *Computer networking: A top-down approach featuring the Internet, 3/E*. Pearson Education India.

Liu, Y., Fang, Z., Cheung, M.H., Cai, W. and Huang, J., 2022. An incentive mechanism for sustainable blockchain storage. *IEEE/ACM Transactions on Networking*, 30(5), pp. 2131–2144.

Owenson, G. and Adda, M., 2017, June. Proximity awareness approach to enhance propagation delay on the bitcoin peer-to-peer network. In 2017 IEEE 37th International Conference on Distributed Computing Systems (ICDCS) (pp. 2411–2416). IEEE.

Serfozo, R., 2009. *Basics of applied stochastic processes*. Springer Science & Business Media.

Sheskin, T.J., 1985. A Markov chain partitioning algorithm for computing steady state probabilities. *Operations Research*, 33(1), pp. 228–235.

Wang, H., Li, H., Ye, Q., Lu, P., Yang, Y., Chong, P.H.J., Chu, X., Lv, Q. and Smahi, A., 2023. A physical topology for optimizing partition tolerance in consortium blockchains to reach CAP guarantee bound. *Transactions on Emerging Telecommunications Technologies*, p. e4820.

Yuan, L., He, Q., Chen, F., Zhang, J., Qi, L., Xu, X., Xiang, Y. and Yang, Y., 2021. Csedge: Enabling collaborative edge storage for multi-access edge computing based on blockchain. *IEEE Transactions on Parallel and Distributed Systems*, 33(8), pp. 1873–1887.

Zhou, M., Zeng, L., Han, Y., Li, P., Long, F., Zhou, D., Beschastnikh, I. and Wu, M., 2023, May. Mercury: Fast transaction broadcast in high performance blockchain systems. In IEEE INFOCOM 2023-IEEE Conference on Computer Communications (pp. 1–10). IEEE.

3

P2P Network in Blockchain

The blockchain network layer typically employs the peer-to-peer (P2P) networking method. This chapter will present three sections introducing the structures, node discovery methods, and broadcast protocols within P2P networks.

3.1 P2P Network Structure

A P2P network can be conceptualized as P2P computing or P2P networking. Within this kind of network, all nodes function as peers, allowing each node to arbitrarily connect with other nodes and engage in bidirectional data exchange. A fundamental distinction between P2P network structure and traditional Client/Server (C/S) structure lies in the absence of a central node (Schollmeier 2001, pp. 101–102). Figures 3.1 and 3.2 illustrate the schematic diagrams of the C/S network structure and the P2P network structure respectively.

P2P network has the advantages of decentralization, scalability, and robustness. Redundant storage of data ensures system resilience, as the failure of a moderate number of nodes or links does not necessarily lead to service unavailability. Its high-cost performance eliminates the need for expensive professional equipment to establish a central server, thus reducing bandwidth costs significantly. It also provides privacy protection for the broadcast of blocked information. For example, in Bitcoin, since it is difficult for others to locate the real IP address behind the Bitcoin address (Parameswaran, Susarla, and Whinston 2001, pp. 31–38), user communication will not be eavesdropped. In addition, the distribution of external access traffic across multiple nodes allows for effective load balancing. These advantages have attracted wide attention in both academia and industry.

Principles and Applications of Blockchain Systems: How to Overcome the CAP Trilemma in Consortium Blockchain, First Edition. Hui Li and Han Wang.

Published 2025 by John Wiley & Sons, Inc.

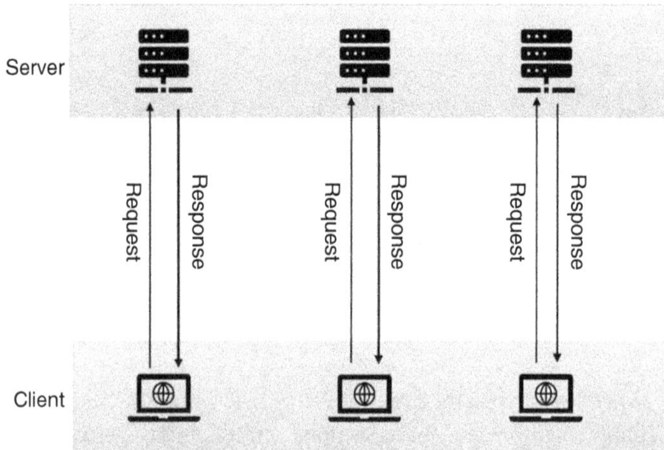

Figure 3.1 Diagram of C/S network structure.

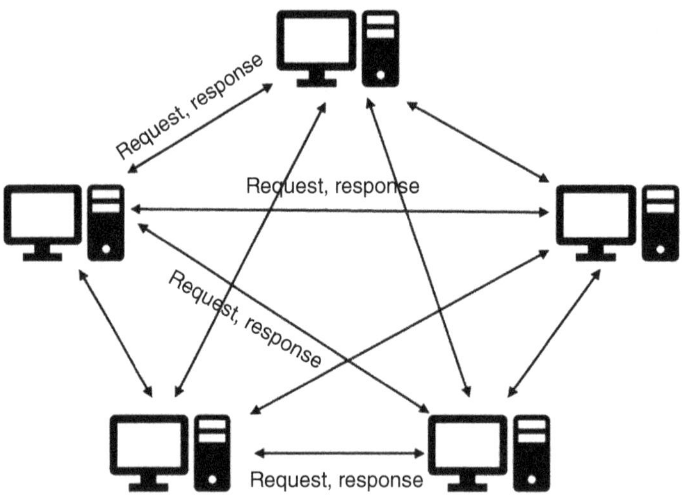

Figure 3.2 Diagram of P2P network structure.

3.1.1 Traditional P2P Network Structure

The origins of P2P technology in industry can be traced back to 1973. However, due to limitations in hardware capabilities at that time, this network structure was not popularized but limited to some high-end industries. It wasn't until the arrival of the 21st century, marked by significant advancements in computer

Table 3.1 Common application fields and representative products of P2P network.

Application fields	Representative products
File sharing system	Napster, Gnutella, eDonkey, eMule, Maze, BT
Computing power and storage sharing	SETI@home, Avaki, Popular Power, Nelbatch, Farsite
Streaming media application	PPStream, PPLive, QQLive, SopCast
Communication information-sharing software	Skype, Crowds, Onion Routing
Collaborative processing with service-sharing platform	JXTA, Magi, Groove

hardware technology enabling full-duplex communication between hosts, that the P2P network became extensively utilized. The main application fields of traditional P2P network include file sharing system, streaming media application, communication information-sharing software, and so on. Table 3.1 lists the common application fields and representative products (Cheng, Zhai, and Dong 2022, pp. 114–124; Dao et al. 2022, pp. 1–38; Yeh et al. 2022, pp. 5234–5245; Ihle et al. 2023) of P2P network.

3.1.2 P2P Network Structure in Blockchain

From the inception of Bitcoin which marks the advent of blockchain to many followed blockchain applications, the network layer predominantly leverages P2P networks. Taking Bitcoin as an example, its utilization of a P2P network structure devoid of a central server facilitates the swift synchronization of data, ensuring the ultimate goal of consistency. The distributed nature of P2P network endows them with the ability to tolerate a single point of failure, embodying principles of equality, autonomy, and decentralization. These attributes make P2P networks the predominant form of networking within blockchain systems. In a P2P network, each node is both a server and a client. The message exchange relies on a group of clients rather than a central server. So, nodes should participate in the relay. The implementation of the service is performed directly between the nodes. Since services are distributed among nodes, the failure of a moderate amount of nodes or links has minimal effect on the remainder of the network. On the other hand, queuing in communication is low, which reduces the resource and time costs caused by centralization.

According to whether the network is decentralized and whether the node network address is structured, P2P networks can be classified into four categories, which are centralized P2P networks, fully distributed unstructured P2P networks, fully distributed structured P2P networks, and semidistributed P2P networks (Yap, Chin, and Klemeš 2023, p. 113170). Table 3.2 introduces the advantages and disadvantages of the four P2P network structures as well as their blockchain applications.

Centralized P2P networks have no typical application in blockchains and will not be analyzed here.

Nodes in a fully distributed P2P network are free to join and leave, and there is no central node. In unstructured P2P networks, the entire network forms a random graph structure without structured uniform node addresses. The typical blockchain application of a fully distributed unstructured P2P network is Bitcoin. The Bitcoin overlay network exhibits the characteristics of an evolutionary random graph (Abdo et al. 2022), suggesting that its structure is dynamic and flexible over time. In contrast, structured P2P networks define the topological relationships of nodes, and the structure of the network is guaranteed by certain protocols between nodes. The typical blockchain application of a fully distributed structured P2P network is Ethereum (Wood 2014, pp. 1–32).

Indeed, in both structured and unstructured P2P networks, such as the World Wide Web (WWW) (Albert, Jeong, and Barabási 1999, pp. 130–131; Barabási,

Table 3.2 Comparison of different P2P network structures.

P2P network structure	Advantages	Disadvantages	Blockchain application
Centralized P2P network	• Simple maintenance • High resource discovery rate	• High system breakdown probability • High central server maintenance costs	None
Fully distributed unstructured P2P network	• Free node access • Fast node discovery	• Large amount of redundant information • High probability of network congestion	Bitcoin
Fully distributed structured P2P network	• Precise node address search	• Complex maintenance mechanism	Ethereum
Semidistributed P2P network	• High resource discovery rate • High system stability	• Frequent entry and exit of nodes • Low system stability	Hyperledger

Albert, and Jeong 2000, pp. 69–77) and Bitcoin transaction network (Tao, Ho, and Dai 2021, pp. 1–5; Serena, Ferretti, and D'Angelo 2022, pp. 839–853), individual nodes are dynamically interconnected. The connections between nodes occur randomly, and the likelihood of link formation adheres to a specific distribution. Consequently, the overall network structure is relatively stable, exhibiting characteristics governed by universal laws and fundamental principles including scale-free properties, small-world phenomena, and power-law distributions.

Semidistributed P2P networks combine the features of structured and unstructured networks. The advantage of semidistributed P2P networks is that they are efficient, scalable, and easy to manage. Its typical blockchain application is Hyperledger (Cachin 2016, pp. 1–4). The semidistributed P2P network is often combined with the delegated mechanism, which also appears in the consensus algorithm. Specifically, it divides nodes into super and ordinary nodes based on evaluation criteria such as computing power, bandwidth, and retention time. Super nodes endorse and supervise ordinary nodes of the organization or institution to which the node belongs, and participate in the core consensus process. Ordinary nodes make transactions through super nodes but do not participate in bookkeeping and voting. The super nodes are equal to each other and there is no frequent joining and leaving problem. At the same time, the number of supernodes in the consortium blockchain is significantly less than that of the public blockchain. Although the original Bitcoin was based on an unstructured and fully distributed P2P network and flooding mechanism, a semidistributed P2P network is better suited as the networking mode of the consortium blockchain from the standpoint of network efficiency.

The above P2P network structures have a wide range of applications across numerous scenarios. We select four typical applications of P2P network structures, namely Bank, Bitcoin, Ethereum and Hyperledger. Table 3.3 conducts a comparative assessment, providing scores ranging from 0 to 5 for each application across five key dimensions: decentralization, system security, privacy protection, node access efficiency and application richness.

Table 3.3 Comparison of different P2P network products.

Rating items	Bank	Bitcoin	Ethereum	Hyperledger
Decentralization	1	4	4	2
System security	4	2	2	3
Privacy protection	2	4	3	3
Node access efficiency	4	2	1	3
Application richness	3	1	4	3

3.2 Node Discovery Method

The spontaneous addition and departure of nodes within the P2P network in the blockchain system establishes the groundwork for its inherent openness. However, upon joining the blockchain network, a new node must first establish network access. Due to the decentralized characteristic of this network, accessing it through a central server is not feasible for newly added nodes. Therefore, an essential aspect of blockchain P2P networking is how to discover and obtain addresses of other nodes within the network after a new blockchain node initiates.

3.2.1 Bitcoin Node Discovery

Bitcoin represents the first decentralized infrastructure and distributed computing paradigm based on blockchain. Due to its complete decentralization, nodes are allowed to freely join or exit. However, this decentralized nature poses challenges for newly added nodes as they cannot obtain addresses to access the network. Therefore, Bitcoin designs the following three primary methods for node discovery:

3.2.1.1 Hard-Coded Seed Nodes

The centralized P2P network employs a central server for indexing, ensuring the stable connection of new nodes to the network (Garnett 2001, pp. 1–5). Although Bitcoin operates without a centralized server, it maintains the stability of certain nodes over an extended period, referred to as seed nodes. The core client of Bitcoin incorporates a method for obtaining seed nodes, with the option for automatic acquisition. Bitcoin hardcodes these seed nodes into its source code, serving as initial entry points into the network during startup. New nodes utilize these seed nodes as intermediaries to connect to other nodes, ensuring continuous access to a list of addresses within the blockchain network.

3.2.1.2 Address Broadcast

Once a node is connected to the network, it can serve as an intermediary for acquiring the addresses of other nodes. The address broadcast encompasses two methods, as illustrated in Figure 3.3:

1) *Actively broadcast the address of node A (push):* In Bitcoin, the active push of node *A*'s address is facilitated through the Net.AdvertiseLocal() method. This process involves a one-way transmission, where node *A* proactively shares its information with other nodes. Node *B*, upon receiving this information, locally stores it without providing a response. Similarly, node *B* can also employ the push mechanism to broadcast its own address to other connected nodes.

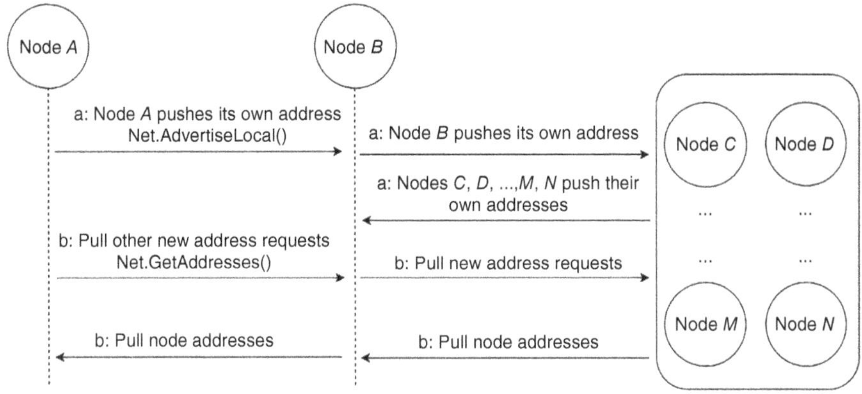

Figure 3.3 The process of address broadcast in Bitcoin.

2) *Actively obtain the addresses of other nodes (pull):* In addition to pushing their own addresses to connected nodes, Bitcoin employs an alternative method for address broadcast by actively pulling addresses through Net.GetAddresses(). In this approach, node *A* initiates a request for addresses and receives the address information from node *B* in response. This process involves one request and one response at a time, effectively preventing the waste of network resources. Node *B* can also expand its address repository by requesting addresses from other nodes. During this pull process, if other nodes have transmitted their address information to node *A* through active broadcast (push) before, these address information will also be returned to the requesting node.

Notably, Bitcoin's two methods of obtaining addresses operate independently, as a safeguard against potential attackers attempting to forge numerous fake addresses and disseminate them widely. This precautionary measure helps maintain the integrity of the Bitcoin network, preventing scenarios where normal nodes might be hindered from accessing the authentic network or inadvertently connecting to a fraudulent one.

3.2.1.3 Addresses Stored in Database

In order to alleviate the limitations on connection numbers and bandwidth of seed nodes, Bitcoin nodes acquire other node information through broadcasting after accessing the network and save it for subsequent use. In the Bitcoin client, nodes store their addresses in the LevelDB format within the peer.dat database system. The LevelDB database uses a Key/Value structure, commonly employed for storing and managing an ordered mapping from string keys to string values. It exhibits efficient read and write performance, making it highly suitable for node address management in the Bitcoin system.

In summary, the above three ways ensure stable network access and achieve the maintenance of the address list for frequently incoming and outgoing nodes. By employing these methods collectively, Bitcoin nodes are reliably free to join the P2P network without a central authority.

3.2.2 Ethereum Node Discovery

Compared to Bitcoin, Ethereum exhibits enhanced functionality and a broader range of applications, necessitating a more flexible and efficient organizational management approach for nodes. However, the implementation of Ethereum relies on the precise discovery of node address as needed, a feature not adequately supported by the unstructured P2P network structure in Bitcoin. To overcome this limitation, Ethereum adopts the structured P2P network with the Kademlia (Kad) protocol, a type of Distributed Hash Table (DHT) technology, for rapid and accurate address retrieval. Ethereum node discovery mainly involves the following core parts:

3.2.2.1 Seed Nodes

Ethereum seed nodes are divided into hard-coded seed nodes and mining pool seed nodes. The former comprises node information, network address, and data protocol, which facilitate new nodes' access to the Ethereum P2P network. The latter aims to meet the efficiency demand of node connectivity in the network. By encouraging organizations or individuals interested in Ethereum projects to share their node addresses, high-quality nodes are filtered out and packaged as mining pool seed nodes for release. Users can download and connect to them stably, thereby enhancing connectivity with the Ethereum network.

3.2.2.2 Addresses Stored in Database

Ethereum maintains an address database of connected nodes and adopts LevelDB's storage format to generate multiple history database files. For a node that initially connects to the Ethereum network, its address database is empty. Through address broadcast, it gradually fills the address list. When reconnecting to the Ethereum network, loadSeedNodes() is employed during startup to read seed nodes and history data for a fast and efficient connection to Ethereum P2P network. This method can help the nodes get the seed nodes and history data quickly, thus speeding up the node joining process.

3.2.2.3 Address Query

The Kad protocol used in Ethereum to query addresses is a specific implementation of DHT. As a dynamic node management and routing protocol within the third-generation P2P network, it employs a globally unique ID for each node. The distance between nodes is measured using XOR values of their respective node IDs, represented as $Dis(M, N) = XOR(M, N)$ (Maymounkov and Mazieres 2002, pp. 53–65). According to the Kad table structure, rapid localization of the queried node ID can be achieved.

3.2.2.4 Address Broadcast

With the Kad table structure, each node in Ethereum has a unique fixed location, thereby precluding active broadcasting of its own address. Instead, the system disseminates node address information through doRefresh() and lookup(). Each node searches for the nearest 16 nodes to establish connections and then randomly generates three target IDs. After a successful connection, nodes engage in two-way communication using pingpong(), as shown in Figure 3.4. The connecting node saves the connected node's information in its own Kad bucket, while the connected nodes store the connecting node's information in the address database. This facilitates the sharing of address information.

3.2.3 Hyperledger Fabric Node Discovery

Bitcoin and Ethereum are typical applications of public blockchains. Apart from the aforementioned methods for initial node access or post-startup node discovery, there exist alternative approaches in current blockchain systems to achieve similar functionality. Hyperledger Fabric, an enterprise-grade blockchain, has different node permissions. For example, transaction processing must go through a super node. The subsequent enumeration presents various node discovery techniques employed by Hyperledger Fabric:

3.2.3.1 Seed Nodes

Seed nodes in Hyperledger Fabric are configured through the core.yaml profile, rather than being hard-coded. Node discovery via profiles is a common way, such as Ethereum's adoption of Viper (Bates and LaNou 2022) as a profile-loading scheme. Hot updates of configuration files are important to Hyperledger Fabric because the super node administrator can dynamically load new configuration item values and make them effective in real time without affecting the operation of the system or having to restart the system.

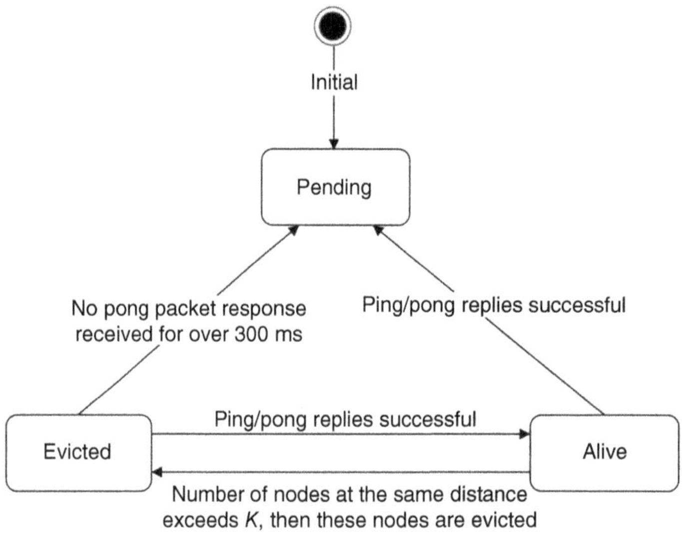

Figure 3.4 Node state in pingpong protocol.

3.2.3.2 Address Broadcast

Hyperledger Fabric adopts Gossip as the P2P network propagation protocol. The broadcast process of Gossip is shown in Figure 3.5. It involves randomly selecting *N* nodes from the node list, pushing requests for node list information, and synchronizing their own node lists. Simultaneously, during the push process, nodes also transmit their own node information to other nodes, broadcasting it throughout the entire network.

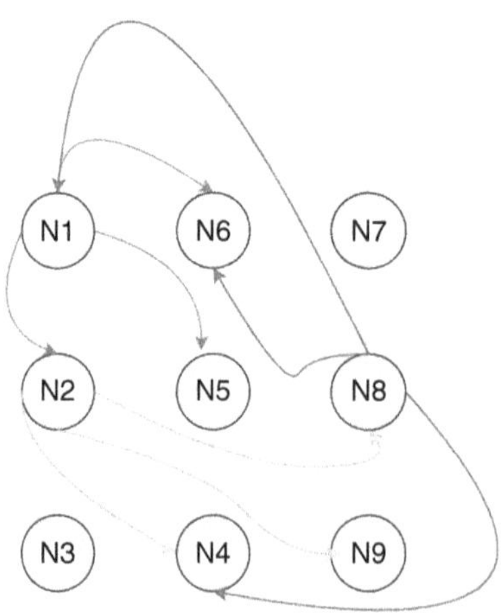

Figure 3.5 Message broadcasting in the Gossip protocol.

3.2.3.3 Specification Through Command Line

A user can pass the address of the specified node to a new node by command.

3.3 Broadcast Protocol

In blockchain, a broadcast protocol is used to spread messages across a network, ensuring uniform message reception and consensus state among all nodes. It typically obeys the P2P communication paradigm, where each node can function as both sender and receiver. This section focuses on the classical Gossip broadcast protocol along with an innovative variant known as Matching-Gossip.

3.3.1 Gossip

Gossip, also referred to as the epidemic protocol, was first proposed at the ACM PODC academic conference in 1987 (Demers et al. 1987, pp. 1–12), and primarily employed for data synchronization among replication nodes in distributed databases. At present, it is extensively used by numerous blockchain systems as a broadcast protocol at the network layer to disseminate transaction and block information.

Gossip protocol, as a consistent protocol, propagates information through random communication between nodes to achieve efficient information dissemination and data synchronization. The basic idea involves the initiator periodically selecting random nodes to receive and pass on information until all nodes in the network have received it. The protocol mainly consists of three processes (Kermarrec and Van Steen 2007, pp. 2–7): node selection, message or node list exchange, and data processing.

The propagation mechanism of Gossip is mainly realized by anti-entropy propagation or rumormongering. Anti-entropy propagation refers to eliminating the data differences in different nodes, so as to increase the similarity of data between nodes and reduce entropy. This is to solve differences between nodes by randomly selecting nodes with a fixed probability to exchange all data, avoiding the inconsistency of cluster metadata caused by packet loss or new node addition. This mechanism involves a vast and infinite number of messages, thereby is usually used only for initializing newly added nodes rather than maintaining dynamic environments with frequent node changes. Figure 3.6 is a diagram of anti-entropy propagation. In this propagation mechanism, nodes only exhibit two states: Susceptible and Infective, hence it is referred to as the SI model.

Rumormongering differs from anti-entropy propagation in that it periodically exchanges new data instead of all data until all nodes store the new data.

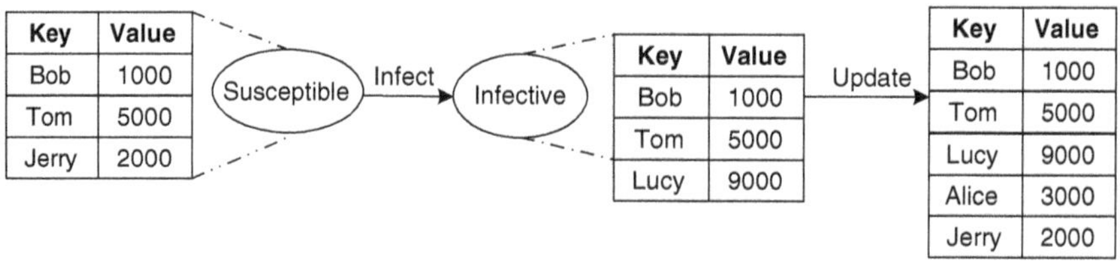

Figure 3.6 Diagram of anti-entropy propagation.

A propagated message contains only the latest information, and at a certain point in time is marked removed and no longer propagated. The cycle of rumormongering may be more frequent than that of anti-entropy propagation because each node requires fewer resources, but there is a probability that the update will not reach all sites. It is usually used for incremental data synchronization between nodes, which is more suitable for distributed systems with dynamic changes. As shown in Figure 3.7, rumormongering includes three node states: Susceptible, Infective, and Removed, so it is called the SIR Model.

According to different specific application scenarios, there are three communication modes between two nodes in the network:

1) *Push-gossip*: As shown in Figure 3.8, node *A* selects node *B* as the target node and sends information to it. Node *B* then updates itself according to the received information.

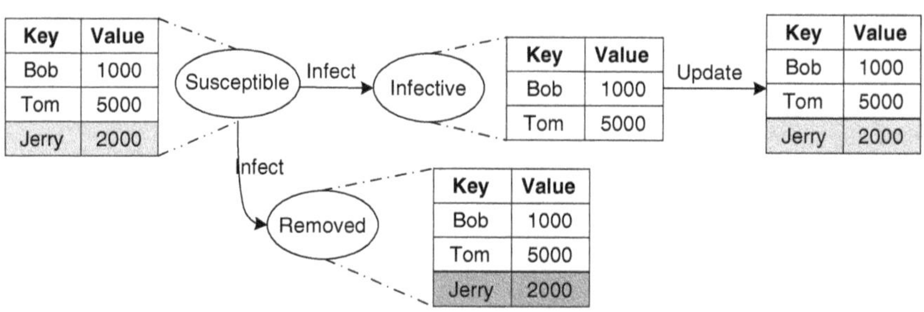

Figure 3.7 Diagram of rumormongering.

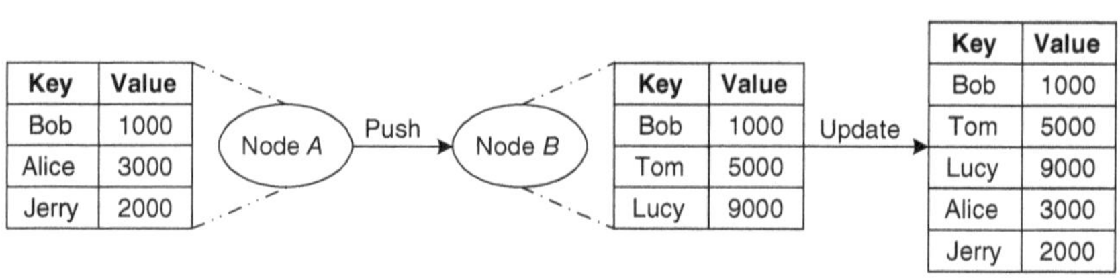

Figure 3.8 Diagram of Push-gossip.

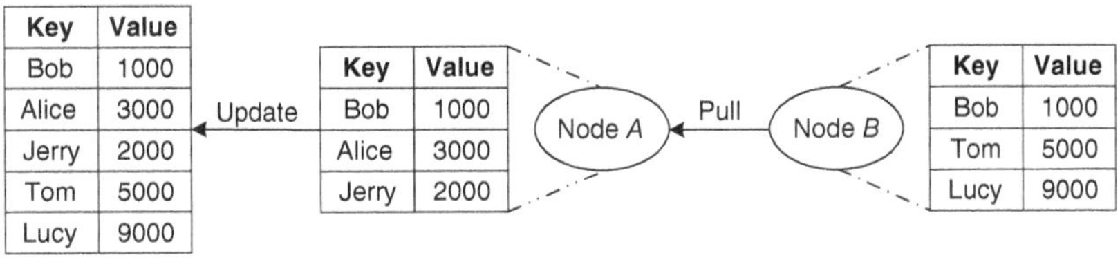

Figure 3.9 Diagram of Pull-gossip.

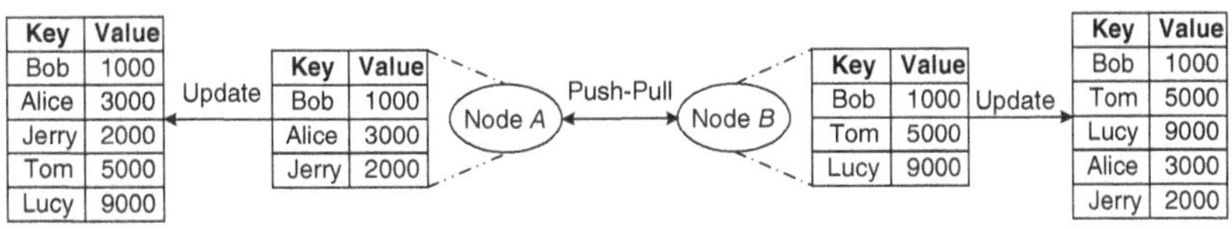

Figure 3.10 Diagram of Push-Pull gossip.

2) *Pull-gossip*: As shown in Figure 3.9, node *A* designates node *B* as the target node, and subsequently receives information from node *B* for updating its own state.
3) *Push-Pull gossip* (Taheri-Boshrooyeh et al. 2022, pp. 1286–1287): This mode is a combination of Pull-gossip and Push-gossip. As shown in Figure 3.10, node *A* initiates the information exchange by sending a message to node *B* while simultaneously obtaining data from it.

Gossip is a decentralized and final consistent protocol that exhibits inherent advantages in terms of scalability and distributed fault tolerance. Instead of directly broadcasting a generated block to all other nodes, it employs a method of randomly selecting neighboring nodes to initiate a chain reaction of information dissemination, ultimately ensuring reception by all network nodes. This random propagation effectively reduces the communication complexity associated with direct broadcasting from each individual node to every other node. Despite the potential for message delay and redundancy, it ensures the efficient dissemination of information throughout the network without necessitating a complex direct communication structure.

3.3.2 Innovative Broadcast Protocol

The proper operation of the P2P system relies primarily on direct P2P connections, with all joining nodes forming an overlay network atop the physical network

(Lua et al. 2005, pp. 72–93). That is, each node establishes a virtual connection at the application layer of the computer network architecture, enabling all nodes in the system to interconnect and form a logical virtual network. This overlay network is dependent upon support from the underlying physical network, while also being independent of it by shielding its details; allowing for node discovery and message or other networking operations according to certain rules within P2P network. The network is built on the underlying physical network and depends on the support of the underlying physical network. At the same time, the overlay network is independent of the underlying physical network, shielding the underlying details, which means that we can discover nodes and send messages or other network operations in accordance with certain rules on the overlay network.

At present, the Gossip protocol is widely used in the field of P2P topology construction and maintenance as well as data distribution. However, the virtual topology constructed by Gossip in the process of node discovery has randomness and cannot match the underlying physical topology. This mismatch problem further leads to the reduction of data distribution efficiency and the blindness of data exchange.

Specifically, the process of constructing an overlay network based on the Gossip protocol is actually managing node relationships during information exchange to maintain a network topology with certain characteristics. However, when nodes join or leave, or when messages are updated, the topological mismatch problem may occur in the Gossip protocol. Such mismatches often result in redundant traffic as messages traverse the same physical link multiple times (Liu et al. 2004, pp. 132–139). For example, in Figure 3.11, (a) and (b) are two logical overlay networks on top of the underlying physical network shown in (c). Assuming that nodes A and B are located on the same Intranet in Beijing, while nodes C and D are on another Intranet in New York, it can be inferred that the delay of the physical link between nodes B and C is much longer than that between nodes A and B or C and D. Obviously, in the topological mismatched overlay network in Figure 3.11a, the update message is broadcast from node B and will pass through the $B-C$ link with the longest delay three times. However, in the topological adaptive overlay network shown in Figure 3.11b, the update message only needs to pass through all physical links once for broadcast. Therefore, constructing a logical overlay network that adapts to the underlying physical topology is crucial for optimizing the Gossip protocol.

In practical application, Gossip protocol will inevitably send messages to duplicate nodes in overlay networks with loops. As shown in Figure 3.12, node O is the source node, which sends the update message to nodes A and B in the first round of broadcast cycle. In the second round, upon receiving the update message, node A forwards it to nodes O and C while node B to nodes A and D. Consequently, both

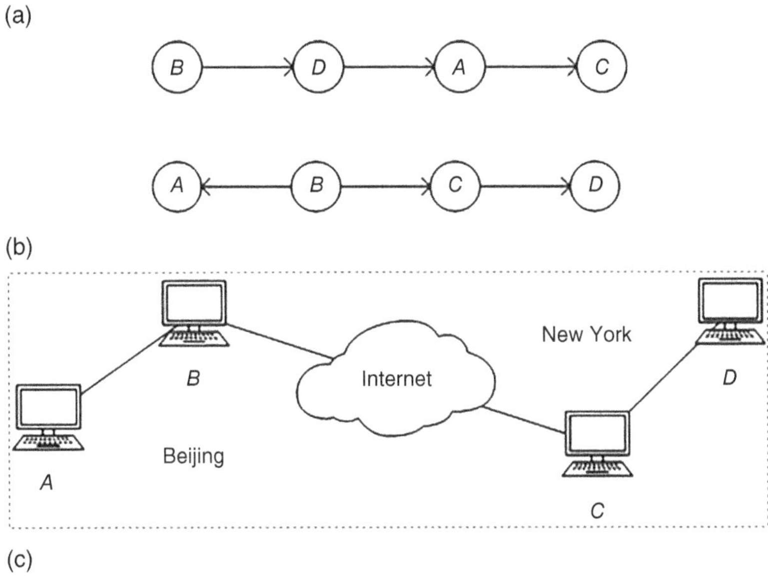

Figure 3.11 Topological mismatch problem. (a) Topological mismatched overlay network. (b) Topological adaptative overlay network. (c) Underlying physical network.

nodes O and A receive redundant copies of the message whereas nodes E and F remain uninformed. This duplication leads to inefficient data synchronization and unnecessary message redundancy.

To solve the above issue, this section presents an optimized Gossip protocol known as Matching-Gossip, including two components for new node joining and message broadcasting. Subsequently, these two components will be individually elucidated.

3.3.2.1 New Node Joining

During the process of new node joining, each node maintains a direct neighbor node list to record its logical neighbor nodes. When a new node is added, it is inserted into the logical neighbor node list of the physically nearest node and becomes its direct neighbor, ensuring consistency between logical and physical network topologies. This adaptation eliminates inefficiencies and redundancies caused by randomly selecting broadcast nodes in Gossip, thereby enhancing broadcast link utilization.

The nearest node refers to the physical closest node. In Matching-Gossip, the network delay between two nodes is used as an indicator to measure inter-node

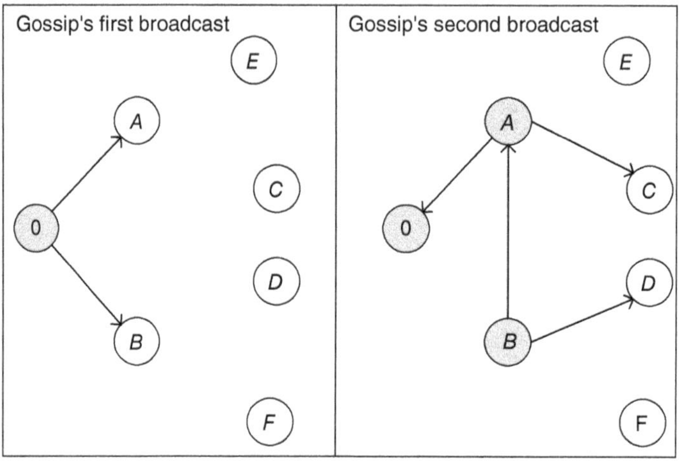

Figure 3.12 Diagram of basic Gossip broadcast in actual practice.

distance. It is closely related to the spatial distribution of nodes in the physical topology. Ideally, a higher network delay implies greater geographical separation between two nodes, and vice versa. When a new node is added, it undergoes detection within the network to measure its delay with existing nodes, which are then sorted from smallest to largest. Subsequently, the nearest nodes insert the new node into their logical neighbor node lists, and all nodes update their direct neighbor node lists accordingly.

The logical neighbor node list and the direct neighbor node list are identical, with the former transforming into the latter once it is populated by the nearest nodes. In order to describe the logical topology concretely, Matching-Gossip proposes a numbering scheme involving binary IDs to identify each unique node. Node numbers also represent the location relationship between nodes. Specifically, a logical distance of 1 is defined between a pair of nodes whose IDs differ by 1 bit.

The process of adding a new node consists of five steps, as shown in Algorithm 3.1. Upon the addition of a new node, the initial step involves detecting and evaluating the current network environment. Subsequently, the network delay from the newly added node to the detected nodes is calculated and arranged in ascending order, followed by selecting the nodes with minimal network delay. The insertion of the new node occurs at the smallest unassigned number positions within the logical neighbor node lists of these nodes, ultimately resulting in an update of all direct neighbor node lists. In case no nodes are detected, initialization of the new node takes place.

Algorithm 3.1 Dynamic Node Joining

```
Input: node_set N,new node A
Output: updated direct neighbor node xiulists
    for each node N_i in N do
       detectNode(A,N_i);
    end for
    if hasNodesDetected() then
       calculateLatency();
       sortDetectedNodes();
       B ←selectLeastLatencyNode();
       addNeighbors(A,B);
       addNeighbors(B,A);
    else
       initializeNode(A);
    end if
```

The addition of a fifth node *E* to the ringed four nodes *A*, *B*, *C*, and *D* is illustrated in Figure 3.13. These nodes are numbered 00, 01, 10, and 11 respectively. In this scenario, *A* is assumed as the nearest node to *E* with minimal network delay, as depicted in Figure 3.13a. Consequently, node *E* is assigned the number 100 and included in the logical neighbor node list of node *A* (00). As shown in Figure 3.13b, the direct neighbor node lists of nodes *A* (00) and *E* (100) become {01, 10, 100} and {000}, respectively; where it should be noted that the node number 00 is equal to 000.

3.3.2.2 Message Broadcasting

In the Gossip protocol, the random selection of broadcast nodes can result in certain nodes receiving redundant messages repeatedly. Although incorporating the direct neighbor node list to establish the logical topology aligned with the physical topology can restrict the choice of broadcast nodes and minimize duplication of information exchange links, it is still possible for different nodes to share common entries in their direct neighbor node lists, thereby making it unavoidable for these nodes to receive duplicate messages. To alleviate this repetition issue, Matching-Gossip introduces a "message-state" data structure based on state bit. Specifically, each node maintains such a data structure, where each state bit corresponds to a specific message. A bit value of 0 represents the initial state, signifying that the corresponding bit has not yet received the message. A bit value of 1 indicates that the message has been received by the node. Consequently, when the same message is resent to the node, it is discarded. Messages are uniquely identified using

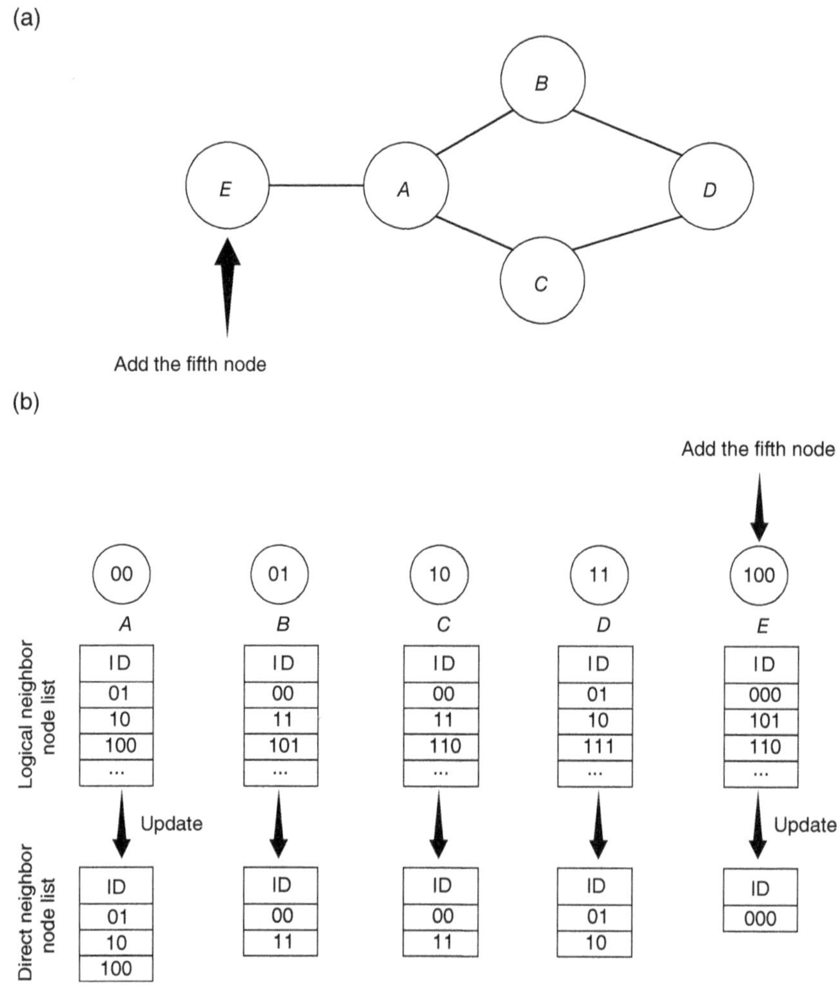

Figure 3.13 Example of new node joining. (a) Physical topology. (b) Logical topology.

Universally Unique Identifiers (UUIDs). Each UUID corresponds to a bit, and all bits share the same Time to Live (TTL). When a state bit transitions from 0 to 1, the TTL countdown begins. After a specified period, the message UUID is cleared, the state bit is reset to 0, and the system enters the next period. The period time, denoted as T, depends on factors such as the node number, topology structure, and network conditions. Given that network conditions are uncontrollable, this section only considers the impact of node number on the duration, indicating a positive correlation between the size of the network and the duration T.

Nodes produce metadata that is broadcast as update messages, each of which is assigned a UUID. The optimized message broadcasting process in Matching-Gossip is shown in Algorithm 3.2.

Step 1: Select the target nodes: As the sender of the initial broadcast round, the node generating metadata selects target nodes from its direct neighbor node list for message propagation.

Step 2: Propagate the message: Upon receiving the message, a node continues to propagate it to nodes in its direct neighbor node list. This facilitates gradual transmission of information across the entire network in successive rounds. This step encompasses two communication mechanisms simultaneously: rumormongering and anti-entropy propagation. While updates are propagated using rumormongering, nodes periodically utilize anti-entropy propagation for validation and correction, aiming to prevent inconsistencies in the metadata arising from packet loss or new node addition.

Step 3: Update the status: When a node receives a new message, it updates its status and sets the corresponding status bit to 1. During the TTL period of the status bit, any subsequent messages with identical UUIDs will be discarded, while those with different UUIDs will continue to trigger updates to status bits. Due to network delay and other reasons, there is a possibility of messages with the same UUID in different TTL periods. As a result, it is crucial to establish an appropriate TTL value to alleviate this phenomenon.

The above three steps iterate continuously until all nodes have received the messages, in order to ensure the consistency of the entire consortium blockchain network.

Algorithm 3.2 Matching-Gossip

```
Input:node_set N, message M, status S, UUIDs, TTL
Output:consistent consortium blockchain network
while allHaveReceivedMessage(N, M)==False do
  for each node N_i in N do
    T_i←constructDirectNeighborNodeList(N_i);
  end for
  for each node N_i in N do
   if isInitialBroadcaster(N_i)then
    for each neighbor j in T_i do
      propagateMessage(M, j);
    end for
   end if
  end for
  for each node N_i in N do
    M'←receiveMessage();
    updateStatus(S_i,M');
    discardIdenticalUUIDs(M', UUIDs, TTL);
  end for
end while
```

3.3.2.3 Adaptability Analysis in Future Network

The traditional Gossip protocol covers the IP network, and most upper-layer applications are also under the TCP/IP architecture. However, with the emergence of metaverse and Web3.0, various future networks such as eXpressive Internet Architecture (XIA) (Anand et al. 2011, pp. 1–6), Information-Centric Networking (ICN) (Xylomenos et al. 2013, pp. 1024–1049; Honda, Nakamura, and Kamiyama 2023, pp. 1–5), and Multi-Identifier Network (MIN) (Li et al. 2020, pp. 36569–36581) have arisen. Therefore, a P2P network protocol should adapt to different types of networks in order to keep up with the development trend and establish a comprehensive ecosystem for future networks. The following will take MIN as an example to analyze the adaptability of Matching-Gossip.

Multi-Identifier Network (MIN) is a new network system that supports content, IP, ground and air identifiers. The new network architecture adopted by the multi-identifier network breaks through the defects of IP resource exhaustion and single semantics in the traditional TCP/IP network and proposes a co-governance domain name management mode based on blockchain technology, effectively preventing network unilateralism monopoly.

MIN supports the coexistence of network identifiers including identity, content, geographic information, and IP address. Identifiers in the network are identity-centric. For example, the content identifiers of all resources are bound to the identity identifiers of their publishers. The protocol architecture of MIN is shown in Figure 3.14.

Constructing an overlay P2P network with the Matching-Gossip protocol in MIN enhances the consistency and reliability of the entire network. Figure 3.15 shows the protocol stack diagram of applying the Matching-Gossip protocol within the MIN architecture.

The protocol stack is divided into two parts, the MIN protocol stack and the consortium blockchain network protocol stack. The MIN protocol stack includes the application layer, multi-identifier layer, data link layer and physical layer, in which the consortium blockchain is built on the application layer. The consortium blockchain network protocol stack contains three layers: interaction logic layer for data synchronization, transmission, verification and message channel; connection layer for node discovery, connection, heartbeat monitoring and failure feedback; propagation layer for data propagation, including single point propagation through Socket point-to-point communication and multi-point broadcast through the Matching-Gossip protocol.

The process of node communication in MIN involves both push and pull modes, which are integrated into the Multi-Identifier Router (MIR). In the conventional

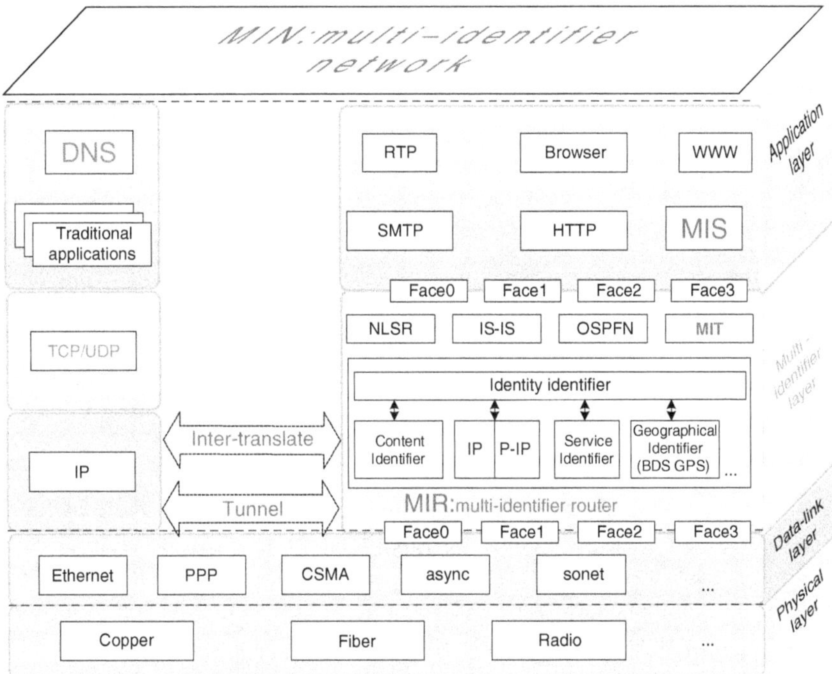

Figure 3.14 The protocol architecture of MIN.

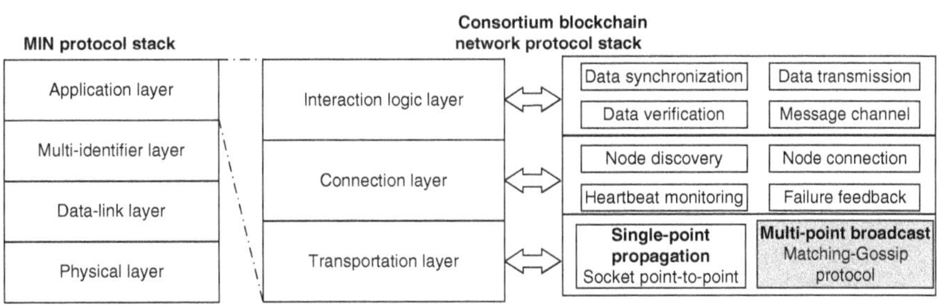

Figure 3.15 Protocol stack diagram of Matching-Gossip in MIN.

push mode, Matching-Gossip can be used for building a P2P overlay network. On the other hand, the novel pull mode is inherently decentralized. Therefore, with the incorporation of the Matching-Gossip protocol, MIN's communication approach consistently aligns with blockchain's original design concept of decentralization.

3.3.2.4 Experiments and Analysis

We have chosen the Memberlist library (Das, Gupta, and Motivala 2002, pp. 303–312) to implement both the basic Gossip protocol and the Matching-Gossip protocol for comparison purposes. This section further evaluates the convergence time and network load across various topologies and different numbers of nodes.

According to Section 3.3.1, in the Gossip protocol, the objective of information propagation is to achieve global state synchronization through communication among nodes. Rumormongering contributes to this process directly, while anti-entropy propagation aims to eliminate the information discrepancies among nodes, thus maintaining the system's consistency. In order to simplify the problem, we assume that only one node in the network initially has a certain message, then the execution process of the Gossip protocol is actually the process of spreading the message to the whole network.

Experiment 1 First, the convergence time of the basic Gossip and Matching-Gossip protocols is measured and compared in different dimensional hypercube topologies. Each node maintains a direct neighbor node list and utilizes a status bit to record whether a message is received. Initially, the status bit of only one node is set to 1, while the remaining nodes' status bits are set to 0. If a node's status bit is 1, it actively infects other nodes, causing their status bits to change from 0 to 1, making them infective. The result is shown in Figure 3.16. A total of 20 groups of experiments have been conducted, and the experimental data has been averaged.

As can be seen from Figure 3.16, the convergence time required by Matching-Gossip protocol is less than that of the basic Gossip protocol on the whole. This can be attributed to the limited selection range of target nodes imposed by the direct neighbor node list and the reduced probability of repeated message dissemination due to status bit. Moreover, this effect becomes more pronounced with an increase in the number of nodes. Specifically, when there are fewer nodes in the network, there are fewer branch paths for spreading, thereby diminishing the impact of broadcast mechanism. However, as the number of network nodes increases, so does the spread of branch paths, and consequently enhances the effectiveness of broadcast mechanism. This enhanced stability is evident from error lines.

Experiment 2 This experiment compares the convergence time between the basic Gossip and Matching-Gossip protocols in various topologies, including bus, ring, and Hypercube. The experiments are conducted under controlled

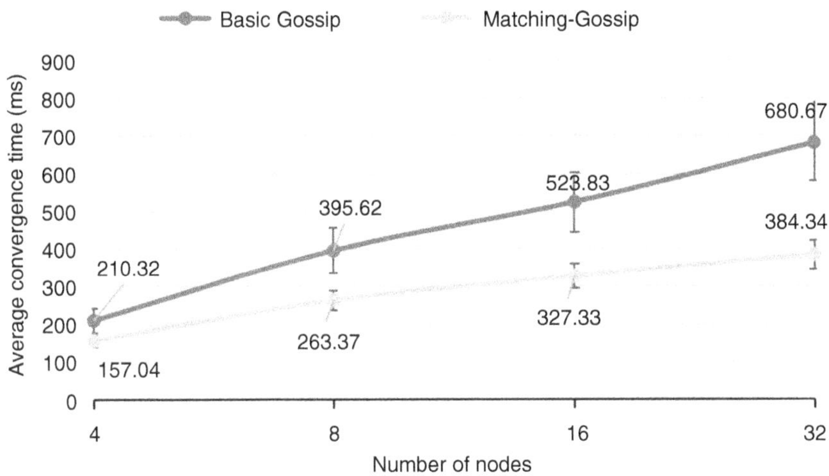

Figure 3.16 Comparison of convergence time under different number of nodes.

conditions with identical topology sizes and communication delays among nodes. In a consistent experimental network environment comprising 16 nodes, 2 target-sending nodes are designated, and the average convergence time is calculated and plotted.

The experimental result is shown in Figure 3.17. A total of 20 groups of experiments have been conducted, and the experimental data has been averaged. The Matching-Gossip protocol demonstrates excellent performance in the bus, ring, and hypercube topologies, exhibiting lower convergence times compared to the Gossip protocol. Especially in the highly structured hypercube topology, where messages can be transmitted through multiple paths allowing for parallel propagation, Matching-Gossip exhibits superior effectiveness due to decreased probability of link redundancy and node repetition.

Experiment 3 The network load of the Matching-Gossip protocol is observed to be lower than that of the basic Gossip protocol in the best-performing hypercube topology, as evidenced by Figure 3.18. A total of 20 groups of experiments have been conducted, and the experimental data has been averaged. The advantage of the Matching Gossip protocol is more pronounced with an increasing number of nodes in the network, owing to a higher probability for duplicate links and nodes in which the basic Gossip spreads redundant messages.

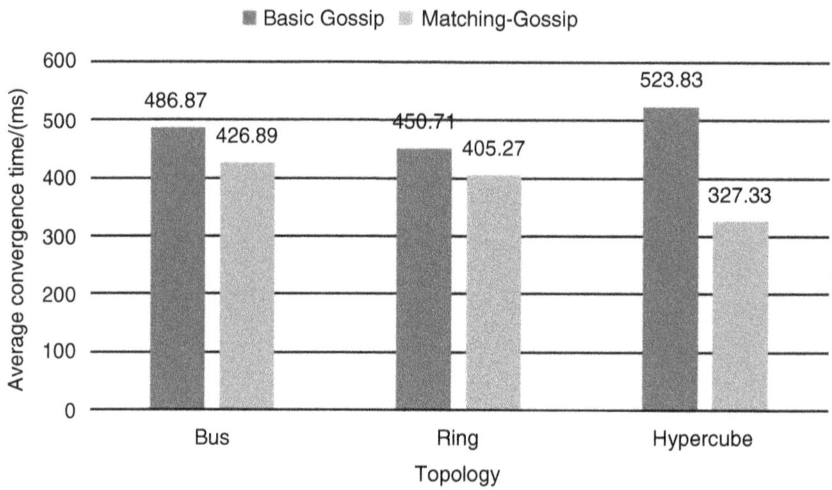

Figure 3.17 Comparison of convergence time in different topologies.

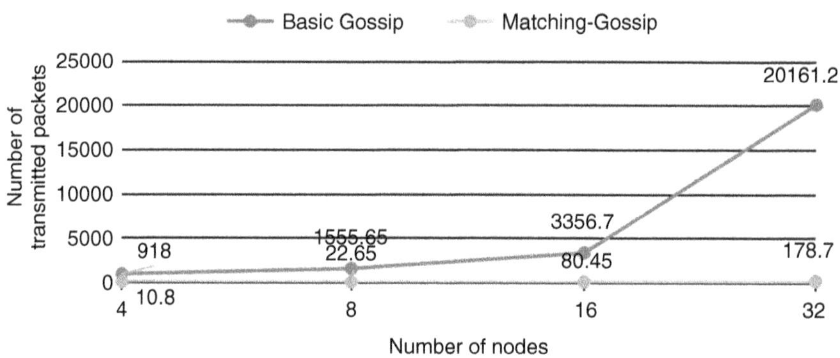

Figure 3.18 Comparison of network load under different numbers of nodes.

The experimental results and analysis presented above demonstrate the excellent adaptability of the Matching Gossip protocol to the underlying network. Based on this, the following conclusions can be drawn:

Conclusion 1: The convergence speed of Matching-Gossip protocol is faster than that of the basic Gossip protocol, and with the increase of the number of nodes, the effect has a better trend.

Conclusion 2: The topology adaptation of the Matching-Gossip protocol surpasses that of the basic Gossip protocol, particularly in hypercube topologies.
Conclusion 3: Compared with the basic Gossip protocol, the network load brought by Matching-Gossip protocol does not increase but greatly decreases.

3.4 Chapter Summary

This chapter introduces the P2P network structures, node discovery methods, and broadcast protocols. Specifically, the traditional P2P network structure is compared with the P2P network structure blockchain to avoid confusion. Sections of node discovery consider three well-known blockchains, including Bitcoin, Ethereum, and Hyperledger Fabric. In terms of broadcast protocol, we first introduce the classic basic Gossip protocol followed by an innovative Matching-Gossip protocol that effectively addresses issues related to topological mismatch and redundant node transmissions. In addition, in conjunction with the Multi-Identifier Network system, we elaborate on how the Matching-Gossip protocol aligns with the future network landscape. The chapter delves into the protocol stack and communication processes specific to Matching-Gossip within the MIN system. Through the presentation of three experiments, we validate and analyze the performance of the Matching-Gossip protocol concerning data distribution, network load, and its adaptability to diverse network topologies.

Discussion Questions

3.1 Briefly outline the classification of blockchain P2P network structures.

A: According to the degree of decentralization and the structure of node addresses, P2P networks can be divided into four categories: centralized P2P networks, fully distributed unstructured P2P networks, fully distributed structured P2P networks and semidistributed P2P networks.

3.2 Briefly describe the method of node discovery.

A: Discovering and obtaining the addresses of other nodes within the network is a crucial aspect of blockchain networking, particularly during the joining of a new node into the network. This is typically achieved through address database, command line specification, seed nodes, hard-coded addresses, or address broadcast.

3.3 Briefly describe the message broadcasting process in Matching-Gossip.

A: The message broadcasting process in Matching-Gossip mainly includes three steps: selecting the target nodes, propagating the message and updating the status. Through the information exchange and propagation between nodes, the consistency of the entire network is ensured.

References

Abdo, J.B., Dass, S., Qolomany, B. and Hossain, L., 2022. Evolutionary random graph for bitcoin overlay and blockchain mining networks. arXiv preprint arXiv:2206.09011.

Albert, R., Jeong, H. and Barabási, A.L., 1999. Diameter of the world-wide web. *Nature*, 401(6749), pp.130–131.

Anand, A., Dogar, F., Han, D., Li, B., Lim, H., Machado, M., Wu, W., Akella, A., Andersen, D.G., Byers, J.W. and Seshan, S., 2011, November. XIA: An architecture for an evolvable and trustworthy Internet. In Proceedings of the 10th ACM Workshop on Hot Topics in Networks (pp. 1–6).

Barabási, A.L., Albert, R. and Jeong, H., 2000. Scale-free characteristics of random networks: the topology of the world-wide web. *Physica A: Statistical Mechanics and its Applications*, 281(1–4), pp.69–77.

Bates, M. and LaNou, C., 2022. *Go fundamentals: Gopher guides*. Addison-Wesley Professional.

Cachin, C., 2016, July. Architecture of the hyperledger blockchain fabric. In Workshop on distributed cryptocurrencies and consensus ledgers (Vol. 310, No. 4, pp. 1–4).

Cheng, F., Zhai, S.C. and Dong, J., 2022. Investigation of Gaussian mixture clustering model for online diagnosis of tip-wear in nanomachining. *Journal of Manufacturing Processes*, 77, pp. 114–124.

Dao, N.N., Tran, A.T., Tu, N.H., Thanh, T.T., Bao, V.N.Q. and Cho, S., 2022. A contemporary survey on live video streaming from a computation-driven perspective. *ACM Computing Surveys*, 54(10s), pp. 1–38.

Das, A., Gupta, I. and Motivala, A., 2002, June. Swim: Scalable weakly-consistent infection-style process group membership protocol. In Proceedings International Conference on Dependable Systems and Networks (pp. 303–312). IEEE.

Demers, A., Greene, D., Hauser, C., Irish, W., Larson, J., Shenker, S., Sturgis, H., Swinehart, D. and Terry, D., 1987, December. Epidemic algorithms for replicated database maintenance. In Proceedings of the sixth annual ACM Symposium on Principles of distributed computing (pp. 1–12).

Garnett, N., 2001. Digital rights management, copyright, and napster. *ACM SIGecom Exchanges*, 2(2), pp. 1–5.

Honda, K., Nakamura, R. and Kamiyama, N., 2023, May. Characteristic analysis of socially-aware information-centric networking. In NOMS 2023–2023 IEEE/IFIP Network Operations and Management Symposium (pp. 1–5). IEEE.

Ihle, C., Trautwein, D., Schubotz, M., Meuschke, N. and Gipp, B., 2023. Incentive mechanisms in peer-to-peer networks – A systematic literature review. *ACM Computing Surveys*, 56(1).

Kermarrec, A.M. and Van Steen, M., 2007. Gossiping in distributed systems. *ACM SIGOPS Operating Systems Review*, 41(5), pp. 2–7.

Li, H., Wu, J., Yang, X., Wang, H., Lan, J., Xu, K., Tan, H., Wei, J., Liang, W., Zhu, F. and Lu, Y., 2020. MIN: Co-governing multi-identifier network architecture and its prototype on operator's network. *IEEE Access*, 8, pp. 36569–36581.

Liu, Y., Zhuang, Z., Xiao, L. and Ni, L.M., 2004, March. A distributed approach to solving overlay mismatching problem. In 24th International Conference on Distributed Computing Systems, 2004. Proceedings (pp. 132–139). IEEE.

Lua, E.K., Crowcroft, J., Pias, M., Sharma, R. and Lim, S., 2005. A survey and comparison of peer-to-peer overlay network schemes. *IEEE Communications Surveys & Tutorials*, 7(2), pp. 72–93.

Maymounkov, P. and Mazieres, D., 2002, March. Kademlia: A peer-to-peer information system based on the xor metric. In *International Workshop on Peer-to-Peer Systems* (pp. 53–65). Berlin, Heidelberg: Springer Berlin Heidelberg.

Parameswaran, M., Susarla, A. and Whinston, A.B., 2001. P2P networking: an information sharing alternative. *Computer*, 34(7), pp. 31–38.

Schollmeier, R., 2001, August. A definition of peer-to-peer networking for the classification of peer-to-peer architectures and applications. In Proceedings First International Conference on Peer-to-Peer Computing (pp. 101–102). IEEE.

Serena, L., Ferretti, S. and D'Angelo, G., 2022. Cryptocurrencies activity as a complex network: Analysis of transactions graphs. *Peer-to-Peer Networking and Applications*, 15(2), pp. 839–853.

Taheri-Boshrooyeh, S., Thorén, O., Whitehat, B., Koh, W.J., Kilic, O. and Gurkan, K., 2022, July. Privacy-preserving spam-protected Gossip-based routing. In 2022 IEEE 42nd International Conference on Distributed Computing Systems (ICDCS) (pp. 1286–1287). IEEE.

Tao, B., Ho, I.W.H. and Dai, H.N., 2021, May. Complex network analysis of the bitcoin blockchain network. In 2021 IEEE International Symposium on Circuits and Systems (ISCAS) (pp. 1–5). IEEE.

Wood, G., 2014. Ethereum: A secure decentralised generalised transaction ledger. *Ethereum Project Yellow Paper*, 151(2014), pp.1–32.

Xylomenos, G., Ververidis, C.N., Siris, V.A., Fotiou, N., Tsilopoulos, C., Vasilakos, X., Katsaros, K.V. and Polyzos, G.C., 2013. A survey of information-centric networking research. *IEEE Communications Surveys & Tutorials*, 16(2), pp.1024–1049.

Yap, K.Y., Chin, H.H. and Klemeš, J.J., 2023. Blockchain technology for distributed generation: A review of current development, challenges and future prospect. *Renewable and Sustainable Energy Reviews*, 175, p. 113170.

Yeh, L.Y., Shen, C.Y., Huang, W.C., Hsu, W.H. and Wu, H.C., 2022. GDPR-aware revocable P2P file-sharing system over consortium blockchain. *IEEE Systems Journal*, 16(4), pp. 5234–5245.

4

Blockchain Consensus

This chapter will initially present the basic concept of distributed consistency, followed by several prominent consensus mechanisms for consortium blockchains, including voting-based consensus, proof-based consensus, and consensus integrating proof and voting. At the end of this chapter, we will provide an evaluation and analysis of these various consensus mechanisms.

4.1 Basic Concepts of Distributed Consistency

The consistency problem lies at the core of distributed systems, defining how multiple nodes manage data states within such systems. In the long stage of the development of distributed agreement protocols, a relatively mature theoretical system has been established, which is also the foundational basis for the design, optimization, and analysis of many blockchain consensus.

4.1.1 SMR Model in Blockchain System

The State Machine Replication (SMR) model, originating from traditional distributed theory, has been adapted to the blockchain system. It can represent that the state machine is composed of multiple replicas, and consensus is achieved among the states on each replica when executing a command.

If the initial state of each replica is the same, the consensus mechanism (Susskind, McKearnen, and Thomas-Lamar 1999) ensures a global agreement on the order of input commands, and the state of each replica will be the same. Specifically, in the basic SMR model, an input command is *tx*, and a bookkeeper packs these *tx*s into a block, each containing the hash of the previous block. The leader sends the proposal, and then the individual nodes participate in the vote to reach a consensus on the order of *tx*s.

Principles and Applications of Blockchain Systems: How to Overcome the CAP Trilemma in Consortium Blockchain, First Edition. Hui Li and Han Wang.

Published 2025 by John Wiley & Sons, Inc.

4.1.2 FLP Theorem

The FLP theorem (Fischer, Lynch, and Paterson 1985, pp. 374–382), introduced by Fischer, Lynch, and Paterson in 1985, is a renowned theorem within distributed systems. It asserts that in fully asynchronous consensus protocols, not even a single unannounced process failure can be tolerated. Consequently, the FLP theorem effectively demonstrates the impracticality of designing an algorithm capable of achieving consensus under any scenario involving asynchronous distributed systems.

4.1.3 Distributed Network Assumption

The basic network assumptions of distributed systems are initially divided into synchronous and asynchronous paradigms. Consensus can be easily achieved in synchronous distributed systems, whereas the complexity arises in asynchronous ones. In reality, due to delay, partition, and other network factors, actual distributed systems rarely operate under ideal synchronization conditions. Considering an asynchronous network system, it is impossible for nodes to reach a consensus according to the FLP theorem. Therefore, the network models of distributed systems are generally based on the assumption of partial synchronization.

Definition 4.1 Synchronization
In the synchronous network state, messages sent by a normal node can reach the target node within a known time interval, that is, the maximum message delay is determined. Consensus in a synchronous distributed system is relatively straightforward, as all nodes execute algorithmic steps simultaneously during a synchronization round.

Suppose the system consists of n nodes, each of which executes a serial algorithm locally. These nodes send and receive messages over a fully connected communication network, with two-way communication channels between each pair of nodes. In addition, the channel is reliable and messages will not be lost, duplicated, or changed.

Several basic communication operations are given below.

1) The process p_i sends a message to the process p_j by calling send m to p_j. The send operation is atomic, that is, regardless of the size of m, it can only be fully executed or not executed at all, and there is no case that only half of the message is sent.
2) The process p_i sends a message to all the processes by calling broadcast m. Unlike the send operation, the broadcast operation is nonatomic. In addition, broadcast termination only ensures that the message m has been sent to all processes, but does not require the sending order.

3) The receive operation is used to receive messages, and this process appears implicitly in the algorithm description.

Synchronization model is a special time assumption. It considers that both message transmission delay and process execution time have known upper limits, thus eliminating time uncertainty in asynchronous systems. Therefore, it can be logically assumed that the process runs in lock-step mode.

"Lock-step" means that distributed synchronization algorithms can be described in terms of a round-based model, where each run is made up of a limited series of rounds, numbered 1, 2, ..., r. Make up. The number of current rounds in the system is represented by a read-only global variable r, the value of which is implicitly maintained by the synchronization hypothesis. A round consists of three successive stages.

1) *Sending phase*: The local algorithm specifies that the process p_i broadcasts a message.
2) *Receiving phase*: Each process receives messages. A basic property is that messages sent by process p_i to process p_j in the r-th round will be received in the same round.
3) *Local computing phase*: The process p_i modifies the current local state according to the historical state and received messages. In addition, the process p_i calculates the messages it will broadcast in the next round.

Figure 4.1 shows an example of a simple synchronous run. Each process broadcasts a message in each round, waits for the message to arrive, and computes locally until the algorithm forces all processes to go to the next round.

Definition 4.2 Asynchronization

In the asynchronous network state, messages sent by a normal node can reach the target node within an unknown time interval, that is, the maximum message delay is undetermined. Since nodes do not know the network's transmission delay and other nodes' behavior, reaching consensus in an asynchronous scenario poses significant challenges, necessitating a robust and effective consensus algorithm.

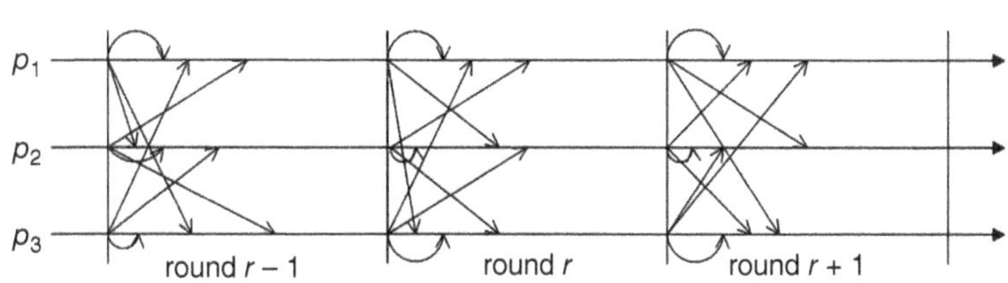

Figure 4.1 A simple synchronous run example.

Let us consider a scenario where one process p is waiting for a message from another process q. In the $AS_{n,t}[\emptyset]$ system model, a process can wait for messages from another $n - t$ process without being permanently blocked, and the main problem process p needs to solve is to stop waiting for messages from process q or to continue waiting. Basically, allowing the wait to stop the process p while the process q is active violates the safety requirements of the distributed system, and forcing the wait of p to continue may cause the liveness of the distributed system to be unsatisfied if q crashes before sending the required message.

Then consider a synchronization system with two processes, p_i and p_j. Synchronization means that the transmission delay has an upper limit, assuming the corresponding upper limit is Δ, and the speed of the process has upper and lower limits. For simplicity and without loss of generality, the processing time can be considered negligible relative to the transfer time and therefore equal to 0.

In the context of this synchronization, consider this problem P. p_i and p_j has the initial value, v_i and v_j, respectively, and they all have to compute a result. If no process crashes, the result is $f(v_i, v_j)$. If p_j crashes, then the result is $f(v_i, \perp)$. If p_i crashes, then the result is $f(\perp, v_j)$.

Each process sends its own value and waits for the value of the other process. When it receives another value, the process will send its own value if it has not yet done so. To avoid waiting forever, the process p_i uses a timer, as shown in Figure 4.2. It sets the timer to 2Δ. When it sends its own value. If no value of p_j is received and the timer expires, p_i will conclude that p_j crashed before sending the value $f(v_i, \perp)$. In another case, it receives the value and returns $f(v_i, v_j)$.

The left execution is error-free and p_j sends its own value at the latest, that is, when it receives the value v_i of p_i. In this case, the timer does not time out and p_i returns $f(v_i, v_j)$. But the execution on the right was different and p_j crashed before sending its own value, causing p_i to return $f(v_i, \perp)$ after the timer expired. If p_j sends its value before the crash, p_i will receive it and therefore return $f(v_i, v_j)$. The uncertainty of p_j's state is controlled by time-out values. Because whether p_j crashes or not are not known by p_i in advance, timeout values are set 2Δ conservatively.

When the processing time is equal to 0, the transfer time is finite but arbitrary. Therefore, the system is asynchronous in terms of messages. A process can adopt

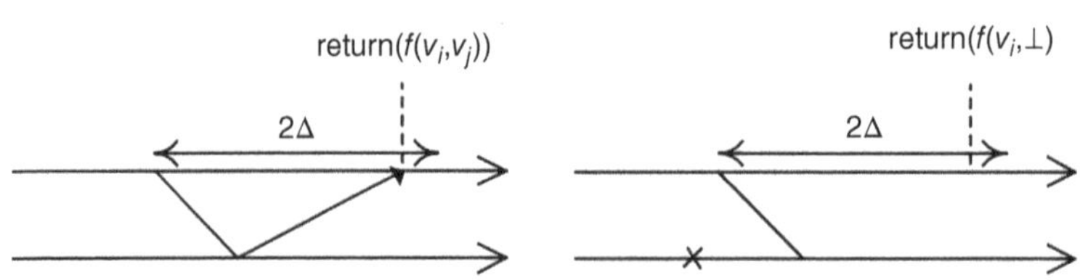

Figure 4.2 Synchronization without uncertainty.

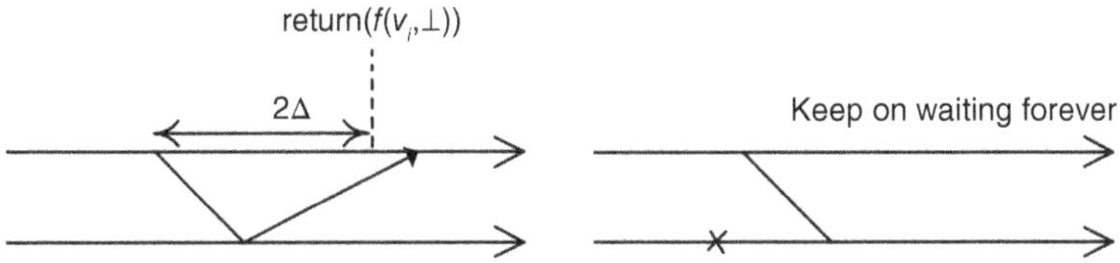

Figure 4.3 Wait or not in asynchronous and failed cases.

an estimate policy for the local clock and round-trip latency, but no matter what this value is, there is no guarantee that the estimate is the upper limit for the current round-trip latency performed. Otherwise, the system will be synchronized.

Using this estimate, several things can happen. In the current execution, the estimate may be accurate, in which case the synchronization assumptions used by the process are correct, as shown in Figure 4.3.

Unfortunately, as mentioned above, there is no guarantee that the estimate used in the process is correct, regardless of its value. This is depicted on the left side of Figure 4.3, which returns $f(v_i, \perp)$ after the timer expires, but actually it should return $f(v_i, v_j)$. In this case, incorrect estimates can undermine the security of the problem. Therefore, the timer cannot be used safely. However, if the timer is not used by p_i, if p_j crashes before sending its value, as shown on the right in Figure 4.3, p_i will wait forever, which violates the liveness requirement for distributed consensus problems.

This simple example shows that when the problem P must be solved in an asynchronous system, it is not possible to guarantee both security and liveness of P. Achieving consensus in an asynchronous distributed system is a seemingly impossible task because transmission delays cannot be accurately estimated, which will cause many problems and lead to the failure of the message exchange between processes, causing the process to return the wrong calculated value. In this case, there is no guarantee that every process can reach a consensus on the state of the application. At the same time, it also shows that in asynchronous distributed systems, security and liveness cannot be obtained at the same time, and if this problem needs to be solved, a more robust distributed system is needed.

Definition 4.3 Partial Synchronization
Consider a system with an uncertain Global Stable Time (GST) and a Δ such that the system is synchronous within time Δ after the end of GST. The network state of this system is called partial synchronization. In the partial synchronization state, any message sent at time x must be delivered before time $\Delta + max(x, GST)$. Informally, in a partially synchronous model, the system is asynchronous before GST and synchronous after GST, as shown in Figure 4.4.

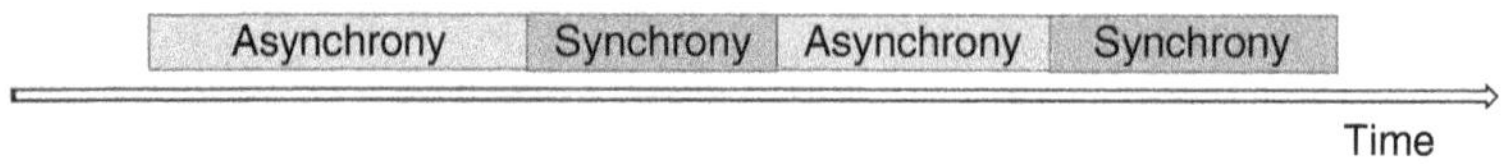

Figure 4.4 Partial synchronization.

4.1.4 Paxos

Paxos (Lamport 2019, pp. 277–317) is a fundamental distributed consensus algorithm proposed by Leslie Lamport, initially introduced in 1988. Paxos is used to construct reliable systems, ensuring that even in the presence of failures or unreliable communication, the system can still operate correctly. To better describe this algorithm, Lamport imagined a scenario of elections in a Greek city-state named Paxos, hence the name of the algorithm. The city-state adopts a democratic process of proposing and voting to reach decisions. However, due to the inability of residents to devote all their time and energy to decision-making, they can only participate in decisions intermittently, follow the progress of voting, and express their voting preferences. The goal of the Paxos algorithm is to reach consensus in a way that the majority prevails.

In the Paxos algorithm, system nodes are mainly divided into three categories:

Proposer: Proposers are responsible for proposing proposals, which include a proposal ID and a value. The proposed value can be any operation, such as "changing the value of A from 0 to 1." There can be multiple proposers, and different proposers can propose different or even conflicting values. However, for the same round of the Paxos algorithm, at most one proposed value can be accepted.

Acceptor: Acceptors can vote on proposals proposed by proposers, and acceptors are completely independent of each other. If more than half of the acceptors vote to approve a certain proposal, then that proposal is chosen, and its proposed value remains unchanged.

Learner: Learners are responsible for learning the agreed-upon values.

The Paxos algorithm consists of two main phases, namely the prepare phase and the accept phase:

4.1.4.1 Prepare Phase

Proposers send prepare(n) messages to a majority or all acceptors. Here, n represents the proposal identifier, which is globally unique and incrementally increasing, greater than any proposal identifier previously used by the proposer. For example, n can be a nanosecond-level timestamp. If a proposer cannot make progress due to a lack of response from the acceptors, the proposer retries with a higher n.

When an acceptor receives a prepare(n) message, it makes a "promise." If it has not previously made a promise to any prepare message, it promises to ignore any requests with proposal identifiers less than n. The acceptor records the value of n and replies with a promise(n) message. On the other hand, if the acceptor has previously made a promise, i.e., has responded to another prepare message with a proposal identifier lower than n, the acceptor performs the following operation:

If the acceptor has not yet received any accept messages from proposers in the accept phase, it records the maximum n and then sends a promise message to the proposer. Otherwise, the acceptor sends the accepted complete proposal along with the promise message to the proposer.

4.1.4.2 Accept Phase

For proposals that have been proposed, proposers wait for responses from acceptors regarding proposal identifier n. Upon receiving responses, proposers need to determine the value v to be sent in the accept message. If the proposer receives one or more promise messages containing complete proposals, it chooses the value v of the proposal with the highest proposal identifier. If the proposer does not receive any promise messages containing complete proposals, it can freely choose any value. Then, the proposer sends an accept message to the acceptors in the form of accept(n, v). Upon receiving the accept(n, v) message, an acceptor performs the following operation:

> If the acceptor previously promised not to accept the proposal identifier, it ignores the message. Otherwise, if the acceptor has responded with the same response to the corresponding prepare request prepare(n), it replies with the accepted(n, v) message, indicating acceptance of the proposal. Finally, the acceptor sends the accepted(n, v) message to all learners. If more than half of the acceptors accept the value v in the proposal, v becomes the decision value of the current round of the protocol, thus reaching consensus.

4.1.5 Raft

Raft (Ongaro and Ousterhout 2014, pp. 305–319) is a consensus algorithm used for achieving distributed consistency, proposed by Diego Ongaro and John Ousterhout in 2014. It aims to enhance the understandability and maintainability of consensus algorithms in design. Compared to other consensus algorithms like Paxos, Raft is easier to understand and implement because of its modular design, clear role definitions, and message-passing patterns.

Raft is an asymmetric protocol based on leader election, where only one node in the system is elected as the leader. The leader receives client requests and manages log replication. If the current leader fails, a new leader is elected. In a Raft cluster, nodes are mainly categorized into three types: leaders, followers, and candidates.

Leader: The leader receives client requests, manages log replication, and communicates with followers.
Follower: Followers respond to Remote Procedure Call (RPC) requests but do not initiate any communication.
Candidate: Candidates attempt to be elected as leaders by requesting votes.

The Raft protocol mainly consists of two phases: leader election and log replication. In the leader election phase, a leader is elected, and in the log replication phase, the leader accepts client requests, updates the log, and sends heartbeat messages to all followers to maintain its leader status.

4.1.5.1 Leader Election

All nodes initially start as followers. As long as followers receive valid RPCs from leaders or candidates, they remain in the follower state. If followers do not receive heartbeat messages from the leader within a certain time period, an "election timeout" is triggered, indicating that the leader node may have failed. The election timeout is randomly set between 150 and 300 ms.

At this point, follower nodes transition to candidates and attempt to become the new leader by starting an election. Candidates vote for themselves and request votes from other nodes by sending RequestVote RPCs. Nodes grant votes only if the candidate's log is at least as up-to-date as the receiver's log. If a candidate receives votes from a majority of nodes, it becomes the new leader and starts sending heartbeat messages to other follower nodes. If another candidate wins the election and becomes the new leader, the previous candidate reverts to the follower role. If no candidate wins and an election timeout occurs, a new round of the election process starts.

Once a leader is elected, the system is ready to accept requests from clients and enters the log replication phase.

4.1.5.2 Log Replication

In Raft consensus, time is divided into terms, which monotonically increase and serve as the logical clock of the system to achieve partial global ordering of events in the absence of a global synchronized clock.

After clients send requests to the leader, the leader assigns a term and index to the request to uniquely identify it in the node's log. The leader then appends this request to its log and replicates it to all follower nodes via AppendEntries RPCs.

When the leader confirms that the request has been replicated to a majority of follower nodes, the entry is considered committed in the cluster. Subsequently, the leader executes the request in its state machine, returns the result to the client, and notifies followers of the committed entry via AppendEntries RPCs, which followers execute in their state machines.

If a follower fails or responds too slowly, the leader retries AppendEntries RPCs until successful. When a follower receives an AppendEntries RPC for log replication, it checks if the term is smaller than the current term. If it is, the follower responds with false. Followers only append new entries not already in the log. If an existing entry at the same index has a different term, the existing entry and all subsequent entries are deleted.

Although the system may experience network delays, packet loss, restarts, or crashes, once a request is committed, the Raft cluster does not lose the request. However, it does not handle Byzantine faults.

Each log entry includes a term number, an index, and a state machine command. The term number helps detect inconsistencies between logs and provides an indication of when the request occurred. The index is used to identify the position of the entry in the log. The command is the content of the client request to be executed.

4.2 Byzantine Generals Problem

The Byzantine generals problem (Lamport, Shostak, and Pease 2019, pp. 203–226), initially proposed by Leslie Lamport in 1982, offers a scenario that illustrates the challenges of achieving distributed consensus. In this problem, divisions of the Byzantine imperial army, led by different generals, must coordinate their actions while stationed outside an enemy city. Communication between generals is limited to messengers, and victory relies on more than half of the generals agreeing on a plan of action. However, some of these generals may be traitors trying to prevent the loyal generals from agreeing on a plan of action. Even more unfortunately, the messengers may also be traitors to alter or forge messages, or cause message loss.

In order to understand the Byzantine generals problem deeply, the following will illustrate it through the example of three generals.

When all three generals are loyal, a unanimous plan of action can be decided by vote. As shown in Figure 4.5, Generals A and B propose to launch an attack by observing the enemy's military situation and judging from their own situation, while General C suggests retreat. In the end, the vote result is attack: retreat = 2:1, so the three generals will attack together to win.

Even one traitor among the three generals can disrupt the normal plan of action. As shown in Figure 4.6, the traitor General C sends conflicting messages to Generals A and B. In this case, General A gets the vote result of attack: retreat = 1:2, and decides to retreat, while General B gets the vote result of attack: retreat = 2:1, and chooses to initiate an attack. Finally, only General B attacks but suffers defeat.

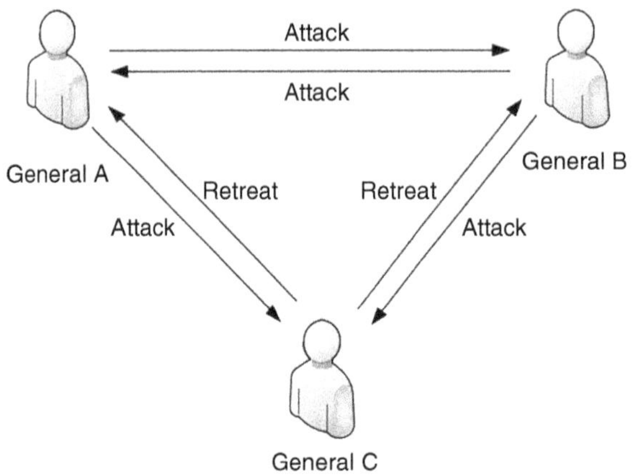

Figure 4.5 A case where all three generals are loyal.

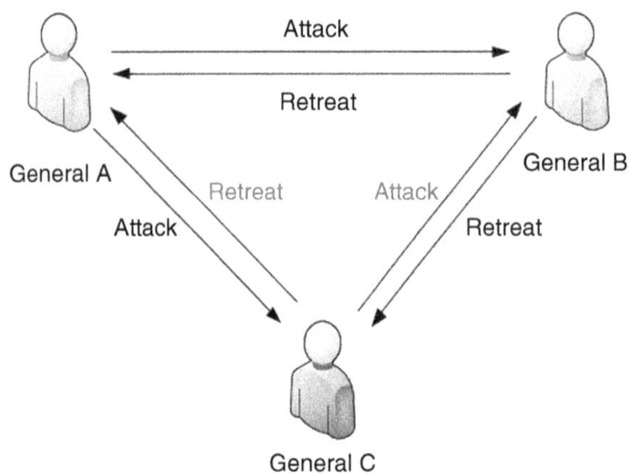

Figure 4.6 A case with a traitor among three generals.

In fact, Leslie Lamport's paper offers a general conclusion: if there are m traitors, it takes at least $3m + 1$ generals to reach an agreed plan of action. This paper further presents two solutions to the Byzantine generals problem, namely the Oral Message (OM) algorithm and the Signed Message (SM) algorithm.

4.2.1 Oral Message Algorithm

First of all, the assumptions regarding oral messages are as follows:

a) Every message sent will reach its intended receiver accurately;
b) The receiver can identify the sender of a message;
c) It's detectable when a message has not been received.

Among them, assumptions a) and b) ensure that the traitor node cannot interfere with the communication between two honest nodes, where Assumption a) focuses on the information transmission process, while assumption b) emphasizes the information itself. Assumption c) prevents traitors from influencing consensus by message manipulation.

Based on the above three assumptions, an oral message is impervious to tampering but susceptible to forgery. According to the derivation of the three generals problem, when there is a traitor, three more loyal generals must be added to achieve the final consistent action. In order to deepen understanding, the following scenario will employ three loyal generals and one traitor to illustrate the OM algorithm.

In the OM algorithm, the initial sender of the message is referred to as the commander, and the remaining generals are adjutants. For the scenario of three loyal generals and one traitor, two rounds of action information negotiation are required, and if no action information is received, the default retreat is made.

Consider the case where the commander is loyal, as shown in Figure 4.7. In the first round of action information negotiation, the commander broadcasts attack messages. In the second round, since Generals A and B are loyal, they transmit similar attack messages as that of the commander; while General C, a traitor, sends retreat messages to disrupt the action plan. Eventually, the commander, General A, and General B agree on a plan of attack with victory.

Consider the scenario where the commander acts as the traitor, as shown in Figure 4.8. In the first round of action information negotiation, the commander sends a retreat message to Generals A and B, but an attack message to General C in order to disrupt his decision. In the second round, since Generals A and B

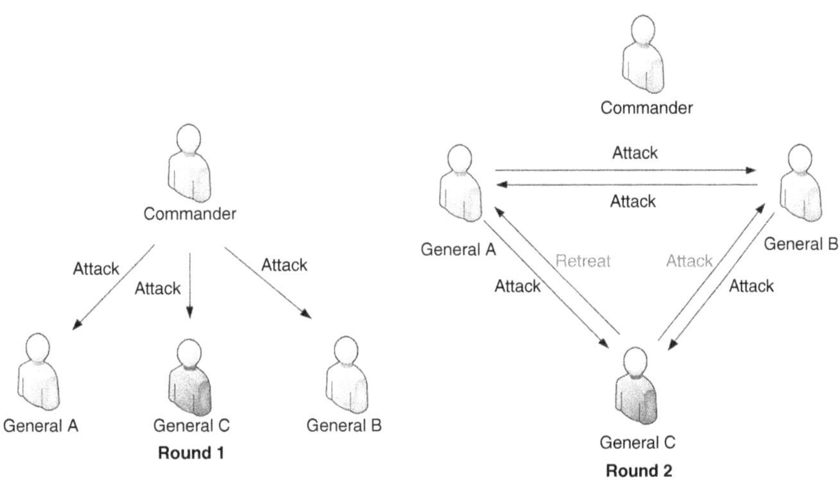

Figure 4.7 The case of a loyal commander.

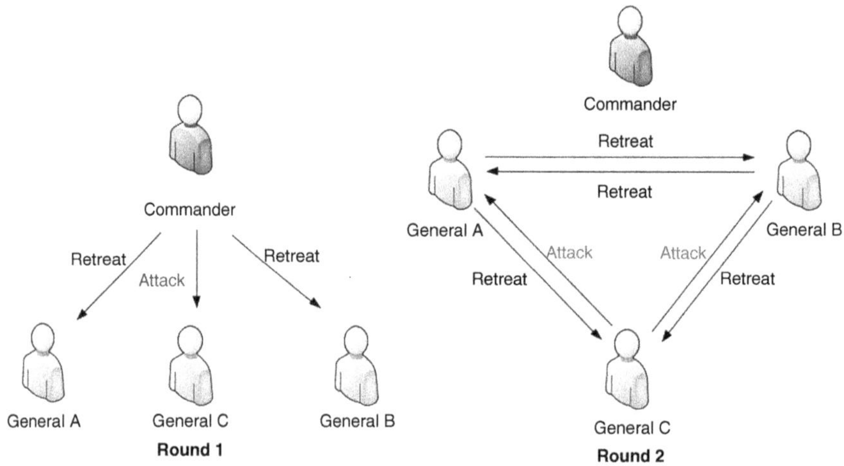

Figure 4.8 The case where the commander is a traitor.

are loyal generals, the messages from the commander are correctly sent to the remaining two adjutants. Eventually, all the loyal generals can agree on a plan to retreat.

As previously mentioned, in the case of the Byzantine generals problem with the OM algorithm, if there are m traitors and not less than $3m + 1$ generals, an agreed plan of action will eventually be reached. It should be noted that in this algorithm, m is a known variable which determines the recursion frequency, that is, m determines the number of rounds $(m + 1)$ required for action information negotiation. This also explains why two rounds of action information negotiation in the above scenario. The communication complexity of this algorithm is denoted by $O(n^m)$, where n represents the node number.

4.2.2 Signed Message Algorithm

The assumptions regarding signed messages are based on those for oral messages, with two additional conditions:

d) It is impossible to forge the signature of a loyal general, and any modification to the content of their SM will be detected;
e) The authenticity of a general's signature can be verified by anyone.

Based on these five assumptions, signed messages cannot be forged or tampered with. In order to further understand the SM algorithm, a similar example from the three generals problem will also be derived. Consider the case in which a loyal general takes the lead in initiating action information negotiations. As shown

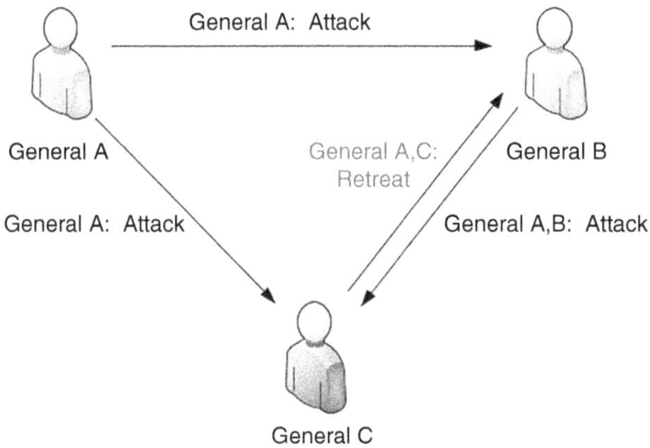

Figure 4.9 A case where a loyal general takes the lead in initiating action information negotiations.

in Figure 4.9, General *A* sends attack messages to Generals *B* and *C*. Once the traitor General *C* manipulates the message from General *A*, General *B* will find this tampering and execute the message from General *A*.

Consider the case in which a traitor general first initiates action information negotiation. As shown in Figure 4.10, the traitor General *C* sends misleading

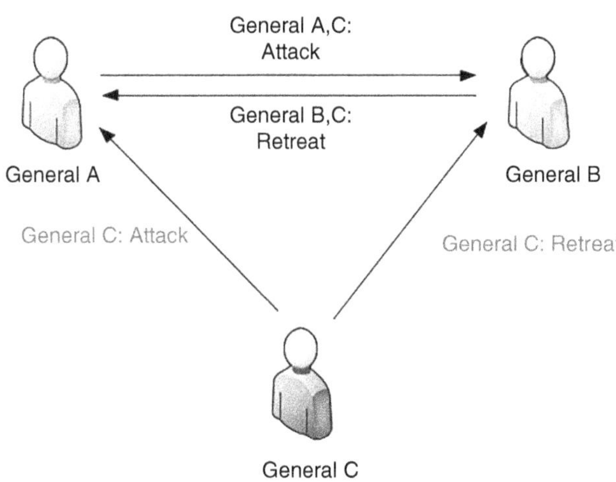

Figure 4.10 A case where a traitor takes the lead in initiating action information negotiation.

action information, and then Generals A and B will identify inconsistencies in the information provided by General C. Consequently, General C will be judged as a traitor and processed before conducting action information negotiation.

Lamport et al. further prove that if the signed messages sent between generals are unforgeable, the SM algorithm can make the loyal generals in any $n > m + 1$ generals reach a consensus, that is, the SM algorithm can handle any scenario with a varying number of traitors. In a broad context, these generals can be perceived as network nodes, while traitors are defined as Byzantine nodes capable of maliciously tampering with data or disseminating disinformation. The communication complexity of this algorithm is $O(nm)$, where n is the total number of nodes and m is the number of Byzantine nodes.

As mentioned above, the Byzantine generals' problem provides a situational description of the distributed consensus problem and is the most complex model in the field of distributed systems. In addition, it provides a framework for understanding and classifying many existing distributed agreement protocols and algorithms. The existing distributed agreement protocols and algorithms can be divided into two main categories:

One is the Crash Fault Tolerance (CFT) algorithms, also known as non-Byzantine fault tolerance algorithms. They solve the consensus problem in distributed systems where there are faults but no malicious attacks. In these scenarios, messages may be lost or duplicated, but not tampered with or forged. Usually applied in LAN environments, such as distributed databases.

The other is Byzantine Fault Tolerance (BFT) algorithms, which address the consensus problem dealing with both faults and intentional attacks in distributed systems. Usually applied in Internet scenarios, such as blockchain systems.

As an open network, there are usually Byzantine nodes within a blockchain system. The consensus mechanism has two ways of dealing with Byzantine failures: One is based on voting, wherein consistency among nodes is achieved through message interaction even in the presence of certain malicious nodes, as exemplified by Practical Byzantine Fault Tolerance (PBFT) (Castro and Liskov 1999, pp. 173–186). The other is based on proof and aims to reduce the likelihood of malicious nodes by increasing the cost associated with malevolent actions, such as Proof of Work (PoW) (Nakamoto 2008) and Proof of Stake (PoS) (King and Nadal 2012). Below, we describe typical consensus mechanisms based on voting, proof, and their integration.

4.3 Voting-Based Consensus

Voting-based consensus is derived from traditional distributed agreement protocols. In a blockchain with strong trust guarantees, it is important for nodes to be easily identifiable and adjustable in order to facilitate message exchange.

In a voting-based consensus algorithm, apart from maintaining a distributed ledger, all nodes in the network must also collaborate to verify blocks or transactions by interacting with each other to determine whether a proposed block can be added to the blockchain. In almost all of these variants, there needs to be a minimum threshold of participating nodes in each consensus round.

4.3.1 Partial Synchronization Class

4.3.1.1 Practical Byzantine Fault Tolerance

A typical voting-based consensus is the PBFT consensus algorithm proposed by M. Castro and B. Liskov in 1999. PBFT addresses the issue of low efficiency in previous BFT algorithms by reducing complexity from exponential to polynomial levels, making it feasible for practical system applications. Since the Hyperledger Fabric project (Cachin 2016, pp. 1–4) adopted an improved version of PBFT (Sukhwani et al. 2017, pp. 253–255) as its consensus mechanism in 2015, there has been widespread discussion within blockchain communities about this tokenless and high-speed verification algorithm.

PBFT assigns nodes to three distinct roles: clients, responsible for sending transaction requests; the primary node, which packages transactions into blocks and leads block consensus (with only one primary node per round); and replica nodes, which participate in block consensus (with multiple replicas per round, each processing similarly). Both the primary and replica nodes are integral components of the consensus mechanism.

All copies work in a rotation process called a view, wherein one node serves as the primary node and the other nodes serve as replica nodes. The primary node is calculated by $p = v \bmod |R|$, where v is the view number and consists of consecutive integers, p is the copy number, and $|R|$ is the number of replica nodes.

The PBFT consensus process consists of three phases: pre-prepare, prepare, and commit. The pre-prepare and prepare phases aim to arrange requests sent in the same view, ensuring that each node in the network accepts and executes them sequentially.

The algorithm is illustrated using a four-replica network with numbers $i = 0, 1, 2, 3$ as an example. In this scenario, replica 0 is the primary node while N represents the number of replica nodes and f represents the number of faulty or Byzantine nodes. Let us consider the consensus process in the absence of any abnormal nodes ($f = 0$), as depicted in Figure 4.11.

Step 1: The client sends a request message m to each replica node. The primary node 0 in the current view assigns a sequence number n to the request after receiving the client request, and broadcasts a pre-prepare message $\langle\langle PRE-PREPARE, v, n, D(m)\rangle, m\rangle$ to all replica nodes. Here, v represents the current view number and D represents the digest of the message content.

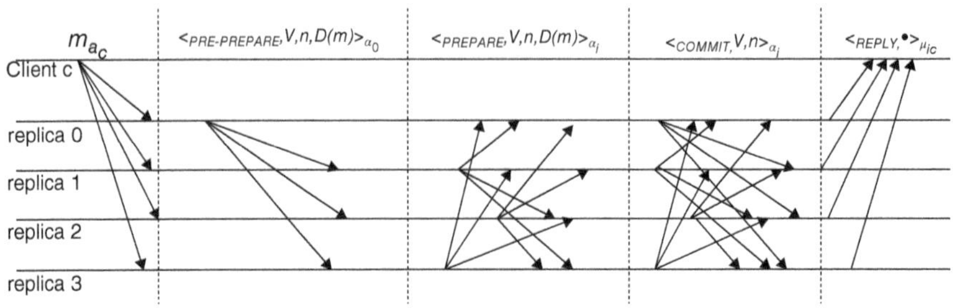

Figure 4.11 Message passing diagram of PBFT.(N = 4, f = 0).

Step 2: In node i, if no prior message with the same n and v but a different abstract D has been received, and if the sequence number n falls within the permissible interval while matching the currently recorded view number for requested view v, then it verifies the success of the pre-prepare message. It accepts the allocation of request m from the primary node, broadcasts a prepare message $\langle PREPARE, v, n, D(m)\rangle$ and logs the pre-prepare and prepare messages. The request m is considered to be in a pre-prepared state in node i when node i sends either the corresponding pre-prepare or prepare message.

Step 3: Node i is considered to enter a prepared state for request m if it receives at least $2f+1$ pre-prepare or prepare messages from distinct nodes, including itself, within a specified time interval.

Step 4: Node i transmits the commit message $\langle COMMIT, v, n\rangle$ to inform other nodes that the request with number n under view v has been prepared locally. Similarly, when node i receives at least $2f+1$ commit messages from different nodes, including itself, request m reaches a committed state in this node.

Step 5: Node i sequentially executes requests in ascending order of number n and feeds back to the client. The client receives identical messages from $f+1$ nodes, indicating successful completion of this consensus round. Also, node i discards requests with timestamps earlier than the latest message in its record.

PBFT requires the node number N to satisfy $N \geq 3f+1$. In the previous example with $N = 4$, it means that a failure tolerance level of $f \leq 1$ can be achieved. Obviously, when the primary node is good and one replica is bad, PBFT ensures the healthy and legal operation of network. Figure 4.12 shows the consensus process in case of node 3 failure.

A primary node issue, such as a timeout or fault, triggers a view change event. The process of view change is also composed of three phases: view-change, view-change-ack, and new-view. Let us continue considering the scenario for $N = 4$, as depicted in Figure 4.13.

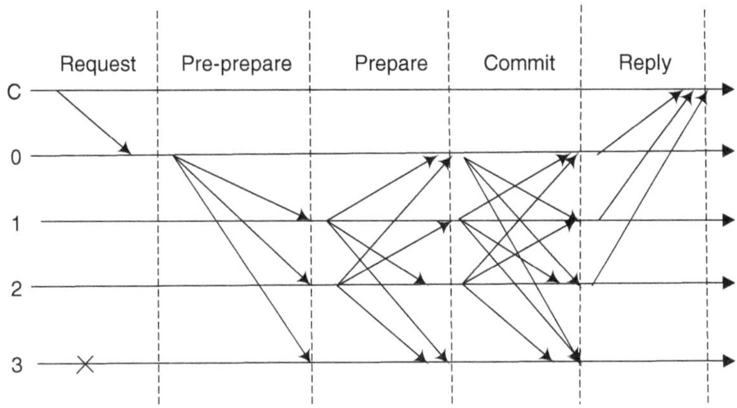

Figure 4.12 PBFT consensus process ($N = 4, f = 1$).

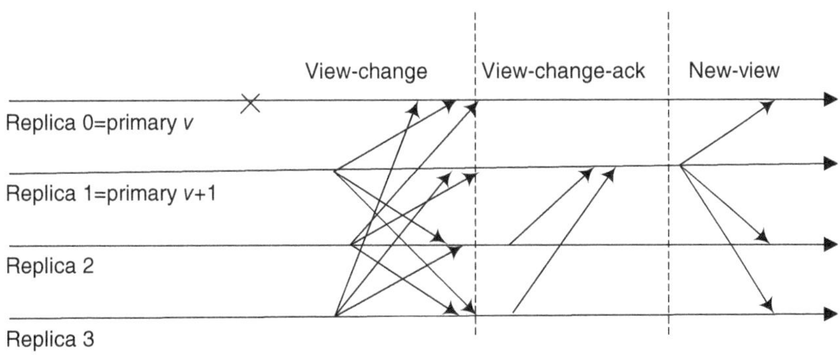

Figure 4.13 View change in PBFT.

Step 1: When a node $i(i = 1, 2, 3)$ detects an anomaly in the primary node, it enters the view $v + 1$ and broadcasts a view-change message $\langle VIEW - CHANGE, v + 1, n, C, P\rangle$. Here, n indicates the stable checkpoint of node i, C contains its checkpoints along with their digests, and P is the set of requests prepared in previous view v with numbers greater than n in node i. The surviving node with the smallest number, in this scenario, namely node 1, assumes the role of the new primary node and updates relevant information in its log.

Step 2: Node $i(i = 2, 3)$ receives a view-change message with a view number not greater than v, and then sends a view change-ack message $\langle VIEW - CHANGE - ACK, v + 1, i, j, D(VIEW - CHANGE)\rangle$ to the primary node 1. Here, j is the sender of the view-change message.

Step 3: Primary node 1 continuously gathers view-change and view-change-ack messages. After $2f-1$ view-change-ack messages regarding j are collected, the validity of the view-change message for j is established, and it is stored in set S.

Step 4: Upon receiving $2f$ view-change messages from other nodes, the primary node 1 broadcasts a new-view message $\langle NEW-VIEW, v+1, S, O\rangle$ to achieve state synchronization among all nodes. Here, O is the pre-prepare message set. After the other nodes verify the new-view message, they continue to process the pre-prepare messages sent by the primary node according to the normal consensus process.

Finally, we introduce the checkpoint and stable checkpoint mentioned in the above steps, which are designed for garbage collection in PBFT. Specifically, after completing requests, replica nodes need to clear the previously recorded log information. Considering potential view changes, a simple cleanup scheme is to broadcast again after each request execution to reach an agreement across the network on whether the information can be erased. An improved optimization scheme involves broadcasting to announce the completion of K consecutive requests after their execution by a node. If most nodes in the network also confirm this execution completion, all related information regarding these K requests will be deleted. The latest request number of node i upon completing these K requests is referred to as its checkpoint. If at least $2f+1$ nodes including themselves agree on this checkpoint, the number of the Kth request will be recorded as the stable checkpoint for node i. All requests prior to this stable checkpoint can then be deleted.

The fact is, when node i broadcasts a checkpoint to the entire network for consensus, it may not receive immediate responses as other nodes might not finish processing the corresponding K requests. Consequently, node i's processing progress will outpace that of other nodes, leading to a divergence in their respective progress rates. In such cases, the concept of high and low water levels is introduced to represent the range of requests that the system allows nodes to process. For node i, its low water level h equals the stable checkpoint, while its high water level $H = h + L$ where L represents a selected value which is usually a multiple of the checkpoint period K. By setting up high and low water levels for request numbers on node i, even if it processes at a fast pace, it must pause when reaching its high water level H until the stable checkpoint changes before proceeding.

The PBFT consensus algorithm enables a tokenless operation of blockchain systems, ensuring real-time and high-throughput performance with a typical consensus delay of approximately 2–5 seconds. However, the communication cost of PBFT is $O(n^2)$, which scales quadratically with the number of nodes. In terms of fault tolerance, PBFT can handle up to 1/3 of Byzantine nodes. If 1/3 or more nodes collude maliciously and divide the remaining nodes into separate network islands, it is possible for an attacker to create a fork. Nevertheless, this attack mode would leave behind cryptographic evidence.

4.3.1.2 Consensus of Trust

The Consensus of Trust (CoT) (Lv et al. 2020, pp. 104–120) consensus algorithm introduces a trust mechanism and quantifies the trust relationship according to data exchanged between nodes. Furthermore, it employs an iterative calculation to determine the trust value of each node, thereby selecting competent bookkeepers and enhancing the efficiency and scalability of consensus. Moreover, CoT ensures that bookkeeper selection is not dependent on computing or token ability, thus preventing the concentration of bookkeeping rights among a select few individuals.

The CoT network model defines four types of nodes: normal nodes, Byzantine nodes, normal representative nodes, and Byzantine representative nodes, as shown in Figure 4.14, where the Byzantine node number is f and the total node number is n, with a constraint that $n > 3f + 1$. Encryption and authentication mechanisms are used to ensure secure communication between the nodes. Each message contains a signature, digest, and verification information. The model also assumes independent malicious behaviors among Byzantine nodes without any collaboration. Additionally, it considers their computational power to be insufficient for brute-forcing encrypted messages, forging signatures, or discovering messages with identical digests.

In the CoT consensus, representative nodes are selected based on the trust relationship between nodes, which mirrors the concept of trust transfer in human society. CoT assumes that a trust relationship always exists between two nodes, and each node independently assesses the varying degrees of trust values toward other nodes. These trust values dynamically change due to interaction behavior and temporal influences. It's important to emphasize that the trust value of a node is not

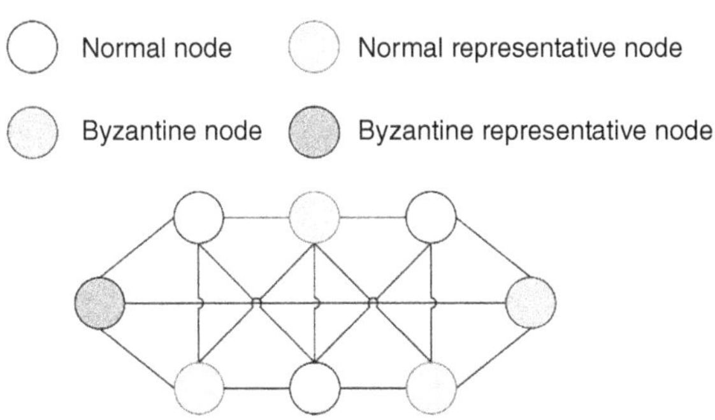

Figure 4.14 Network model of the CoT consensus algorithm.

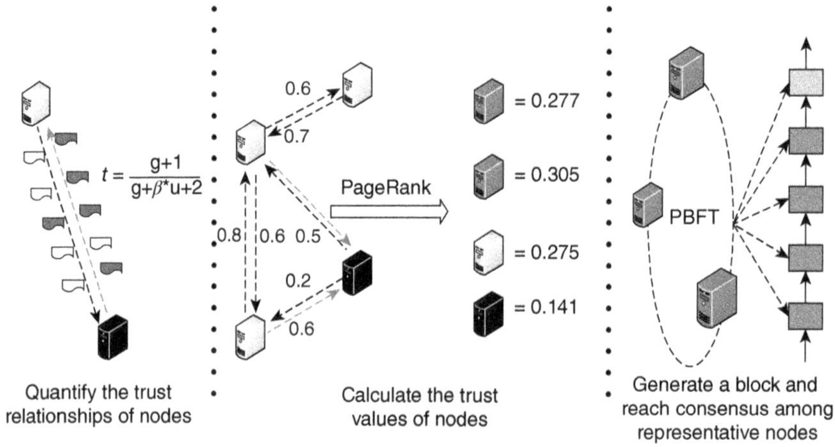

Figure 4.15 CoT consensus process.

absolute but rather represents a probability, serving as a basis for judgment by other nodes.

As shown in Figure 4.15, the CoT consensus process is divided into four steps:

Step 1: Each node in the network continuously monitors transaction and block interaction messages from its neighbors, establishes corresponding trust relationships, and quantifies these relationships into real numbers ranging from 0 to 1. A higher value indicates a greater degree of trust. When a node sends a valid transaction or block message to another node, the recipient's trust toward the sender increases. Conversely, trust will be reduced.

Step 2: Based on the trust relationships among all network nodes, the trust relationship graph is constructed and the trust matrix is generated.

Step 3: Calculate the trust value iteratively for each node using the PageRank (Page et al. 1998) algorithm. Select the nodes with high trust values as the representative nodes eligible for bookkeeping rights and block generation.

Step 4: PBFT with a fault tolerance capability of 1/3 is executed among representative nodes. Through a three-phase negotiated vote, consistency of block data between representative nodes is achieved. In the pre-prepare message, each node locally stores the complete block received from the primary node and replaces it with its hash value in subsequent prepare and commit messages to minimize communication overhead. Only blocks that complete this PBFT consensus can be broadcast to the blockchain network and accepted by other nodes, ensuring both security and availability of the consensus algorithm.

The communication cost in the classical BFT algorithm increases proportionally with the number of nodes. In the CoT consensus algorithm, only representative nodes participate in the consensus process, while normal nodes cannot generate blocks or vote but can observe the complete consensus process. Consequently, network traffic involving node interaction is reduced and system scalability is enhanced. Additionally, representative nodes in the CoT consensus are strictly selected based on trust relationships between nodes, exhibiting high degrees of trust values. In summary, CoT demonstrates a Byzantine fault tolerance capacity higher than 1/3, surpassing that of the classical BFT algorithm.

4.3.2 Synchronization Class

4.3.2.1 RPCA

The Ripple protocol, developed and launched by Ripple Labs, a Silicon Valley start-up, is an Internet-based open-source payment protocol aimed at facilitating seamless and instantaneous exchange of global currencies and diverse assets. It introduces the RPCA (Schwartz, Youngs, and Britto 2014, p. 151), which synchronizes transactions in the network with a preference for data correctness. RPCA is based on several special nodes that are initially identified. Subsequent nodes must be confirmed by at least 51% of these initial nodes before they participate in the core consensus process. Therefore, RPCA exhibits weak decentralization characteristics.

The roles of nodes in the Ripple network are shown in Figure 4.16. Transactions are initiated by clients and spread across the network by tracking or validating nodes. A tracking node primarily serves to disseminate transaction information and corresponding ledger requests from clients. In addition to containing all the functions of a tracking node, a validating node also contributes to appending new data into the ledger through a consensus process.

In RPCA, consensus is reached between validating nodes, each of which is pre-configured with a list of trusted nodes called a Unique Node List (UNL).

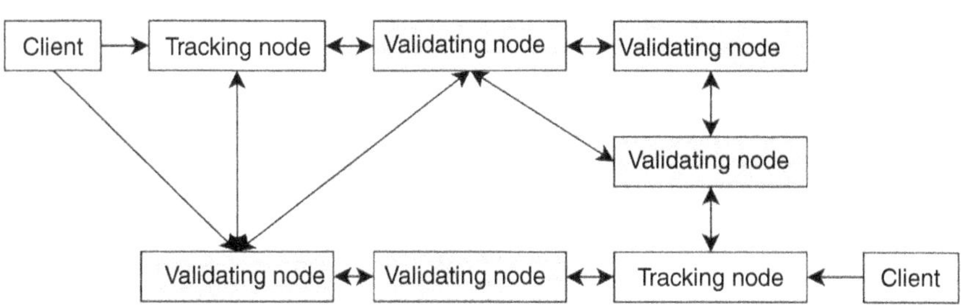

Figure 4.16 Interaction of node roles in RPCA.

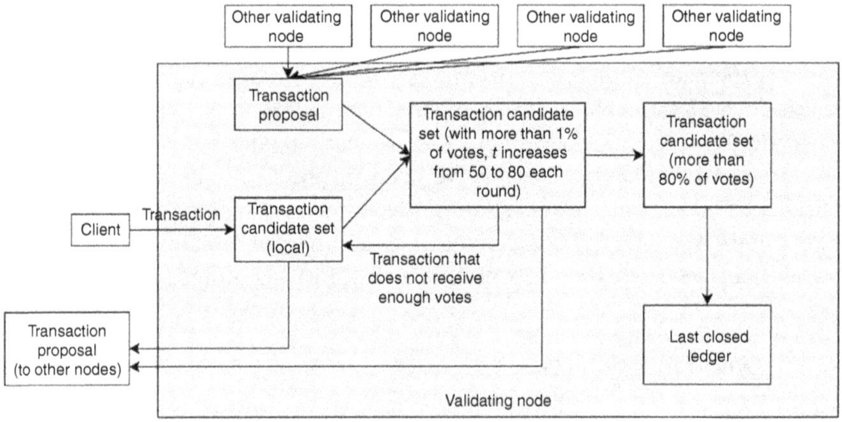

Figure 4.17 Consensus process of RPCA.

A validating node only communicates with other nodes in its UNL. It is required that the intersection size of any two distinct nodes' UNLs should be no less than 1/5 of the total network size. Figure 4.17 describes the consensus process of RPCA.

Step 1: Each validating node continuously receives transactions from the network, and after verification according to the local ledger data, it directly discards illegal transactions while aggregating legal ones into the transaction candidate set. At the same time, the transaction candidate set also contains remaining transactions that cannot be confirmed in the previous consensus process.

Step 2: Each validating node sends its local transaction candidate set as a proposal to the other validating nodes.

Step 3: Upon receiving a proposal, the validating node checks whether the source of the proposal is included in its UNL. If not, it ignores the proposal. If yes, it compares the transactions in the proposal with its local transaction candidate set. In case of a matching transaction, it receives one vote. Within a certain time period, only if a transaction gets more than 50% of votes does it proceed to the next round. Transactions that fail to gather more than 50% of votes are deferred for the next consensus process.

Step 4: The validating nodes send transactions with more than 50% of votes as proposals to other nodes while increasing the required vote threshold to 60%. Repeat Steps 3 and 4 until the threshold reaches 80%.

Step 5: The validating node formally writes the transaction confirmed by at least 80% of votes into the local ledger, which subsequently becomes the last closed ledger representing the final state of the system.

The advantage of RPCA lies in its ability to maintain the effectiveness and consistency of the entire network without any hard forks while enabling real-time transaction verification. The Byzantine fault tolerance of RPCA is $\frac{n-1}{5}$, namely it can tolerate up to 20% Byzantine nodes without compromising final correctness. This consensus algorithm solves the problem of high latency in asynchronous communication among network nodes by using a subnetwork based on collective trust. It achieves low latency and high robustness in environments with minimal trust and connectivity. Currently, Ripple has evolved into a global financial settlement network built upon blockchain technology.

4.3.2.2 SCP

The Stellar Consensus Protocol (SCP) (Mazieres 2015, pp. 1–45) is based on the federated Byzantine agreement. Unlike the traditional Byzantine agreement, it utilizes a set of nodes known as quorum slices for communication among validating nodes. Validating nodes may belong to one or multiple quorum slices. In order to ascertain the validity of a transaction, a node must seek confirmation from other nodes within the same quorum slice. If all nodes in the quorum slice successfully verify the transaction, it will also be deemed valid by that node.

Figure 4.18 depicts the hierarchical quorum slice through an example. In this instance, a node in Group 1 constructs a quorum slice by including two other different nodes from the same group. Similarly, in Group 2, a node establishes a quorum slice with one node from Group 1 and another from Group 2; In Group 3, it includes two nodes from Group 1 and one node from Group 2 to form its quorum slice. Furthermore, Groups 1 and 2 are positioned at the upper level and hold priority for transaction validation. Assuming Nodes 1, 2, 7, and 10 form a quorum slice. When Node 10 wants to validate a transaction, it must seek consensus among the other nodes within its quorum slice, that is, Nodes 1, 2, and 7. If all other nodes agree on the transaction, it can also be considered valid by Node 10.

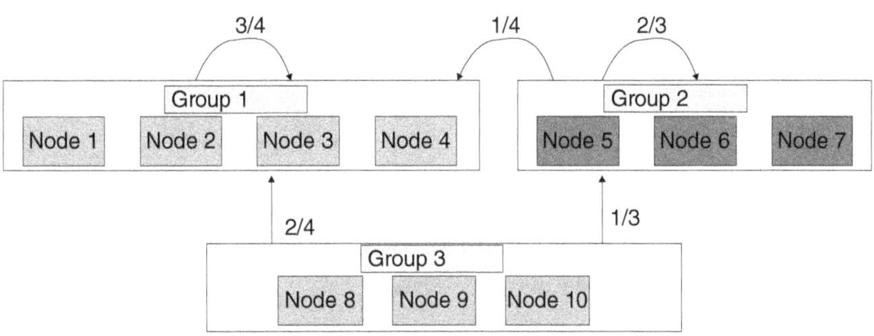

Figure 4.18 Quorum slice in SCP.

4.3.3 Asynchronous Class

Partial synchronization and synchronous BFT consensus mechanisms are introduced in the previous sections. These two consensus mechanisms perform well in stable network environment and ensure the consistency and reliability of the system. However, these mechanisms can be challenged in the face of extreme network conditions, such as uncertain network latency or frequent disconnections. An asynchronous class BFT consensus with high robustness is introduced next. This type of consensus mechanism does not rely on strict time constraints and can maintain the continuous operation and consistency of the blockchain in an environment where the network state is uncertain.

4.3.3.1 HoneyBadgerBFT

The success of cryptocurrencies has led to the continuous application of the BFT Consensus protocol in those important areas, especially in the financial industry. Traditional PBFT is a weakly synchronous consensus protocol because its reliability depends heavily on the time processing delay in the network. In other words, network liveness is largely affected by network conditions.

HoneyBadgerBFT (Miller et al. 2016, pp. 31–42), as an asynchronous BFT consensus protocol, claims to be independent of the dependence on time conditions in the network and has significantly improved efficiency compared with traditional PBFT consensus protocols. HoneyBadgerBFT assumes that there is a reliable communication channel connection between every two nodes, and the final delivery status of messages is entirely dependent on the adversary, but messages between honest nodes are always delivered eventually. The total number of nodes in the entire network, denoted as N, must be greater than three times of the adversary node number F, i.e., $N \geq 3F + 1$.

HoneyBadgerBFT implements Atomic Broadcast (ABC) through Asynchronous Common Subset (ACS). ACS can be implemented through Multi-value Validated Byzantine Agreement (MVBA), but the MVBA original protocol is too time-consuming, so HoneyBadgerBFT considered an alternative route: Reliable Broadcast (RBC) combined with Asynchronous Binary Agreement (ABA).

The ACS protocol is described in detail in Algorithm 4.1. ACS protocol is built around an instance of ACS centralized, in order to obtain scalable efficiency, the protocol chooses a batch processing strategy. Assume a batch size and commit transactions per epoch. Each node selects a transaction from its queue. In order to avoid excessive overlap of selected transactions, nodes are randomly selected from the previous transaction in each queue.

Algorithm 4.1 HoneyBadgerBFT

```
B = Q(AN2 log N); // batch size parameter
PK, SK_i = TPKE.Setup(); // Let PK be the public key
  received from TPKE.Setup () executed by a dealer, and
  let SK_i be the secret key for node Pi;
buf :=[]; // Let buf :=be a FIFO queue of input
  transactions
// Step 1: Random selection and encryption
encrypt x := TPKE.Enc(PK, proposed); // let proposed be
  a random selection of ⌊B/N⌋ transactions from the frst
  B elements of buf
// Step 2: Agreement on ciphertexts
v_j (j∈S) = ACS[r](x) ; // s⊂[1...N],in consecutive
  epochs numbered r
// Step 3: Decryption
for each j∈S do
   e_j := TPKE.DecShare(SK_i,v_j);
   Multicast(DEC(r,j,i,e_j));
   // wait to receive at least f + 1 messages of the
     form DEC(r,j,k,e_j.k)
   y_j := TPKE.Dec(PK, {(k,e_(j,k))}); //Decryption
end for
block_r:= sorted(∪_(j∈S) {y_j}); //such that block, is
  sorted in a canonical order
buf := buf - block;
```

The total communication cost of ACS instantiation is $O(N^2|v| + \lambda N^3 logN)$, where the size of any node input is limited by $|v|$. Therefore, the author chooses a batch size $B = \Omega(\lambda N^2 logN)$ to ensure that each node's contribution (B/N) can accommodate this additional overhead.

In order to prevent the attack of adversary nodes, HoneyBadgerBFT uses a threshold encryption scheme. That is, each node selects a set of transactions and encrypts them. Each node then passes the encryption result as input to the ACS subroutine. Thus, the output of ACS is a ciphertext vector. Once ACS is complete, the ciphertext is decrypted. This ensures that the set of transactions is fully determined before the adversary node acquires the specifics of the proposal made by each node. This also ensures that an adversary cannot selectively prevent a transaction from being submitted at the front of a queue with enough correct nodes.

4.3.3.2 Dumbo

Dumbo protocol (Guo et al. 2020, pp. 803–818) was jointly completed by Professor Tang Qiang from New Jersey Institute of Technology, Chinese Academy of Sciences and Jingdong Innovation Lab. After a detailed analysis of the performance of HoneyBadgerBFT, the Dumbo authors found that a bottleneck affecting the performance of HoneyBadgerBFT was ABA. Since each node runs N instances of ABA in each round of consensus, each instance has to verify $O(N^2)$ threshold signatures, which is very CPU-consuming. As shown in Figure 4.19, the running time of RBC is almost negligible compared to ABA, and as N increases, the time required to run ABA becomes longer and longer. Therefore, how to reduce the number of ABA instances that need to be run in each round of consensus is the key to improving the efficiency of asynchronous consensus.

Along this line of thought, Dumbo gives two solutions, Dumbo1 and Dumbo2.

Dumbo1's idea is shown in Figure 4.20: Since the goal is to select a common subset, why not select a committee of k ($k < N$) members and each member propose a subset so that only one binary consensus on each proposal is needed to reduce the number of instances running ABA from N to k. Dumbo1's key problem then became how to randomly elect a committee of k individual members with a high probability that at least one of them would be honest.

Dumbo2's goal was even more radical: Could the number of ABA's directly be reduced to a constant?

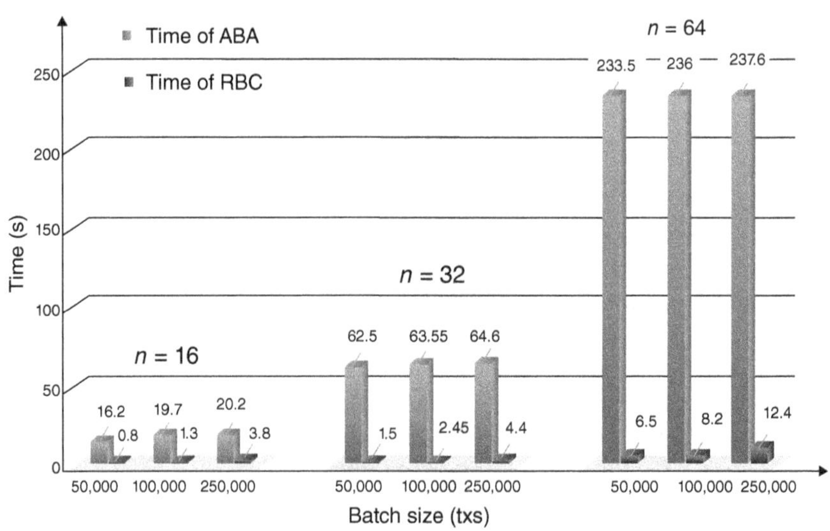

Figure 4.19 Time cost of RBC and ABA in HoneyBadgerBFT.

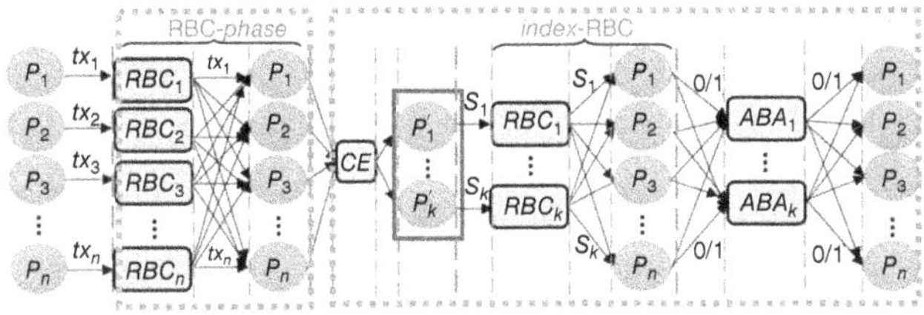

Figure 4.20 Dumbo1-ACS structure.

Dumbo2 considers using MVBA, that is, let each node propose a subset subject to certain conditions, and then choose one from N subsets as the consensus result (see Figure 4.21). The problem is that the communication complexity of existing MVBA schemes is higher, reaching $O(N^2 \mid m \mid + \lambda N^2 + N^3)$, where $|m|$ denotes the input size of MVBA. In many cases, $|m| > \lambda N log(N)$, thus the dominating term of communication complexity is $O(N^2 \mid m|)$. It can be seen that the key to the complexity of MVBA communication is the size of $|m|$. If the value of $|m|$ is small enough, then implementing ACS using MVBA, which only contains a constant number of ABA runs is much better than the combination of RBC and ABA used by HoneyBadgerBFT. Dumbo2's solution was to make $|m|$ as small as possible.

Overall, the Dumbo protocol proposes two solutions for ABA bottlenecks, namely Dumbol and Dumbo2, through in-depth analysis of HoneyBadgerBFT performance. The core idea of the solution is to reduce the number of ABA instances that need to be run in each round of consensus, thereby improving the efficiency of asynchronous consensus. Dumbol reduces the number of ABA instances to the constant level by selecting a committee with a small number of members, while Dumbo2 considers reducing the number of ABA instances directly to the constant level, although its implementation faces the challenge of MVBA communication complexity.

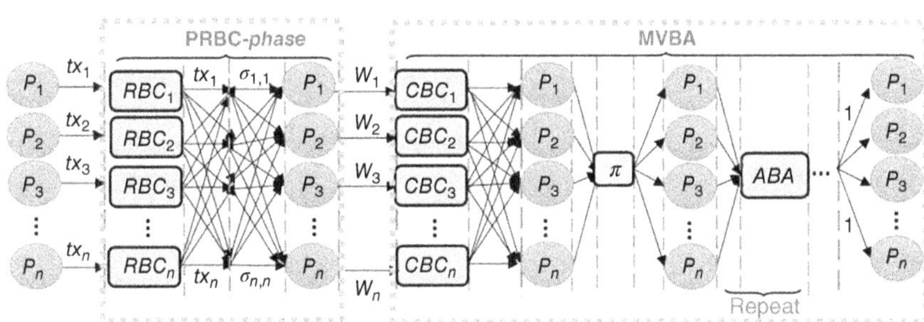

Figure 4.21 Dumbo2-ACS structure.

4.3.3.3 Dumbo-NG

Dumbo-NG (Gao et al. 2022, pp. 1187–1201) is an efficient asynchronous Byzantine fault-tolerant consensus algorithm, which solves the limitations of traditional asynchronous BFT algorithms in terms of processing power and response time through innovative design. The core advantage of Dumbo-NG is its ability to achieve high throughput while maintaining low latency at different system sizes, from 4 to 64 nodes. Dumbo-NG can handle transaction volumes up to 100 k tx/s without sacrificing consensus node latency. In addition, Dumbo-NG introduces a throughput-insensitive metric that allows it to handle maximum throughput while still maintaining an almost constant latency. Dumbo-NG demonstrates significant performance benefits in wide area network (WAN) Settings compared to other state-of-the-art asynchronous BFT protocols. Through extensive experiments, the paper not only tested on Amazon's EC2 cloud platform but also verified its performance in a controlled latency/bandwidth environment, demonstrating the potential and robustness of Dumbo-NG in practical applications.

The rationale for Dumbo-NG is to deal with the broadcast of transactions, namely sending and receiving, separately from the ordering of transactions via MVBA.

Broadcast phase: Each node continuously broadcasts transaction batches to the network. These batches are called "blocks," and each block comes with a certificate that is co-signed by the nodes in the network, ensuring the validity and reliability of the batch.

Sorting phase: In the MVBA phase, the system sorts these blocks to ensure that they are added to the blockchain in a certain order. This stage is not bandwidth dependent and can therefore be run independently of the broadcast process, reducing latency across the system.

As shown in Figure 4.22, the top half shows the flow of different nodes continuously broadcasting transaction blocks. As you can see, although transactions are issued consecutively, each node does so independently and does not suspend its own broadcast because of the broadcast of other nodes. The bottom half shows how to sort the transaction blocks of these broadcasts through multiple MVBA cycles. In each cycle, the node decides which block will be accepted into the blockchain. This decision is based on the results of the previous cycle and the new certificates received in the current cycle. This means that each MVBA cycle is somewhat dependent on the previous cycle, as it requires data that has been sorted in the previous cycle to help determine the ordering of the current cycle.

In summary, Dumbo-NG is an efficient asynchronous Byzantine fault-tolerant consensus algorithm, and through its innovative design, it overcomes the limitations of traditional asynchronous BFT algorithms in terms of processing power and response time. Its core advantage is the ability to achieve high throughput while maintaining low latency and being less affected by throughput in systems

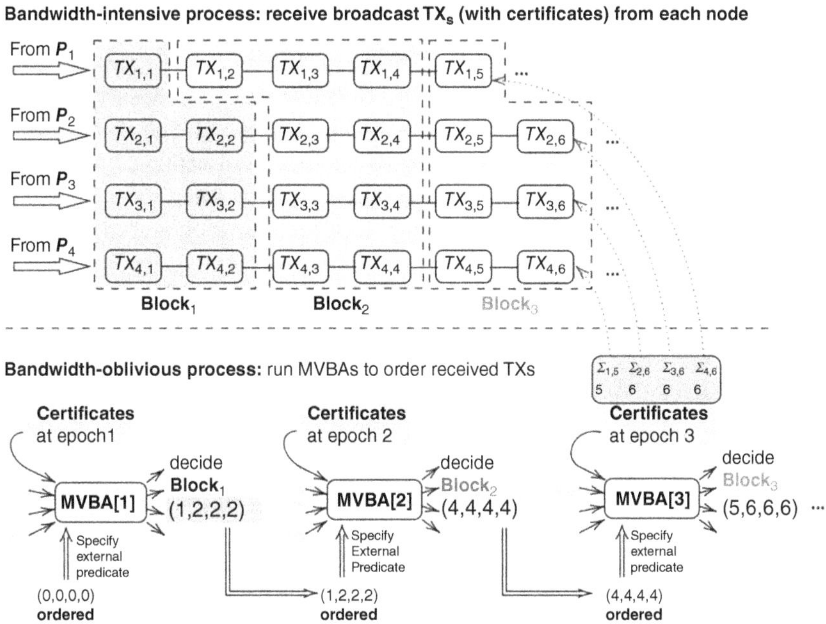

Figure 4.22 Complete sequencing process for incoming broadcasts by performing a series of MVBAs.

of different sizes. By handling the broadcast and ordering of transactions separately, Dumbo-NG achieves efficient transaction processing and ordering while reducing latency in the system.

4.4 Proof-Based Consensus

Proof-based consensus algorithms are unique to blockchain technology. In blockchains with weak trust guarantees and fully decentralized environments, they generally exhibit superior scalability and fairness compared to voting-based consensus algorithms. These algorithms effectively address the Byzantine generals problem by increasing the cost of malicious behavior and reducing the probability of malicious nodes. Since each bookkeeper has the right to generate blocks, it is crucial to impose a nontrivial cost for block generation in order to ensure fair bookkeeping rights among participants and prevent network congestion caused by competitive bookkeeping activities. Current approaches toward proof-based consensus design can be broadly divided into three categories: proof of work, proof of stake, and other proofs based on publicly accessible resources.

4.4.1 PoW

The PoW consensus algorithm requires all network nodes to solve a cryptographic puzzle with dynamically adjusted difficulty. The node that first finds the solution acquires the right to generate a new block and gets a reward. Specifically, prior to solving the puzzle, a node includes its verified transactions, *Prev_Hash*, *Timestamp*, and other related information within a block. Then it finds a secret random number satisfying the puzzle of this block based on the above information and inserts it into the *nonce* field. Figure 4.23 depicts the process of calculating such a random number. All the information in the block header is combined into the SHA256 hash function, and the PoW block is judged by the condition $F(nonce) < Target$. If the output value of the function is lower than the difficulty threshold *Target*, the random number is accepted. Otherwise, the node guesses the random number again until it gets the correct solution.

When a node successfully finds a correct random number, it will propose the corresponding block and broadcast it to other nodes. At this point, a bookkeeper who receives this message and has not yet found a solution for its puzzle stops attempts. Subsequently, it checks the validity of this block. If valid, it appends the block to its current blockchain and continues to solve the next puzzle.

The first transaction in a block is a special transaction called the coinbase transaction. Unlike normal transactions, the coinbase transaction has no input and does not consume Unspent Transaction Output (UTXO). The sole purpose of its input, known as Coinbase, is to generate new Bitcoins. Its output is the address of the successful bookkeeper. Taking the Bitcoin system as an example, Figure 4.24 shows the process of transactions from generation to ultimate inclusion on-chain.

Step 1: The owner of a Bitcoin *A* uses its private key to sign the previous transaction, which denotes the source of the Bitcoin, as well as the recipient *B*. Subsequently, *A* appends this signature to the Bitcoin in order to generate a transaction.

Step 2: *A* broadcasts the transaction to the whole network. The system transfers the Bitcoin to *B*, and each node includes the received transaction in its generated

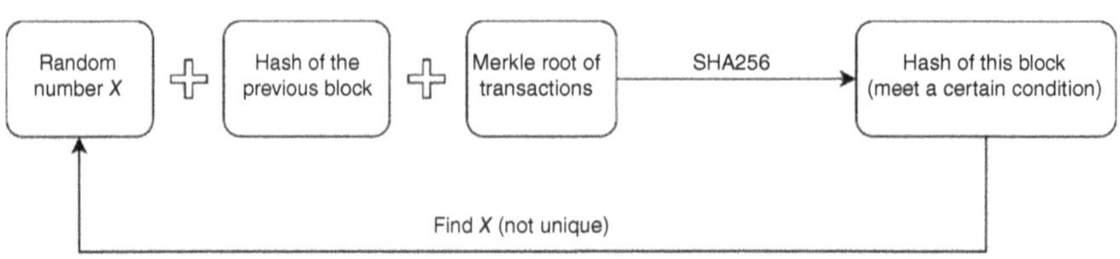

Figure 4.23 Node calculates a random number in PoW.

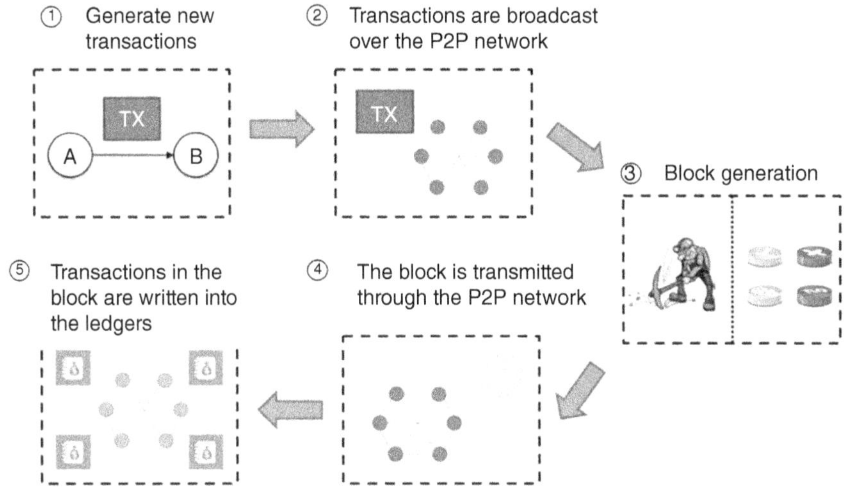

Figure 4.24 Bitcoin transaction process.

block. For *B*, the Bitcoin is instantly displayed in its wallet but remains unspendable until a block is confirmed successfully.

Step 3: Each node solves a mathematical puzzle to compete for generating the new block. The successful node will be rewarded, and this process leads to the creation of new Bitcoins.

Step 4: Once a node finds a solution, it broadcasts its generated block containing time-stamped transactions across the network for verification by other nodes. The inclusion of a timestamp ensures the existence of a specific block at a designated moment, and in order to determine an accurate timestamp, the Bitcoin system aggregates timestamps from more than five nodes and calculates their intermediate value.

Step 5: Other nodes in the network validate the block, and then compete for the next block, thereby forming a legal ledger commonly referred to as a blockchain. The system automatically adjusts the difficulty for generating a block based on recent time differences observed across 2016 generated blocks, ensuring an average generation time of approximately 10 minutes per block. This time is not absolute and may vary due to fluctuations in the overall computing power of the network.

However, there is another competition situation where certain nodes successfully solve the puzzle before receiving a valid block. Motivated by the block generation reward, these nodes choose to still broadcast their blocks. Consequently, when other nodes receive multiple conflicting blocks, they will prioritize the

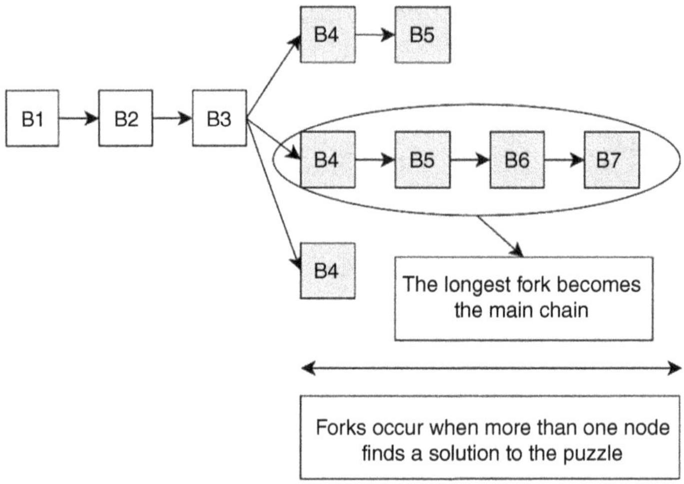

Figure 4.25 Forking issue in PoW consensus.

earliest arriving ones and disregard subsequent conflicting ones, resulting in forks. To address this forking issue, nodes are allowed to continue generating blocks on different forks until one fork becomes the longest blockchain. In other words, when forks occur, all nodes are subject to the longest main chain rule, as shown in Figure 4.25.

PoW is characterized by its simplicity in logic and ease of implementation, enabling nodes to reach consensus without the need for additional message exchange. Its robust security features make disrupting the system a costly endeavor. Furthermore, its primary advantage lies in complete decentralization for nodes, granting unrestricted access and exit. However, PoW also exhibits certain drawbacks. For instance, it suffers from low efficiency and long delays, often leading to forks and compromising finality. Additionally, the generation of blocks within PoW results in significant resource wastage. Consequently, Bitcoin has currently attracted most of the world's computing power while other blockchains utilizing PoW struggle to attain comparable computational resources necessary for ensuring their own security.

4.4.2 Variants of PoW

One of the biggest obstacles in the implementation of PoW consensus algorithm is low throughput and high latency, which is not suitable for real-time application scenarios. Therefore, it is necessary to reduce transaction latency. Two possible solutions include increasing the number of transactions in the block and reducing the difficulty of the puzzle to be solved. However, the former requires a longer network propagation time, while the latter reduces the time to generate blocks, but can lead to nonconsistent bifurcation of the chain and double spending attacks.

4.4.2.1 Bitcoin-NG

Ittay Eyal et al. proposed a scaling solution for PoW called Bitcoin-NG (Eyal et al. 2016, pp. 45–59). This consensus algorithm builds upon the trust model of PoW and improves performance by decoupling consensus operation into two components: leader election and transaction serialization, that is, writing transactions to the blockchain. Specifically, Bitcoin-NG divides traditional blocks into two types, key block and microblock, as shown in Figure 4.26.

When a node finds a correct solution to its puzzle, it broadcasts its key block to the other nodes. This node is a leader until another node discovers a correct solution, thereby ensuring that there is one and only one rotating leader per time segment. During the time segment, the leader can continue to write microblocks containing transaction information to the blockchain at a set rate less than a predefined maximum value. The maximum rate is deterministic and may be much larger than the average interval between key blocks. In particular, a microblock is invalid if its timestamp is in the future or if its time difference from the previous block is less than the minimum. The above limitations prevent malicious, greedy, or destructive leaders from using microblocks to overwhelm the system.

As puzzle-solving is not required by microblocks, leaders are able to generate them swiftly and inexpensively, thereby causing the split of the system brain and potentially leading to a double-spend attack where different nodes believe the same coin was spent by different transactions. To disincentivize this behavior, the Bitcoin-NG consensus algorithm uses poison transaction to invalidate the payoffs of fraudulent leaders. The poison transaction serves as evidence of fraud by including the first block header from the pruned fork. It must be inserted within the maturity window of the misbehaving leader's key block and before the

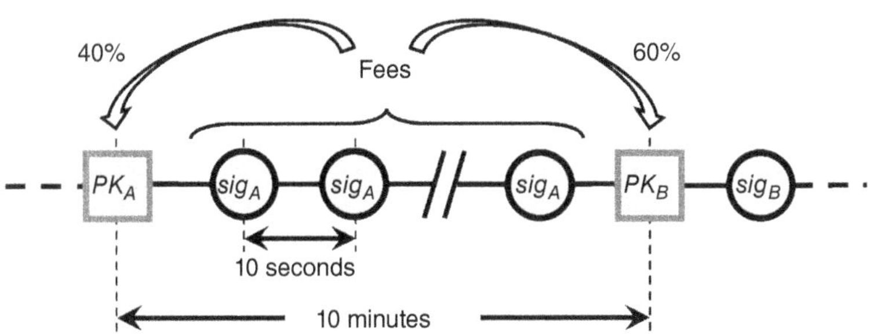

Figure 4.26 Blockchain structure of Bitcoin-NG.

malicious leader's reward is spent. Besides nullifying the rewards of the leader responsible for the fork, the poison transaction also provides partial compensation to the current leader.

When a node generates a key block, it may not receive all of the microblocks generated by the previous leader. If microblocks are generated frequently, this situation may be common when leaders change. This scenario often leads to short microblock forks. Any node accepting a microblock before the new key block is propagated can observe this fork. However, once the key block reaches that node, the fork disappears, as depicted in Figure 4.27. Consequently, users encountering a microblock should wait for network propagation time before considering its addition to the main chain, ensuring it will not be pruned by new key blocks.

The Bitcoin-NG consensus algorithm can achieve a higher transaction verification rate because many microblocks are created while waiting for the next leader to create a new key block. Experiments show that the consensus delay of Bitcoin-NG is limited only by network propagation delay, and the bandwidth is limited only by node processing capacity.

It is undeniable that Bitcoin-NG provides a novel idea for scaling blockchain. Despite its partial enhancement of PoW performance, the expansion remains limited and fails to meet the demand adequately. Although there has been a significant enhancement in the speed of microblock generation, resulting in faster transaction packaging, both key blocks and microblocks still reside on the same blockchain. As a result, caution must be exercised when setting the speed of microblock generation too high as it may lead to more frequent forks and longer transaction confirmation time. Moreover, excessive time would be wasted on pruning forks while computational power becomes dispersed across multiple forks, thereby compromising system security. Furthermore, since the system continues to rely on PoW as its foundation, energy wastage persists as an issue.

4.4.2.2 GHOST

The Greedy Heaviest-Observed Sub-Tree (GHOST) algorithm (Sompolinsky and Zohar 2015, pp. 507–527) proposed a strategy to deal with forking and prevent double-spend attack to reduce the time of writing a new block to the blockchain. This algorithm organizes all blocks in a tree structure, keeping those on forks that are

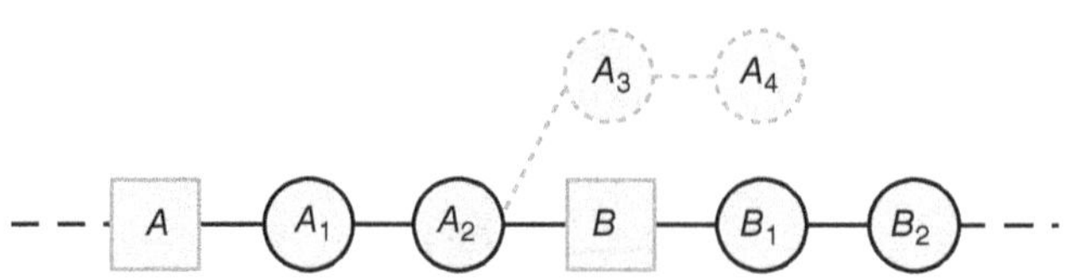

Figure 4.27 Microblock fork in the Bitcoin-NG consensus algorithm.

not selected for the main chain. The shape of the tree is determined by nodes successfully generating blocks through their selection of extended blocks.

Unlike the longest main chain rule in PoW, a node selects the main chain based on the highest cumulative weights of blocks, each determined by the density of a block's subtrees. In other words, the main chain encompasses the greatest number of blocks, including those that have forked from it.

Forked blocks that are included in the longest chain, such as 3E and 3C in Figure 4.28, are not discarded but instead processed as follows:

a) **An orphan block** is a block that holds no value and provides no rewards to its generator. Forked blocks in the PoW consensus algorithm are treated as orphan blocks.
b) **An uncle block** is a block that is followed by blocks within a certain range, and its generator receives partial profit.

The GHOST consensus algorithm has a higher resistance to a double-spend attack than PoW. In the case of Figure 4.28, where chain $0 \leftarrow 1B \leftarrow 2D \leftarrow 3F \leftarrow 4C \leftarrow 5B$ should be chosen according to the longest main chain rule, it is observed that the attacker's secret chain surpasses this main chain in length, resulting in a successful attack. However, adhering to the heaviest chain rule of GHOST, the winning chain becomes $0 \leftarrow 1B \leftarrow 2C \leftarrow 3D \leftarrow 4B$ due to its greater weight than the attacker's secret chain. This victory by the main chain can be attributed to GHOST considering forked blocks when evaluating block counts.

4.4.3 PoS

In 2011, Quantum Mechanic, a fervent advocate of digital currencies, proposed the PoS consensus algorithm on the Bitcointalk forum. Following extensive

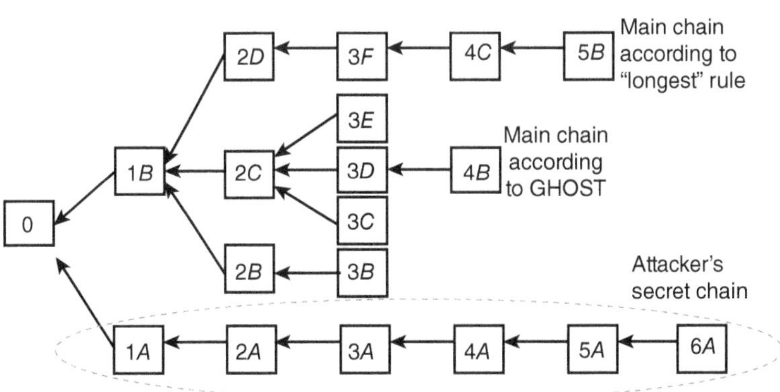

Figure 4.28 Forking issue in GHOST consensus algorithm.

deliberation and discourse, this algorithm gained widespread recognition for its practicality and viability within the academic community.

PoS is an upgraded consensus algorithm derived from PoW, which also relies on hash operations to compete for bookkeeping rights. Its main idea revolves around adjusting the difficulty of a node in solving cryptographic puzzles based on its stake in the network. This adjustment takes into account both the proportion and duration of tokens held by each node, aiming to reduce difficulty proportionally and accelerate random number generation. While the PoW consensus process primarily hinges on computational power competition, where higher computing power increases a node's likelihood of generating a block, the PoS consensus process emphasizes balance, granting nodes with larger amounts of digital currency greater probabilities for block generation.

The primary distinction between PoS and PoW is their criteria for validating blocks, namely $F(Timestamp) < Target \times Balance$. Compared with PoW, the search space in PoS changes from random number (*Nonce*) to *Timestamp*. The range of random numbers is essentially infinite, and the timestamp of a valid block must be within the specified range of the previous block timestamp, and blocks generated too early or too late will not be accepted by other nodes. In addition, the target threshold (*Target*) introduces a multiplication factor *Balance*. As *Balance* increases, so does the overall target value ($Target \times Balance$), thereby increasing the probability of finding a valid block.

PoS solves the shortcomings of energy waste and computing power centralization in PoW, thereby partially reducing the time required for consensus. However, PoS introduces a concern known as the "nothing-at-stake" problem. Specifically, when forking occurs, nodes can generate blocks on multiple forks simultaneously at low cost to maximize their benefits, as shown in Figure 4.29. This creates a new confusion, where malicious nodes have an incentive to create new forks to support or initiate illegal transactions. At this time, a malicious node does not even need to hold 51% stakes to launch a successful double-spend attack.

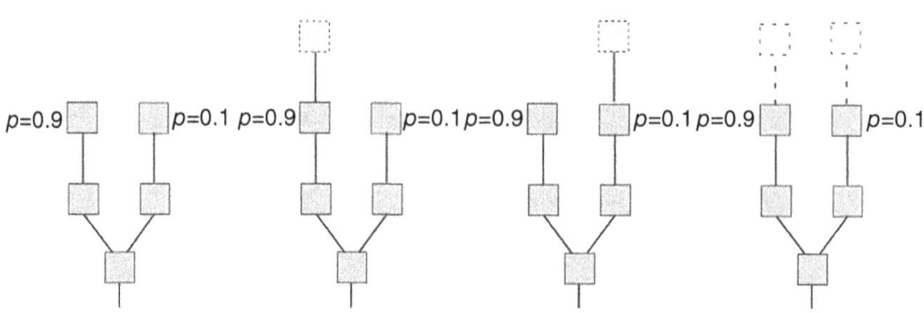

Figure 4.29 Nothing-at-stake problem in PoS.

PoS encompasses a diverse range of strategies, with Peercoin representing one of the most classic implementation ideas.

In the Peercoin system, there are two types of blocks: PoW blocks and PoS blocks. In addition, the founder Sunny King has specially designed core concepts for Peercoin, such as Coinstake, Kernel, Stake Modifier, Modifier Interval, Coin Age, Stake Reward, and other related elements.

4.4.3.1 Coinstake Transaction

To achieve PoS consensus, Sunny King borrowed from the Coinbase transaction of the Bitcoin system and designed a special type of transaction called Coinstake transaction. The structure of the Coinstake transaction is shown in Figure 4.30.

In the Bitcoin system, a Coinbase transaction requires that the number of inputs equal to 1, and the output of the previous transaction corresponding to this input (Prevout) must be empty while ensuring that the number of outputs is greater than or equal to 1. Referring to Coinbase transactions, a Coinstake transaction requires that the number of inputs is greater than or equal to 1. Additionally, it mandates that the Prevout field of the first input (Input0), also known as Kernel, cannot be empty. Furthermore, it stipulates that the number of outputs is greater than or equal to 2 with an obligatory condition for the first output (Output0) being empty.

According to Nakamoto's design, Coinbase can only appear on the first transaction of a block. Sunny King adds a rule to this: The second transaction in a PoS block must be a Coinstake transaction. Otherwise, the Coinstake transaction cannot be included anywhere else in the block. In other words, as long as the second transaction is a Coinstake transaction, the block is treated as a PoS block.

4.4.3.2 Kernel Protocol

Kernel is the first input of a Coinstake transaction, which plays an important role in PoS block determination. Specifically, the judging condition for a valid PoS blocks is $SHA256D(nStakeModifier + txPrev.\ block.\ nTime + txPrev.\ offset + txPrev.\ nTime + txPrev.\ vout.\ n + nTime) < bnTarget \times nCoinDayWeight$. Among them, *nStakeModifier* is a regulator specifically designed for PoS consensus. In order to ensure that PoS nodes engage in blind exploration akin to PoW nodes and

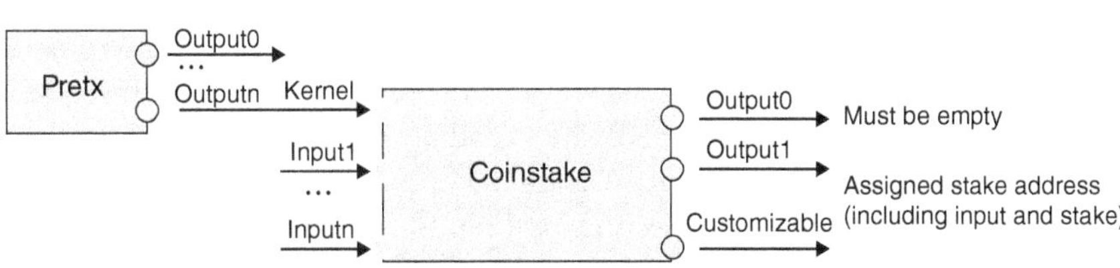

Figure 4.30 Coinstake transaction structure.

maintain real-time blockchain functionality, each block is assigned a relatively fixed *nStakeModifier* value, which changes according to the *Modifier Interval* period. The *txPrev* represents the previous transaction corresponding to Kernel. The *txprev. block. nTime* indicates the timestamp of the block where *txPrev* resides, preventing nodes from taking advantage of prediction to generate a large number of transactions in advance. The *txPrev. offset*, *txPrev. nTime*, and *txPrev. vout. n* represent the offset of *txPrev* in the block, the construction time and the output subscript of Kernel in *txPrev*, respectively, to reduce the probability that nodes in the network generate Coinstake transactions at the same time. In addition, *bnTarget* is the current target difficulty benchmark value of the whole network, analogous to the current difficulty value in PoW. The *NCoinDayWeight* indicates the coin age of Kernel.

When a node creates a block, it first selects one of its UTXOs as a Kernel and constructs a Coinstake transaction. If the transaction does not meet the above condition, the construction process is repeated until a valid PoS block is found. Sunny King aims to provide sufficient randomness to all PoS nodes while strictly confining the search space within the boundaries of Coinstake transaction timestamps, thereby ensuring that coin age of Kernel is the primary determinant in finding a valid block.

4.4.3.3 Coin Age

Peercoin uses Coin Age, also known as Coin Days, instead of directly considering the balance in order to determine difficulty. For instance, if an account holds 1.5 coins for 10 days, its age value is $Coinage = 1.5 \times 10 = 15$. Once a UTXO is spent, its age is cleared to zero, that is, the age of a new UTXO is calculated from this baseline value.

4.4.3.4 Stake Reward

The Stake Reward is calculated as $StakeReward = ((0.01 \times nCoinAge)/365) \times Coin$, where *nCoinAge* is the cumulative age of all inputs for Coinstake transactions, with an annual interest rate of 1%.

4.4.4 Variants of PoS

While the PoS consensus does enhance the performance of PoW consensus to some extent, it also relinquishes certain inherent advantages of PoW and becomes more susceptible to forking, thus necessitating additional confirmations for transactions to ensure adequate security. On the other hand, establishing a rigorous mathematical demonstration of security and fault tolerance in PoS proves challenging. To address these concerns, this section introduces prominent variations of PoS consensus.

4.4.4.1 Ouroboros

Ouroboros (Kiayias et al. 2017, pp. 357–388) is the first PoS consensus framework that has been proven to possess complete security guarantees. Its fundamental idea is to take a snapshot of the stake holdings of each node after a set time epoch. To establish a random seed, nodes engage in a multi-party coin-tossing protocol and employ the follow-the-satoshi random function to select the leader based on their proportionate stake ownership. This approach renders it arduous for an attacker to predict the outcome of a leader election through simulation. In addition, fairness is enhanced by assigning only block creation responsibilities to the elected leader while transaction addition tasks are delegated to other participants within the current time epoch. Irrespective of being chosen as a leader or not, all participants equally share in the rewards they receive.

As shown in Figure 4.31, the specific execution process of the Ouroboros consensus algorithm is as follows:

Step 1: In the genesis block of each *epoch* on the chain, hardcode some public keys, the corresponding stakes, and the initial random seed ρ. This base information is used by the flow to run the next *epoch*.

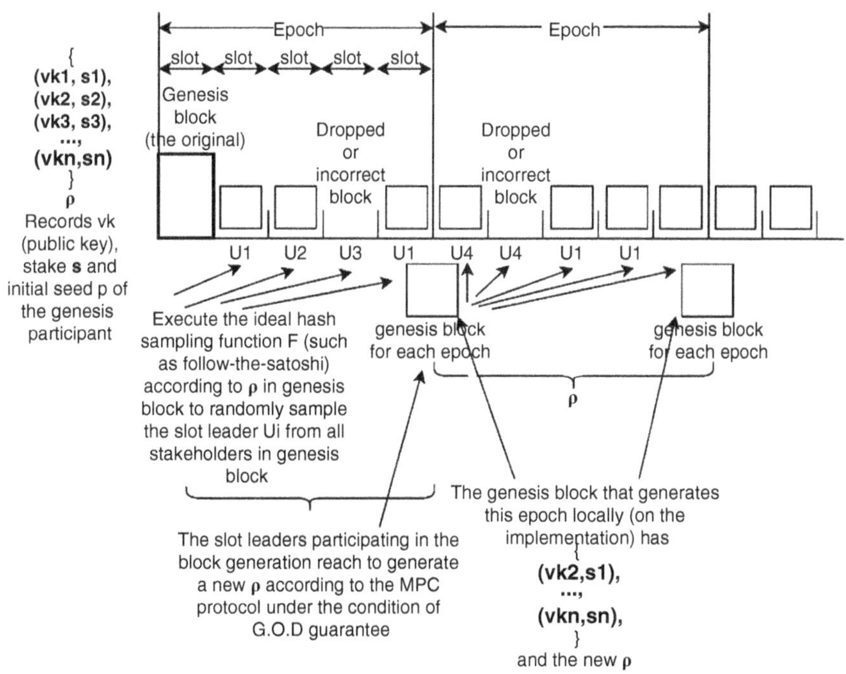

Figure 4.31 The execution process of Ouroboros.

Step 2: Each node independently executes a random function F, such as follow-the-satoshi, based on the random seed ρ of the current *epoch*. The function takes into account the stakes in the genesis block, the random seed, and the slot index as input parameters to determine the designated slot leader.

Step 2.1: If a node finds that it is its turn, it performs actions such as packaging blocks. In addition, it generates a random number and records its commitment on-chain.

Step 2.2: In the event that it is not the leader's turn, it waits for the leader to generate and broadcast a block. Upon receipt of this block, validation is performed. However, if an extended period elapses without receiving the block beyond the current *slot*, the block pertaining to said *slot* is deemed abandoned.

Step 3: Repeat Step 2 continuously in the current *epoch* until all slots in this *epoch* end.

Step 4: A random seed ρ that is agreed upon by all participants is generated throughout the *epoch*.

Step 5: Record the random seed ρ acquired in Step 4, along with the participants, that is, slot leaders, of the next *epoch* obtained in Step 2 in local memory. Commence the next *epoch*, and proceed to Step 2.

4.4.4.2 DPoS

The idea of the Delegated PoS (DPoS) consensus algorithm (Song and Zhao 2018, pp. 1–8) was first proposed by Larimer. He believes that the decentralization of PoS can be realized by relying on a certain number of representative nodes instead of all shareholder nodes. In April 2014, Larimer's team formally introduced DPoS and published a white paper. Compared with PoS consensus, DPoS consensus further reduces the waste of computing power while strengthening the security of the blockchain system.

In DPoS, a certain number of representative nodes called delegates are selected by the coin holders to operate the network. Typically, there are 101 delegates determined by the project side, with a minimum requirement of 11. Delegates possess the authority for bookkeeping, which involves verifying transactions and generating blocks. To qualify as valid and be appended to the blockchain, newly generated blocks must gain recognition from more than 2/3 of the delegates. Once on-chain, these blocks become permanently valid. All delegates have equal rights and take turns according to an established schedule. They also share all benefits resulting from their work, as shown in Figure 4.32.

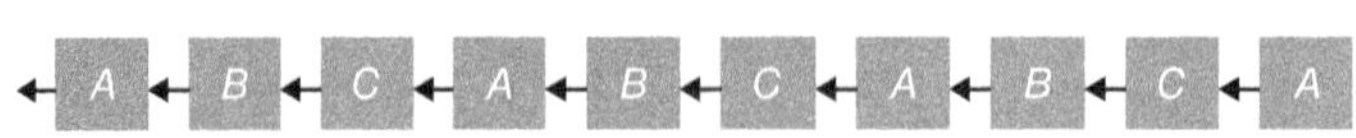

Figure 4.32 The execution process of DPoS.

In particular, the basic steps of the DPoS consensus are as follows:

Step 1: Become a representative node. To become a representative node, you must first register a public key on the network and then be assigned a 32-bit unique identifier that will be referenced by the header of each transaction.

Step 2: Shareholder nodes authorize votes. Shareholder nodes can set the option to vote for one or more nodes in the wallet and rank them. Once set, each transaction made by the shareholder node transfers votes from "input delegates" to "output delegates." Given transaction fees, in general, nodes do not create transactions specifically for the purpose of voting. But in an emergency, the DPoS system does not prohibit certain nodes from changing their votes by paying a fee in a more active way.

Step 3: Keep the representative nodes honest. Each wallet has a status indicator that informs the shareholder node about the performance of support nodes. If a support node misses too many blocks, the system will recommend the shareholder node to replace it with a new support node. Once a representative node is found to have generated an invalid block, all standard wallets will require a new representative node to be elected before conducting further transactions.

The DPoS consensus algorithm also uses the longest main chain rule, where a representative node that misses an opportunity to generate a block means that it is on a shorter chain than a potential competitor. In other words, once 51% of the subsequent 100 blocks following a transaction are produced, it can be deemed securely positioned on the main chain. In a DPoS system, blocks are generated every 30 seconds, and it takes up to 5 minutes to determine whether a node is on a branch chain. The DPoS consensus algorithm allows no more than 50% of nodes to be malicious or faulty; Otherwise, forking occurs as shown in Figure 4.33.

DPoS reduces the potential loss of forks by timely detection and warning. Since representative nodes get paid for generating blocks, they will stay close to 100% online to prevent losing revenue by being voted out of office. Therefore, it is safe to assume that if 1 or 2 blocks in the past 10 blocks miss production, then some part of the network may be experiencing connectivity issues, and the shareholder nodes should be particularly alert to this and ask for additional confirmation. If more than 5 out of 10 blocks miss production, then this means that the supporting node

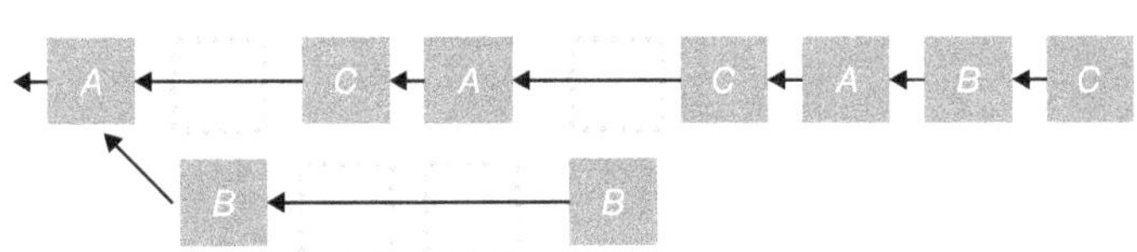

Figure 4.33 Forking issue in DPoS.

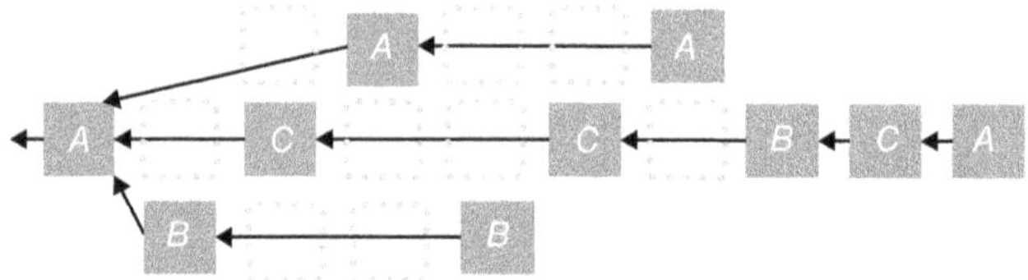

Figure 4.34 Network partitioning in DPoS.

of the shareholder node is likely on a branch chain, at which point all transactions should be stopped until the fork is resolved.

When the network is partitioned, it is highly probable that no single chain will constitute the majority of all blocks, as shown in Figure 4.34. In this scenario, the node in the longest chain will be the largest minority node group. Upon restoration of network connectivity, relatively small groups of nodes will naturally switch to the longest chain, leading to a definitive consensus reinstatement.

It is worth noting that the number of representative nodes must be odd. This is to prevent the situation where the two largest branch chains have the same length when network partitioning occurs.

In terms of resisting attacks, the top 101 representative nodes possess equal bookkeeping rights. So, it is impossible to centralize power to a single representative node by obtaining more than 1% of votes. Since the number of representative nodes is only 101, we can imagine an attacker taking turns in a Distributed Denial of Service (DDoS) attack on each representative node that has been granted bookkeeping rights. The utilization of public keys rather than IP addresses for node identification increases the complexity of DDoS attackers aiming to target specific nodes. The potential direct connections between representative nodes will also complicate attackers' attempts to obstruct block generation processes.

4.4.4.3 Conflux

Conflux (Li et al. 2018) is an advanced public blockchain system designed to address common challenges in existing blockchain networks such as scalability, security, and decentralization. At its core are the Tree-Graph ledger structure and the Greedy-Heaviest-Adaptive-SubTree (GHAST) chain selection rule. This mechanism allows for parallel processing of blocks and transactions, reducing the time and resources required to reach consensus and increasing the overall capacity of the network.

In distributed ledgers, concurrent block handling, namely block forking, needs to be addressed. Bitcoin and Ethereum use the longest chain rule to select one fork and discard all others. Discarded blocks neither enhance the system's security nor

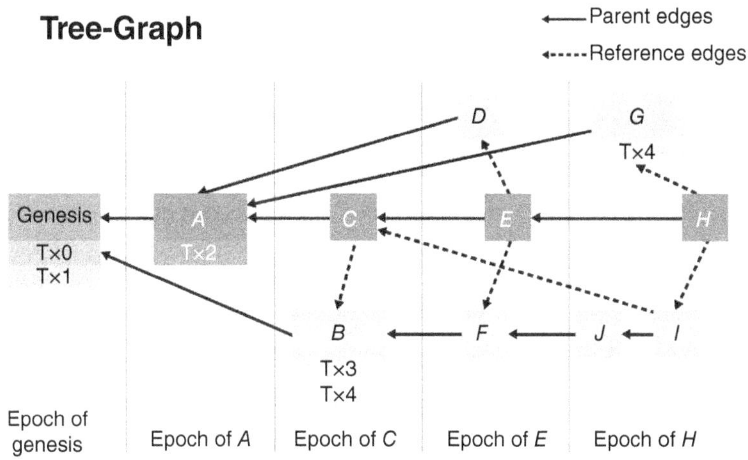

Figure 4.35 Tree-Graph ledger structure of Conflux.

improve its throughput. Consequently, there exists an inherent conflict between the scalability and security of these blockchains.

As depicted in Figure 4.35, in the Conflux system, each block contains a reference edge list to previous blocks, in addition to a single parent edge. This introduces new information regarding the temporal relationships between blocks. This structure is essentially a directed tree embedded in a Directed Acyclic Graph (DAG), hence the name Tree-Graph for Conflux's ledger structure.

Conflux merges all concurrent blocks into its ledger, thereby enhancing its security and performance. Specifically, Conflux replaces the longest chain rule with the GHAST chain selection rule. By employing this rule, fork selection is no longer solely based on on-chain computational power but also considers computational power within subtrees. Specifically, the GHAST mechanism involves the heaviest chain rule but with a modified block weighting system. Block types are determined based on the historical tree-graph structure of blocks, rather than being determined by miners.

Under the GHAST mechanism, the heaviest chain rule is implemented by selecting the sub-block with the highest weight from the subtree of the current last main chain block. Sub-block weights are computed not only based on block quantity but also include the sum of weights. By allowing miners to generate special blocks, the GHAST mechanism increases block difficulty and slows down block production, helping mitigate liveness attacks.

The core components of the GHAST mechanism can be summarized as follows:

The heaviest chain rule is applied, but the block has three different weights: 0, 1, X, where X is a relatively large number, for example, $X = 1000$, ignoring the situation involving adjustment of mining difficulty. There are two types of blocks in the network: normal blocks and special blocks. The weight of the normal block is always 1; the weight of the special block is determined according to the difficulty of the block – there are $1/X$ special block weights of X, while the rest are 0. Mining a normal block has the same difficulty as a special block. The block type is determined by the historical Tree-Graph structure of the block. As the generator of a block cannot arbitrarily specify the block type. In the absence of an attack, all newly generated honest blocks should become normal blocks; after the attacker conducts any kind of "liveliness attack" and continues for a long enough time, all newly generated honest blocks become special blocks.

4.4.5 PoX

A novel category of consensus algorithms, known as PoX, typically substitutes the competition based on computing power with valuable work derived from publicly accessible resources or even eliminates the need for computing altogether. Prominent examples of PoX consensus algorithms include Proof of Elapsed Time (PoET) (Chen et al. 2017, pp. 282–297), Proof of Luck (PoL) (Milutinovic et al. 2016, pp. 1–6), Proof of Space (Proof of Space, PoSpace) (Dziembowski et al. 2015, pp. 585–605), and Proof of Bandwidth (PoB) (Ghosh et al. 2014).

From Sections 4.2 and 4.3, it can be observed that a common feature of proof-based consensus algorithms is the likelihood of generating forks for each node with a proof when considering the same previous block. These conflicting blocks are then resolved in such a way that only one ultimately attains validity, showcasing the final consistency inherent in proof-based consensus algorithms. Conversely, voting-based consensus algorithms rely on message interaction among nodes, resulting in each consensus round generating a single block without forks and thus exhibiting strong consistency. To sum up, while proof-based consensus algorithms find general applicability in permissionless blockchains with numerous nodes, voting-based consensus algorithms are generally suitable for small-scale permissioned blockchains.

4.5 Consensus Integrating Proof and Voting

The performance bottlenecks of consensus algorithms based on proof and those based on voting are, respectively, attributed to the computational capabilities of nodes and communication resources. Thus, each type of algorithm has its own merits in terms of scale and efficiency. The consensus integrating proof and voting utilizes a representative mechanism to assign different rights to nodes, thereby combining the advantages of both types of consensus algorithms, achieving large-scale scalability.

4.5.1 PoV

The primary idea of the PoV consensus algorithm (Li et al. 2017, pp. 466–473) is to divide the rights of consensus nodes within the blockchain network into bookkeeping and voting. The bookkeeping right grants a node the ability to write, thus referred to as the bookkeeper. The voting right grants a node the power to decide, thus referred to as the voter. A single consensus node can possess one or both rights. Ordinary nodes without rights do not participate in the consensus process but have the same reading capabilities as bookkeepers and voters. If an ordinary node wishes to participate in the consensus process, it can apply to join as a bookkeeper candidate and subsequently compete in the election for bookkeepers.

Assuming the number of voters is N_v, the number of bookkeepers is N_b, the number of bookkeeper candidates is N_c, the number of ordinary nodes is N_o, and the total number of system nodes is N_{all}. Since a node might possess both rights, the total number of system nodes is less than the sum of these four respective counts, in other words, $N_{all} \leq N_v + N_b + N_c + N_o$. Unless otherwise specified, blockchain nodes generally refer to all types of nodes mentioned above.

The election process for candidates is conducted by voters. In the last phase of the previous tenure, each voter needs to vote for candidates and the N_b bookkeeper candidates with the most votes will become the bookkeepers for the next tenure. Each successfully elected bookkeeper will receive an assigned number, starting from 0 up to $N_b - 1$. Assuming the tenure of a bookkeeper is T_w, there are $B_w + 1$ blocks generated within each tenure. Bookkeepers rotate in a random order to produce blocks during their tenure, with each creation of a block referred to as a consensus round. The bookkeeper responsible for producing a block within a round is called the duty bookkeeper. The last block of each tenure is a special one, recording the voting results, specifically the server information and numbers for the bookkeepers elected for the next term. The duty bookkeeper generates a block within a designated consensus round, which is the block encapsulation period T_b. Figure 4.36 depicts the consensus model for one tenure.

The consensus process for block generation involves both bookkeepers and voters, as illustrated in Figure 4.37. Each block comprises a block header and a variable number of transactions. Within a consensus round, the duty bookkeeper initially extracts a certain number of transactions from its transaction pool and packages them into a pre-block. The distinction between a pre-block and a formal block is that the pre-block lacks a timestamp, voter's voting information, and the

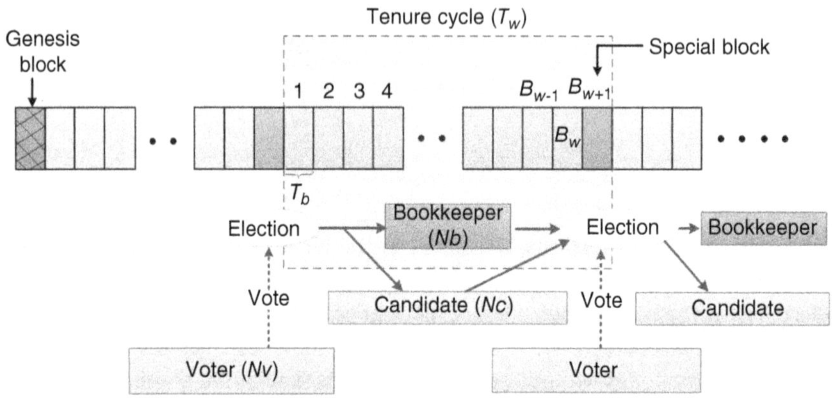

Figure 4.36 PoV tenure cycle.

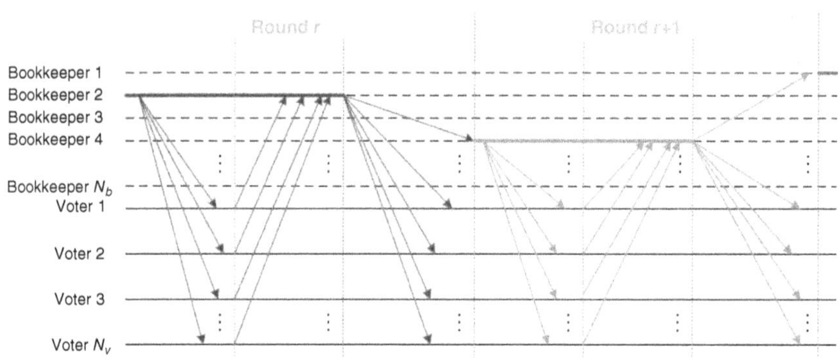

Figure 4.37 PoV consensus flowchart.

identifier of duty bookkeeper in next round. After generating the pre-block, the duty bookkeeper dispatches it to all voters for validation. Voters are responsible for inspecting the pre-block header and transaction details. If approved, they sign the pre-block header and send it back to the duty bookkeeper as their votes. Once the duty bookkeeper accumulates votes from more than half of the voters, the pre-block can be augmented to a formal block and then disseminated throughout the network.

Algorithm 4.2 provides a pseudo-code for a node to run the overall PoV algorithm. After a series of initialization processes, the node determines its own state and decides to run PoV processes of different identities according to its own state and configuration.

Algorithm 4.2 PoV State Machine Running Flow

```
System_init;
{gen_com_list}← set_commissioner_list_genesis();
{Block_list}← BLOCK_SYNC();
examine({com_list},{bul_list},{bc_list},{user_list});
myaddr← key_manager.get_my_public_key(); //Gets the
local node address, which is the public key
if my_addr ∈{com_list}∪{bc_list} then
  if my_addr ∈{com_list} then
     Run the work process of voter;
  end if
  if my_addr ∈{bc_list} then
     Run the work process of bookkeeper candidate;
  end if
  else if my_addr ∈{user_list} then
     Run the work process of ordinary node;
  else then
     Forward_block_and_message();
  end if
```

Algorithm 4.3 describes the execution process of the voters, including the genesis block generation stage and the normal stage.

Algorithm 4.3 Working Process of Voters

```
while is_connecting_to_network==true do
  {Block_list}← BLOCK_SYNC(); //Synchronize the latest
  blocks and update system variables and memory pools
 Height← make_get_height_request_msg (); //Request
 latest height
 if Height == NULL then //No blocks exist in the
 network yet
    send Tx_PERMISSION;
    if is_needed_to_be_bulter==true then
       send Tx_PERMISSION;
    end if
    if my_addr== min (sort({com_list})) then
       Create the genesis block;
    end if
 else then
    The voters enter the block generation stage;
   end if
end while
```

Algorithm 4.4 describes the execution flow of the bookkeeper candidates.

Algorithm 4.4 Working Process of the Bookkeeper Candidates

```
while is_connecting_to_network==true do
  {Block_list}← BLOCK_SYNC(); //Synchronize the latest
  blocks and update system variables and memory pools
  Process the received voting transactions and put them
  into the memory pool after verification;
  Process the received identity change transactions and
  put them into the memory pool after verification;
  Process received ordinary transactions, verify them
  and put them into the memory pool;
  Process other messages of the system, verify the
  validity and forward;
  Process new blocks received, verify the legitimacy of
  blocks, and update information;
  if my_addr ∈{bul_list} then
     The bookkeeper candidate process enters the
     bookkeeper tenure phase;
  end if
end while
```

The supplementation of information in the pre-block header depends on the voters' signatures. Within PoV, it is specified that the block's generation time is dictated by the timestamp of the most recent voter signature. The identifier of duty bookkeeper for the next round is derived by hashing the signature and timestamp and then modulo operation. The mechanism for electing the next duty bookkeeper capitalizes on the randomness and unforgeability of the signature operation. Since each voter's signature is generated randomly, the computed identifier for the next duty bookkeeper is also imbued with randomness.

Compared to consensus algorithms such as PoW and PoS, the PoV consensus algorithm forsakes the reliance on computational power, enabling shorter block generation time and achieving higher Transaction Per Second (TPS) rates. In terms of partition tolerance, as long as more than half of the voters in the network are operating honestly, coupled with an honest-working bookkeeper, the continuous operation of the PoV consensus can be ensured without any forks. Furthermore, when compared to the PBFT consensus, the communication complexity of PoV is only $O(N_v)$, significantly lower than $O\left(N_{all}^2\right)$ of PBFT.

Considering that PoV is initially an efficient consensus algorithm based on consortium blockchains, operating in network environments with minimal presence of Byzantine nodes or malicious attack behavior, the efficient and reliable consortium nodes can form a block by receiving more than 51% of votes, establishing a threshold of 1/2. Furthermore, when faced with network environments containing Byzantine nodes exhibiting arbitrary behaviors resulting in issues such as message loss, delay, repeated propagation, and out-of-order occurrences within an asynchronous setting, PoV demonstrates dynamic adaptability by generating a block valid threshold tailored to specific needs. This adaptation necessitates at least 2/3 of total voters to achieve consensus on a block, effectively countering Byzantine attacks and providing robust Byzantine fault tolerance. Although this adjustment may introduce communication delays for PoV implementation, it ensures the utmost security during the consensus process.

4.5.2 PPoV

In most consensus algorithms, each round of consensus requires the selection of a single bookkeeper to be responsible for generating blocks, leaving other bookkeepers inactive. As a result, the overall consensus process operates sequentially. Compared to the data throughput of traditional distributed systems, there is still room for enhancing the performance of blockchain consensus mechanisms.

To mitigate the performance constraints resulting from the sequential nature of consensus algorithms, this section introduces the PPoV consensus algorithm (Bai et al. 2021, pp. 147–154). It improves the data structure and consensus procedure utilized in PoV consensus, allowing multiple bookkeepers to generate blocks concurrently, thereby enhancing the throughput of the blockchain system.

In PPoV, blockchain data is organized into block groups, comprising a block group header and a block group body. The block group header includes the current block group's height and the associated voting outcomes. Only blocks that have successfully passed the voting process are included in the block group body. Each individual block within this structure contains the hash value of the previous block group, Merkle root, generator's public key, and timestamp, among other information, as well as a set of transactions. Since blocks within a block group do not have any interrelation, an unbalanced tree can be used to depict the block dependency relationships in PPoV, as illustrated in Figure 4.38.

PPoV designates all operations required to produce a block group as one consensus round. Since every bookkeeper can generate a block within a single consensus round, PPoV introduces a new consensus right, the aggregation right, which grants certain nodes the responsibility to gather and organize votes. These nodes possessing the aggregation right are referred to as aggregators.

The PPoV consensus process is illustrated in Figure 4.39, with the following steps in each consensus round.

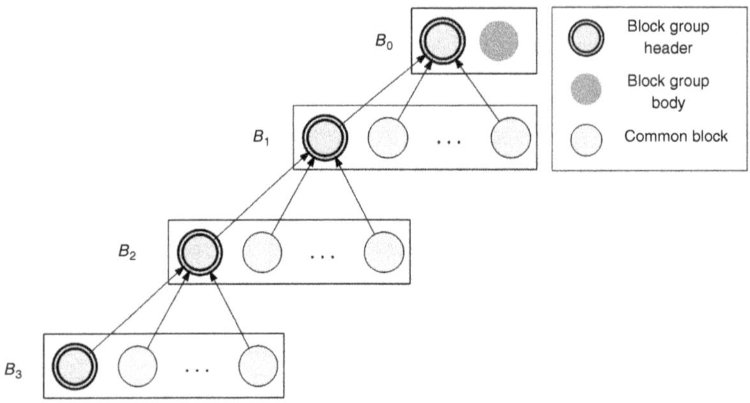

Figure 4.38 PPoV block dependency relationship.

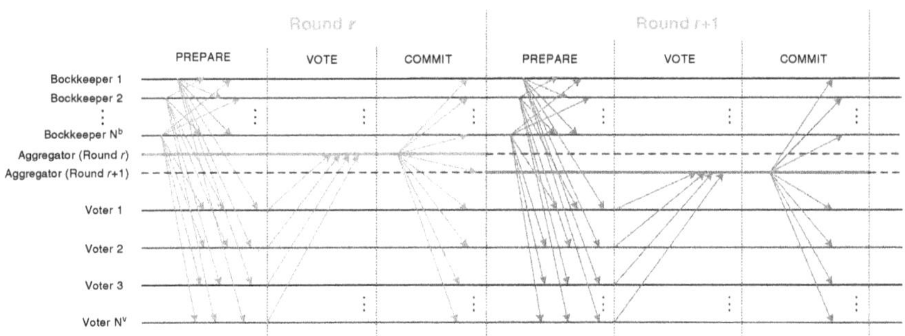

Figure 4.39 PPoV consensus flowchart.

4.5.2.1 Prepare Phase

Step 1: Each bookkeeper independently generates a block with a specific transaction allocation rule and releases it to the network. Blockchain nodes collect blocks produced by all bookkeepers. The transaction allocation rule ensures that transaction pools of bookkeepers are distinct, resulting in entirely unique blocks generated by each individual bookkeeper. The pseudo-code is shown in Algorithm 4.5.

Algorithm 4.5 Prepare (publishing blocks)

```
if do_prepare=true do
    h← getBlockChainHeight()+1;
    gen_block_group_num← h%(Bw+1);
    if gen_block_group_num=0 and I_am_duty_worker do
        VoteForNextWorkers();
    end if
    block← GenerateBlock();
    Msg_Block← GenerateBlockMsg(block);
    for node in node_list do
        SendMessage(node, Msg_Block);
    end for
    do_prepare=false;
end if
return
```

4.5.2.2 Vote Phase

Step 2: Upon collecting the blocks from the bookkeepers, a voter casts individual votes for each block and creates a comprehensive voting message to send to the aggregator. The voting message contains the hash value of every block, an opinion indicating agreement or disagreement (−1, 0, 1), and additional signature information. The pseudo-code is shown in Algorithm 4.6.

Algorithm 4.6 Vote

```
if do_vote=true do
    received_block_num← getLen(received_block_set);
    Nw← getWorkerAmount();
    if received_block_num< N_w and N_epoch=0 do
        return
    end if
    Initial Vote_Ticket to a list with N_w {null, 0} elements;
    for block in received_block_set do
        block_num← getBlockNum(block);
        header← getHeader(block);
        hash← getHash(block);
        opnion← VerifiedBlock(block);
        Vote_Ticket[block_num]←Pair(hash,opinion);
    end for
    Msg_Vote←getVoteMsg(Vote_Ticket);
```

```
    node←getDutyWorkerNode();
    sendMessage(node, Msg_Vote);
    do_vote=false;
end if
return
```

4.5.2.3 Commit Phase

Step 3.1: The aggregator consistently waits for voting messages and counts the results. When the number of affirmative or negative votes in each block surpasses 2/3 of all voters, these tally results are added along with their respective voting messages into the block group header. Subsequently, the aggregator generates a random number, which serves as the aggregator number for the next consensus round and incorporates it into the block group header that is then broadcasted. The pseudo-code is shown in Algorithm 4.7.

Algorithm 4.7 Propose (the block group header)

```
if do_Propose=true do
    Can_Generated_Result, Result_List←VoteList
Statistic(Vote_List);
    if Can_Generated_Result=false do
        return
    end if
    block_group_header←GenerateBlockGroupHeader
(Vote_List, Result_List);
    Msg_Block_Group_Header←getBlockGroupHeaderMsg
(block_group_header);
    for node in node_list do
        sendMessage(node, Msg_Block_Group_Header);
    end for
    do_propose=false;
end if
return
```

Step 3.2: Once a blockchain node receives all blocks produced by bookkeepers along with the block group header from the aggregator, it locally assembles them into a block group and saves them to the database. Following this, nodes execute transactions present in valid blocks within the block group. Besides executing transactions, they also update variables like the start time for the next consensus round, the next aggregator number, and the current consensus height, based on the block group header. The pseudo-code is shown in Algorithm 4.8.

Algorithm 4.8 Commit (the block group)

```
satisfied_commit_condition← true;
received_block_group_header← hasBlockGroupHeader
(block_group);
if received_block_group_header=false do
   satisfied_commit_condition← false;
else
   block_group_header← getBlockGroupHeader
(block_group);
   Vote_Result← getVoteResult(block_group_header);
   Nw← getWorkerAmount();
   has_all_block← true;
  for i in 1 to Nw do
      opinion← getOpinion(i, Vote_Result);
      if opinion=1 do
         if hasBlock(block_group, i)=false do
            satisfied_commit_condition← false;
            break
         end if
         block← getBlock(block_group,i);
         header← getHeader(block);
         m_hash← getHash(header);
         hash← getVoteResultHash(i, Vote_Result);
         if hash!=m_hash do
            satisfied_commit_condition←false;
            break
         end if
      end if
   end for
end if
if satisfied_commit_condition do
   AddBlockGroupToBlockChain(block_group);
   UpdateVariables(block_group);
   do_prepare=true;
   do_vote=true;
   do_propose=true;
```

```
else
    if Nepoch>0 do
        TimeoutProcess();
    end if
end if
return
```

In comparison with PoV, the PPoV consensus enhances the concurrent storage capacity of the blockchain as an append-only database. As shown in Figure 4.40, ensuring security and scalability, its throughput peak surpasses 280,000 TPS. Benchmarking against the renowned efficient consensus HotStuff, PPoV consensus not only meets a similar throughput performance level but also boasts a transaction confirmation latency of just half that of HotStuff. In blockchain system functionality and performance tests conducted by the China Academy of Information and Communications Technology, the PPoV blockchain platform consistently achieved over 30,000 TPS single-chain with zero errors.

4.5.3 Lightweight PPoV

The Lightweight PPoV (Wang et al. 2023, pp. 150–157) addresses the data scalability issue in the chained append-only structure utilized by the original PPoV. This

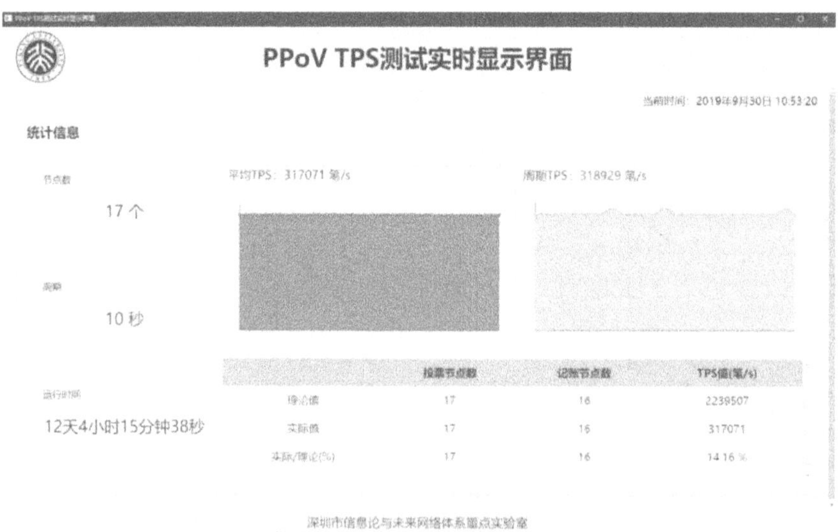

Figure 4.40 Measured interface showcasing the actual performance of PPoV. *Source:* Peking University Shenzhen Graduate School.

includes comprehensive compression of data at each consensus phase and implementation of aggregate signature to effectively manage signature volume as the number of nodes increases.

Specifically, Lightweight PPoV adopts a cooperative storage approach that integrates erasure codes. This technique alleviates the burden of storing all data in its entirety at every node and is particularly effective in environments with Byzantine nodes, including both crash and malicious nodes. In this cooperative storage scheme, each node stores fragments of transaction data and collaboratively reconstructs complete blocks in real-time when necessary.

To optimize access efficiency, it's advisable to encode only the block body, which primarily comprises transactions, leaving the block header untouched. For instance, in Figure 4.41, a Reed-Solomon (RS) code (Wicker and Bhargava 1999) is employed, assuming a total of n ($n = 4$) nodes with at most f ($f = 2$) nodes being Byzantine. An $(n - f, f)$ RS code is used to facilitate access by communicating with $(n - f)$ active nodes. In this setup, each node independently encodes the block body into n chunks $\{C\}_{c=1}^{n}$, comprising $(n - f)$ data chunks $\{C\}_{c=1}^{n-f}$ and f parity chunks $\{C\}_{c=n-f+1}^{n}$. Data chunks contain segments of the original block body, each storing a certain number of transactions. Parity chunks serve as redundant parts for recovery purposes. At each block height, each node stores one or multiple chunks. Consequently, the maximum theoretical compression ratio achievable for the block body is $1/(n - f)$.

As far as we understand, read requests in blockchain demonstrate two key characteristics: (a) Temporal locality: This refers to the tendency for accessing data within block bodies to decrease gradually as it ages. (b) Random hotness: Some data exhibits higher read value due to frequent access, but this does not correlate directly with block height. In light of these characteristics, this section introduces two optimization methods tailored to address them.

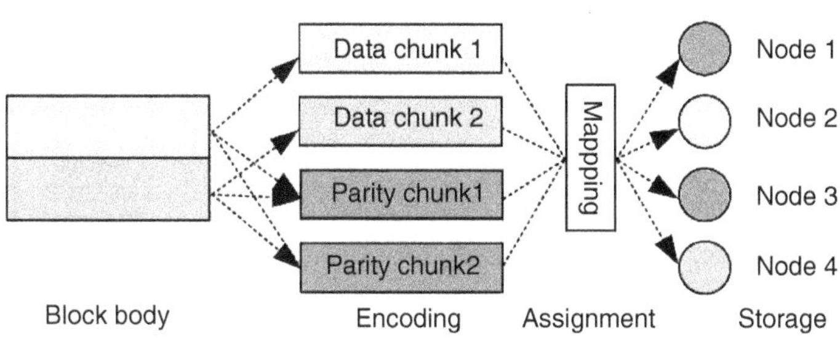

Figure 4.41 Process of Lightweight PPoV, taking (2,2) RS code as an example.

4.5.3.1 Adaptive Timeline Adjustment Method

Leveraging the temporal locality of read requests in blockchain, a timeline mechanism was introduced by Wang et al. (2021, pp. 3656–3662). This mechanism categorizes blocks into hot, warm, and cold spaces according to their heights and employs distinct chunk storage and block caching strategies for each space, as depicted in Figure 4.42.

The timeline mechanism essentially aims to strike a balance between storage and read performance. The designation of a hot space implies prioritizing read performance at the expense of storage. A prolonged hot space signifies a strong demand for accessing recently generated blocks, while a warm space offers read protection for blocks that are only partially accessible. However, in practice, this balance is dynamic. Therefore, an adaptive timeline adjustment method is proposed to optimize this mechanism, as illustrated in Figure 4.43. The core concept is to dynamically adjust the timeline based on changing factors. For instance, as the rate of invalidated requests on newly generated blocks declines rapidly, the hot space should be shortened to facilitate compression. Similarly, if interest in reading a warm block diminishes rapidly, reducing the warm space can expedite its transition to the cold space with the highest compression ratio.

To regulate the length of the hot space, this section introduces a pair of parameters α_{uf} and α_{df}. The up factor α_{uf} is determined by the ratio between the average times to request blocks in the original hot space and those in the expected expanded hot space. Conversely, the down factor α_{df} is the ratio between the

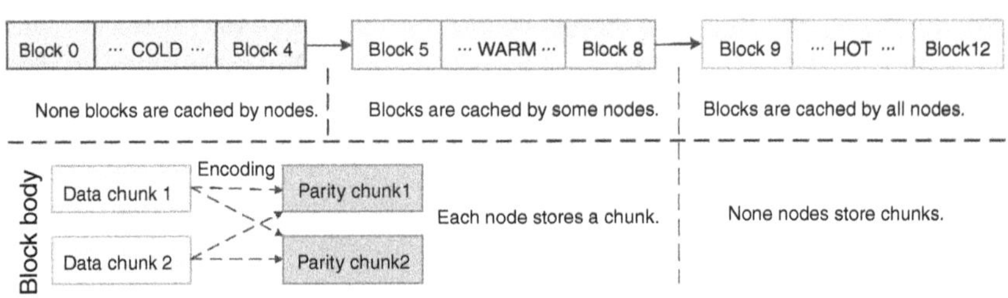

Figure 4.42 The timeline mechanism for the blockchain.

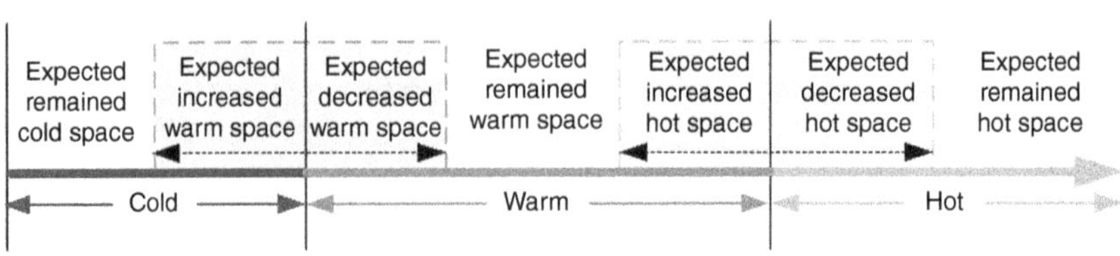

Figure 4.43 The adaptive timeline adjustment method.

average times to request blocks in the expected reduced hot space and those in the expected maintained hot space. These parameters indicate the discrepancy in visitation rates between the hot and warm spaces, serving as difficulty coefficients for adjusting the length of the hot space. A higher-up factor α_{uf} facilitates the extension of the hot space, reflecting an optimistic storage strategy that prioritizes reads. Conversely, a smaller down factor α_{df} suggests a tendency for the hot space to contract, indicating a cautious approach toward block expiration and storage reduction. Unlike the consideration of request times for the hot space, the adjustment parameter for the length of the warm space depends solely on whether the block is reachable within the expected space. This distinction arises because the categorization of warm and cold spaces is determined solely by whether a block is encoded or not.

Through periodic monitoring of block requests in each space, the system adjusts the length using the aforementioned parameters. If multiple successive adjustments occur in the same direction (either increase or decrease), the expected space length undergoes exponential expansion. For instance, if 1 block height is added to the hot space in the first period, the monitoring extends to 2 block heights in the second period, and so forth. Conversely, if the system changes direction, the monitoring length for that direction is set to 1. For instance, if the system increases the block height by 2 in the second period and then decreases it by 1 in the third period, then at most 1 block can be added in the fourth period. This exponential adjustment method enables rapid convergence of the timeline to an appropriate length. Furthermore, progressive adjustment offers the advantage of precise regulation of the timeline, particularly when the current and previous periods exhibit contrasting trends.

4.5.3.2 Tentative Transaction Query Method

In scenarios where random hot transactions are dispersed across the blockchain without clear patterns, direct access from cache proves effective when transactions are situated within the hot space. However, if a transaction resides in the warm or cold space, decoding may become necessary for recovery. A conventional approach involves tallying transaction requests and sorting them to identify random hot transactions, but this method can lead to substantial storage and bandwidth consumption. To address this issue, this section proposes a best-effort tentative transaction query method that minimizes global overhead. This method involves querying the cache or data chunk of the target node for missing transactions. The target node for each transaction is efficiently located using a consistent hash ring.

Consistent hashing, an advanced hash algorithm, operates within a defined address range typically denoted as $[0, 2^{32} - 1)$. During initialization, nodes within the network are positioned onto a hash ring based on the hash values derived from their public keys. Each node then takes charge of transactions falling within its designated forward space along this ring. To ensure that each node's hash space remains uniformly sized, the introduction of virtual nodes helps counteract potential skewness. Furthermore, nodes maintain local queues to manage the query requests they receive. Figure 4.44 depicts the process of querying a transaction using consistent hashing.

Step 1: When node *C* receives a query request for transaction *TX*3, it first checks its local cache or data chunk for the transaction. If unsuccessful, it locates the nodes responsible for storing the data chunks of *TX*3 and queries them. If successful, *TX*3 is returned and cached locally. If not, proceed to Step 2.

Step 2: Node *C* attempts to request *TX*3 from nodes that recently queried for it. It hashes *TX*3 into the ring and proceeds clockwise until it establishes a connection with the first responding node, say node *A*. Upon receiving the query request for *TX*3 from node *C*, node *A* needs to check if it is locally cached and return it if found. Otherwise, node *A* checks the query queue and obtains a list of nodes that have recently queried for the same transaction. Meanwhile, node *A* adds the mapping relation between *TX*3 and node *C* to the end of the query queue.

Step 3: Node *C* sends query requests to the nodes in the list sequentially until successfully obtaining transaction *TX*3. If all attempts fail, decoding is performed for recovery. Additionally, node *C* caches *TX*3 for future responses.

Step 4: Node *C* dynamically monitors the number of queries from different nodes for transactions. Once it exceeds a certain threshold, denoted as $(2f + 1)$, the

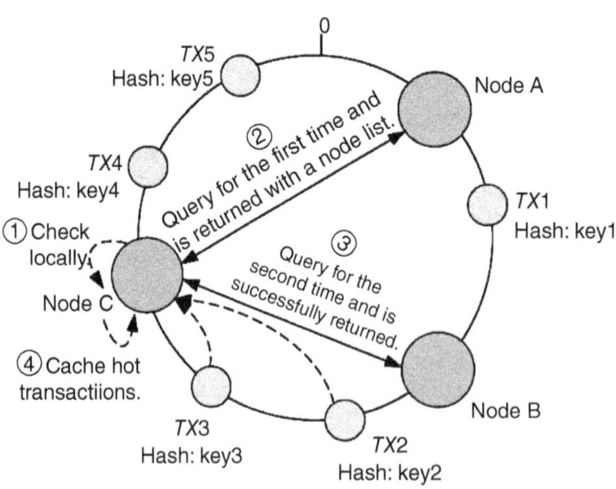

Figure 4.44 An example of the transaction query method based on consistent hashing.

transaction is considered hot. This threshold prevents malicious nodes from wasting storage space. For a hot transaction, node C actively executes Steps 2 and 3 to cache it locally, preparing for potential requests.

4.5.4 Mimic PPoV

PPoV, through role-based authorization, enhances consensus speed by substituting consensus process across the entire network with a subset of nodes. However, solely attempting to minimize network-wide consensus will inevitably diminish decentralization and subsequently compromise the overall security of the system. This section introduces Mimic PPoV algorithm (Xiao et al. 2022, pp. 3215–3224) which integrates the concept of mimic defense. Drawing inspiration from the dynamic heterogeneous redundancy architecture in mimic defense, a consensus framework combining mimic defense tailored for BFT-like consensus is proposed.

The consensus process of Mimic PPoV is divided into three phases: propose, vote, and commit, as illustrated in Figure 4.45.

The propose phase within each shard follows the same process as PPoV, where bookkeepers package transactions from local pools into batches in parallel and broadcast them as proposal messages. For S shards, let $batch_{i,j}^r$ denote the batch generated by bookkeeper $Bookkeeper_{i,j}$ in shard s_i during the r-th consensus round, where i $(1 \ll i \ll S,\ i \in N)$ and j $(1 \ll j \ll N_b,\ j \in N)$ represents the shard number and bookkeeper number, respectively. Under normal circumstances, bookkeepers with the same number in different shards generate identical batches, that is, $batch_{1,j}^r = batch_{2,j}^r = \ldots = batch_{S,j}^r$. It is ensured by the input agent.

The vote phase is also analogous to PPoV, where a voter assumes the responsibility of verifying and voting on proposals received from bookkeepers. Subsequently, it generates a voting message with the digests of the proposals and transmits it to the leader of the corresponding shard.

The commit phase encompasses the adjudication of votes and the commitment of block. During adjudication, the leader of each shard forms a group and engages in iterative negotiations to compute the final voting results, which are recorded in a block header. The block header is then broadcast across all network nodes for block assembly, as well as commitment activities such as storage of blocks and execution of transactions.

In particular, the leader in each shard forms a group known as the leader group, which exhibits an undirected connected graph structure denoted by $G = (LG, E)$. Here $LG = \{leader_i\}_{i=1}^{S}$ represents the set of leaders, while E represents the set of links, as depicted in Figure 4.46.

In the simplest scenario, for the leader $leader_i$ in shard s_i during the r-th consensus round, let vt_i^r represent the count of approval votes it receives for an arbitrary

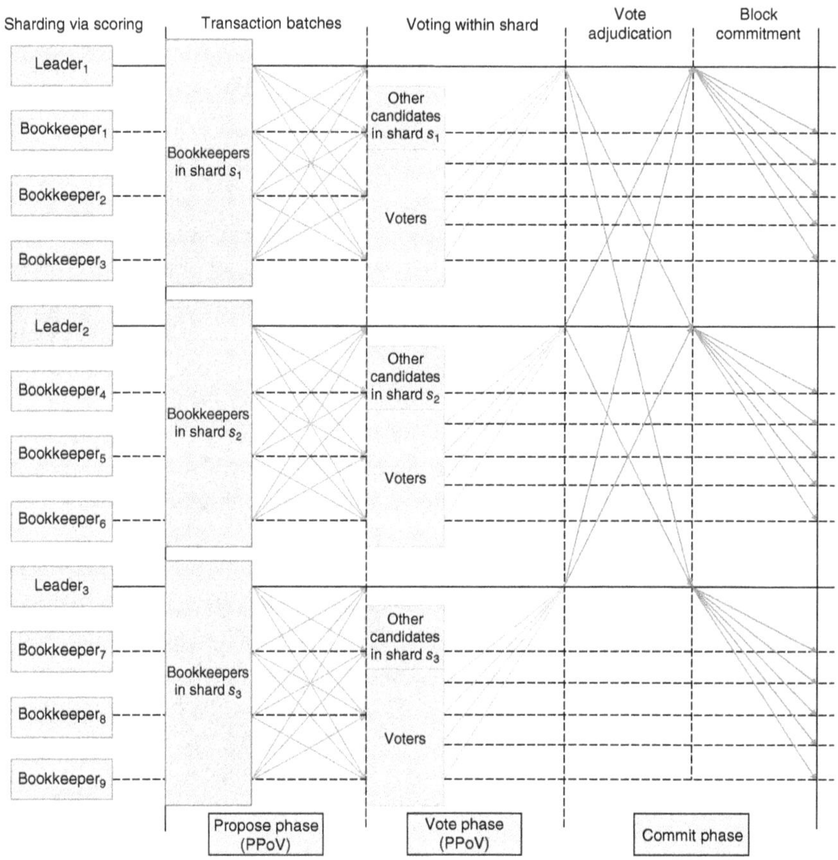

Figure 4.45 Consensus process of the Mimic PPoV protocol.

batch. The fundamental adjudication condition is expressed as Equation (4.1), which, if met, validates the batch. Otherwise, the batch is considered invalid.

$$\textit{Adjudication condition}\ 1: \frac{vt_i^r}{N_v} > 2/3. \tag{4.1}$$

However, due to our network assumptions, leaders of different shards may receive inconsistent votes. To ensure a uniform adjudication result for the batch, the leader group will negotiate over multiple rounds of iterations. Specifically, for the k-th ($k \in N^*$) negotiation round, the voting result $vt_i^r(k)$ in leader $leader_i$ is updated as

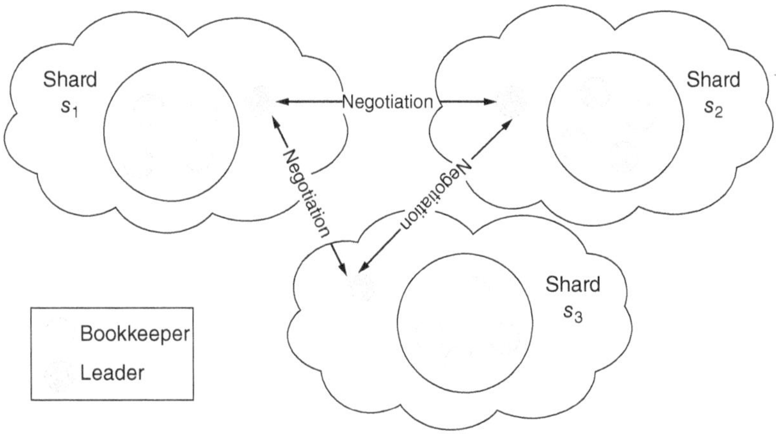

Figure 4.46 Leader group from multiple shards.

$$vt_i^r(k) = \sum_{i'=1}^{i'=S} \omega_{ii'} \bullet vt_{i'}^r(k-1), \tag{4.2}$$

where $vt_i^r(0) = vt_i^r$, and $\omega_{ii'}$ represents predetermined fixed-weight parameters with $\sum_{i'=1}^{i'=S} \omega_{ii'} = 1$.

Obviously, after multiple rounds of iterations, the voting result of each leader will ultimately converge to $vt_1^r(\infty) = vt_2^r(\infty) = \cdots = vt_S^r(\infty)$. The adjudication condition is then modified, in accordance with Equation (4.1), to

$$\textit{Adjudication condition } 2: \frac{vt_i^r(\infty)}{N_v} > 2/3. \tag{4.3}$$

Because the voting results of all leaders are convergent, their adjudication results based on Equation (4.3) exhibit uniformity. Compared to the regular BFT consensus protocol requiring the approval message to be received from more than 2/3 of the nodes, the adjudication condition in Mimic PPoV is stricter.

4.5.5 HotStuff

HotStuff (Yin et al. 2019, pp. 347–356) is a BFT-like consensus algorithm employing a three-phase voting procedure. It incorporates threshold signatures during the voting process, aggregating the data packets confirmed by $(n - f)$ node signatures and the view number into a Quorum Certificate (QC). This achieves a communication complexity of $O(n)$.

HotStuff operates on a view-based SMR model. Within a view, there exists a deterministic leader who orchestrates consensus through three voting phases, during which one or multiple blocks can be generated. The system then transitions to the next view to commence the subsequent round of consensus. If an abnormal situation occurs, like a timeout before achieving consensus, it also shifts to the next view to continue the consensus process.

4.5.5.1 Basic HotStuff

The Basic HotStuff represents the fundamental version of the consensus algorithm. The confirmation for a block necessitates three voting phases, after which the consensus for the next block commences, as depicted in Figure 4.47.

4.5.5.1.1 Prepare Phase

Step 1.1: At the commencement of each view, the new leader gathers *new_view* messages sent by $(n-f)$ nodes. Each *new_view* message contains the highest *PrepareQC* from its respective node.

Step 1.2: The leader selects the highest *PrepareQC* from the received *new_view* messages, designating it as *HighQC*. Subsequently, a new block is generated based on this branch, which is then broadcast to the entire network as a *proposal.*

Step 1.3: Upon receipt of the *proposal* message from the current leader, replica nodes check its safety and validity. If deemed legal, replicas return their *Prepare – Vote* signed with their private keys.

4.5.5.1.2 Precommit Phase

Step 2: Following the issuance of the proposal, the leader awaits signatures from $(n-f)$ nodes for that proposal. Once these signatures are accumulated, they are merged into a new signature. A *PrepareQC*, storing this aggregate signature, is

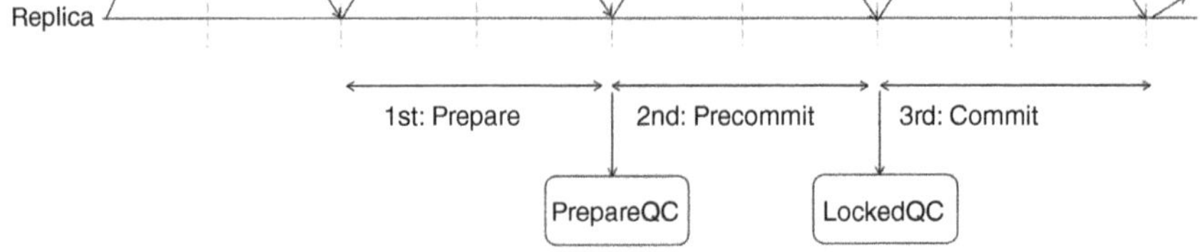

Figure 4.47 Basic HotStuff consensus process.

saved locally and subsequently embedded in a *precommit* message broadcasted to replica nodes.

4.5.5.1.3 Commit Phase

Step 3.1: Upon receipt of $(n - f)$ *Precommit – Vote* messages for the current proposal, the leader amalgamates these votes into a *PrecommitQC*. This is then transmitted via a *commit* message broadcast.

Step 3.2: After receiving the *commit* message, replicas generate and send back *Commit – Vote* messages signed by them. Simultaneously, the local *LockQC* is updated with the received *PrecommitQC*.

4.5.5.1.4 Decide Phase

Step 4.1: After obtaining $(n - f)$ *Commit – Vote* messages, the leader fuses them into a *CommitQC* and broadcasts a *decide* message subsequently.

Step 4.2: Upon receipt of the *CommitQC* within the *decide* message, replicas perceive the current proposal as definitive. Transactions on the confirmed branch are executed. The view number increments by 1, ushering in a new consensus round.

4.5.5.2 Chained HotStuff

In Basic HotStuff, each of the three voting phases involves dispatching messages followed by accumulating votes. Considering this, Chained HotStuff streamlines the protocol through pipelining.

During the prepare phase, the votes are gathered by the corresponding leader of current view (*leader*1), creating a *PrepareQC* upon completion. This *PrepareQC* is then dispatched to the leader of subsequent view (*leader*2), who utilizes it to commence its own prepare phase while simultaneously serving as precommit phase for leader1. By extension, *leader*2 generates a new *PrepareQC* and sends it to *leader*3 of subsequent view. This marks the beginning of prepare phase of *leader*3, commit phase of *leader*1 and precommit phase of *leader*2.

Consequently, the consensus process for an operation set (*cmd*) is collaboratively achieved over three views. This can be comprehended as a complete consensus for a *cmd* necessitating the generation of three block rounds. Each block comprises a *QC* and a *cmd*, with *cmd* consensus organized in a pipelined fashion. Specifically, the consensus processes for leaders and nonleaders are as follows:

Leader: Await *new_view* messages → Issue proposal → Wait for votes from other replicas → Send *new_view* message to the subsequent leader.

Nonleader: Await proposal from the leader → Examine *QC*, as well as update local variables such as *PrepareQC* and *LockedQC* → Vote → Send *new_view* message to the next leader.

The rules for updating variables are elucidated in detail below. If a block *b* is sequentially followed by *k* blocks, this blockchain segment is designated as a k-chain for block *b*. Owing to pipelined consensus mechanism of Chained HotStuff, for a new block, nodes inspect for the formation of 1-chain, 2-chain, or 3-chain. Upon detecting a 1-chain status indicating the creation of a new *PrepareQC*, nodes are required to refresh their local *PrepareQC*. Similarly, a 2-chain status signifies the establishment of a new *PrecommitQC* and prompts nodes to update their local *LockedQC* accordingly. Last, a 3-chain status indicates the emergence of a new *CommitQC*. As an incoming *cmd* enters the commit phase with this fresh information, nodes proceed to execute specific transaction details.

4.5.6 VaaP

Votes-as-a-Proof (VaaP) (Fu, Wang, and Shi 2022, pp. 4964–4973) is tailored for consortium blockchains, prioritizing high transaction processing efficiency and scalability. In VaaP, each node maintains its own block chain. At the onset of a consensus round, a node compiles its transactions into blocks and simultaneously gathers votes from other nodes. Consensus on a block is achieved when a node generates a proof indicating that over 2/3 of the nodes have validated the block. In VaaP, every node executes a straightforward consensus process based on voting concurrently. If a node is faulty, it only impacts its own access to the consensus service without affecting the overall consensus process.

In a consortium blockchain setup, each node creates and maintains its own blockchain, with blocks added in parallel. Every node possesses a complete copy of all blockchains and can serve as a leader for its own blockchain or act as a replica of others' blockchains. As illustrated in Figure 4.48, all blockchains operate independently and expand autonomously. Block addition occurs through voting rounds for each blockchain. In each round, the leader is tasked with generating a block containing its transactions, gathering votes for the block, and appending it to its respective blockchain. The remaining nodes function as replicas, voting for legitimate blocks.

Nodes in the system are categorized as correct or faulty, with faulty nodes falling into two types: crash or Byzantine. Crash nodes may experience message delivery failures, while Byzantine nodes exhibit arbitrary behavior. VaaP, as a blockchain consensus protocol, is designed to be Byzantine fault-tolerant and assumes the presence of at most f Byzantine nodes among $N = \{N_1, N_2, ..., N_{3f+1}\}$ full nodes in the network. The protocol aims to ensure that the number of Byzantine nodes

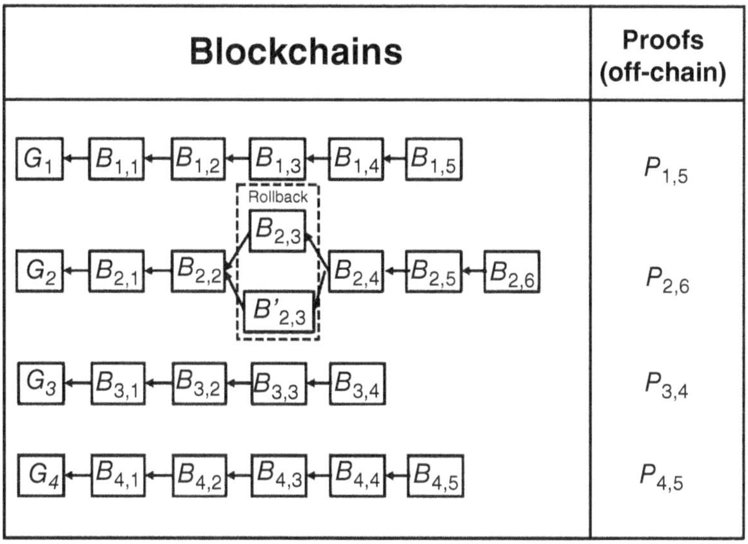

Figure 4.48 The chain structure of VaaP.

remains below 1/3 of the total node count. Additionally, VaaP assumes a strong adversary capable of coordinating Byzantine nodes to disrupt consensus service.

Correct nodes will not vote for a forked blockchain. When a correct node serves as the leader, achieving consensus requires more than half of the votes, namely $\lfloor (n-1)/2 \rfloor + 1$ including the leader, representing the majority. However, in cases where the leader is faulty, it may introduce a fork by generating two conflicting blocks (B and $B^{'}$) and distributing one to some replicas while sending the other to the remaining replicas. In such scenarios, faulty nodes may vote for both blocks. To ensure safety, it's crucial to ensure that at most one of the two blocks can achieve consensus. According to quorum theory, the number of votes required for a block to reach consensus is $2f + 1$.

Specifically, consensus for a block is achieved via two voting rounds: the prepare and commit phases. Block generation occurs at regular intervals, and there is no distinction in voting between the two phases. As a result, the consensus process is structured to be pipelined: the commit phase for a block also serves as the prepare phase for the subsequent block.

More precisely, depicted in Figure 4.49, the consensus mechanism for each node operates in a fully asynchronous manner. Each node assumes the dual role of being the leader of its own blockchain and a replica of the blockchains maintained by other nodes.

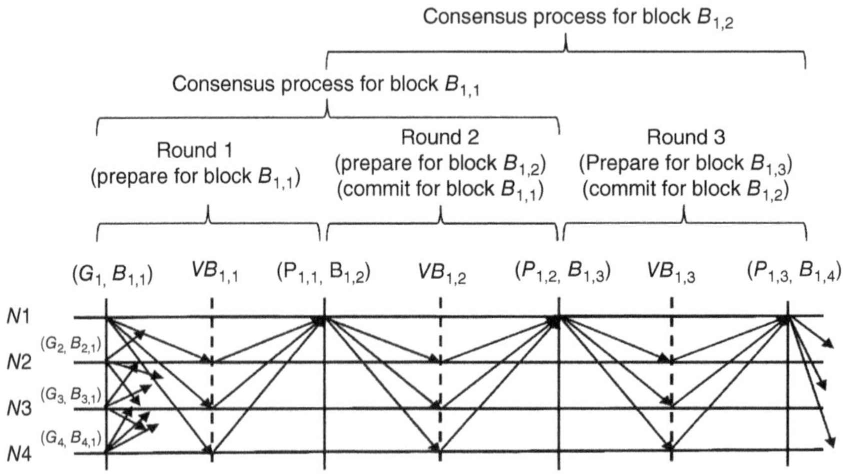

Figure 4.49 The pipeline confirmation consensus process.

4.5.6.1 Processing at Leader

In each round, the leader $N_i(1 \leq i \leq 3f+1)$ initiates by assembling its transactions into a block. The structure of a block $B_{i,j}$ is illustrated in Figure 4.50. Typically, there exists only one block at a specific block-height. The blockchain's block-height increases monotonically. The pre-hash denotes the hash of the preceding block, while the timestamp indicates the block's generation time. All transactions included in a given block are exclusively generated by its corresponding creator. Optionally, the leader can append the block-heights of other nodes from its viewpoint, aiding replicas in validating the block. With the block-heights of other nodes provided, replicas can validate the block based on the leader's perspective. Otherwise, they must validate the block based on their own perspective, potentially leading to disparate validation outcomes among nodes.

Subsequently, the leader distributes the block $B_{i,j}$ to all replicas and awaits their votes. Once it has gathered no fewer than $2f+1$ votes, including its own, the leader generates the proof $P_{i,j}$ demonstrating that $B_{i,j}$ has been validated by over 2/3 of all nodes. This concludes the prepare phase of $B_{i,j}$. The leader then initiates the commit phase of $B_{i,j}$ and the prepare phase of $B_{i,j+1}$ by sending $P_{i,j}$ and $B_{i,j+1}$ to the replicas. The consensus process of $B_{i,j}$ is finalized when the leader obtains no fewer than $2f+1$ votes for $B_{i,j+1}$, indicating that no fewer than $2f+1$ nodes have received $P_{i,j}$. The pseudo-code outlining the leader's actions is illustrated in Algorithm 4.9.

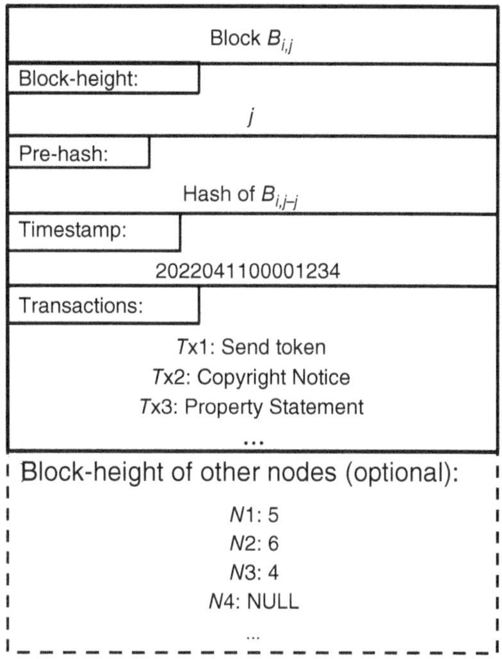

Figure 4.50 The block structure of VaaP.

Algorithm 4.9 The Algorithm Runs in the Node as a Leader

```
while The node N_i has transactions to send && P_(i,j-1)
  of B_(i,j-1) is generated do
   Package the transactions into a new block B_(i,j) and
   connect it to B_(i,j-1) on its blockchain;
   Broadcast B_(i,j) and P_(i,j-1) to other nodes;
   while The number of votes < 2f+1 do
      Collect votes VB_(i,j) from other nodes;
   end while
   Generate a proof P_(i,j) for B_(i,j) and add B_(i,j)
   to its Blockchain;
end while
```

4.5.6.2 Processing at Replicas

A correct replica $N_k(1 \leq k \leq 3f+1,\ k \neq i)$ receives blocks and proofs from other nodes and votes for these blocks after validating them. Block $B_{i,j}$ is considered valid if it meets the following criteria:

1) All transactions within $B_{i,j}$ are legal.

2) $B_{i,j}$ is signed by N_i, ensuring its authenticity.
3) $P_{i,j-1}$ is legal, confirming that $B_{i,j-1}$ is prepared.
4) The timestamp of $B_{i,j}$ falls within an acceptable error range. (The error between the timestamp and the local system time is less than t.)
5) N_k has not voted for any block in block-height j from N_i.

Algorithm 4.10 presents the pseudo-code for the node as a replica.

Algorithm 4.10 The Algorithm Runs in the Node as a Replica

```
while The node N_k receives B_(i,j) and P_(i,j-1) from
  N_i (k ≠ i) do
  Validate B_(i,j) and P_(i,j-1);
  if B_(i,j) and P_(i,j-1) pass the validation then
     Send a vote  to N_i;
  else
      Delete B_(i,j) and P_(i,j-1);
  continue
  end if
end while
```

To optimize storage, proofs are not retained on the blockchain. Additionally, for each chain, only the latest proof is required to be stored. This implies that a node can discard old proofs after receiving the latest one. It's important to note that if a block $B_{i,j}$ does not include the block-height of any other nodes (as depicted by the dotted line zone in Figure 4.50), the transactions within $B_{i,j}$ can be verified based on the replica's perspective itself. However, if $B_{i,j}$ contains the block-height of another node (as indicated by the "block-height of other nodes" zone in a block), the transactions must be validated based on the perspective provided by the block generator. For instance, if $B_{i,j}$ includes the block height of N_k, which is m, it signifies that transactions in $B_{i,j}$ must not conflict with those in $B_{k,x} (x \leq m)$, otherwise $B_{i,j}$ is considered illegal. The "block-height of other nodes" zone in a block furnishes a "world state" of the block generator, serving as a prerequisite for the block's legitimacy. Hence, replicas must obtain all blocks representing the "world state" of the block generator before validating the block (any missing blocks can be requested from neighboring nodes).

As described above, confirming a block involves two phases: the prepare phase, where the proof is received, and the commit phase, where the proof is stored by over 2/3 of all nodes. A node can ascertain the confirmation status of a block solely based on its local blockchain data. The prepare phase is easily verified by examining the signatures of the voters. However, to validate the commit phase, a node must await the proof of the next block, as a vote for $B_{i,j}$ from N_k indicates that the proof $P_{i,j-1}$ has already been obtained by N_k. Consequently, there's no necessity for nodes to communicate with each other to confirm a block.

In summary, VaaP stands out as a consensus protocol tailored for consortium blockchains, offering high throughput, scalability, and low latency. Its consensus process is straightforward: gathering votes from the majority. While Byzantine faulty nodes might marginally affect performance, they cannot compromise the system's safety and liveness. Faulty nodes only hinder their own access to the consensus service since each node collects votes for its own blocks. Moreover, VaaP is deliberately crafted to be easily understandable and straightforward to implement.

4.6 Evaluation and Analysis of Blockchain Consensus

So far, extensive research has been conducted in the field of consensus algorithms, leading to a continuous emergence of novel algorithms. Some offer incremental improvements over existing ones, while others introduce substantial changes and innovative approaches. This chapter aims to review the development of mainstream consensus algorithms and provide an evaluative analysis from both algorithmic and systemic perspectives.

4.6.1 Evolution

This section categorizes the development of blockchain consensus into three main lines, as shown in Figure 4.51. The first encompasses a series of voting-based consensus algorithms derived from BFT. The second comprises a sequence of proof-based consensus algorithms derived from PoW. The third introduces novel consensus algorithms integrating both proof and voting first proposed by the authors of this monography. Subsequently, we will present each of these three development main lines in turn.

4.6.1.1 Main Line One: Development of Voting-Based Consensus

In 1982, Lamport et al. proposed the famous Byzantine Generals Problem and suggested two solutions: the BFT consensus algorithms based on oral and signed messages. However, due to their high communication complexity, respectively $O(n^m)$ and $O(nm)$, they are difficult to use. In 1999, Castro and Liskov proposed the PBFT consensus algorithm, which was further improved in 2002. PBFT assumes an asynchronous network and reduces the communication complexity of the BFT consensus algorithm to $O(n^2)$ by adopting a master–slave backup design. To address Byzantine fault tolerance concerns, PBFT also designed a subprotocol for switching the primary node when it becomes abnormal, ensuring that switches caused by

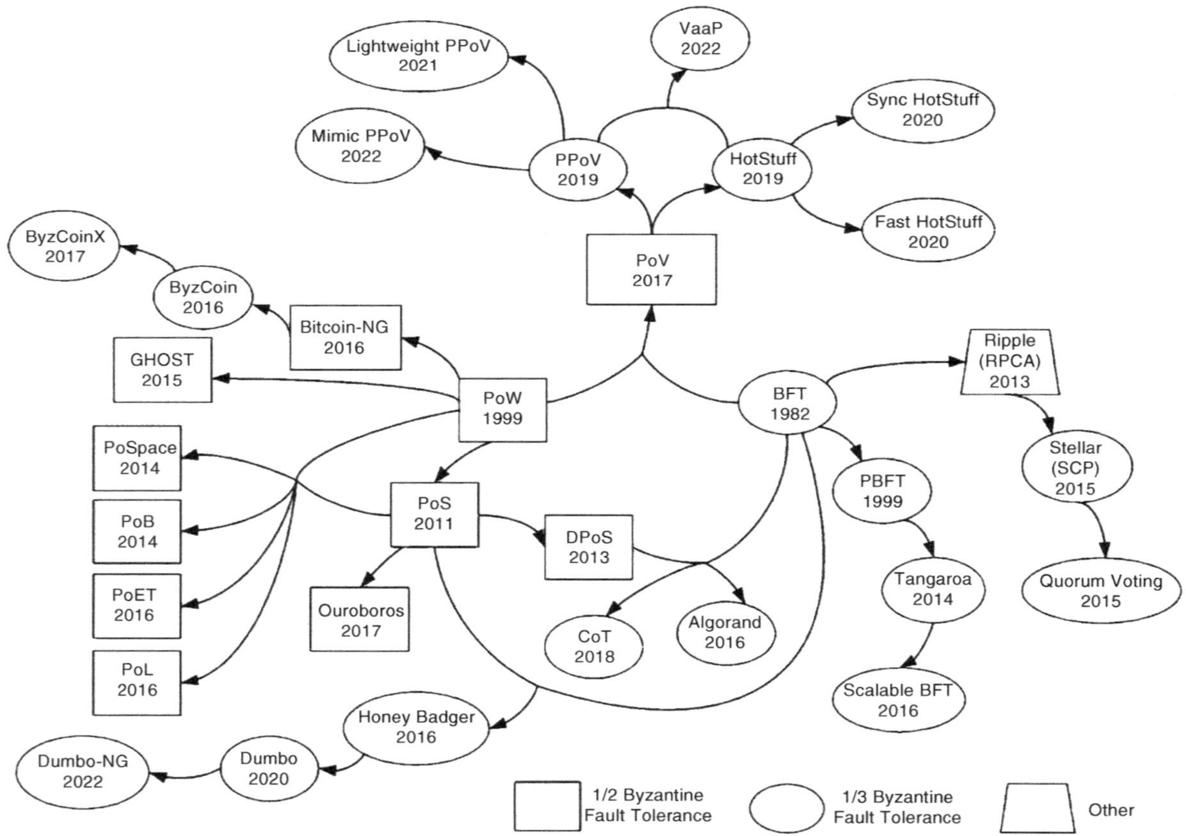

Figure 4.51 Evolutionary trajectory of consensus algorithms.

Byzantine behaviors will not deactivate the cluster. Either the original PBFT in 1999 or its optimization in 2002 requires collecting a large number of historical consensus message logs and completing safe master node switchover through complex information exchange and message verification. In an optimal situation, the communication complexity of completing the switch would require $O(n^3)$. In 2014, Christopher Copeland et al. improved Raft by combining it with PBFT and proposed the Tangaroa algorithm (Copeland and Zhong 2016). Tangaroa inherits Raft's characteristics of simplicity and ease of understanding while possessing Byzantine fault tolerance. Later, the Scalable BFT (Jalalzai, Busch, and Richard 2019, pp. 308–313) algorithm, inspired by Tangaroa, demonstrated better performance than Tangaroa in subsequent developments.

In 2013, Ripple (RPCA) proposed utilizing a subnetwork of collective trust to implement low-latency and highly robust Byzantine fault-tolerant consensus. Subsequently, Stellar (SCP) was introduced as an advancement of Ripple, incorporating elements from the BFT algorithms, thus establishing itself as the pioneering consensus protocol with proven security. In 2015, the Quorum Voting algorithm was proposed as an extension of Ripple and SCPs to enable immediate transaction status determination.

4.6.1.2 Main Line Two: Development of Proof-Based Consensus

Since the inception of Bitcoin in 2008, a plethora of blockchains utilizing proof-based consensus algorithms have emerged continuously. PoW is a pioneering solution to address the Byzantine fault tolerance problem in Internet-scale distributed systems. It achieves consensus through competition in computing power to ensure data consistency while maintaining the security and decentralization. However, it results in significant power resource consumption. In 2015, Israeli scholars Yonatan and Aviv proposed GHOST, which ensures high throughput while maintaining security. Furthermore, protocols such as Bitcoin-NG and its optimization called ByzCoin (Kogias et al. 2016, pp. 279–296), as well as ByzCoinX (Kokoris-Kogias et al. 2018, pp. 583–598) with sharding technology enhance the scalability of blockchain systems from various perspectives.

In 2011, PoS was proposed based on proof and stake that partially addressed the issue of power resource consumption associated with PoW. In 2013, DPoS was proposed as an enhanced version of PoS. The primary distinction between the two lies in how bookkeeping rights are obtained: while PoS relies on the number and duration of coins held by a node, DPoS delegates these rights to bookkeepers through stakeholder voting, resembling a representative mechanism in politics. Consequently, DPoS enhances scalability compared to PoS but reduces decentralization. Later, Algorand (Chen and Micali 2019, pp. 155–183) and CoT were proposed based on the ideas of DPoS and BFT. Algorand is a blockchain protocol proposed by Silvio Micali et al. in 2016. The name "Algorand" combines "algorithm" and "random," representing a consensus protocol based on a random algorithm. Algorand aims to create a distributed ledger that is low-energy, scalable, and decentralized. CoT selects nodes with high trust degrees as representatives according to the trust relationships between them, essentially reflecting the concept of transferring trust relationships in human society. Ouroboros, introduced in 2017 by Kiayias et al., is the first PoS consensus protocol with provable security.

In 2016, Miller et al. proposed Honey Badger (Miller et al. 2016, pp. 31–42), the first practical asynchronous BFT consensus algorithm. By introducing multiple rounds of random numbers, the algorithm enables each node to achieve consensus results with high probability after repeating multiple rounds of consensus. Additionally, as an asynchronous consensus algorithm, Honey Badger does not have a specific master node. In each consensus round, every node can initiate a proposal and the commitment of each round is composed of final selected proposals. To improve efficiency, each node packages a slice of transactions to prevent duplicate transactions. However, since the asynchronous BFT consensus algorithm requires multiple repeated rounds of consensus before obtaining commitment results, it has high latency which becomes particularly evident in wide-area networks where the consensus delay exceeds 1 minute in certain scenarios. In 2020, Dumbo (Guo et al. 2020, pp. 803–818) identified that the limited performance in Honey Badger primarily stemmed from increased running time caused by numerous randomized submodule calls. It then conducted targeted optimizations and significantly reduced algorithmic delays thereby making the asynchronous BFT algorithm practically applicable. Dumbo-NG (Gao et al. 2022, pp. 1187–1201) represents further improvements over Dumbo.

4.6.1.3 Main Line Three: Development of Consensus Integrating Proof and Voting

As the first consensus algorithm which integrates proof and voting, PoV was proposed in 2017. Compared with consensus algorithms such as PoW and PoS, PoV eliminates the reliance on computing power, resulting in shorter latency and higher throughput. In terms of security, just more than half of properly functioning voters and at least one honest bookkeeper in the network ensure continuous operation of the PoV consensus process without forks. The network communication complexity of PoV is only $O(N_\upsilon)$, which is significantly lower than PBFT's $O\left(N_{all}^2\right)$. In 2019, PPoV was proposed as an improved version of PoV. It enhances both the data structure and consensus process by allowing multiple bookkeepers to generate blocks simultaneously and optimizes the overall throughput of the blockchain system. Subsequently, Lightweight PPoV and Mimic PPoV consensus algorithms were successively proposed.

In 2019, Yin et al. proposed HotStuff, a chained BFT consensus algorithm utilizing aggregate signatures. The main contribution of HotStuff lies in achieving linear communication complexity for view change. According to this algorithm, a proposal can only be submitted after three rounds of interaction. Although it slightly increases delay, this design simplifies the complex process of view change in PBFT and facilitates practical implementation. Subsequently, improvement algorithms like Sync HotStuff and Fast HotStuff were proposed. In particular, both ideas of parallelization in PPoV and pipelining in HotStuff are concurrently manifested within VaaP.

4.6.2 Evaluation and Comparison

The consensus algorithms of blockchain can be classified from multiple dimensions. As previously mentioned, according to the consensus principle, they can be divided into voting-based consensus, proof-based consensus, and their integration. Furthermore, they can also be divided into BFT consensus and non-BFT consensus based on fault tolerance type; public blockchain consensus, consortium blockchain consensus, and private blockchain consensus based on deployment mode. Additionally, considering the degree of consistency, they can also be distinguished as strong consistent consensus and weak or final consistent consensus. According to the hypothesis of network model, consensus algorithms can be divided into three categories: synchronous network consensus, partially synchronous network consensus and asynchronous network consensus, of which the partially synchronous network model is the most commonly used model of blockchain consensus mechanism.

Referring to these classification dimensions, this section divides current mainstream consensus algorithms into three categories based on differences in application scenarios, node permissions, and fault tolerance. These categories include permissionless blockchain consensus with full decentralization, BFT variant consensus, and non-BFT consensus based on traditional distributed agreement algorithms. Each category makes distinct compromises to achieve consensus on the state of blockchains. Specifically, permissionless blockchain consensus algorithms sacrifice external resources such as computing power in PoW for consistency, which is often used in public blockchains. BFT variant consensus algorithms obtain consistency through multiple phases involving proposal and commitment. Non-BFT consensus algorithms balance consistency and security by restricting permissions and establishing trusted environments. Table 4.1 shows a comparison of their features, where note [Syn] indicates the synchronous network consensus algorithm and the uncommented algorithms are the partially synchronous network consensus algorithms.

Furthermore, many blockchain systems have designed consensus algorithms unique to specific scenarios. A comprehensive evaluation of these consensus algorithms from a system perspective is presented in Table 4.2.

Table 4.1 Comparative analysis of mainstream consensus algorithms.

Consensus classification	Permissionless blockchain consensus	BFT variant consensus	Non-BFT consensus
Mainstream algorithm	PoW, Bitcoin-NG, GHOST, PoS, DPoS, Ouroboros	PBFT, RPCA[Syn], SCP[Syn], CoT, PoV, PPoV, Lightweight PPoV, Mimic PPoV, HotStuff, VaaP	Paxos, Raft
Decentralization degree	Strong	Middle	Weak
Suitable deployment mode	Public blockchain	Public blockchain, Consortium blockchain, Private blockchain	Consortium blockchain, Private blockchain
Authentication requirement	No	Yes	Yes
Token requirement	Yes	Unnecessary	No
Free to join or exit	Yes	Depend on node role	Depend on node role
Consistency	Yes	Yes	Yes
Supported network scale	Large	Middle	Middle
Regulatory	Weak	Middle	Strong
Efficiency performance	High latency and low throughput	Low latency and high throughput	Low latency and high throughput
Finality	No	Probabilistic	Yes
Resource consumption	High	Low	Low
Fault tolerance	Allow server failures, and accommodate the presence of malicious nodes possessing no more than 50% of computational power	Allow server failures, but the fault tolerance of malicious nodes varies depending on different algorithms	Allow server failures, but prohibit malicious nodes

4.7 Chapter Summary

This chapter commences by exploring the concepts of distributed systems and agreement issues, elucidating the theoretical foundation of blockchain consensus.

Table 4.2 Evaluation of consensus algorithms from the perspective of blockchain systems.

Blockchain system	Open source	Consensus resource	Strong consistency	Security: DoS attack resilience	Security: Adversary model	Performance: Throughput	Performance: Scalability	Performance: Latency	Experimental environment
Hyperledger	✓	Permission	✓	●	33%	1,000–2,000[a]	✗	<1s[a]	Real
Ripple	✓	Permission	✓	●	20%	3,400	✗	—	Real
Stellar	✓	Permission	✓	●	33%	-	✗	—	—
Bitcoin	✓	PoW	✗	●	50%	7	✗	600s	Real
Bitcoin-NG	✗	PoW	✗	◐	50%	7	✗	<1s	Real
GHOST	✗	PoW	✗	●	50%	—	✗	—	—
ByzCoin	✓	PoW	✓	◐	33%	1,000[b]	✗	10–20s[b]	Real
Solidus	✗	PoW	✓	◐	33%	—	—	—	—
Blackcoin	✓	PoS	✗	●	50%	—	—	64s	Real
EOS	✓	PoS	✗	●	50%	—	—	0.5s	Real
Ouroboros	✗	Lottery	✗	●	50%	257.6[c]	✗	20s	Simulation
Algorand	✗	Lottery	✓	●	33%	90[d]	✗	40s[d]	Real
RSCoin	✓	Permission	✓	●	33%	2,000[e]	✓	<1s[e]	Real
Elastico	✗	PoW	✓	●	33%	16 blocks in 110s[f]	✓	110s for 16 blocks[f]	Real
Omniledger	✗	PoW	✓	●	33%	≈10,000[g]	✓	≈1s[g]	Real
Chainspace	✓	—	✓	◐	33%	350[h]	✓	<1s[h]	Real

(*Continued*)

Table 4.2 (Continued)

Blockchain system	Open source	Consensus resource	Strong consistency	Security: DoS attack resilience	Security: Adversary model	Performance: Throughput	Performance: Scalability	Performance: Latency	Performance: Experimental environment
Diem	✓	Vote	✓	●	33%	1,000	✓	—	Real
PPoV	✓	Vote	✓	●	33%	30,000[i]	✓	<5s	Real
Praos	✗	PoS	✗	◐	50%	—	—	—	—
Snow-White	✗	PoS	✗	◐	50%	100–150[c]	✓	—	Simulation
PermaCoin	✓	PoW	✗	●	50%	—	✗	—	—
SpaceMint	✓	PoS	✗	●	50%	—	✗	600s	Simulation
Intel PoET	✓	TH	✗	●	TH	1,000[j]	✓	—	Real
REM	✗	TH	✗	●	TH	—	✓	—	Real
DECORHOP	✗	PoW	✗	●	50%	30	✗	60s	Simulation
Specter	✗	PoW	✗	●	50%	—	✗	—	—

[a] 2 peer ndoes and 2 orderer nodes.
[b] 144 nodes/committee.
[c] 3 nodes/committee. 10 committees.
[d] 100 nodes/committee. 16 committees.
[e] 72 nodes/committee (12.5% adversary). 25 committees.
[f] 4 nodes/committee. 15 committees.
[g] 4 nodes.
[h] 40 nodes.
[i] 50 k nodes/committee.
[j] Trusted hardware.

Then, it discusses prominent blockchain consensus algorithms, including voting-based and proof-based consensus, as well as their integration. Voting-based consensus algorithms have evolved from traditional distributed agreement protocols where a node must possess knowledge about a certain threshold number of nodes in a consensus round. Proof-based consensus algorithms are unique to blockchain. They reduce the probability of malicious nodes by increasing the cost of misbehavior while also adjusting block generation difficulty to ensure relative fairness among nodes and avoid network congestion caused by competitive bookkeeping. Consensus algorithms integrating proof and voting combine the advantages of both categories by allocating permissions to representative nodes, thereby achieving large-scale scalability. Finally, we analyze and contrast the attributes of various consensus algorithms, evaluating them from a holistic system perspective with an aim to assist developers in designing and optimizing efficient, secure, and scalable blockchains.

Discussion Questions

4.1 Discuss the differences between voting-based consensus and proof-based consensus algorithms.

A: Voting-based consensus algorithms, derived from traditional distributed agreement protocols, require all nodes in the network to jointly validate blocks and transactions. They determine the inclusion of a proposed block on-chain through mutual information exchanges. In almost all these variants, the number of nodes a participant needs to observe during a consensus round must exceed a certain threshold to tolerate faults. Conversely, proof-based consensus algorithms are exclusive to blockchain technology. The approach to solving the Byzantine generals problem is to increase the cost of malfeasance to reduce the probability of malicious nodes emerging. As a result, in blockchains with weak trust assurances, proof-based consensus algorithms generally outperform voting-based ones in terms of scalability, fairness, and security.

4.2 Provide a concise overview of the distinctions between Bitcoin-NG and GHOST's enhancements to PoW.

A: The PoW consensus requires all nodes in the network to solve a cryptographic puzzle with dynamically adjusted difficulty. The first node to solve it gains the right to add a block to the current chain. One of the significant obstacles to implementing PoW lies in its limited throughput and high latency. Bitcoin-NG improves performance by dividing the consensus process into leader election and transaction serialization. On the other hand, the

GHOST algorithm reduces the time to write new blocks on the chain by retaining blocks not selected for inclusion in the main chain in a tree structure. In contrast to PoW's longest main chain rule, nodes select as their main chain path with maximum total weight, where each block's weight is determined by its subtree density.

4.3 Provide a concise overview of the distinctions among PoV, PPoV, Lightweight PPoV, and Mimic PPoV, highlighting their respective characteristics.

A: The PoV consensus principally divides the rights of consensus nodes within the blockchain network into bookkeeping and voting, both collaborating to generate blocks. The PPoV consensus enhances the data structure and flow of consensus in PoV, enabling multiple bookkeepers to simultaneously generate blocks for increased throughput. Lightweight PPoV further compresses data at each phase of the consensus process to achieve a lightweight purpose. Mimic PPoV draws inspiration from the dynamic heterogeneous redundancy architecture concept utilized in mimic defense, aiming to strengthen the inherent security of blockchain systems.

References

Bai, Y., Zhi, Y., Li, H., Wang, H., Lu, P. and Ma, C., 2021, March. On parallel mechanism of consortium blockchain: Take pov as an example. In 2021 The 3rd International Conference on Blockchain Technology (pp. 147–154).

Cachin, C., 2016, July. Architecture of the hyperledger blockchain fabric. In Workshop on distributed cryptocurrencies and consensus ledgers (Vol. 310, No. 4, pp. 1–4).

Castro, M. and Liskov, B., 1999, February. Practical byzantine fault tolerance. In OsDI (Vol. 99, No. 1999, pp. 173–186).

Chen, J. and Micali, S., 2019. Algorand: A secure and efficient distributed ledger. *Theoretical Computer Science*, 777, pp. 155–183.

Chen, L., Xu, L., Shah, N., Gao, Z., Lu, Y. and Shi, W., 2017. On security analysis of proof-of-elapsed-time (poet). In Stabilization, Safety, and Security of Distributed Systems: 19th International Symposium, SSS 2017, Boston, MA, USA, November 5–8, 2017, Proceedings 19 (pp. 282–297). Springer International Publishing.

Copeland, C. and Zhong, H., 2016. Tangaroa: A byzantine fault tolerant raft.

Dziembowski, S., Faust, S., Kolmogorov, V. and Pietrzak, K., 2015, August. Proofs of space. In Annual Cryptology Conference (pp. 585–605). Berlin, Heidelberg: Springer Berlin Heidelberg.

Eyal, I., Gencer, A.E., Sirer, E.G. and Van Renesse, R., 2016. {Bitcoin-NG}: A scalable blockchain protocol. In 13th USENIX symposium on networked systems design and implementation (NSDI 16) (pp. 45–59).

Fischer, M.J., Lynch, N.A. and Paterson, M.S., 1985. Impossibility of distributed consensus with one faulty process. *Journal of the ACM (JACM)*, 32(2), pp. 374–382.

Fu, X., Wang, H. and Shi, P., 2022. Votes-as-a-Proof (VaaP): Permissioned blockchain consensus protocol made simple. *IEEE Transactions on Parallel and Distributed Systems*, 33(12), pp. 4964–4973.

Gao, Y., Lu, Y., Lu, Z., Tang, Q., Xu, J. and Zhang, Z., 2022, November. Dumbo-ng: Fast asynchronous bft consensus with throughput-oblivious latency. In Proceedings of the 2022 ACM SIGSAC Conference on Computer and Communications Security (pp. 1187–1201).

Ghosh, M., Richardson, M., Ford, B. and Jansen, R., 2014, July. A TorPath to TorCoin: Proof-of-bandwidth altcoins for compensating relays. In Workshop on Hot Topics in Privacy Enhancing Technologies (HotPETs).

Guo, B., Lu, Z., Tang, Q., Xu, J. and Zhang, Z., 2020, October. Dumbo: Faster asynchronous bft protocols. In Proceedings of the 2020 ACM SIGSAC Conference on Computer and Communications Security (pp. 803–818).

Jalalzai, M.M., Busch, C. and Richard, G.G., 2019, July. Proteus: A scalable BFT consensus protocol for blockchains. In 2019 IEEE international conference on Blockchain (Blockchain) (pp. 308–313). IEEE.

Kiayias, A., Russell, A., David, B. and Oliynykov, R., 2017, July. Ouroboros: A provably secure proof-of-stake blockchain protocol. In Annual International Cryptology Conference (pp. 357–388). Cham: Springer International Publishing.

King, S. and Nadal, S., 2012. Ppcoin: Peer-to-peer crypto-currency with proof-of-stake. Self-published paper, August, 19(1).

Kogias, E.K., Jovanovic, P., Gailly, N., Khoffi, I., Gasser, L. and Ford, B., 2016. Enhancing bitcoin security and performance with strong consistency via collective signing. In 25th USENIX Security Symposium (USENIX Security 16) (pp. 279–296).

Kokoris-Kogias, E., Jovanovic, P., Gasser, L., Gailly, N., Syta, E. and Ford, B., 2018, May. Omniledger: A secure, scale-out, decentralized ledger via sharding. In 2018 IEEE symposium on security and privacy (SP) (pp. 583–598). IEEE.

Lamport, L., 2019. The part-time parliament. In Concurrency: The Works of Leslie Lamport (pp. 277–317).

Lamport, L., Shostak, R. and Pease, M., 2019. The Byzantine generals problem. In Concurrency: The Works of Leslie Lamport (pp. 203–226).

Li, K., Li, H., Hou, H., Li, K. and Chen, Y., 2017, December. Proof of vote: A high-performance consensus protocol based on vote mechanism & consortium blockchain. In 2017 IEEE 19th International Conference on High Performance Computing and Communications; IEEE 15th International Conference on Smart

City; IEEE 3rd International Conference on Data Science and Systems (HPCC/SmartCity/DSS) (pp. 466–473). IEEE.

Li, C., Li, P., Zhou, D., Xu, W., Long, F. and Yao, A., 2018. Scaling nakamoto consensus to thousands of transactions per second. arXiv preprint arXiv:1805.03870.

Lv, S., Li, H., Wang, H. and Wang, X., 2020. CoT: A secure consensus of trust with delegation mechanism in blockchains. In Blockchain Technology and Application: Second CCF China Blockchain Conference, CBCC 2019, Chengdu, China, October 11–13, 2019, Revised Selected Papers 2 (pp. 104–120). Springer Singapore.

Mazieres, D., 2015. The stellar consensus protocol: A federated model for internet-level consensus. *Stellar Development Foundation*, 32, pp. 1–45.

Miller, A., Xia, Y., Croman, K., Shi, E. and Song, D., 2016, October. The honey badger of BFT protocols. In Proceedings of the 2016 ACM SIGSAC Conference on Computer and Communications Security (pp. 31–42).

Milutinovic, M., He, W., Wu, H. and Kanwal, M., 2016, December. Proof of luck: An efficient blockchain consensus protocol. In Proceedings of the 1st Workshop on System Software for Trusted Execution (pp. 1–6).

Nakamoto, S., 2008. Bitcoin: A peer-to-peer electronic cash system. Decentralized business review.

Ongaro, D. and Ousterhout, J., 2014. In search of an understandable consensus algorithm. In 2014 USENIX Annual Technical Conference (USENIX ATC 14) (pp. 305–319).

Page, L., Brin, S., Motwani, R. and Winograd, T., 1998. The pagerank citation ranking: Bring order to the web. Technical report, Stanford University.

Schwartz, D., Youngs, N. and Britto, A., 2014. The ripple protocol consensus algorithm. *Ripple Labs Inc White Paper*, 5(8), p. 151.

Sompolinsky, Y. and Zohar, A., 2015. Secure high-rate transaction processing in bitcoin. In Financial Cryptography and Data Security: 19th International Conference, FC 2015, San Juan, Puerto Rico, January 26–30, 2015, Revised Selected Papers 19 (pp. 507–527). Springer Berlin Heidelberg.

Song, T.Y. and Zhao, Y., 2018. Comparison of blockchain consensus algorithm. *Computer Applications and Software*, 35(8), pp. 1–8.

Sukhwani, H., Martínez, J.M., Chang, X., Trivedi, K.S. and Rindos, A., 2017, September. Performance modeling of PBFT consensus process for permissioned blockchain network (hyperledger fabric). In 2017 IEEE 36th Symposium on Reliable Distributed Systems (SRDS) (pp. 253–255). IEEE.

Susskind, L.E., McKearnen, S. and Thomas-Lamar, J., 1999. *The consensus building handbook: A comprehensive guide to reaching agreement.* Sage Publications.

Wang, Z., Li, H., Wang, H., Xiao, Z., Lu, P., Yang, Z., Zhang, M. and Chong, P.H.J., 2021, December. A data lightweight scheme for parallel proof of vote consensus. In 2021 IEEE International Conference on Big Data (Big Data) (pp. 3656–3662). IEEE.

Wang, H., Li, H., Wang, Z., Zhao, F., Yao, Y., Chen, Y., Qin, T., Lu, P. and Shi, J., 2023, October. Optimizing read performance in lightweight blockchain with cooperative storage scheme. In 2023 Fifth International Conference on Blockchain Computing and Applications (BCCA) (pp. 150–157). IEEE.

Wicker, S.B. and Bhargava, V.K. eds., 1999. *Reed-Solomon codes and their applications.* John Wiley & Sons.

Xiao, Z., Li, H., Wang, H., Yang, G., Ye, Q., Zou, S., Lu, P. and Lyu, Q., 2022, December. Optimizing parallel proof of vote consensus based on mimic security in consortium blockchains. In 2022 IEEE International Conference on Big Data (Big Data) (pp. 3215–3224). IEEE.

Yin, M., Malkhi, D., Reiter, M.K., Gueta, G.G. and Abraham, I., 2019, July. HotStuff: BFT consensus with linearity and responsiveness. In Proceedings of the 2019 ACM Symposium on Principles of Distributed Computing (pp. 347–356).

5

Smart Contract and Its Security in Blockchain

Smart contracts are programs that run on the blockchain and play a vital role in advancing Web 3.0 across various areas such as the future network and digital finance. However, they encounter notable security vulnerabilities that could lead to potential threats and financial losses. In this chapter, an overview of the inherent vulnerability of smart contracts is provided, including typical vulnerabilities in smart contract applications, as well as vulnerabilities specific to Web 3.0 applications. After that, we systematically categorize technologies based on core methodologies for identifying vulnerabilities within smart contracts. Furthermore, we perform a comparative evaluation of existing tools, comparing their detection effectiveness, vulnerability coverage, integration capabilities, and open-source availability.

5.1 Concept of Smart Contracts

After the success of Bitcoin, which first proposed the concept of blockchain, Ethereum blockchain introduced smart contract technology. Smart contracts were first conceptualized in the 1990s by computer scientist Nick Szabo as a set of promises expressed in digital form. The definition of smart contracts changed somewhat after the advent of Ethereum, and the smart contracts studied in this chapter refer specifically to Ethereum smart contracts, which are computer programs that run on the EVM (Wang et al. 2019, pp. 136951–136961; Gupta et al. 2021, pp. 1877–1890). Ethereum has now evolved into one of the most popular blockchains in the world and boasts millions of smart contracts. As of April 2023, there are already over 430,899 verified smart contracts on the Ethereum blockchain.

Smart contracts have emerged as a widely used technology across diverse domains like the Internet of Things, supply chain finance, and network

Principles and Applications of Blockchain Systems: How to Overcome the CAP Trilemma in Consortium Blockchain, First Edition. Hui Li and Han Wang.

Published 2025 by John Wiley & Sons, Inc.

management due to their advantages of decentralization and programmability. In the field of network management, Multi-Identifier System (MIS) serves as the management layer for a future network called Multi-Identifier Network (MIN). It employs the identifier management contract based on EVM, offering enhanced rule-making functions and flexible identifier capabilities (Li and Yang 2021, p. 257). In addition, in the data layer, MIS supports the management of diverse identifier types including content, service, IP address, and hyperbolic routing, among others. At the consensus layer, MIS utilizes the Parallel Proof of Vote (PPoV) consensus algorithm to maintain a uniform global state, encompassing transaction and contract states (Wang et al. 2023a).

With the development of smart contract businesses on blockchain, many security problems are emerging. One notable incident occurred in June 2016, when a project called "The DAO" on the Ethereum blockchain suffered from a reentrancy vulnerability in its contract code, resulting in the unauthorized theft of millions of Ethereum coins valued at over $60 million. To recover the losses, Ethereum was compelled to undergo a hard fork. Another more serious incident was the Parity multi-signature wallet breach in 2017, which involved two attacks (Mehar et al. 2019, pp. 19–32). The first attack on Parity, an Ethereum wallet contract, was due to an overriding flaw in its code, which allowed attackers to steal around $30 million worth of ether. In the second attack, because a library contract had saved state and defined a self-destruct function, someone managed to make the library contract self-destruct, causing all wallet contracts that called the library contract to not work properly, resulting in about $150 million worth of ether locked in the contract. Security incidents caused by smart contracts are still emerging today. In 2022, there were a total of 116 security events related to vulnerabilities in smart contracts, constituting approximately 27% of the total number of security incidents within the blockchain domain, and the loss value exceeded $1.7 billion.

Vulnerabilities are common in traditional nonblockchain computer programs. However, when such flaws occur in smart contracts deployed on blockchains, as demonstrated above, the consequences can be far more severe. This is mainly because smart contracts tend to manage and preserve the digital currency on the blockchain, providing a strong incentive for attackers to attempt to steal the funds illegally, and also making contract owners liable for losses in the event of a security incident. At the same time, due to the public nature of blockchains, anyone can see the contracts that have been deployed on-chain, and attackers may even directly download and analyze the contract bytecode to identify vulnerabilities (Cao et al. 2022, pp. 1–21). As for the owner of a contract, there is no way to make any fixes to the deployed contract unless some scalable contract writing model is used before deployment. It is almost impossible to expect developers to write an absolutely secure contract since it requires not only extensive experience but also strong awareness to avoid vulnerable coding modes.

Therefore, it is imperative to investigate the vulnerability detection technology of smart contracts.

5.2 Vulnerability in Smart Contracts

An overview of vulnerabilities in traditional smart contracts is provided, concentrating on three different layers: the block layer, the EVM layer, and the Solidity layer, as noted in Ethereum. Furthermore, we explore distinct vulnerabilities that emerge within the realm of Web 3.0 applications, considering their respective properties.

5.2.1 Solidity Layer

Solidity is a high-level programming language for smart contracts, widely used in Ethereum and other EVM-compatible blockchain platforms. Developers use Solidity to write the logic and functionality of smart contracts, defining the contract's state variables, functions, and events, among others. Vulnerability detection at this layer focuses on logical issues, security vulnerabilities, and potential weaknesses in the contract code.

5.2.1.1 Reentrancy

The Reentrancy Attack exploits the characteristics of reentrant functions in the contract, which is a specific form of security vulnerability affecting smart contracts (Grossman et al. 2017, pp. 1–28). This attack maliciously controls the execution order of the contract through repeatedly calling the function of external address or another contract during the execution. By employing improper methods, the attacker can obtain unauthorized control over extra assets or carry out malicious activities.

5.2.1.2 Integer Error

Integer errors occurring in smart contracts involve sign errors, arithmetic errors, and truncation errors (Lai and Luo 2020, pp. 110–115). Arithmetic errors include scenarios such as modulus by a zero, division by a zero, and integer overflow. Like other programming languages, fixed-length representations for integers are defined within a specific range in Solidity. If the outcome of an integer operation surpasses this range, it leads to the error of integer overflow.

5.2.1.3 Exception Handling

Vulnerabilities related to exception handling in smart contracts refer to inadequate design or flaws in the implementation of contracts when handling erroneous or abnormal situations, which can result in unexpected outcomes or security risks

(Dwivedi et al. 2021, pp. 1–34). In cases where exceptional circumstances are encountered in a smart contract, if the mechanism for handling errors is insufficient or vulnerable, attackers can utilize these vulnerabilities to carry out malicious actions or interrupt the normal execution of the smart contracts.

5.2.1.4 Logical Error

The logical error refers to implementation or design errors in a smart contract that causes the contract to exhibit undesired or unexpected behavior under certain conditions (Zupan et al. 2020, pp. 73–98). These bugs stem from defects in the reasoning or logical structure within the contract, resulting in unexpected outcomes or inconsistencies during the execution of the contract.

5.2.1.5 Access Control

It refers to the flaw in the application's authorization check, which allows attackers to use some methods to bypass permission checks and access or operate other users or higher permissions after obtaining low-privilege user accounts.

5.2.1.6 Unchecked Call Return Value

When a smart contract invokes a function in another contract, if the function and parameter types do not match those of the called contract, the Fallback function in the contract will be called by default. Attackers can hide malicious operations in the Fallback function.

5.2.2 EVM Layer

EVM is the virtual machine of Ethereum, responsible for executing the bytecode of Ethereum smart contracts. At the EVM layer, the contract code is compiled into bytecode and executed in the virtual machine. Vulnerability detection at this level focuses on the execution flow of bytecode and the sequence of operations that may lead to abnormal behavior or vulnerabilities.

5.2.2.1 Short Address

Short Address Attack (Chen et al. 2019, pp. 37575–37586) is a kind of vulnerability in which attackers utilize the property of address encoding algorithms to disregard the last characters in the encoded string. Through the generation of a targeted encoded string that fully matches the prefix segment of a valid address, attackers mislead users into utilizing the address under the attacker's control for carrying out operations or sending funds. This kind of malicious action leads to abnormal functionalities or financial losses within the contract.

5.2.2.2 Tx.origin

Tx.origin acts as a global variable used to preserve the external account's address that initiated the current transaction. It represents the authentic initiator of the transaction, especially the account address that triggered the contract call (Ji et al. 2021, pp. 492–501). By exploiting the vulnerability of Tx.origin, attackers are able to mimic the intended contract invoker by utilizing Tx.origin and creating intermediary contracts. By utilizing this form of manipulation, attackers can carry out a Tx.origin vulnerability attack.

5.2.2.3 Call-Stack Overflow

Call-stack overflow happens when improper usage of local variables or recursive calls results in the depletion of the available call stack. Attackers can leverage the vulnerability to manipulate contracts or initiate attacks (Samreen and Alalfi 2021).

5.2.3 Block Layer

In the Ethereum network, smart contracts are deployed on-chain, and each block contains a set of transactions that may include the execution of the smart contracts. The execution outcome of the smart contract is influenced by factors like the consensus mechanism and transaction sequence within the blockchain. Vulnerability detection at the block layer can focus on issues such as the order of transactions, the impact of the consensus algorithm, and the potential inconsistencies in contract states.

5.2.3.1 Timestamp Dependency

Timestamps are commonly used to record the generation and execution time of contracts or transactions (Wang et al. 2023b, pp. 1–13). Attackers exploit the reliance of a contract on forthcoming timestamps to manipulate the execution order or modify the result by controlling the generation of future blocks or tampering with the system time.

5.2.3.2 Transaction Order Dependency

The transaction order dependency, also known as transaction ordering attack, is a kind of security vulnerability found in blockchain systems. The vulnerability stems from the intrinsic uncertainty in processing transaction orders. Attackers exploit this uncertainty to carry out malicious operations or obtain undue advantages.

5.2.3.3 Block Parameter Dependency

Block parameters have historically been utilized for various applications, such as generating random numbers, securing funds for a specific duration, and implementing conditional statements for time-dependent state changes. Miners have the ability to adjust timestamps slightly, which could pose significant risks if the wrong block timestamp is used in a smart contract.

5.2.4 Web 3.0 Vulnerabilities

Web 3.0 strives to create a secure network ecosystem built on blockchain technology, shared data, decentralization, and user-centricity. However, risks of network security have become more noticeable in this context as well. Several vulnerabilities unique to Web 3.0 applications are highlighted in the following section.

5.2.4.1 Identifier Verification

The identifier management (Wei et al. 2021, pp. 1–6) contract primarily handles write operations associated with identifiers, including registration, renewal, update, restoration, revocation, and deletion. For instance, each write operation requires registration of a username or identity verification of the source in MIS. However, attackers can manipulate the system by using a nonidentifiable owner's address as the recipient address for transfers, thus enabling the theft of funds.

5.2.4.2 Rent Tampering

Throughout the process of registering and renewing the identifier, users must make rent payments, while deleting the identifier leads to the remaining rent being returned to the owner's address. The rent value is directly linked to the duration of the lease. By leveraging the capability to manipulate the lease duration, attackers can extend the validity period of token without the need for rent payment, thus gaining profits from a rent amount that exceeds the inherent value of the token.

5.2.4.3 Single Oracle

Decentralized Finance (DeFi) encompasses a range of financial applications built on a decentralized and open platform, where all business processes are executed through on-chain interactions (Qin et al. 2021, pp. 3–32). Flash loans have emerged as a recently emerged type of unsecured lending in the DeFi ecosystem. They allow users to borrow funds from on-chain liquidity pools, with the condition of returning the borrowed amount together with a minimal transaction fee in the same transaction (Cao et al. 2021). Nonetheless, the vulnerability of flash loan products stems from relying on a single oracle, thereby exposing them to the potential risks of price manipulation. Attackers take advantage of the vulnerability by utilizing significant amounts of funds to buy certain tokens and intentionally boost their prices within a relatively short timeframe. Through controlling the token market, attackers exploit arbitrage chances for their personal benefit.

5.2.4.4 Sandwich Attack

In a sandwich attack, the attacker takes advantage of status or price fluctuations to insert their own transactions between two trades, thereby gaining undue economic benefits. This type of attack is frequently found in decentralized exchanges (DEX) and other smart contract platforms (Wu et al. 2023, pp. 37–49). Sandwich attacks can cause traders to execute transactions at unfavorable conditions or prices, leading to financial losses. The attack exploits the inherent lack of certainty in the transaction orders within the transaction pool and delays during the transaction execution, allowing attackers to rapidly generate profit.

5.3 Taxonomy of Approaches to Detecting Vulnerabilities

We conduct a comprehensive review and analysis of pertinent literature on the technology for detecting vulnerabilities in smart contracts, carefully selecting representative approaches for detection in this section. Based on their core methodologies, these approaches can be classified into six categories: symbolic execution, formal verification, fuzzing, taint analysis, machine learning, and improved integration of symbolic execution and machine learning.

5.3.1 Formal Verification

Formal verification is one of the important technologies for smart contract security analysis. At present, formal verification technology has been successfully employed in fields with high safety requirements such as nuclear power and aerospace. By applying formal methods to detect vulnerabilities in smart contracts, it becomes possible to impose normative constraints on the generation and execution of these contracts, thereby ensuring their credibility and reliability. Common formal verification methods include model checking and deductive verification. Model checking involves exhaustively exploring the state space by enumerating all possible states and systematically checking each one to verify whether a contract exhibits the desired properties. On the other hand, deductive verification relies on theorem proving. It utilizes logical formulas to describe the system and its properties and employs inference rules to prove that the system satisfies specific properties.

As an effective approach for deterministic verification of smart contracts, the formal verification method generally consists of the following steps, as shown in Figure 5.1. First, the input smart contract source code is converted into bytecode. Second, the source code and bytecode are modeled into a formal language and processed using mathematical and logical methods. Subsequently, Formal tools are

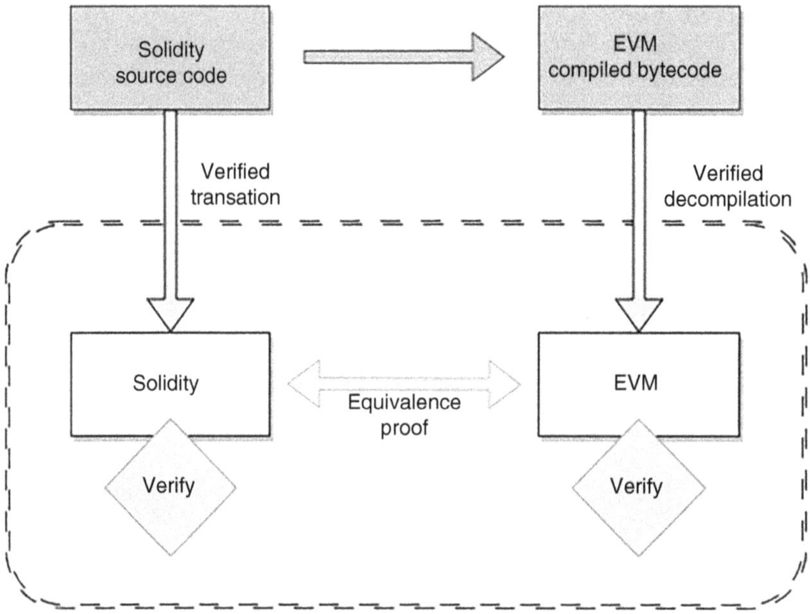

Figure 5.1 Conversion process between EVM bytecode and Solidity code in formal verification.

used to model, analyze, and verify the smart contract, perform semantic consistency testing, and finally generate verified contract code.

Based on the above steps, formal verification methods provide a comprehensive analysis of all potential states and execution paths within the system. By converting the concepts, judgments, and reasoning in the contract into a formal model, ambiguity and nonuniversality in the contract can be eliminated. Further, by integrating rigorous logic and proofs, both individual functions and the whole smart contract can undergo thorough correctness and security inspection.

In 2018, Grishchenko et al. (2018, pp. 243–269) first tried to formally describe Ethereum instructions in a functional programming language F∗ with interactive proof function, and then conducted program verification based on this language. Compared with traditional static analysis and dynamic testing, the F∗ framework provides higher accuracy and credibility with more vulnerabilities, while providing formal proof to support the correctness of the contract. Furthermore, in 2018, Albert et al. proposed EthIR (2018, pp. 513–520), an Ethereum bytecode analysis framework based on Oyente. They performed decompilation on the bytecode to generate a Rule-Based Representation (RBR). Then the control flow graph of the smart contract is constructed, and symbolic execution technology is used to analyze it. When a potential vulnerability in a contract is discovered, EthIR generates a vulnerability report that includes the type, location, and recommended fixes. Next, in response to the problem that existing smart contract vulnerability detection technology lacks accurate memory models and only partially supports inter-contract analysis, in 2020, Frank et al. proposed ETHBMC (2020, pp. 2757–2774), a bounded model checking technology on the basis of symbolic execution. They verified such vulnerabilities on private Ethereum networks, thereby mitigating false positives encountered during smart contract vulnerability detection.

5.3.2 Symbolic Execution

The symbolic execution method involves substituting the input parameters of the program with predefined symbols, followed by simulating the execution environment and traversing the path, known as symbolic execution. Throughout this process, the corresponding path constraints are maintained. After execution, use the constraint solver to solve the path constraints and find the possible values of the input parameters, which are the solutions to the constraints. In symbolic execution, control flow graphs are often constructed to help with program analysis.

As depicted in Figure 5.2, the process of symbolic execution method in smart contract vulnerability detection is: First, the variable values in the contract are symbolized. Then, the program instructions are interpreted and executed sequentially. During the interpretation process, the execution state is updated, and path constraints are collected. Next, the assembly code of the contract is executed step by step, while the current path is checked for the presence of specific vulnerability patterns based on predefined rules. Finally, a solver is employed to solve the path constraints and identify security issues.

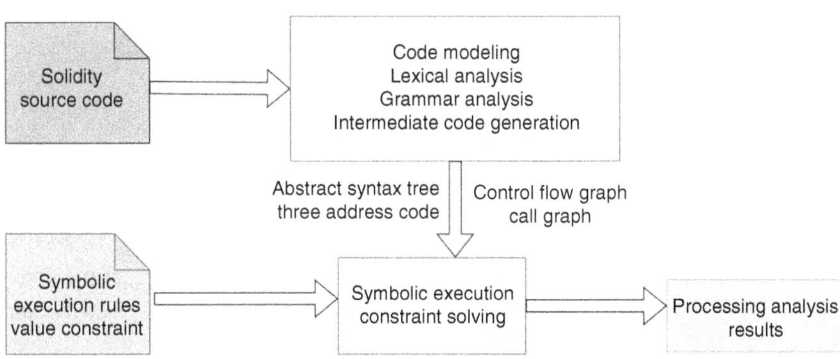

Figure 5.2 Flowchart of symbolic execution technique used in vulnerability analysis.

By using symbolic analysis, we can get a detailed vulnerability detection report. However, symbolic execution encounters challenges such as complex path expressions and explosion of execution paths. The number of paths increases exponentially with the growth of branches in the contract, which may lead to analysis timeout and a high false negative rate.

In 2016, Oyente (Luu et al. 2016, pp. 254–269) introduced the first technique for identifying vulnerabilities in smart contracts and proposed the first utilization of symbolic execution technology for this purpose. It analyzes symbol states and paths on the basis of the predefined attributes of four different vulnerabilities and performs reachability testing through the acquired constraints to minimize the false positive rate. Then, in 2018, Krupp and Rossow proposed teEther, a vulnerability exploit and detection technology based on symbolic execution (2018, pp. 1317–1333). It first finds the critical path to reach the four critical instructions from the control flow graph generated by bytecode, and then conducts symbolic execution from the root node of the control flow graph to obtain the path constraint. Finally, the Z3 constraint solver is used to address the combined limitations of the critical path and the state change path to generate vulnerability exploitation samples, so that the vulnerability in the contract can be detected more accurately by searching for sensitive instructions. Nikolić et al. proposed MAIAN (2018, pp. 653–663) to detect trace vulnerabilities in 2018 by using symbolic execution analysis and verifying execution based on specific path values. MAIAN uses a symbolic execution engine to perform symbolic analysis on all paths of the smart contract bytecode to detect whether there are paths that violate the activity or security of trace characteristics. In addition, in order to support the ERC-20 token standard, FSPVM (Yang et al. 2020, pp. 21411–21436) is proposed as a static analysis tool implemented in Coq. FSPVM symbolically analyzes the reliability code of Ethereum smart contracts and checks for security vulnerabilities by employing Hoare-style logic within Coq. FSPVM is based on an extension of the Curry-Howard isomorphism that combines virtual machine platforms with static security issue checking.

5.3.3 Fuzzing

Fuzzing test is a form of dynamic analysis method that examines the contract's response to abnormal or malicious input by performing random or semi-random mutation operations on smart contract inputs, thereby discovering possible vulnerabilities. It is a method for identifying software faults by constructing unexpected input data and monitoring abnormal results during program operation. It operates as a black box testing technology, but unlike traditional ones, it does not need to understand the internal structure and implementation details of the program under test. It only needs to provide input data and then observe the output results of the program to detect the contract. By generating a large amount of random and diverse input data while simulating various contract execution situations, fuzzing test methods can track the execution process to find possible vulnerabilities and errors.

During fuzzing test of a smart contract, a random engine is used to generate a large amount of random data to form an executable transaction. Referring to the feedback from the test results, the random engine dynamically adjusts the generated data to explore as much of the smart contract state space as possible. Based on the finite state machine, the status of each transaction is analyzed to detect whether there is an attack threat. Figure 5.3 depicts the main process of traditional fuzzing tests. The working process is composed of four main stages, including test case generation, test case running, program execution state monitoring, and analysis of exceptions. Fuzzing is independent of the contract source code but examines the execution outcomes on the basis of the input. Thus, it can be utilized in smart contracts without binary files or source code of contracts.

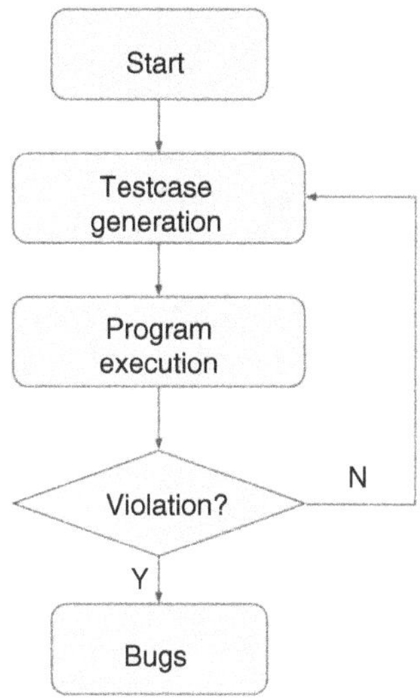

Figure 5.3 The main process of traditional fuzzing.

In 2018, ContractFuzzer (Jiang et al. 2018, pp. 259–269) proposed by Jiang et al. was the first vulnerability detection technology for smart contracts using fuzzing test approach. It first conducts static analysis on the bytecode of the smart contract and application binary interface, and then tests and examines the instruction calls, contract status and other data recorded by the EVM during the contract execution to identify vulnerabilities in the contract. Then, Nguyen et al. proposed sFuzz (2020, pp. 778–788), a fuzzing technology that adapts on the basis of feedback guidance in 2020 to address the issue of creating effective test scenarios for smart contracts. It first initializes the initial test input derived from the existing transaction information of the contract, subsequently tracks the execution progress of the initial test, and integrates the adaptability function with a lightweight multi-objective search technique based on the feedback data to optimize the test seed, thereby improving code coverage and efficiency in testing smart contracts. Additionally, Medeiros et al.'s Harvey (2015, pp. 54–69) is a directional gray-box fuzzing technique designed specifically for smart contracts that captures comprehensive structural information about contract code along with logic coverage through program instrumentation techniques. It calculates the distance from optimal execution to different program points to predict tests that meet high code coverage.

Furthermore, ILF (He et al. 2019, pp. 531–548) employs an imitation learning framework to efficiently and rapidly generate fuzzers from symbolic execution. During the learning process, symbolic execution experts generate large amounts of high-quality input, improving coverage of thousands of programs. Then, the fuzzy policy represented by a suitable neural network architecture is trained on the generated dataset. In order to enable all stages to work individually or together to analyze Ethereum smart contracts, GasGauge (Nassirzadeh et al. 2022, pp. 143–167) was developed as a static analysis tool in 2021. It uses fuzzing tests to identify vulnerabilities. It effectively detects denial-of-service vulnerabilities within smart contracts based on the Ethereum blockchain and has been validated through testing on a set of 1000 real-world Solidity smart contracts.

5.3.4 Taint Analysis

Taint analysis is a static analysis method that detects potential vulnerability sources and the paths of code may be influenced by analyzing and tracking the propagation of taints in data streams. Essentially, it is a data flow analysis technology for tainted variables. It can be abstracted into the form of a triplet <sources, sinks, sanitizers>. Among them, source is the taint source, which means directly introducing untrusted or confidential data into the system; sink is the taint collection point, which means directly generating security-sensitive operations or leaking private data to the outside world; sanitizer means harmless processing methods such as encryption or removal of harmful operations to prevent data dissemination from harming the information security within the software system. Taint analysis is to analyze whether the data introduced by the taint source in the program can be directly propagated to the taint collection point without harmless processing. If not, it indicates that the system is information flow safe; otherwise, it implies security issues such as privacy data leakage or dangerous data operations.

The taint analysis process includes three stages, as depicted in Figure 5.4. First, it is essential to pinpoint the sources of tainted data and the points where taint convergence occurs. Next, the paths through which tainted data propagates in the contract program are analyzed. Last, the data is sanitized to minimize the total number of taint marks within the system. Nevertheless, the range of taint analysis is constrained, and it may not successfully identify certain specific vulnerabilities. Thus, its key role is to enhance the accuracy of data flow analysis, often necessitating combination with other methodologies.

The earliest utilization of taint analysis techniques for detecting vulnerabilities in smart contracts was pioneered by Rodler et al., who introduced an approach known as Sereum (2018). Sereum is a technique designed to protect contracts against reentrancy attacks on the extended EVM client. It utilizes the

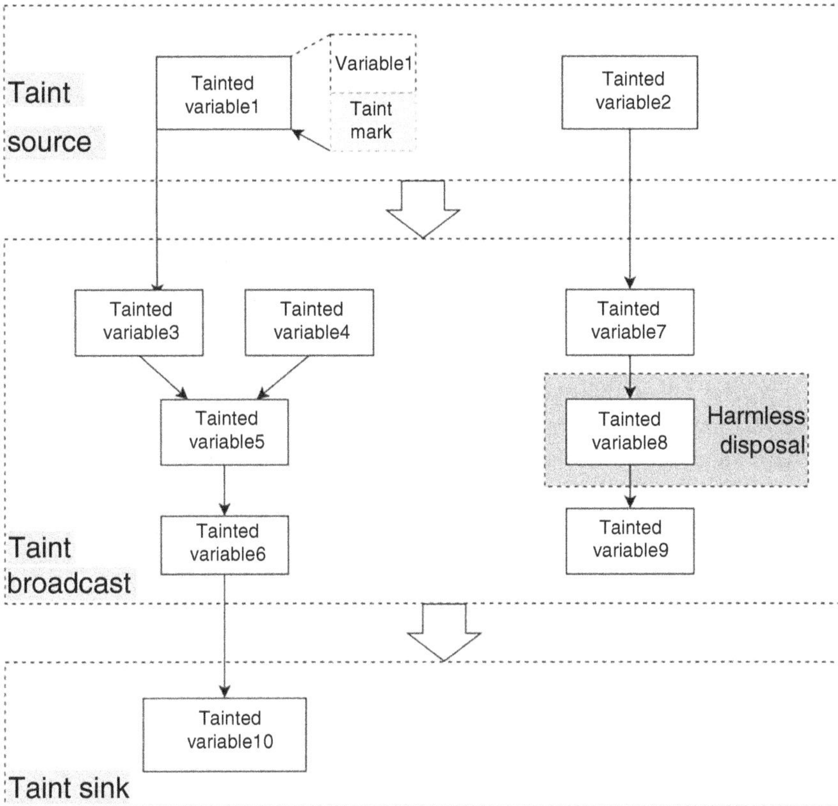

Figure 5.4 Schematic diagram of three steps in the taint analysis process.

K-framework as a symbolic execution engine and infers vulnerability conditions along the execution path by gathering and restricting symbolic values. Then, Brent et al. proposed Ethainter (2020, pp. 454–469), a harmless handling technique for capturing compound vulnerability data using taint analysis. Ethainter leverages taint analysis to abstract the transfer, loading, and storing of variables between operations in an abstract language onto persistent storage. It then captures the compound vulnerability data by applying predefined information flow rules. Ashouri combined taint analysis and execution, and proposed Etherolic (2020, pp. 353–356), a technology capable of identifying smart contract vulnerabilities and exploiting them to trigger unknown errors. Based on the data of taint analysis, it generates transactions that trigger vulnerabilities for the vulnerable code segments in the test contract, thereby realizing the discovery of vulnerabilities in the contract.

5.3.5 Machine Learning

Early methods for detecting vulnerabilities in smart contracts relied on fixed rules or patterns defined by experts. However, expert-defined rules are susceptible to errors and may not cover complex patterns effectively. Additionally, the scalability of rule-based detection tools is limited, reducing their applicability as the number of smart contracts continues to grow exponentially. To address these challenges, machine learning techniques offer a higher level of automation and efficiency. Drawn inspiration from the success of artificial intelligence in multiple fields, machine learning approaches are increasingly being adopted for the task of smart contract vulnerability detection.

Since 2018, an increasing number of machine learning algorithms have been employed for vulnerability detection in smart contracts. Compared with traditional methods, the introduction of machine learning technology can mitigate the substantial human resource requirements and address the relatively high rates of false positives and false negatives. It is also suitable for application scenarios of large-scale complex software systems, but its dependence on data sets and algorithms also brings problems such as insufficient source code semantic modeling and poor interpretability of detection results.

In 2018, Tann et al. proposed a machine learning method (2018) for sequence learning of smart contract vulnerabilities using the Long Short-Term Memory (LSTM) model. This method uses code vectors to model smart contract opcode sequences. Given a set of smart contract opcode data, the LSTM model learns the vector relationships initialized by the embedding algorithm. In addition, Gradel et al. introduced S-gram (2018), a semantic-aware security audit technology that combines N-gram language modeling and lightweight static semantic tags. The working method of S-gram consists of two stages: model construction and security audit. In the model construction stage, the language model of S-gram is trained. In the security audit stage, irregular subsequences are identified as potential vulnerabilities by scanning token sequences from the target contract.

In response to the current limitations in scalability performance of machine learning-based detection technology, Lutz et al. proposed Escort (2021), a comprehensive and scalable framework that utilizes deep neural networks for detecting multiple types of vulnerabilities. In 2022, Zhang et al. introduced MODNN (2022, p. 109289), a multi-target detection neural network designed to identify a wider range of smart contract vulnerabilities. This advanced tool offers enhanced scalability by verifying multiple identified threats and identifying unknown types without requiring expertise or pre-definition through implicit signatures and multi-target detection knowledge. Furthermore, it supports parallel detection of multiple vulnerabilities, eliminating the need for separate models for each vulnerability type and significantly reducing time and labor costs. In order to further improve network capacity, in 2023, You et al. (2023) proposed an attention-based deep learning module tailored for smart contract detection tasks that effectively captures long-range dependencies in inputs while enabling parallel processing capabilities. The authors also incorporated an optional symbolic execution module after the deep learning module to improve interpretability of classification results as elaborated upon in subsequent sections.

5.3.6 Improved Integration of Symbolic Execution and Machine Learning

Since traditional methods represented by symbolic execution and formal verification have problems such as slow reasoning efficiency and high computational cost, some researchers have begun to use deep learning methods for smart contract detection. However, our investigation into previous studies on deep learning-based vulnerability detection in smart contracts has revealed two issues. First, some approaches simply use LSTM models to perform sequence learning on preprocessed smart contracts, lacking the ability to extract long-range features and support parallel processing of inputs. Second, deep learning-based approaches for detecting vulnerability in the smart contract lack result interpretability. While vulnerability classification results are obtained based on deep learning intelligence, no specific explanation can be obtained. In order to solve these problems, You et al. (2023) propose a vulnerability detection method for smart contract that integrates symbolic execution and machine learning, as shown in Figure 5.5.

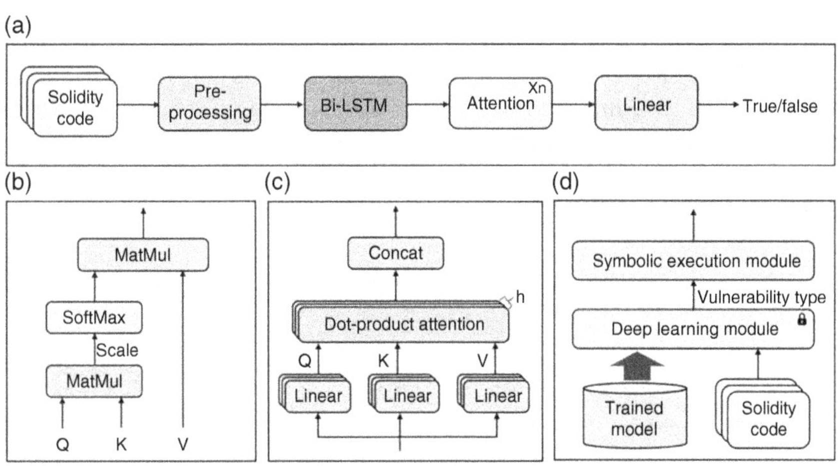

Figure 5.5 Architecture for a smart contract vulnerability detection solution that integrates symbolic execution and machine learning. (a) The deep learning module. (b) The dot-product attention. (c) The multi-head attention. (d) Overall design.

The method mainly consists of two core modules: a deep learning module and a symbolic execution module. The deep learning module is predominantly composed of an LSTM network and an attention network, enabling the capture of long-range relationships and achieving global modeling. The symbolic execution module calls the corresponding vulnerability detection model based on the classification results of the deep learning module to obtain a specific detection report. In practice, Mythril (Sharma 2022) serves as our chosen symbolic execution module. In addition, in order to convert the input smart contract source code into the required format, a data processing module is built. Next, we will introduce the deep learning, symbolic execution, and data processing modules in sequence.

5.3.6.1 Deep Learning Module

The function of this module is mainly to use the deep learning network for smart contract classification. As shown in Figure 5.5a, the machine learning module primarily comprises the Bidirectional Long Short-Term Memory (Bi-LSTM) network (Tann et al. 2018) and the attention network. The attention network is specific to the Dot-Product Attention shown in Figure 5.5b, which we will introduce in detail next. This module extracts opcodes as input sequences, treating them akin to natural language that can be processed using natural language processing techniques. In a sentence of natural language, not only are there important relationships between adjacent sentences, but words that are far apart may also have important semantics. Therefore, Bi-LSTM is mainly used to capture the contextual relationship between inputs, while the attention network is mainly used to model the long-range relationship of inputs.

To detect Solidity source code, first preprocess it into an input vector using a module shown in Figure 5.6. The preprocessing involves converting the input Solidity source code into bytecode and then decompiling it into opcode. These opcodes are further converted into an input vector via Word2Vec (Rong 2014).

Then, utilize the Bi-LSTM module to extract contextual relationships between input vectors. Next, h attention modules are used to globally model the input

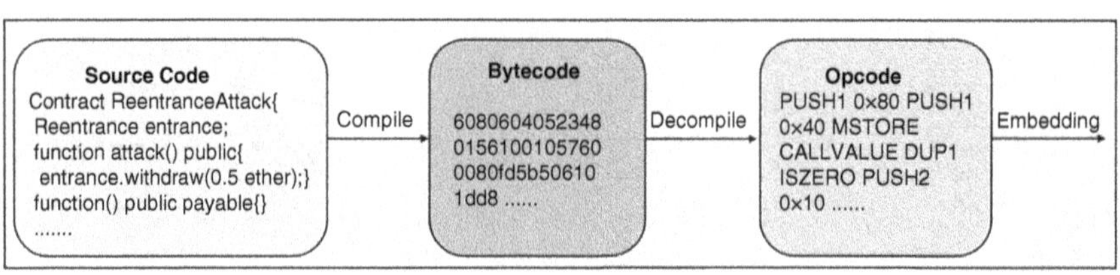

Figure 5.6 Convert smart contract code into data flow.

vector and extract long-range dependencies. Furthermore, inspired by ResNet (He et al. 2016, pp. 770–778), this method applies residual connections to the attention module. In practice, a multi-head attention network is adopted as shown in Figure 5.5c. Afterwards, a linear network processes the input vector with a sigmoid activation function applied. Finally, the cross-entropy loss is utilized as a loss function.

For the attention module in Figure 5.5a, the initial matrix $e \in \mathbb{R}^{n \times d}$ is got as input, where n is the number of embeddings and d is the length of the embedding. Then the matrix e is transformed through a fully connected layer to obtain Q, K and V. The self-attention function is computed on the transformed results. The mathematical form is as follows:

$$Attention(Q, K, V) = Softmax\left(\frac{QK^T}{\sqrt{d}}\right)V. \tag{5.1}$$

In fact, the multi-head self-attention is adopted to improve the representation space of the model. Divide Q, K, and V into h heads in parallel to implement the Dot-Product attention. The Dot-Product attention for each head is calculated individually. The mathematical form is as follows:

$$MHSA = ConCat(head_1, head_2, ..., head_h)W^O, \tag{5.2}$$

$$head_i = Attention\left(QW_i^Q, KW_i^K, VW_i^V\right), \tag{5.3}$$

where W^O is the learnable matrix. Subsequently, a feedforward network is used to capture the relationships within the embedding. By doing so, the deep learning module effectively extracts global relationships among input vectors and captures long-range dependencies.

5.3.6.2 Symbolic Execution Module

The main function of this module is to invoke the security model of the corresponding symbolic analysis tool based on the classification results of the deep learning module. Therefore, it can give a more detailed vulnerability detection report than a separate deep learning module. In specific experiments, Mythril is used as a symbolic analysis module. Given that the previous deep learning module has already identified the specific type of vulnerability, this method only needs to load the detection module for that particular vulnerability based on its identification by deep learning. According to the classification of Smart Contract Weakness Classification (SWC), the Mythril tool can detect up to 13 types of vulnerabilities, including integer overflow vulnerability, unprotected self-destruct instruction, arbitrary storage location write vulnerability, and so on.

5.3.6.3 Data Processing Module

The main function of this module is to preprocess the input data. Similar to traditional software development, smart contracts use high-level languages for coding purposes. Currently, there are numerous platforms available that support the deployment of smart contracts, with Solidity being the language predominantly used for most platforms including Ethereum. Prior to deployment on the EVM, smart contract source code needs to undergo compilation. In the context of smart contracts, source code compilation involves converting Solidity code into bytecode which can be understood by computers. Subsequently, during contract execution, the EVM decompiles bytecode into corresponding opcodes and completes their execution. Throughout our development process, we utilized Remix and Opcode-tool provided by Ethereum platform for implementing source code to bytecode compilation and bytecode to opcode decompilation, respectively. Finally, the opcodes are converted into word embeddings as input to the machine learning module.

5.4 Detection Tools for Smart Contract Vulnerability

Drawing upon the classification of existing detection methods for smart contract vulnerability outlined in Section 5.3, this section introduces several relevant tools. Moreover, a comprehensive comparison is conducted among these tools, accounting for factors including vulnerability coverage, availability of open-source information, integration capabilities, and detection accuracy.

5.4.1 Traditional Tools

We conducted extensive research on current detection tools for smart contract vulnerability, and picked the five most prominent tools below for a detailed introduction.

5.4.1.1 VaaS

Vulnerability as a Service (VaaS) is a type of cloud-based service model designed for vulnerability detection and analysis in smart contracts (Lianantech 2020). Users can upload their self-built smart contracts on the VaaS platform, which conducts static code analysis to detect coding errors, recognized vulnerability patterns, and potential security problems in the contracts. Furthermore, dynamic execution is conducted on the contracts by simulating different execution paths and inputs to observe their behavior and state changes, with the aim of detecting any existing vulnerabilities or abnormal behavior.

5.4.1.2 Mythril

Mythril is a security tool for smart contracts, which is specifically developed by ConSensys. Its primary purpose is to examine smart contracts on blockchains that are compatible with the EVM, such as Ethereum, Quorum, Tron, Hedera, Roostock, and Vechain. Mythril utilizes an integration of Satisfiability Modulo Theories (SMT) solving, symbolic execution, and taint analysis techniques to detect vulnerabilities within the smart contract codes. As time passes, it has become one of the most widely used security analysis tools for Ethereum smart contracts.

5.4.1.3 Securify

Securify (Tsankov et al. 2018, pp. 67–82) is a kind of tool employed for analyzing the security performance of Ethereum contracts, proficient in verifying contract security for the given characteristics. It thoroughly examines contract compliance and identifies potential security vulnerabilities by deriving accurate semantic information from the codes and analyzing the contract's dependency graph. The security analysis process of the Securify tool comprises two primary stages. First, it conducts a symbolic analysis of the contract's dependency graph and derives semantic information from its codes. Second, it examines violation patterns and compliance to derive necessary conditions, thereby establishing the validity of the specified properties. Advantages offered by Securify include scalability, high accuracy, and complete automation in its assessments.

5.4.1.4 Manticore

Manticore (Mossberg et al. 2019, pp. 1186–1189) is an open-source framework specifically designed for dynamic symbolic execution, analyzing Ethereum smart contracts and binary files. The core engine component of Manticore operates based on specific assumptions regarding the underlying execution model. The native binary symbolic execution module achieved the expected high-level execution interface, which is required by the core engine.

5.4.1.5 Slither

Slither is a kind of static analysis framework designed for smart contracts, offering more than 30 vulnerability detection models. It can detect code optimization problems that could be missed by compilers and offer recommendations for optimization. In addition, Slither is capable of creating visual representations including method invocation graphs and inheritance topology diagrams, aiding developers in understanding the structure and relationship of codes.

5.4.2 Detecting Vulnerabilities in Smart Contracts for Web 3.0

Considering the diverse characteristics of Web 3.0 scenarios and the potential application of MIS, this section focuses on smart contract vulnerability detection within MIS. The key emphasis lies in conducting a comprehensive security check before deploying an identifier management contract on-chain, aiming to mitigate security vulnerabilities as much as possible. To achieve this, MIS utilizes Mythril, a customized symbolic execution vulnerability detection tool and adds a module for identifying specific vulnerabilities in identifier management contracts.

The identifier management contracts in MIS consist mainly of two types: an EMIS contract and identifier contracts, as shown in Figure 5.7. (1) The EMIS contract plays a pivotal role by maintaining the username table, as well as supporting registration, update, revocation, transfer, and authorization of usernames. Moreover, the interfaces of the identifier contracts are integrated into the EMIS contract in order to make it easier for the user to call functions uniformly. (2) To manage and resolve identifiers of different types, corresponding contracts are designed such as the identity identifier contract, the content identifier contract, and the service identifier contract. Each identifier contract maintains an identifier table.

The written operation in identifier contracts includes registration, update, revocation, renewal, transfer, and others. In this context, two security aspects are taken into consideration. First, every write operation necessitates verification of the source's identity identifier for regular identifiers or a registered username for identity identifiers. Second, it is imperative to safeguard funds within the identifier management contracts since users are required to pay rent for registering and renewing their identifiers. Furthermore, if an identifier is revoked, any remaining rent will be returned to its owner. Although the original Mythril tool is well-suited for detecting general contract vulnerabilities, it lacks validation modules specifically addressing these two security issues in identifier management contracts. Therefore, the following presents a vulnerability detection algorithm based on symbolic execution for identifier management contracts.

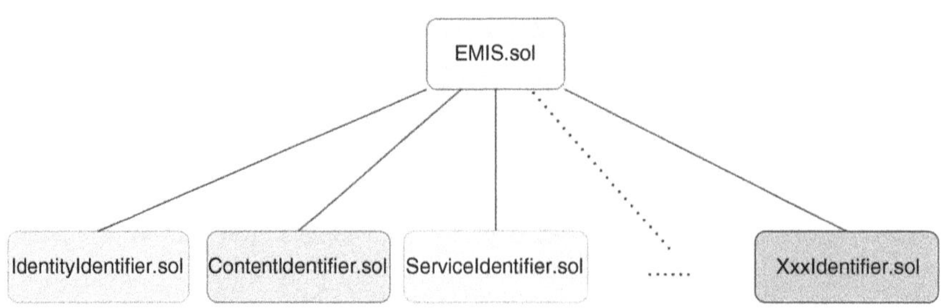

Figure 5.7 Structure of MIS identifier management contracts.

The vulnerability detection module for identifier management contracts utilizes annotation and hook methods. Two types of annotations are defined in this module: HashAnnotation, which records the slot position data used by the SHA3 opcode during hash calculation, and CallAnnotation, which stores information such as owner, sender, value of attached money amount, and a flag decStore to record reduced state variable. The vulnerability-related opcodes defined in the module to hook include "CALL," "SHA3," and "SSTORE." There are two restrictions on the status variable, one is to verify the address of the transaction sender, and the second is that it belongs to the lease type, and the increase or decrease involves the transfer of funds. The specific steps and pseudo-code of the detection algorithm are as follows:

Step 1: Based on the global state, determine if the current contract is an identifier management contract. If not, proceed to Step 2. If it is, verify if the opcode is "CALL" and in prehook; If this condition is not met, return an empty report. If the condition is satisfied, further check whether the third element at the top of the stack in the machine state equals 0. A value of 0 indicates that there has been an external call to a specific identifier contract. In such cases, retrieve from persistent storage the owner address corresponding to the username provided in the call parameter data and add a CallAnnotation to record relevant information in the global state including owner's address, sender's transaction address, and attached Ether amount. Conversely, if this third element does not equal 0, it implies a transfer transaction to other accounts has occurred. In such instances, read and examine previously saved CallAnnotation from global state while ensuring that reduction flag bit of related state variable remains false throughout this process. A false flag signifies that identifier lifetime-related variables have not been reduced during contract transfer – indicating rent for said identifier should be returned without deletion of identifier itself – thus representing an abnormal vulnerability scenario requiring resolution through path constraint analysis along with addition of vulnerability report accordingly. Finally, validate whether destination address for current transfer matches saved owner address within annotation. Any mismatch would also be considered as a vulnerability necessitating path constraint resolution and inclusion within vulnerability report.

Step 2: The current execution is a nonspecific-identifier contract. Verify if the current state is in the post-hook, otherwise proceed to Step 3. Check for opcode "SHA3," or else move on to Step 5. Read the slot position saved in the global state HashAnnotation, add it to the symbol variable at the top of the stack, and save its value, thus transferring the annotation from global state onto expression atop stack.

Step 3: Currently, in pre-hook, judge whether the opcode is "SHA3." If not, jump to Step 4. Otherwise, read the parameters of the hash function from the top two positions on the stack, denoting the byte offset and length of data derived from the hash value in memory. Extract the last 32 bytes of this data, referred to as slot1, which corresponds to a specific position defined for the map variable in the source code. Then add a HashAnnotation for the global state where slot1 is saved.

Step 4: Verify if the opcode is "SSTORE," otherwise jump to Step 5. Try to read the HashAnnotation of the top position expression on the stack. If it does not exist, indicating that the storage location to be written is not calculated by hashing and the write operation does not involve a map variable, return an empty report. Subtract slot1 saved in the annotation from the top element of the stack to get the relative slot position of data in the structure, denoted by slot2. According to slot1 and slot2, check whether verifying sender address of message call transaction is necessary for modifying state variables. If required, extract addresses of identifier owner and transaction sender from the annotation and determine whether these two addresses can be different under current path constraint. A successful solution indicates vulnerability, requiring inclusion of a vulnerability report. Next, ascertain whether state variable belongs to lease type. If so, evaluate size change before and after modification by reading unmodified value from storage space and modified value at second position on top of stack. In case where state variable increases, representing renewal for identifier validity period extension, verify whether the amount carried by the transaction can be 0 under the current path constraint. If the solution is successful, it indicates that there is a path that enables the user to extend identifier's validity period without providing rent. So, a vulnerability report will be saved here. Conversely, if the state variable decreases, indicating revocation or deletion of identifier, set decStore flag as true in CallAnnotation.

Step 5: Collect all reports and return.

Algorithm 5.1 MIS Vulnerability Detection Algorithm

```
Input: globalState
Output: issues
   issuses←[];
   opcode←globalState.getOpcode();
   1: if globalState.environment.activeAccount.
      contractName="EMIS" then
   2: if opcode≠"call" or isPrehook=false then
   3: return []
```

```
end if
if globalState.mstate.stack[-3]=0 then
owner←getOwner(calldata);
globalState.annotate(CallAnnotation(owner,msg.
sender,msg.value));
else
callAnnotation←globalState.getAnnotations
(CallAnnotation)[-1];
if callAnnotation.decStore=false then
issues←getIssues(globalStae,globalState.worldState.
constraints);
end if
owner←callAnnotation.owner;
constraints←And(globalState.worldState.
constraints,owner≠globalState.mstate.stack[-2]);
issues←getIssues(globalState,constraints);
else if isPrehook()=true then
if opcode="SHA3" then
offset←globalState.mstate.stack[-1];
size←globalState.mstate.stack[-2];
slot1←globalState.mstate.memory[offset+size-32:
offset+size];
globalState.annotate(HashAnnotation(slot1));
else if opcode="SSTORE" then
hashAnnotations←stack[-1].getAnnotations
(HashAnnotation);
callAnnotation←globalState.getAnnotations
(CallAnnotation)[-1];
if hashAnnotations=[] then
return []
end if
slot1←hashAnnotations[-1].slot1;
slot2←globalState.mstate.stack[-1]-slot1;
if requireAuth(slot1,slot2)  then
owner←callAnnotation.owner;
sender←callAnnotation.sender;
constraints←And(globalState.worldState.
constraints,sender≠owner);
issues←getIssuse(globalState,constraints);
end if
if transferRecord(slot1,slot2)=false then
```

```
return issues
end if
beforeVal←globalState.environment.activeAccount.
    storage[stack[-1]];
afterVal←globalstate.mstate.stack[-2];
if afterVal>beforeVal then
value←callAnnotation.value;
constraints←And(globalState.worldState.
    constraints,value=0);
issues←getIssues(globalState,constraints);
else if afterValthen
callAnnotation.decStore←true;
end if
end if
else if opcode="SHA3" then
slot1←globalState.getAnnotations(HashAnnotation)
    [-1].slot1;
globalState.mstate.stack[-1].annotate
    (HashAnnotation(slot1));
end if
return issues
```

5.4.3 Comparison of Existing Tools

The following presents a comparative evaluation of the previously mentioned smart contract detection tools. Table 5.1 presents 17 widely used tools and compares their characteristics of open-source availability, detection effectiveness, integration capabilities, and vulnerability coverage.

The detection status in Table 5.1 is obtained from the results of detection experiments offered by the respective original authors of each tool in their respective research papers. These results have been aggregated and synthesized. In addition, some papers incorporate comparisons between different tools. For example, this section discusses the comparison of vulnerability detection coverage and accuracy between Oyente and other tools based on its improvements. This section uses these comparative analyses as references for supplemental tables.

Specifically, we discuss the existing tools from the following four aspects.

5.4.3.1 Vulnerability Coverage

Vulnerability coverage refers to the tool's capability to pinpoint and detect different types of vulnerabilities in smart contracts, such as integer overflows,

Table 5.1 A comparison of vulnerability detection tools for smart contracts.

Detection tools	Detection approach	Supported type of vulnerabilities									Open-source language	Detection accuracy
		Solidity layer			EVM layer			Block layer				
		Reentrancy	Integer error	Exception handling	Logical error	Short address attack	Tx. origin	Call-stack overflow	Timestamp dependency	Transaction order dependency		
F* framework	Formal verification	√	√	√	–[a]	–	–	–	√	√	–	Medium
EthIR		√	√	√	–	–	–	–	√	√	Python	Medium
EthBMC		√	–	–	–	–	–	–	√	√	Python	High
Oyente	Symbolic execution	√	√	√	–	√	–	√	√	√	Python	Low
teEther		√	√	√	√	√	–	–	–	–	Python	Medium
Slither		√	–	√	–	–	√	√	√	–	Python	High
Manticore		√	√	–	–	√	–	–	–	–	Python	Medium
ContractFuzzer	Fuzzing	√	√	–	–	√	–	–	√	–	Go	Medium
sFuzz		√	√	–	√	√	–	–	√	–	C++	Medium
Harvey		√	√	–	√	√	–	–	√	–	Solidity	Medium
Sereum	Taint analysis	√	√	√	–	–	–	–	√	√	Java	High
Ethainter		√	√	–	–	–	–	–	√	–	Solidity	High
Vaas	Integrated	√	√	√	–	–	√	–	√	–	Solidity	High
Mythril		√	√	–	–	–	√	–	√	–	Python	High
Securify		√	–	√	√	√	√	√	√	√	Solidity	Medium
Mythx		√	√	–	–	–	√	–	√	–	Python	High
MIS contract vulnerability detection system		√	√	–	–	–	√	–	√	–	Python	High

[a] "–" implies that the approach is incapable of detecting the corresponding vulnerability, or lacks open-source availability.

permission control problems, reentrancy attacks, and uninitialized variables. A reliable vulnerability detection tool should provide extensive coverage of vulnerabilities, enabling it to effectively identify potential security problems, and improving the overall security of smart contracts.

Regarding the types of vulnerabilities, the majority of detection tools focus on identifying vulnerabilities that have led to significant contract attack events, such as Ethereum freeze vulnerabilities, integer error vulnerabilities, reentrancy vulnerabilities, and others. Nevertheless, there is a relatively limited number of tools available for detecting less common but easily mitigatable vulnerabilities, including denial of service, short address, and permission control vulnerabilities. Among the frequently detected and easily identifiable vulnerabilities, most detection tools provide support for detecting short-address vulnerabilities.

5.4.3.2 Detection Effectiveness

Detection effectiveness indicates the precision and accuracy of a detection tool in identifying vulnerabilities. An effective tool should reduce the occurrence of false negatives and false positives, providing accurate and specific vulnerability reports. This enables developers to promptly identify and resolve potential security issues, thereby enhancing the security of smart contracts.

The Oyente tool was the pioneering tool that employed symbolic execution for detecting potential security vulnerabilities. Out of the 19,366 Ethereum contracts analyzed, it identified 8833 contracts as vulnerable. Nevertheless, the tool demonstrated a relatively considerable proportion of false positives in its detection outcomes. On the other hand, MAIAN, a dynamic symbolic executor, was specifically developed to uncover self-destructing contracts. It utilized inter-procedural symbolic analysis and concrete validation to uncover real vulnerabilities. By examining approximately one million contracts, MAIAN successfully identified real vulnerabilities with an 89% accuracy in detecting true positives on a subset of 3759 contracts, leading to the detection of vulnerabilities in 3686 contracts.

TeEther utilized a combination of binary slicing and symbolic execution techniques to analyze execution paths that contained vulnerable instructions. It produced exploit samples and effectively analyzed 85.65% of the 784,344 accounts, identifying 1532 accounts that were vulnerable to exploitation. In contrast, ETHBMC functioned as a symbolic execution-based automated analysis framework for smart contracts. In comparison to teEther, ETHBMC detected an extra 10.3% of susceptible accounts and discovered 22.8% more vulnerabilities in a shorter time frame. Furthermore, ETHBMC demonstrated the capability to detect false positives in teEther and identified additional vulnerabilities in comparison to MAIAN.

5.4.3.3 Open-Source Availability

Open-source availability refers to whether the tool is open-source and extensively utilized by smart contract developers and auditors. Open-source tools provide greater credibility and transparency, enabling a larger number of individuals to contribute to their maintenance and improvement.

In the aforementioned section about techniques for detecting smart contract vulnerabilities, certain detection tools provide the actual technical source code, while others offer Web interfaces for utilizing the corresponding techniques. Smart contract developers can evaluate the security capability of their smart contracts on these Web platforms.

Python is predominantly utilized as a development language, while Solidity, Go, and C++ are employed by specific tools. The main reasons for selecting a programming language encompass ease of operation, developers' familiarity, performance requirements, and language compatibility. Diverse programming languages can offer unique features and functionalities. For example, Python provides an extensive tool ecosystem and library that simplifies various tasks including vulnerability detection, formal verification, and symbolic execution in smart contracts. Solidity, specifically designed for composing Ethereum smart contracts, has the capacity to directly evaluate the logic and code structure of smart contracts.

5.4.3.4 Integration Capabilities

From the preceding discussions, it becomes apparent that integrated tools demonstrate enhanced performance when it comes to detection accuracy and vulnerability coverage. Detection tools that depend on a single detection technique have certain restrictions, such as the path explosion in symbolic execution (Coward 1988, pp. 229–239), the issues of under-tainting and over-tainting in taint analysis (Dai et al. 2018, pp. 118–123), and the low path coverage in fuzzing (Cadar et al. 2011, pp. 1066–1071). Integrated tools proficiently combine the advantages of each method while mitigating their respective shortcomings to boost overall detection performance. For example, EthPloit (Zhang et al. 2020, pp. 116–126) integrates fuzzing test and taint analysis techniques. By establishing the dependency correlation between variable control flow and variable data within the source codes using taint analysis, EthPloit improves the fuzzing test cases by considering this dependency relationship. Consequently, the efficiency of vulnerability discovery and the path coverage of fuzzing are improved.

5.5 Chapter Summary

Smart contracts are currently regarded as one of the most promising technologies, offering a robust, secure, and trusted decentralized application scenario. This aligns with the practical significance of financial technology and future networks in various fields. However, the presence of security issues has significantly impeded its development, making smart contract vulnerability detection technology an emerging research focus. This chapter presents a comprehensive overview of smart contract vulnerability detection technologies proposed by researchers, categorizing existing techniques into formal verification, symbolic execution, fuzzing, taint analysis, machine learning, and integration. Additionally, it provides an in-depth examination of current smart contract vulnerability detection tools falling under these six categories while discussing the improvements of these methods within the context of the Web 3.0 era. Furthermore, we analyze existing tools based on their vulnerability coverage, detection effectiveness, open-source availability, and integration capabilities to provide a more nuanced understanding of their strengths and weaknesses.

Discussion Questions

5.1 What categories of smart contract vulnerabilities can be classified based on the layers of blockchain?

A: Smart contract vulnerabilities can be divided into the following categories according to their layers in blockchain: Solidity layer, EVM layer, and block layer. At the Solidity layer, developers write source code of smart contracts to define their behavior and logic. Vulnerability detection at this layer concentrates on logical issues, security vulnerabilities, and potential weaknesses in contract code. At the EVM layer, contract code is compiled into bytecode and executed in virtual machines. Vulnerability detection at this layer focuses on the flow of bytecode execution as well as the sequence of operations that can cause unusual behavior or vulnerabilities. In the Ethereum network, smart contracts are deployed on-chain with each block containing a set of transactions that may execute smart contracts. The blockchain's consensus mechanism and transaction sequence also affect the execution outcome of smart contracts. As a result, vulnerability detection at the block layer emphasizes aspects such as transaction ordering, impact analysis of consensus algorithms, and potential inconsistencies in contract states.

5.2 What are the emerging vulnerabilities in smart contracts during the Web 3.0 era?

A: Common smart contract vulnerabilities in the era of Web 3.0 encompass identifier verification, rent tampering, and single Oracle exploitation. In the vulnerability related to identifier verification, an adversary could illicitly employ a nonidentifier owner address as the destination for fund transfers with the intention of pilfering funds. Regarding rent tampering vulnerability, an attacker can manipulate rental time to extend identifier validity without providing adequate rent, thereby generating more profit than the actual value of the identifier itself. The single Oracle vulnerability allows an assailant to utilize substantial funds for purchasing a specific token and artificially inflate its price within a short timeframe to exploit arbitrage opportunities and manipulate the token market dynamics.

5.3 What are the various methodologies employed for detecting vulnerabilities in smart contracts?

A: Methods for detecting vulnerabilities in smart contracts include formal verification, symbolic execution, fuzzing, taint analysis, machine learning, and their combinations. Formal verification is a rigorous mathematical and logic-based approach employed to verify the correctness of computing systems, software, or hardware. Symbolic execution involves executing the bytecode instructions of a smart contract in symbolic form, constructing the symbolic execution path, and analyzing the symbolic constraints on this path to identify potential vulnerabilities. Fuzzing is a dynamic analysis technique in which random or semi-random variation operations are performed on smart contract inputs to explore the contract's response to abnormal or malicious inputs, thereby discovering possible vulnerabilities. Taint analysis is a static analysis technique that identifies possible sources of vulnerability and code paths that could be affected by tracking and analyzing the propagation of tainted data within a stream. Machine learning technology, on the other hand, has the potential to address the limitations of traditional methods such as resource-intensive manual efforts and high rates of false positives and negatives. It can also adapt well to complex software systems at scale. However, its reliance on datasets and algorithms introduces challenges like inadequate semantic modeling of source code and limited interpretability of detection results.

References

Albert, E., Gordillo, P., Livshits, B., Rubio, A. and Sergey, I., 2018, September. Ethir: A framework for high-level analysis of ethereum bytecode. In International symposium on automated technology for verification and analysis (pp. 513–520). Cham: Springer International Publishing.

Ashouri, M., 2020, March. Etherolic: A practical security analyzer for smart contracts. In Proceedings of the 35th Annual ACM Symposium on Applied Computing (pp. 353–356).

Brent, L., Grech, N., Lagouvardos, S., Scholz, B. and Smaragdakis, Y., 2020, June. Ethainter: A smart contract security analyzer for composite vulnerabilities.

In Proceedings of the 41st ACM SIGPLAN Conference on Programming Language Design and Implementation (pp. 454–469).

Cadar, C., Godefroid, P., Khurshid, S., Păsăreanu, C.S., Sen, K., Tillmann, N. and Visser, W., 2011, May. Symbolic execution for software testing in practice: Preliminary assessment. In Proceedings of the 33rd International Conference on Software Engineering (pp. 1066–1071).

Cao, Y., Zou, C. and Cheng, X., 2021. Flashot: a snapshot of flash loan attack on DeFi ecosystem. arXiv preprint arXiv:2102.00626.

Cao, X., Zhang, J., Wu, X. and Liu, B., 2022. A survey on security in consensus and smart contracts. *Peer-to-Peer Networking and Applications*, pp. 1–21.

Chen, W., Zheng, Z., Ngai, E.C.H., Zheng, P. and Zhou, Y., 2019. Exploiting blockchain data to detect smart ponzi schemes on ethereum. *IEEE Access*, 7, pp. 37575–37586.

Coward, P.D., 1988. Symbolic execution systems – A review. *Software Engineering Journal*, 3(6), pp. 229–239.

Dai, P., Pan, Z. and Li, Y., 2018, December. A review of researching on dynamic taint analysis technique. In 2018 3rd Joint International Information Technology, Mechanical and Electronic Engineering Conference (JIMEC 2018) (pp. 118–123). Atlantis Press.

Dwivedi, V., Pattanaik, V., Deval, V., Dixit, A., Norta, A. and Draheim, D., 2021. Legally enforceable smart-contract languages: A systematic literature review. *ACM Computing Surveys (CSUR)*, 54(5), pp. 1–34.

Frank, J., Aschermann, C. and Holz, T., 2020. {ETHBMC}: A bounded model checker for smart contracts. In 29th USENIX Security Symposium (USENIX Security 20) (pp. 2757–2774).

Gradel, A.K.J., Porsgaard, T., Lykkesfeldt, J., Seested, T., Gram-Nielsen, S., Kristensen, N.R. and Refsgaard, H.H.F., 2018. Factors affecting the absorption of subcutaneously administered insulin: Effect on variability. *Journal of Diabetes Research*, 2018, 1205121.

Grishchenko, I., Maffei, M. and Schneidewind, C., 2018. A semantic framework for the security analysis of ethereum smart contracts. In Principles of Security and Trust: 7th International Conference, POST 2018, Held as Part of the European Joint Conferences on Theory and Practice of Software, ETAPS 2018, Thessaloniki, Greece, April 14–20, 2018, Proceedings 7 (pp. 243–269). Springer International Publishing.

Grossman, S., Abraham, I., Golan-Gueta, G., Michalevsky, Y., Rinetzky, N., Sagiv, M. and Zohar, Y., 2017. Online detection of effectively callback free objects with applications to smart contracts. *Proceedings of the ACM on Programming Languages*, 2(POPL), pp. 1–28.

Gupta, B.B., Li, K.C., Leung, V.C., Psannis, K.E. and Yamaguchi, S., 2021. Blockchain-assisted secure fine-grained searchable encryption for a cloud-based healthcare cyber-physical system. *IEEE/CAA Journal of Automatica Sinica*, 8(12), pp. 1877–1890.

He, K., Zhang, X., Ren, S. and Sun, J., 2016. Deep residual learning for image recognition. In Proceedings of the IEEE Conference on Computer Vision and Pattern Recognition (pp. 770–778).

He, J., Balunović, M., Ambroladze, N., Tsankov, P. and Vechev, M., 2019, November. Learning to fuzz from symbolic execution with application to smart contracts. In Proceedings of the 2019 ACM SIGSAC Conference on Computer and Communications Security (pp. 531–548).

Ji, M., Liang, G., Li, M., Zhang, H. and He, J., 2021. Security analysis of blockchain smart contract: Taking reentrancy vulnerability as an example. In Advances in Artificial Intelligence and Security: 7th International Conference, ICAIS 2021, Dublin, Ireland, July 19–23, 2021, Proceedings, Part III 7 (pp. 492–501). Springer International Publishing.

Jiang, B., Liu, Y. and Chan, W.K., 2018, September. Contractfuzzer: Fuzzing smart contracts for vulnerability detection. In Proceedings of the 33rd ACM/IEEE International Conference on Automated Software Engineering (pp. 259–269).

Krupp, J. and Rossow, C., 2018. {teEther}: Gnawing at ethereum to automatically exploit smart contracts. In 27th USENIX Security Symposium (USENIX Security 18) (pp. 1317–1333).

Lai, E. and Luo, W., 2020, January. Static analysis of integer overflow of smart contracts in ethereum. In Proceedings of the 2020 4th International Conference on Cryptography, Security and Privacy (pp. 110–115).

Li, H. and Yang, X., 2021. *Co-governed sovereignty network: Legal basis and its prototype & applications with MIN architecture* (p. 257). Springer Nature.

Lianantech, 2020. VaaS. https://www.lianantech.com.

Lutz, O., Chen, H., Fereidooni, H., Sendner, C., Dmitrienko, A., Sadeghi, A.R. and Koushanfar, F., 2021. ESCORT: Ethereum smart contracts vulnerability detection using deep neural network and transfer learning. arXiv preprint arXiv:2103.12607.

Luu, L., Chu, D.H., Olickel, H., Saxena, P. and Hobor, A., 2016, October. Making smart contracts smarter. In Proceedings of the 2016 ACM SIGSAC Conference on Computer and Communications Security (pp. 254–269).

Medeiros, I., Neves, N. and Correia, M., 2015. Detecting and removing web application vulnerabilities with static analysis and data mining. *IEEE Transactions on Reliability*, 65(1), pp. 54–69.

Mehar, M.I., Shier, C.L., Giambattista, A., Gong, E., Fletcher, G., Sanayhie, R., Kim, H. M. and Laskowski, M., 2019. Understanding a revolutionary and flawed grand experiment in blockchain: The DAO attack. *Journal of Cases on Information Technology (JCIT)*, 21(1), pp. 19–32.

Mossberg, M., Manzano, F., Hennenfent, E., Groce, A., Grieco, G., Feist, J., Brunson, T. and Dinaburg, A., 2019, November. Manticore: A user-friendly symbolic execution framework for binaries and smart contracts. In 2019 34th IEEE/ACM International Conference on Automated Software Engineering (ASE) (pp. 1186–1189). IEEE.

Nassirzadeh, B., Sun, H., Banescu, S. and Ganesh, V., 2022, July. Gas gauge: A security analysis tool for smart contract out-of-gas vulnerabilities. In The International Conference on Mathematical Research for Blockchain Economy (pp. 143–167). Cham: Springer International Publishing.

Nguyen, T.D., Pham, L.H., Sun, J., Lin, Y. and Minh, Q.T., 2020, June. sfuzz: An efficient adaptive fuzzer for solidity smart contracts. In Proceedings of the ACM/IEEE 42nd International Conference on Software Engineering (pp. 778–788).

Nikolić, I., Kolluri, A., Sergey, I., Saxena, P. and Hobor, A., 2018, December. Finding the greedy, prodigal, and suicidal contracts at scale. In Proceedings of the 34th Annual Computer Security Applications Conference (pp. 653–663).

Qin, K., Zhou, L., Livshits, B. and Gervais, A., 2021, March. Attacking the defi ecosystem with flash loans for fun and profit. In International Conference on Financial Cryptography and Data Security (pp. 3–32). Berlin, Heidelberg: Springer Berlin Heidelberg.

Rodler, M., Li, W., Karame, G.O. and Davi, L., 2018. Sereum: Protecting existing smart contracts against re-entrancy attacks. arXiv preprint arXiv:1812.05934.

Rong, X., 2014. word2vec parameter learning explained. arXiv preprint arXiv:1411.2738.

Samreen, N.F. and Alalfi, M.H., 2021. A survey of security vulnerabilities in ethereum smart contracts. arXiv preprint arXiv:2105.06974.

Sharma, N., 2022. A survey of mythril, a smart contract security analysis tool for EVM bytecode. *Indian Journal of Natural Sciences*, 13, pp. 51003–51010.

Tann, W.J.W., Han, X.J., Gupta, S.S. and Ong, Y.S., 2018. Towards safer smart contracts: A sequence learning approach to detecting security threats. arXiv preprint arXiv:1811.06632.

Tsankov, P., Dan, A., Drachsler-Cohen, D., Gervais, A., Buenzli, F. and Vechev, M., 2018, October. Securify: Practical security analysis of smart contracts. In Proceedings of the 2018 ACM SIGSAC Conference on Computer and Communications Security (pp. 67–82).

Wang, S., Huang, C., Li, J., Yuan, Y. and Wang, F.Y., 2019. Decentralized construction of knowledge graphs for deep recommender systems based on blockchain-powered smart contracts. *IEEE Access*, 7, pp. 136951–136961.

Wang, H., Li, H., Smahi, A., Zhao, F., Yao, Y., Chan, C.C., Wang, S., Yang, W. and Li, S. Y.R., 2023a. MIS: A multi-identifier management and resolution system in the metaverse. *ACM Transactions on Multimedia Computing, Communications, and Applications*, 20, pp. 1–25.

Wang, C., Jiang, H., Wang, Y., Huang, Q. and Zuo, Z., 2023b. Research on smart contract vulnerability detection method based on domain features of solidity contracts and attention mechanism. *Journal of Intelligent & Fuzzy Systems*, 45, pp. 1–13.

Wei, G., Li, H., Bai, Y., Yang, X., Zhang, H., Que, J. and Li, W., 2021, July. Co-governed space-terrestrial integrated network architecture and prototype based on MIN. In 2021 International Conference on Computer Communications and Networks (ICCCN) (pp. 1–6). IEEE.

Wu, J., Lin, K., Lin, D., Zheng, Z., Huang, H. and Zheng, Z., 2023. Financial crimes in Web3-empowered metaverse: Taxonomy, countermeasures, and opportunities. *IEEE Open Journal of the Computer Society*, 4, pp. 37–49.

Yang, Z., Lei, H. and Qian, W., 2020. A hybrid formal verification system in coq for ensuring the reliability and security of ethereum-based service smart contracts. *IEEE Access*, 8, pp. 21411–21436.

You, X., Li, H., Wang, H. and Faisal, M., 2023. SmartDT: An effective vulnerability detection system of smart contracts based on deep learning. In 2023 IEEE International Conference on Big Data(Big Data). IEEE.

Zhang, Q., Wang, Y., Li, J. and Ma, S., 2020, February. Ethploit: From fuzzing to efficient exploit generation against smart contracts. In 2020 IEEE 27th International Conference on Software Analysis, Evolution and Reengineering (SANER) (pp. 116–126). IEEE.

Zhang, L., Wang, J., Wang, W., Jin, Z., Su, Y. and Chen, H., 2022. Smart contract vulnerability detection combined with multi-objective detection. *Computer Networks*, 217, p. 109289.

Zupan, N., Kasinathan, P., Cuellar, J. and Sauer, M., 2020. Secure smart contract generation based on petri nets. In *Blockchain Technology for Industry 4.0: Secure, Decentralized, Distributed and Trusted Industry Environment* (pp. 73–98). Singapore: Springer Singapore.

6

Multi-Identifier System Based on Large-Scale Consortium Blockchain

This chapter presents an innovative Domain Name System (DNS) that combines blockchain technology to manage multiple types of identifiers. It primarily encompasses the background, motivation, system architecture, and core functions. Finally, we explore a potential application scenario of this novel system aimed at fostering the development of a worldwide community of shared future in cyberspace.

6.1 Background Introduction and Requirement Analysis

Originally envisioned as a decentralized and inclusive network, the Internet's current DNS retains centralized elements due to its dependence on nonautonomous structures. Despite the distributed nature of its servers, DNS is centralized at its core, especially in the management of its root zone. Control over domain name resolution ultimately rests with a central entity, as the root zone is under the stewardship of IANA and ICANN. This centralized hierarchical model exposes the conventional DNS to a host of issues, such as operational inefficiencies, service disparities, susceptibility to data tampering, and reduced resilience against Distributed Denial of Service (DDoS) attacks. These vulnerabilities could jeopardize the security of national information infrastructure. Comprehensive studies and practical experiences have demonstrated that neither the current DNS nor the various efforts to optimize or replace it have been able to completely eliminate the risks associated with centralization, nor fully satisfy the foundational principles of an open Internet that facilitates equitable participation.

A growing cohort of institutions and groups is eager to engage in domain name services while advocating for the equitable treatment of data on the internet. The emergence of blockchain as a prominent technological innovation provides features like distributed control, tamper-resistant record-keeping, and enhanced

Principles and Applications of Blockchain Systems: How to Overcome the CAP Trilemma in Consortium Blockchain, First Edition. Hui Li and Han Wang.

Published 2025 by John Wiley & Sons, Inc.

security measures. The application of blockchain to foster a collaboratively managed, transparent, and collectively maintained distributed DNS framework is crucial in propelling the evolution of nascent internet technologies (Kalodner et al. 2015, pp. 1–23).

However, the integration of blockchain technology into the development of DNS alternatives faces some challenges (Syed et al. 2019, pp. 176838–176869):

1) *Data storage limitations*: The append-only structure of blockchain means that all state changes are recorded on the blockchain, and all nodes participating in the network must maintain complete copies of the blockchain records. This imposes constraints on the scalability of blockchains supported by current commercial hardware technology.
2) *Slow writes*: The processing speed of transactions is influenced by the blockchain consensus protocol. For example, in public blockchains, new transactions typically take minutes to hours to be committed.
3) *Bandwidth constraints*: The total number of transactions in each block is determined by the block's size. To maintain fairness, all nodes should roughly receive newly published blocks at the same time. Therefore, block size is usually limited by the uplink bandwidth of nodes. For the Bitcoin system, the current bandwidth is 1 MB (approximately 1000 transactions) per new block (Nakamoto 2008).

Recognizing the need for equitable participation in domain name management among countries, as well as worldwide organizations and institutions, this section explores novel blockchain technologies that facilitate certified, easy-to-manage and highly trustworthy solutions. The aim is to establish a globally co-governed and nationally self-governed management system for domain name services within Multi-Identifier System (MIS). Overcoming these challenges requires integrating technologies such as distributed computing, encryption techniques, peer-to-peer networks, and consensus protocols. The Peking University Lab for the China Environment for Network Innovations (CENI) has pioneered a highly secure alternative to traditional DNS, termed MIS, which offers both manageability and control. Within this system, "identifier" denotes the network's resource data labels, encompassing domain names.

6.2 System Architecture

Based on large-scale consortium blockchains, MIS uses a basic single-chain architecture as its core while simultaneously employing a hierarchical architecture to support large-scale networks (Wang et al. 2023).

6.2.1 Basic Single-Chain Architecture

The underpinning architecture of the MIS rests on a consortium blockchain model, crafted to uniformly maintain a myriad of identifiers along with their corresponding resource data, overseen by a cadre of dependable central nodes. Figure 6.1 represents the system's organization as a stratified four-tier hierarchy. Competing candidate nodes aspire to be promoted to core nodes by earning the right to generate blocks. These core nodes are responsible for implementing a streamlined consensus protocol and capturing changes in resource states as transaction entries. Meanwhile, resource details along with metadata are organized in a hierarchical manner and are stored off-chain. This design not only enhances scalability but also maintains a modular relationship among the levels, enabling updates to be made to individual layers without disrupting the functional logic of the rest.

6.2.1.1 Tier 1: Network Tier for Blockchain Nodes

Consortium blockchain nodes fill the lowest layer. The basic MIS consists of nodes, which are endowed with three distinct privileges related to message handling which can be flexibly rearranged or merged, granting a node the potential to hold multiple privileges simultaneously.

1) *Bookkeeping*: Bookkeeping privilege involves recording transactions on the blockchain. Specific nodes called bookkeepers have the ability to accept transaction proposals from others and add them to a local pool. Once a consensus round begins, a bookkeeper selects transactions $Tx\_List = \{t_1, t_2, \cdots, t_{total}\}$ to propose as a transaction set. This includes encapsulating the block height h, timestamp Ts, and hash of the preceding block Pre_Hash. The bookkeeper then disseminates a prepare message $\langle Prepare - Tx\_List \rangle$ across the network for a collective voting process. If the vote is favorable, the proposed transaction set Tx_List will be written into next block on the blockchain.

   A tenure-based mechanism regulates the allocation of bookkeeping privileges. As a term concludes, the performance of bookkeepers is evaluated by voters who communicate their assessments to a central tallying node. This node aggregates the evaluations to ensure a continual reappointment of the highest-scoring bookkeepers, while those at the lower end of the scale $(1 - ratio_{bookkeeper})$ are substituted by the most senior candidates $ratio_{bookkeeper}(\%)$ from the queue. This process maintains a balance between the dynamism and constancy of the network's nodes. The roster of incoming bookkeepers is inscribed into a designated transaction $Tx\_Permission$ $(Bookkeeping)$ to formalize the shift in bookkeeping responsibilities.

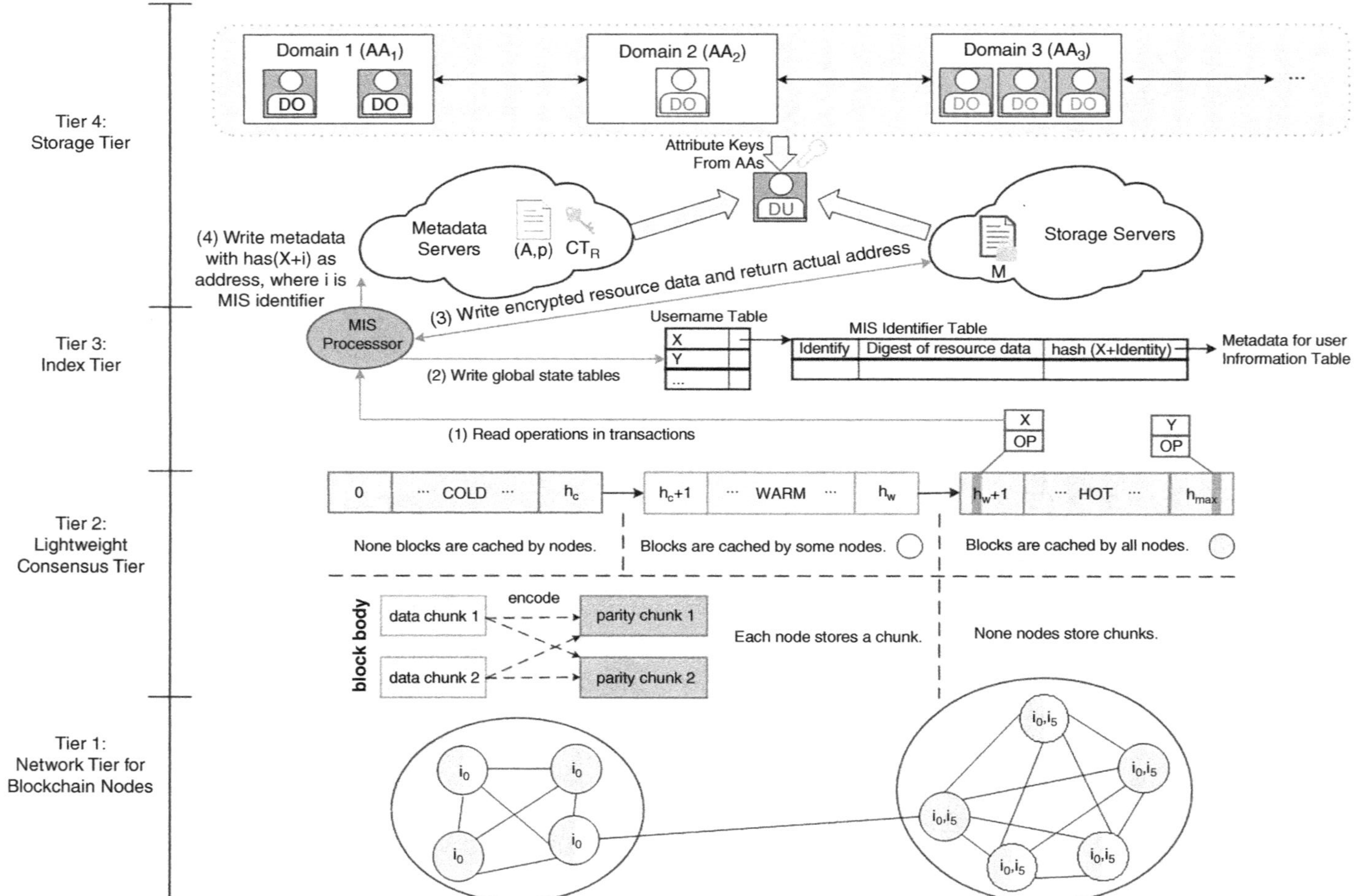

Figure 6.1 MIS's basic 4-tier architecture.

2) *Voting*: Voting is a right granted to particular nodes, allowing them to participate in the consensus round by appraising the transaction sets *Tx_Lists* from bookkeepers. Should a bookkeeper act malevolently or encounter a failure, a voter may not receive all the sets, prompting them to hold off for a specified duration before casting incomplete votes. A voter's verdict on each set is recorded as affirmative, negative, or abstained and this collective judgment *Vote_List* is then encrypted and submitted to the central tallying node as part of the voting process.

   Nodes express their interest to become voters through a specific transaction type *Tx_Permission* (*Voting*). Contrasting with usual transactions or those seeking bookkeeping permissions, this *Tx_Permission* (*Voting*) necessitates unanimous consent from existing voters before being recorded on the blockchain. Once ratified, the node is endowed with voting rights from the subsequent consensus round, expanding the voter base. This method mirrors the BFT consensus model but with the most stringent entry criterion, reflecting the existing voters' confidence.

3) *Aggregating*: Aggregating is a privilege held by nodes responsible for vote tallying. The central tallying node compiles votes *Vote_Lists* and begins the counting process after a set waiting period. A transaction set is conclusively deemed valid or invalid based on the majority vote exceeding two-thirds. Should the majority not be achieved, the node seeks the outstanding votes. Given that all votes are authenticated by the voters, the node compresses these votes and their endorsements, broadcasting the conclusive message $\langle Commit \rangle$ network-wide.

   The role of aggregation is a critical privilege within the network. As each consensus round is facilitated by an individual node serving as the aggregator, any failure or malicious attack on this node could significantly disrupt the network's service provision. It is therefore essential to ensure the aggregator role is not easily assumed by malevolent actors. Currently, aggregators are chosen in a rotating fashion from a group of nodes that have been deemed reliable. The chances of a compromised node being appointed as the next aggregator, *Agg*, are low due to the random nature of the selection process and the unpredictability of vote receipt timing. Furthermore, any aggregator found engaging in harmful activities will face sanctions and the subsequent revocation of their privileges.

4) *No right*: Nodes without privileges are excluded from the consensus mechanism. Nonetheless, these nodes retain the capability to request or acquire transaction sets and headers, paralleling the functions of bookkeepers and voters. Upon receipt of a transaction set *Tx_List*, a node verifies the identifiers and authenticates both the bookkeeping privilege and signature. If an aggregator's commit message $\langle Commit \rangle$ is received, the node checks for the inclusion of all *Tx_Lists* referenced in the block header (*BH*). Should any be absent, the node

procures them from adjacent nodes. Subsequently, the node compiles the block and archives it in adherence to a predefined temporal framework.

6.2.1.2 Tier 2: Lightweight Consensus Tier

The consortium blockchain architecture positions the lean consensus layer atop the network stratum. This rudimentary model incorporates the Parallel Proof of Vote (PPoV) protocol, which is a streamlined Byzantine Fault Tolerant (BFT) consensus mechanism, to manage and authenticate ledger activities including creation, modification, cancellation, renewal, and asset exchange. The integration of PPoV into a DNS surrogate framework is beneficial as it utilizes blockchains, which are progressively acknowledged as foundational layers for disseminating status amendments, with the consensus mechanism's role being confined to facilitating sequential organization. PPoV uniquely distinguishes the voting process, granting participants the autonomy to endorse transactions on the ledger based on individual criteria, thereby promoting a more equitable consensus.

Nevertheless, the practice of archiving every vote and signature as validation in the block's preamble incurs considerable storage overheads. It's also important to note that each custodian affixes their endorsement to the transaction batch they prepare. The PPoV protocol is streamlined in the MIS through three distinct approaches:

In addressing the bulkiness of digital endorsements, the first method of streamlining within the MIS's PPoV mechanism involves the adoption of the Boneh-Lynn-Shacham (BLS) signature framework (Boneh, Lynn, and Shacham 2001, pp. 514–532). This approach supersedes the conventional Elliptic Curve Digital Signature Algorithm (ECDSA), amalgamating multiple signatures into a singular, reduced footprint within the block's header.

A further refinement entails the reengineering of the PPoV block's architecture, delineated in Table 6.1, to diminish the associated storage expanse. This reconfiguration is designed to enhance the block's succinctness and operational efficacy.

Table 6.1 Lightweight block structure of PPoV.

Block header	Height	Pre-hash	Timestamp
	Vote_result	Votes	Voters' aggregate signature
	Bookkeepers'	Merkle Root_0+Tamestamp_0	
	Aggregate	...	
	Signature	Merkle Root_h+Tamestamp_h	
Block body		Tx_Lists{0,1...,h}	

Optimizing the signature size and structural design of a block presents a practical approach for streamlining. In the traditional PPoV model, the cumulative size of signatures escalates with the increase in the number of validators or bookkeepers. Nonetheless, the redesigned BH incorporates a fixed-size aggregate signature that remains unaffected by the number of participating nodes. Consequently, the restructured, more compact block is substantially smaller than its PPoV predecessor.

The third facet of PPoV streamlining within the MIS framework is the minimization of redundancy. Standard configurations necessitate that each node retains a complete dataset, which can strain node storage capacity. Yet, the likelihood of accessing archival blocks is comparatively rare. In a consortium blockchain with n nodes, where at most f nodes may be faulty (with ($n > 3f$)), the algorithm leverages this infrequency to enhance storage optimization.

Recognizing that BHs are frequently retrieved by nodes, the algorithm selectively compresses only the transaction data within the body of block leveraging an ($n - 2f$, $2f$) Reed-Solomon (RS) coding scheme (Wicker and Bhargava 1999). RS coding is advantageous in that it can reconstruct original data from only ($n - 2f$) portions of data, making it apt for blockchain environments that may contain Byzantine nodes.

Through this compression of block body transactions, node storage demands are lessened, particularly for less-accessed older blocks. Conversely, the BH, which houses critical information and undergoes more frequent access, is not compressed to enable swift retrieval.

MIS integrates these three elements – BLS signatures for signature aggregation, block structure redesign, and RS coding for block body compression – to accomplish a refined PPoV consensus. These enhancements contribute to reduced storage requirements, heightened efficiency, and sustained consensus security, even with Byzantine nodes present.

To further address the decline in query efficiency that may occur when compressing the transactions of newly minted blocks – which typically experience higher access rates – MIS implements a tiered storage strategy. This method stratifies blocks into three temperature-based categories relative to their age: hot for the newest, warm for intermediate, and cold for the oldest. This temporal stratification ensures that while the most recent blocks remain quickly accessible, older blocks benefit from compression, optimizing storage without compromising access times.

1) Nodes should cache a copy of hot blocks due to their frequent access. The length of the hot space is denoted as L_h, and the biggest block height is represented by h_{max}. Blocks with heights falling within the range $(h_{max} - L_h, h_{max}]$ are classified as hot.
2) Warm blocks, which occupy the range between the most recent (hot) and the least recent (cold) blocks, are subject to an intermediate access frequency. The

span of the warm segment is signified by L_w, and blocks with heights within the interval $(h_{max} - L_h - L_w, h_{max} - L_h]$ are categorized as warm. As a block transitions from the hot to the warm state, nodes undertake a process to encode the warm block into $(n - 2f)$ data chunks, denoted as $\{C\}_{i=1}^{n-2f}$, and $\{C\}_{i=n-2f+1}^{n}$ representing $2f$ parity chunks. Subsequently, each node retains the BH along with a solitary, distinct chunk. In the event of a chunk's failure, a node is capable of retrieving any other $(n - 2f)$ chunks to reconstruct the original block.

To reduce the dependency on decoding operations, the MIS designates a number of nodes to maintain a cache of the warm blocks. The variable n_w represents the tally of nodes responsible for caching a given warm block. The need to decode is only precipitated if all n_w caching nodes become inaccessible. As the likelihood of requesting a warm block wanes over time, it logically follows that the quantity of caching nodes should correspondingly diminish. The freshest warm block is preserved in the caches of $(2f + 1)$ nodes, which allows for transaction queries without the necessity of decoding, even in scenarios where up to $2f$ caches are nonfunctional. Conversely, to prevent undue storage consumption, the oldest warm block is cached on a single node only. The relationship between cache quantity n_w and block height h is given by

$$n_w(h) = \left\lfloor (h + L_w - h_{max} + L_h - 1) \cdot \frac{2f}{L_w - 1} \right\rfloor + 1.$$

3) Cold blocks, with heights in the range $[0, h_{max} - L_w - L_h]$, have a low probability of being accessed. At this stage, nodes retain only block headers and chunks generated in the warm space, removing caches. However, for frequently visited important old blocks, the node monitors the access count and preserves the cache from deletion.

This section theoretically computes the total on-chain storage cost for the general case to illustrate the efficacy of the coding and timeline strategies. Denote the size of the redesigned block head as $size_{BH}$. Assume the block body is populated with transactions of $size_{BD}$, where $size_{BD}$ is significantly larger than $size_{BH}$. For the hot space with complete caching, the storage cost is given by $size_h = L_h n (size_{BH} + size_{BD})$. In the warm space, blocks are subject to both encoding and caching. Among them, the size of the encoded data chunks is $size_w^{chunk} = L_w n \left(size_{BH} + \frac{size_{BD}}{n-2f}\right)$, and that of the cached copies is $size_w^{cache} = (size_{BH} + size_{BD}) \sum_{h=h_{max}-L_h-L_w+1}^{h_{max}-L_h} n_w(h) \leq (size_{BH} + size_{BD}) \left[\sum_{h=h_{max}-L_h-L_w+1}^{h_{max}-L_h} (h - h_{max} + L_h + L_w - 1) \cdot \frac{2f}{L_w - 1} + L_w\right] = (size_{BH} + size_{BD}) L_w (f + 1)$. Therefore, the cost of the warm space is $size_w = size_w^{cache} + size_w^{chunk} \leq L_w\left[(n + f + 1) \cdot size_{BH} + \frac{nf + 2n - 2f^2 - 2f}{n - 2f} \cdot size_{BD}\right]$. For the cold space with full encoding, the cost is $size_c = \left(size_{BH} + \frac{size_{BD}}{n-2f}\right) n (h_{max} - L_h - L_w + 1)$. In summary, the total cost is

$$size_{total} = size_h + size_w + size_c \leq size_{BH}[n(h_{max} + 1) + L_w(f + 1)] + size_{BD} \left[(f + 1)L_w \frac{n}{n - 2f}(h_{max} + 1) + \left(n - \frac{n}{n - 2f}\right)L_h\right]. \tag{6.1}$$

In order to compare with the original storage cost of on-chain data $size'_{total} = n(h_{max} + 1)(size_{BH} + size_{BD})$, calculate their difference as

$$\Delta_{size} = size'_{total} - size_{total} \geq size_{BD}\left[\left(n - \frac{n}{n - 2f}\right)(h_{max} - L_h + 1) - (f + 1)L_w\right] - size_{BH}(f + 1)L_w. \tag{6.2}$$

Since $n > 3f$ and $size_{BD} \gg size_{BH}$, get

$$\Delta_{size} \gg size_{BH}(f + 1)(L_w + 3L_c), \tag{6.3}$$

where L_c is the length of cold space.

Equation (6.3) demonstrates that the coding and timeline strategies significantly decrease the storage consumption of on-chain data, primarily due to the compression of warm and cold spaces. As the number of blocks grows, the overall compression ratio converges to that of the encoded block body, which is $1/(n - 2f)$.

6.2.1.3 Tier 3: Index Tier

The index layer serves as the foundation for the MIS by keeping a comprehensive record of who owns which identifiers and how they connect to data resources that are not on the blockchain. Within the system, an entity is associated with several identifiers that are updated as changes occur in the network. The MIS uses a noSQL database architecture, featuring a table for user names and several tables dedicated to MIS identifiers, which are arranged according to key-value pairs.

At this level, the MIS processor is responsible for handling the logic concerning identifiers. Its initial step is to pinpoint the blockchain operation where a user, referred to as "X," registers their identity. Following this, it incorporates a record for "X" into the username database and initiates a new MIS identifier table specifically for "X," which includes a record labeled "Identity." This procedure also entails securing the metadata address through a hash function combining "X" and "Identity," along with capturing a summary of the resource data. Afterward, the processor encrypts and stores the user information table on designated storage servers and dispatches the metadata to servers. This systematic approach ensures the decoupling of identity identifiers from their corresponding data, streamlining the indexing process and reinforcing the integrity of verification.

Within the fundamental structure of the MIS, it is imperative that each entity is equipped with an identity identifier. This identifier acts as a distinct marker, akin to a "passport number," affirming the entity's identity. Additionally, this identity identifier lays the groundwork for other types of identifiers, serving as the primary reference and anchoring point.

6.2.1.4 Tier 4: Storage Tier

At the apex of the system's structure lies the storage tier, which serves as the repository for the fully off-chain resource data connected to multi-identifiers. It is imperative that any resources containing sensitive personal details, such as tables of user information, are encrypted within this tier to preserve user privacy.

This tier is designed to be versatile, supporting a variety of storage technologies, devices, and replication methodologies. Such adaptability enables the MIS processor to consistently store and administer metadata across a network of metadata servers that are geographically dispersed.

Metadata files housed within this tier are comprehensive, encompassing details such as the storage locations, credentials for authentication, encrypted access keys, and policies governing who may access the actual data or services. To facilitate seamless access for all users, metadata servers are equipped with the full spectrum of identifiers.

MIS adopts a data storage and access scheme for cyberspace that utilizes multi-authority Attribute-Based Encryption (ABE), enabling secure and controllable off-chain storage. In this scheme, a Data Owner (DO) encrypts the resource data using a symmetric key, which is then encrypted with an access control policy through the MIS processor. Considering unique user traits, encompassing biological and spatiotemporal factors, access to decrypt resource data is exclusively granted to Data Users (DUs), who fulfill the specified access policy and hold the appropriate attribute keys. To ensure fair attribute management, MIS establishes an Attribute Authority (AA) for each domain. The AA authenticates users and generates the corresponding attribute keys. The scheme comprises four modules, which are described below.

1) During the setup phase, the processor of the MIS takes in the security parameter, represented by λ, and creates the global parameter, known as GP, through a local randomization process. Subsequently, for each domain m_i (with i being integers such as 1, 2, 3, and beyond), the corresponding AA crafts a distinctive pair of keys (apk_i, ask_i) using GP as the foundation. These elements, GP along with each apk_i, are then disseminated across the network.
2) *Attribute key distribution*: The AA of the domain m_i inputs the global parameter GP, a DU's attribute att_j ($j = 1, 2, 3, \ldots$), the DU's identity identifier X, the time *period*, and its private key ask_i to outputs the attribute key $sk_{att_j,X}^{period,i}$. The time *period* restricts attribute key's lifetime, and the AA updates the key upon

expiration. Illegal DUs are added to the revocation list rl_i, denying them access to subsequent attribute keys.

3) *Encryption*: The MIS processor selects a symmetric key R to encrypt the resource data M randomly. It then generates the access structure (A, ρ), where A represents the matrix of access control policy and ρ represents the mapping from attributes to rows of the matrix. Next, the symmetric key R is encrypted using the access structure (A, ρ), the time *period*, and the public key $\{apk_i\}$ to obtain the ciphertext CT_R. The MIS processor writes (A, ρ) to the metadata server together with the ciphertext CT_R.
4) *Decryption*: During the process of resource data fetching, the DU accesses the corresponding metadata file and verifies if its attribute set $\{att_j\}$ meets the access structure (A, ρ) requirement. It will use the attribute key set $\left\{sk_{att_j,X}^{period,i}\right\}$, the identity identifier X, the time *period*, and the global parameter GP, to decrypt the ciphertext CT_R and get the key R if so. Simultaneously, the encrypted resource data are received by the DU from the address listed in metadata file. Parallel read is enabled for large resources to maximize efficiency. Finally, the original resource data plaintext is recovered by decrypting with R.

6.2.2 Hierarchical Architecture for Large-Scale Network

A fundamental single-threaded MIS can be expanded into a tiered framework, as exemplified by the Multi-Identifier Network (MIN). MIN facilitates the simultaneous presence of various network identifiers, encompassing user identity, data content, geographical data, and IP addresses. Within this network, the focus is on the identification of entities, with content identifiers for all items being linked to their originators' identity markers.

Refer to Figure 6.2 for a depiction of the network's stratified configuration. This structure categorizes the entire network into levels of domains in descending order. Entities within the apex domain are part of key national organizations that collaboratively manage a shared blockchain ledger. Lower-tier domains are under the jurisdiction of their respective local organizations. Within these domains, the operational mode for registering and overseeing identifiers, along with the precise modalities of execution, may differ. This loose integration ensures the network's integrity and allows for domain-specific tailoring.

A primary node's role in the network encompasses managing user activities within its domain, overseeing the blockchain-based registration of identifiers, and facilitating translation and resolution services across domains. The network also includes supervisory nodes distinct from individual and corporate user nodes. These supervisory nodes act as data exchange portals bridging hierarchical domains and possess a suite of identifiers each.

The MIN framework is structured into a management layer and a data layer. The management layer is tasked with creating and handling identifiers. Once

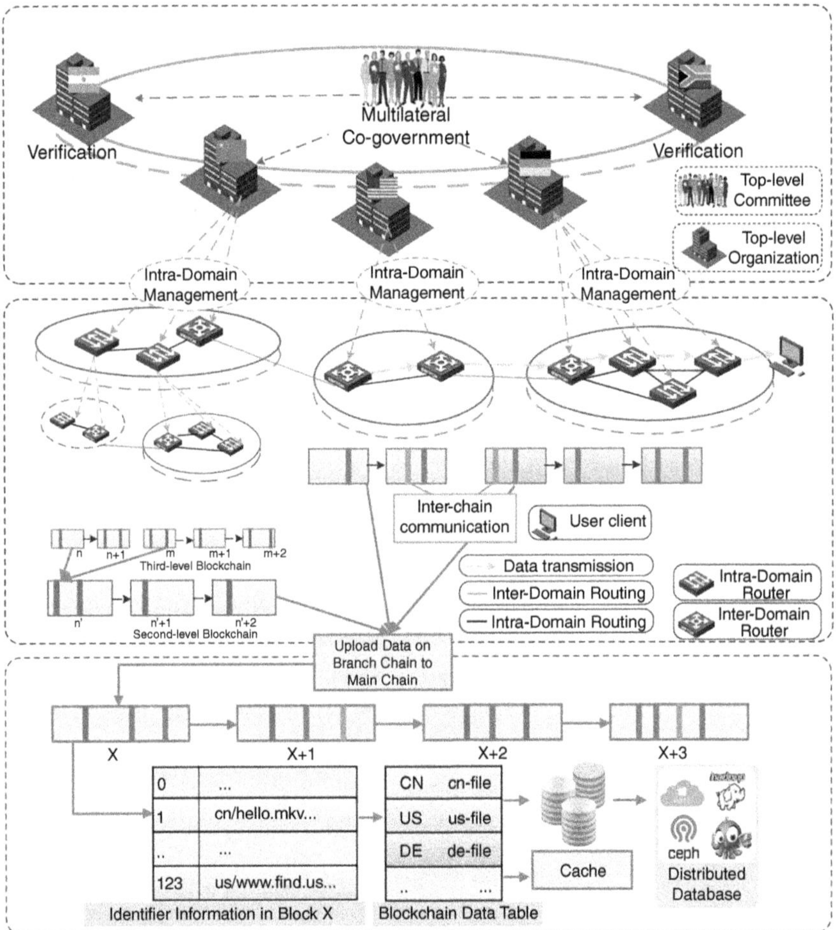

Figure 6.2 Hierarchical architecture framework of MIN.

supervisory nodes authenticate these identifiers and achieve consensus via the consensus protocol, they log pertinent ownership and activity data on the blockchain, ensuring network-wide consistency, immutability, and auditability. Storing only critical data on-chain optimizes efficiency, while comprehensive identifier information is held off-chain. The data layer is responsible for resolving various identifiers – identity, content, geographic, etc. – as well as managing data transmission and filtering. For performance optimization, MIS employs a multi-tiered caching system with bi-daily sync to minimize network traffic impact, ensuring that cached data does not interfere with network routing.

As networks like MIN evolve both in technological sophistication and organizational structure, they will form a pivotal infrastructure, facilitating global connectivity and collaborative governance. The integration of blockchain technology breaks through the constraints of traditional networks, fostering interconnectedness and broadening participation in the evolution of the Internet by a diverse array of stakeholders. This evolution represents a critical stride toward the Internet's globalization, driving our global society toward heightened levels of openness and cooperation.

6.3 Core Functions

MIS undertakes multiple roles associated with identifier creation and oversight, encompassing identity administration, access regulation, as well as the registration, modification, annulment, and resolution of identifiers, including their inter-conversion.

6.3.1 Identity Management and Access Control

Table 6.2 delineates the structure of identifiers within MIN. To accommodate prospective enhancements, MIN's identifier schema integrates a version field specific to identities, facilitating straightforward expansion in subsequent iterations. The identity's cryptographic key is bifurcated into dual segments to ensure uniform formatting across various platforms and stages of use, thus eliminating redundant

Table 6.2 MIN identity format.

Identity field	Meaning
Name	Identity name
Version	Identity version
IdentityID	Unique identifier number
Attributes	Attribute information
Status	Status information, which can be selected as Active, Suspended, Revoked, etc.
Identifiers	A list of identifiers with two fields: type and value
KeyParam	Cryptographic algorithm to adopt
PrivateKey	Decrypted private key, which is the plaintext
PrivateKeyEncrypt	Ciphertext of encrypted private key
PublicKey	Public key information
Cert	Certificate of Identity

definitions of identity formats. The "PrivateKeyEncrypt" segment denotes the user-specific encrypted private key, while the "PrivateKey" segment contains the unencrypted private key available during operational runtime. The latter is stored in an encrypted state within serialized file repositories. Should the identity be utilized exclusively for packet verification purposes, both segments are left unpopulated.

To manage identity and control access, MIN integrates identity information and provides a unified Access Management System called MIN-AMS, which offers fine-grained control down to the level of network communication packets. It supports access management under both push-based and pull-based communication semantics.

Taking the context of content-centric communication as an illustration, the system achieves access control based on attributes by integrating the Ciphertext-Policy Attribute-Based Encryption (CP-ABE) algorithm. Specifically, the setup step is executed by the service provider. When the content consumer initiates a request, the service provider evaluates whether the content consumer meets the access conditions according to the access policy. Subsequently, the consumer accesses the corresponding content with the authorization token, and the service provider encrypts the content according to the access policy. The CP-ABE algorithm saves the access structure into the encrypted ciphertext and returns it to the content consumer.

Permission management consists of two core elements set by the server provider: the allocation of users' attributes and the setting of access policies. The former is combined with Identity Management System (IMS) platform, while the latter is according to attribute information and corresponding access requirements. The Action field of access policy is shown in Table 6.3, which can be flexibly configured by administrators to align with specific system environments.

Table 6.3 Action field of access policy.

Scope	Example	Description
Network layer	MIN:Pull, MIN:Push	Communication semantics, such as push or pull, both of which are currently supported in MIN.
Identity layer	Application	The corresponding identity is allowed. Usually, the service provider adds the application, so as to obtain the application Id and application key, etc.
Application layer	Read/Write	Operations based on specific requirements, such as reading or writing files.

Table 6.4 Identifier matching rules.

Matching model	Match symbol	Example
Exact matching	/<component>	/min/pkusz/lab/a.txt
Component-rule matching	/*	/min/pkusz/lab/*, which means that all child signs under /min/pkusz/lab are matched.
Component-level matching	/?number	/min/pkusz/lab/?2, means that only components with a maximum of two levels under /min/pkusz/lab can be matched. For example, /min/pkusz/lab/test1/test2 is a match, while /min/pkusz/lab/test1/test2/test3 is not.

To better support flexible policy configuration, Table 6.4 presents various matching methods in the field of content identifier. Note that these methods are primarily designed for interest and content identifiers, but can be extended to other types of identifiers based on them.

In the realm of algorithm design, a tree-based resource matcher has been engineered to efficiently ascertain whether an identifier meets the identifier matching rules in access management. A comprehensive depiction of its data structure is available in Figure 6.3.

The resources discussed here encompass both MIN resources and IP resources. MIN resources are represented by hierarchical identifiers, such as /min/pku/test. IP resources are displayed in the form of Classless Inter-Domain Routing (CIDR), for example, 10.119.0.1/24.

The MIN resource matcher is built upon the hierarchical service identifier, which consists of multiple string components separated by "/." Contrastingly, the IP resource matcher employs a trie tree as opposed to a multiplexed identity matching tree resulting from word segmentation.

6.3.2 Registration, Update, and Revocation of Identifiers

Identity is the fundamental element in the MIS. While devices receive predetermined identities, users must complete a registration protocol. This involves generating a key pair with robust security, followed by submitting an identity application. This application encompasses a username, desired identity, Time-to-Live (TTL), fee for registration, timestamp, signature, and other pertinent data to a chosen record-keeper in the identifier realm. Users can select any record-keeper managing the relevant identifier class, as the network maintains a cohesive identity environment.

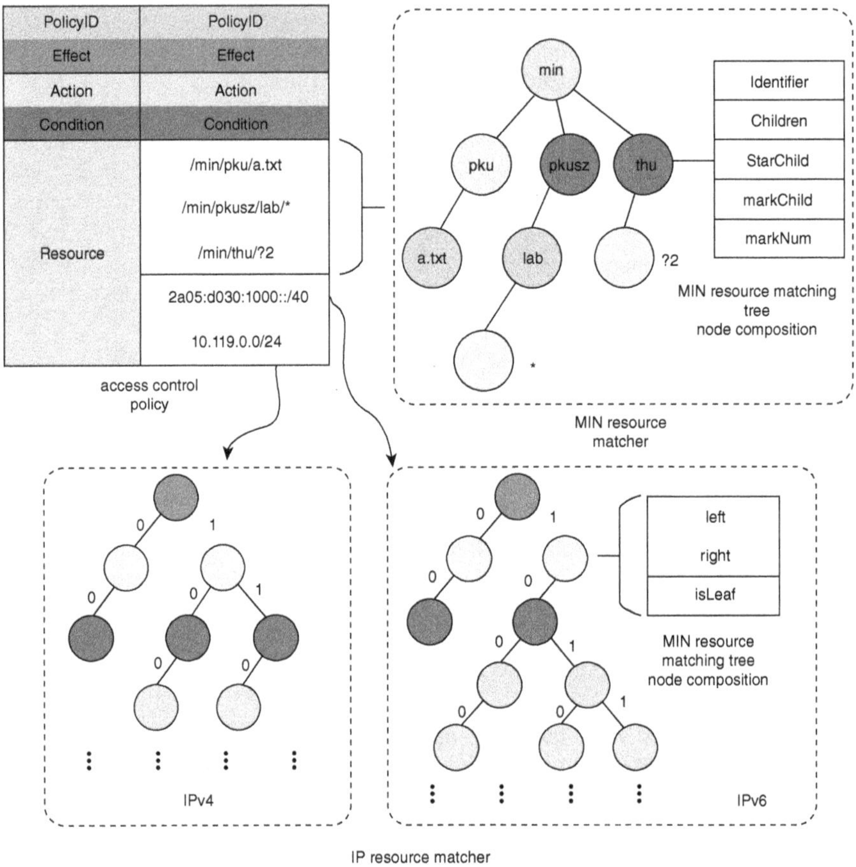

Figure 6.3 Resource matcher for the access policy.

The record-keeper examines the application for both formatting and content integrity, ensuring no existing identifier duplicates in the global directories. If the application is validated, those with higher registration fees are given precedence and added to the local transaction pool for an expedited consensus process. After achieving consensus, the MIS engine extracts usernames and other vital details from sanctioned registration transactions to update the global directories. If the registration includes "AboutMe" information, it is also encoded and stored separately in the off-chain personal information database.

Securing an identity empowers the user to register further labels, covering content and services. These labels remain under the sole control of the identity holder during their validity period, allowing the owner to alter or revoke them as needed. Expired or withdrawn labels can be reapplied for through a similar registration mechanism as the original identity request. All such procedures rely on the collective consent governed by the consortium blockchain's rules.

6.3.3 Resolution of Identifiers

In environments where a singular identifier space is maintained, basic MIS functions analogously to DNS by providing identifier resolution services. Resolving an identifier enables user access to a storage server or the pertinent resource. The resolution procedure is delineated below:

Step 1: Users consult the global state tables to retrieve the metadata hash address – created from the concatenation of Username and Identifier – and digest details of the resource linked to the identifier.

Step 2: Utilizing the metadata address, users connect to the metadata server and are furnished with the metadata file. This file delineates the storage server locations and includes additional metadata such as access control measures and the symmetric encryption key.

Step 3: With the metadata file in hand, users appeal to the network to deliver the encrypted resource data tied to the identifier. This resource request can be executed using either push or pull methods, both incorporated in the Multi-Identifier Router (MIR). Notably, during pull transactions, users do not directly engage with the storage server locations specified in the metadata file.

Step 4: Upon receipt of the resource linked to the identifier, users decrypt the data using the symmetric key and validate its integrity using the provided digest. Successful verification signifies resolution completion. Any integrity issues necessitate a return to Step 3 for repeated attempts.

While IP address identifiers in MIS differ from traditional network IP addresses, MIS retains compatibility with legacy DNS systems. This is achieved by defining domain names in MIS as identifiers that are tied to web resources, with their corresponding IP addresses cataloged within the metadata file. MIS also records special usernames in the format DNS_cache:i (where i is a sequential number) to store DNS resource data.

To resolve a domain name, a user or device queries the MIS identifier table associated with the DNS_cache:i username record. Should this query be unsuccessful, the MIS processor relays the request in standard fashion to a DNS server, subsequently caching the DNS server's response within the metadata file corresponding to the domain name identifier in the global state tables for future referencing.

It should be noted that the domain name resolution process relies on traditional DNS servers for domain name control, not on users or devices within the basic MIS. Consequently, the caching of domain name resolutions proceeds without waiting for consensus, in contrast to the consensus requirements for registering identities and other identifiers. The reliability of domain name resolution services thus hinges on the DNS infrastructure itself.

6.3.4 Inter-Translation of Identifiers

In recognition of the need to support diverse functions and requirements, future networks will incorporate a variety of identifier types, each with its own communication mode. Content identifiers, for instance, are particularly beneficial for managing data-centric resources such as videos and web pages. Service identifiers, on the other hand, enhance the adaptability, decoupling, and reusability of services. For mobile devices that frequently change locations, identity and location identifiers are especially apt.

With this evolution, Internet resource providers are urged to register for multiple identifiers and publish their resources widely to create a rich tapestry of identifier spaces. The basic MIS facilitates user access to these varied identifier types through an inter-translation service, enabling the resolution of identifiers and retrieval of associated resources. This concept is depicted in a diagram, referred to as Figure 6.4.

In the scenario presented in Figure 6.4, the identity identifier space, labeled C_0, contains a specific identity, denoted as (i_0). The space C_1, in addition to housing the

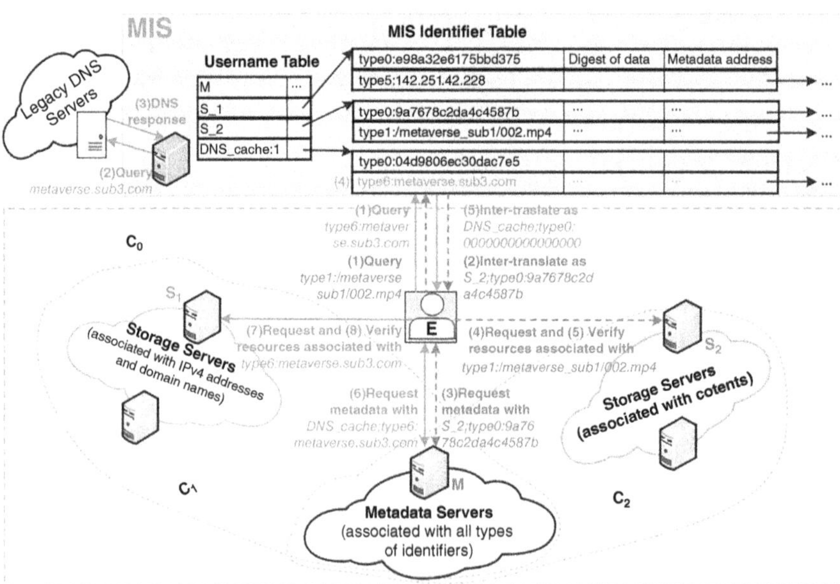

Figure 6.4 An example of inter-translation.

basic identity (i_0), also includes an IPv4 address (i_5) and a domain name (i_6). Similarly, the space C_2 comprises the identity (i_0) along with a content identifier (i_1). Metadata servers, within this framework, manage all these types of identifiers – (i_0), (i_1), (i_5), and (i_6). An ordinary individual end-user, referred to as E, possesses only the essential identity and exists within the identifier space C_0.

This framework supports a multi-faceted Internet where resources are more accessible and services more dynamic, catering to the ever-changing landscape of online content and user interaction.

If user E seeks to resolve the domain name ($type6 : metaverse.\ sub3.\ com$) within identifier space C_1, the procedure unfolds as follows:

Initial query: User E queries the global state tables for the domain name.

Resolution process: If the initial query is unsuccessful, the MIS processor engages to resolve the domain name, returning the inter-translated result to user E. This result includes both the username ($DNS\_cache : 1$) and the associated identity ($type0 : 04d9806ec30dac7e5$), rendering the domain name recognizable in identifier space C_0.

Metadata server request: Subsequently, user E requests from the metadata server M the IPv4 address associated with the domain name, ($type5 : 142.251.42.228$), as detailed in the metadata file.

Communication with storage server: With the identity ($type0 : 04d9806ec30dac7e5$) and the IPv4 address ($type5 : 142.251.42.228$) in hand, user E communicates with the storage server S_1, utilizing the appropriate routing mechanism to access the resource linked to ($type6 : metaverse.\ sub3.\ com$).

User E can similarly resolve content identifiers, such as ($type1 : /metaverse\_sub1/002.\ mp4$) in identifier space C_2. The distinction lies in the data retrieval method: the identity and IPv4 address information is procured via push mode, while content data is retrieved using pull mode. This necessitates an adjustment in the communication mode during the resolution process.

The MIN incorporates a communication modality within the protocol stack that supports both push and pull semantics. To facilitate this, one or more edge routers are established within each identifier space. These routers are tasked with processing packets directed to different identifier spaces, which involves recognizing the type of identifier and switching the communication semantics accordingly.

In essence, the inter-translation service provided by the MIS allows for the same resource data to exist in multiple formats, ensuring accessibility for users across various identifier spaces. This functionality supports seamless interaction within domains, as users can navigate and access resources despite the underlying complexity of different identifier systems.

6.4 Building a Community of Shared Future in Cyberspace with Sovereign Blockchain

A community of shared future in cyberspace founded on sovereign blockchains will pave the way for an Internet governance system with equality, consensus, and co-governance. This represents an inevitable trend toward fostering equitable collaboration in cyberspace and upholding a well-regulated Internet environment. MIS, characterized as a high-performance hierarchical blockchain for multilateral co-management and co-governance, not only achieves cross-chain transmission functionally but also facilitates interoperability with other homogenous or heterogeneous blockchains. Additionally, it can serve as a relay chain to connect diverse blockchains, thereby supporting the establishment of a community of shared future in cyberspace among sovereign entities.

6.4.1 Background Introduction

The concept of a community of shared future in cyberspace, initially proposed in 2015, constitutes a crucial component of novel ideas and strategies for Internet governance. It represents a scientific pathway in the new era to ensure national data security with profound implications and extensive influence. In the process of global Internet development, human society will establish a community of shared future in cyberspace based on the principle of respecting network sovereignty, which necessitates support from sovereign blockchains.

Given the rapid advancement of blockchain technology, a multitude of blockchain applications with distinct functionalities and features have emerged across various sectors such as clearing and settlement, cross-border payments, supply chain finance, the Internet of Things, judicial arbitration, and governmental legal affairs. Each application can be supported by its respective explicit or implicit sovereignties within the global Internet system. Collectively, these applications form a globally interconnected sovereign blockchain network.

However, these blockchain applications operate autonomously and lack interconnectivity, leading to the formation of information silos that restrict requirement diversity and system scalability. Users need to interact with different blockchains in order to access various functionalities. Moreover, the absence of bidirectional communication confines users' assets and data within individual blockchains, significantly diminishing their utilization. Consequently, a mechanism is imperative to facilitate transfer of assets and data across diverse blockchains. These needs can be collectively referred to as blockchain interoperability. To achieve this interoperability, cross-chain protocols have emerged, building bridges for facilitating communication between global blockchain applications.

The introduction of cross-chain communication among sovereign blockchains has the potential to revolutionize their inherent isolation, thereby transforming them into an extensive interconnected network. Cross-chain technology enables smooth data exchange and information sharing between sovereign entities, thereby promoting trust and consensus while strengthening global blockchain network governance as a part of Internet governance. Ultimately, it lays the foundation for a community of shared future in cyberspace with openness, transparency, and mutual trust.

6.4.2 Cross-Chain and Sovereign Internet

In the ecosystem of public blockchains, a cross-chain bridge serves as the primary solution for cross-chain interaction. The security of these bridges is directly linked to the security of cross-chain assets, and various attacks on cross-chain bridges have emerged in practice (Lee et al. 2023, pp. 1–14). To ensure the security of cross-chain protocols, the optimal approach involves performing native verification through light nodes, or reducing verification overhead through zero-knowledge proof technology (Xie et al. 2022, pp. 3003–3017).

Through the joint research and development of academia and industry, there are currently six mainstream cross-chain technologies: Hash-Locking (HL), sidechains, notary schemes, relay, Distributed Private Key Control (DPKC), and Communication Protocol Suites (CPSs).

6.4.2.1 Hash-Locking

HL is a technology designed for asset exchange between blockchain networks. To ensure the security of assets on each blockchain during the exchange process, asset transfers must either be fully completed or not completed at all, with no intermediate states. HL operates without reliance on a trusted coordinator. Suppose there are users of two blockchains A and B, attempting to exchange asset α located on chain A and asset β located on chain B. The specific cross-chain process is shown in Figure 6.5.

Step 1: A first chooses a secret random number S, calculates the hash value H of S using a specific hash algorithm, then sends H to B. Meanwhile, A and B negotiate two time points T_0 and T_1, ensuring that $T_0 > T_1$.

Step 2: A creates an asset lock smart contract LockContractA based on H and T_0. This smart contract will lock asset α, which can be unlocked with S and transferred to B. If it is still not unlocked before T_0, the lock will be automatically canceled, and there will be no asset transfer.

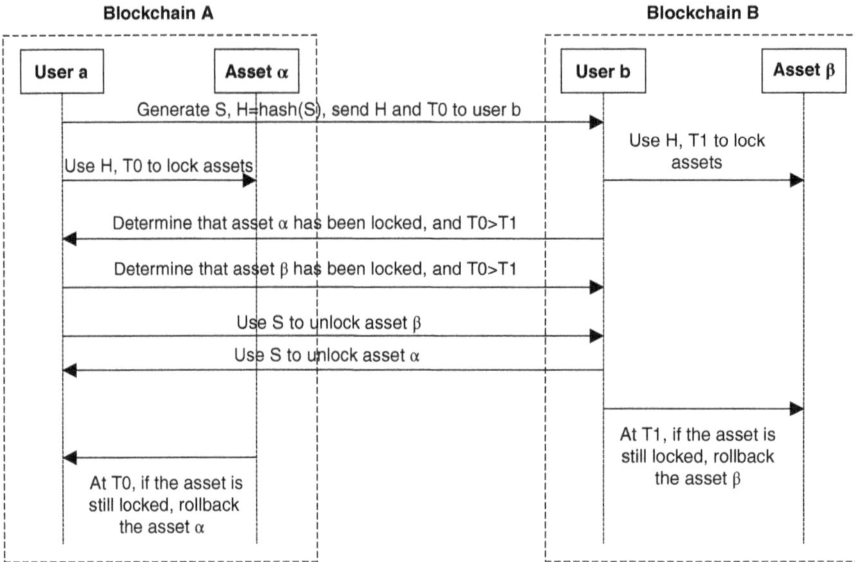

Figure 6.5 Cross-chain process of hash-locking.

Step 3: B creates an asset lock smart contract LockContractB based on H and T_1. This smart contract will lock asset β, which can be unlocked with S and transferred to A. If it is still not unlocked before T_1, the lock will be automatically canceled, and there will be no asset transfer.

Step 4: A uses the secret random number S to call the smart contract LockContractB on B, transferring asset β to A. After the above steps, B obtains the secret random number S. B uses S to call the smart contract LockContractA on A, transferring asset α to B. The asset exchange is completed.

Step 5: If either A or B fails to perform the operation in time, after the specified time T_0 or T_1, the locked assets will be automatically returned to the original owner. This ensures the atomicity of cross-chain asset exchange.

In summary, HL for cross-chain transactions involves one party locking assets using a hash value. If the original hash number can be provided within a specified time, the assets can be acquired. Another party locks assets using the same hash value and sets the same unlocking conditions. One party uses the hash number to unlock and acquire assets, while the other party uses the same hash number to acquire assets. HL is currently the most widely adopted cross-chain asset technology. Lightning Network (Poon and Dryja 2016), Zcash XCAT (Hopwood et al. 2016, p. 32), and WeCross (Ou et al. 2022, p. 109378) are examples of platforms that use HL to facilitate cross-chain asset exchanges.

6.4.2.2 Sidechains

The sidechain is a blockchain that fully possesses the main chain's functionality and runs parallel to it. A sidechain can read and verify information on the main chain, but the main chain cannot perceive it. Sidechains are implemented via two-way pegging technology, which temporarily locks digital currency in the main chain while releasing equivalent digital assets in the sidechain. The biggest challenge in implementing two-way pegging is that the protocol modification must be compatible with the existing main chain without disrupting its operations. Specific implementation methods include Single Management (SM) mode, Consortium Management (CM) mode, Simplified Payment Verification (SPV) mode, Drive Chain (DC) mode, and Mix Mode (MM).

The SM mode is the simplest way to transfer assets between the main chain and the sidechain, as shown in Figure 6.6. Assets on the main chain are sent to a single custodian (such as an exchange), which then activates equivalent digital assets on the sidechain after receiving them. After use, the remaining digital assets are returned to the main chain through the same process. However, a significant drawback of SM mode lies in its excessive centralization.

The CM mode resembles the SM mode, with the distinction that the custodian of assets is transferred from a single entity to a consortium of multiple parties, as shown in Figure 6.7. Members in this consortium act as notaries for asset transfers, hence it is referred to as the Notary Consortium. Each notary signs the asset transfer employing multi-signature technology. The advantage of CM mode is its relative security because hackers would have to compromise several notaries to steal the locked assets. However, it should be noted that CM mode represents a weakly centralized solution and there exists a significant possibility of internal disagreements within the notary consortium leading to an initiation of "mutiny."

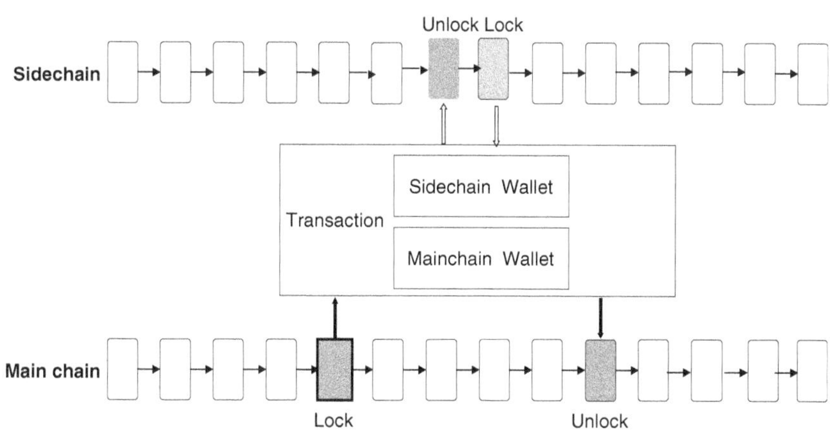

Figure 6.6 Single management mode sidechain.

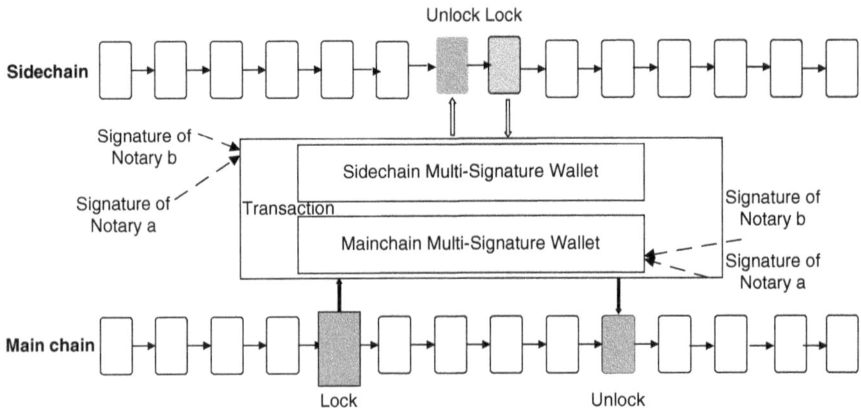

Figure 6.7 Consortium management mode sidechain.

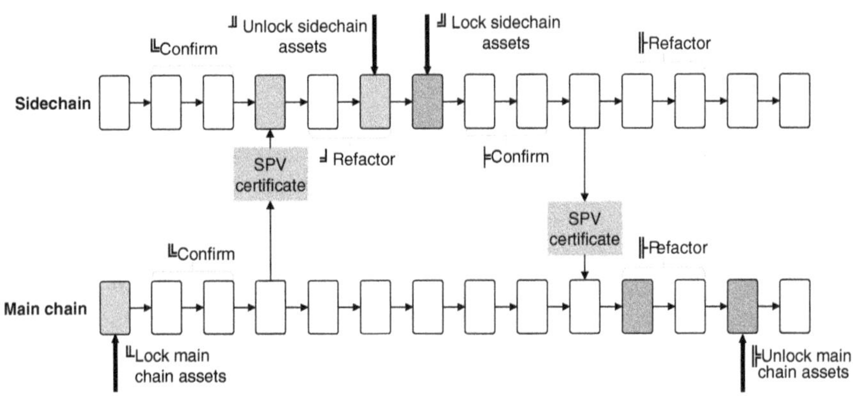

Figure 6.8 Verification process of SPV sidechain.

The SPV mode differs from the aforementioned custody modes as it eliminates the need for a custodian and solely relies on both the main chain and sidechain, as shown in Figure 6.8. A user first makes an SPV output on the main chain, transferring assets to a multi-signature address to lock them. Once the transaction is confirmed, the SPV certificate is broadcast to the sidechain, prompting its nodes to release the corresponding assets and write the transaction into a block. After the refactor phase, the transaction from the main chain to the sidechain is complete, and the transaction from the sidechain to the main chain follows the same principle.

In the DC mode, digital asset miners assume the role of custodians for assets and are entrusted with the authority to supervise them. They exercise voting rights to determine when assets should be unlocked and where to be transferred.

The MM effectively integrates the aforementioned sidechain methods, employing the most appropriate mode for blockchains with diverse structures, such as utilizing SPV for the main chain and DC for the sidechain.

In summary, sidechain technology facilitates relatively straightforward cross-chain implementations; however, its unidirectional access imposes limitations on its potential. Pegged Sidechains (Back et al. 2014, pp. 201–224) serve as the initial technical prototype of sidechains, while RootStock (RSK Infrastructure Framework Whitepaper v1.21), BTCRelay (Ethereum and Consensys), Loom (Campbell and Konstantopoulos 2018), Elements (BlockStream), and Lisk (Lisk Foundation 2023) also leverage sidechain technology to enable cross-chain transactions.

6.4.2.3 Notary Schemes

Notary mechanisms are prevalent in facilitating cross-chain transactions within the cryptocurrency exchange domain, paralleling the function of notaries in traditional settings. When two parties, labeled "a" and "b," lack mutual trust, they may opt to involve a reliable intermediary known as a notary. This intermediary could be a single central authority or a consortium of nodes that both parties trust within the blockchain environment. The intermediary's duties are not limited to gathering data; they also include the affirmation and scrutiny of transactions. There are three main types of notary approaches: Centralized Notary Schemes (CNSs), Multi-Signature Notary Schemes (MNSs), and Distributed-signature Notary Schemes (DNSs).

Focusing on CNS, or single-signature notaries, an appointed autonomous entity or organization is charged with the compilation of data, as well as the ratification and examination of transactions. In this model, the notary operates both as the guarantor of transactions and the mediator in case of disputes, effectively substituting technical trust mechanisms with a central authority. Although this framework provides the advantages of quick processing times, high compatibility with various systems, and straightforward technical design, the security and dependability of the entire system hinge critically on the central authority, presenting a significant risk to overall system robustness.

MNSs require multiple notaries to jointly sign on their respective ledgers to reach a consensus before completing cross-chain transactions. Each node of the multi-signature notary has its own key. Only when a certain number or proportion of notary signatures is reached, the cross-chain transaction can be confirmed. Notaries are an alliance composed of a group of institutions, and the transfer of cross-chain funds is controlled by this alliance. This method is more secure than the single signature mode. If a few notaries are attacked or do evil, it will not affect the normal operation of the system. But both chains themselves need to support multi-signatures.

The primary difference between the DNSs and the MNS resides in their signature methods. The former adopts the concept of Multi-Party Computation (MPC), which enhances security at the expense of increased implementation complexity. It generates a unique cryptographic key in the system and splits it into multiple fragments distributed to randomly selected notaries (no notary in the group would possess the complete key). Even if all notaries assemble their fragments, they cannot deduce the entire key. A certain proportion of notaries can jointly sign to piece together the complete key, thereby accomplishing a more decentralized "data collection verification" process, similar to the threshold signature mechanism. The DNS thoroughly safeguards key security while offering enhanced flexibility and resilience against attacks or errors affecting only a minority of nodes.

In conclusion, notary schemes conduct cross-chain transactions on individual blockchains, mainly by using trusted third parties who have accounts on both blockchains to perform the notarization process. The advantages and disadvantages of notary schemes are clear. An advantage lies in its ability to effectively support cross-chain asset interactions among diverse heterogeneous blockchains. However, a disadvantage is the necessity to identify a mutually trusted third party by both transaction participants. Corda (Brown 2018) employ the notary scheme for cross-chain transactions.

6.4.2.4 Relay

The relay technology is an extension of sidechain technology, incorporating notary mechanisms and other technologies to enable cross-chain interoperability. Unlike relying solely on the verification judgment of a trusted third party, the relay mechanism self-verifies by collecting data states from different blockchains through intermediaries. In this mechanism, application chains connect to the relay through protocol specifications. When initiating a cross-chain operation, an application chain submits transaction information for review through the relay, which then conveys this information to achieve cross-chain interoperability with the target application chain. Over time, two modes have emerged in relay cross-chain development: relay chain mode and relay mode. The former employs one blockchain as a consensus-based intermediary for verifying and forwarding cross-chain data, while the latter combines the CPS technology to forward cross-chain messages via routing without requiring an actual blockchain as an intermediary.

Typical relay cross-chain projects include Cosmos (Kwon and Buchman 2019) and Polkadot (Burdges et al. 2020). Cosmos, founded on the Inter-Blockchain Communication (IBC) protocol and Hub, operates as a relay chain where parallel blockchains connect to the Hub via IBC for facilitating verification and transfer of cross-chain transactions. Currently, Cosmos has implemented an official Hub called Cosmos Hub, as shown in Figure 6.9. While it offers convenience in committing cross-chain transactions for Cosmos SDK-based blockchains, non-Cosmos SDK-based blockchains necessitate the Peg Zone to establish a bridge with the Hub, which not only presents development challenges but also demands considerable effort.

Figure 6.10 illustrates that Polkadot operates as a central relay chain that anchors the parachain architecture. Parachains enable simultaneous transaction processing, which contrasts with linear processing. Distinct State Transition

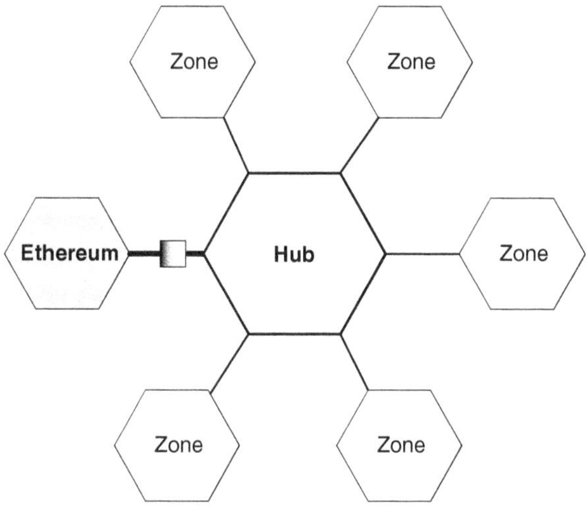

Figure 6.9 Cosmos hub.

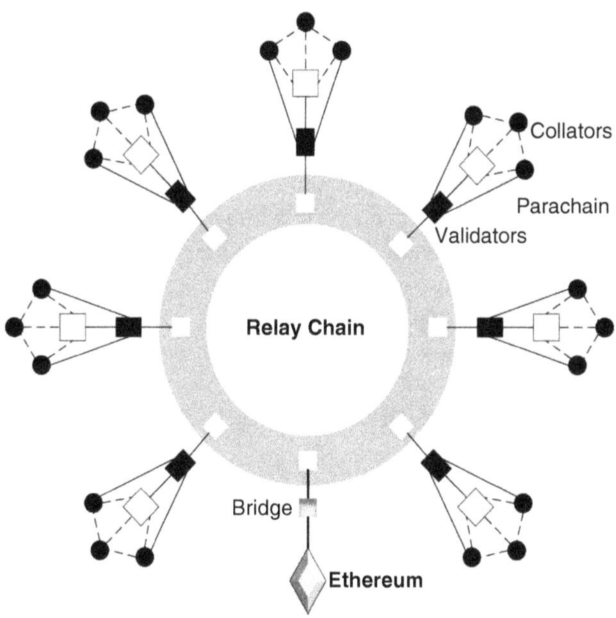

Figure 6.10 Polkadot structure.

Functions (STFs) are characteristic of each individual parachain within the ecosystem. At the heart of Polkadot lies the relay chain, serving as the primary backbone. Polkadot's architecture permits the integration of any blockchain into its network, provided that the blockchain's protocol can be translated into WebAssembly (Wasm) and is compatible with the Relay Chain Application Programming Interface (API). Despite Polkadot's flexibility in accommodating a variety of cross-chain transaction types, such an arrangement presents integration hurdles for numerous pre-existing blockchain frameworks.

At present, relay cross-chain is the most widely used and relatively safe cross-chain technology, applicable to various scenarios and compatible with heterogeneous blockchain systems. However, it still faces challenges in mitigating 51% of attacks under both the relay chain mode and the relay mode.

6.4.2.5 Distributed Private Key Control

The DPKC technology essentially integrates MPC and threshold secret sharing mechanisms, enabling the splitting of the relay chain account's private key into redundant parts that are distributed among validators. This approach effectively mitigates the risk of a single validator engaging in malicious activities during cross-chain asset exchanges, as it requires a combination of multiple validators to possess the private key.

As can be seen from Figure 6.11, DPKC is to map digital assets from various blockchains onto a new blockchain, enabling the exchange of digital assets between different blockchains on this new blockchain. This is done by creating source chain accounts for destination chain users and vice versa. The private keys for these created accounts are distributed and stored by multiple nodes, and only after the transaction is complete do users a and b gain access to the respective account's private key. Furthermore, cross-chain development necessitates adherence to the characteristics specific to each application chain, posing significant challenges in implementation. In addition, cross-chain operations are subject to prolonged confirmation times for application chain transactions, resulting in inefficiencies. Notable projects include FUSION (Yang et al. 2022, pp. 29–43) and Wanchain (Lu et al. 2017, p. 34).

6.4.2.6 Communication Protocol Suites

The Cosmos network, as an early proposer of the IBC protocol, enables direct cross-chain communication between parachains. By specifying a series of communication data formats and protocol standards for blockchain integration, the CPS gradually began to develop as an individual cross-chain technology. Aion (Spoke and NE Team 2017), Block Collider (Block Collider Team 2018), and OneLedger (OneLedger) have successfully implemented cross-chain interoperability using

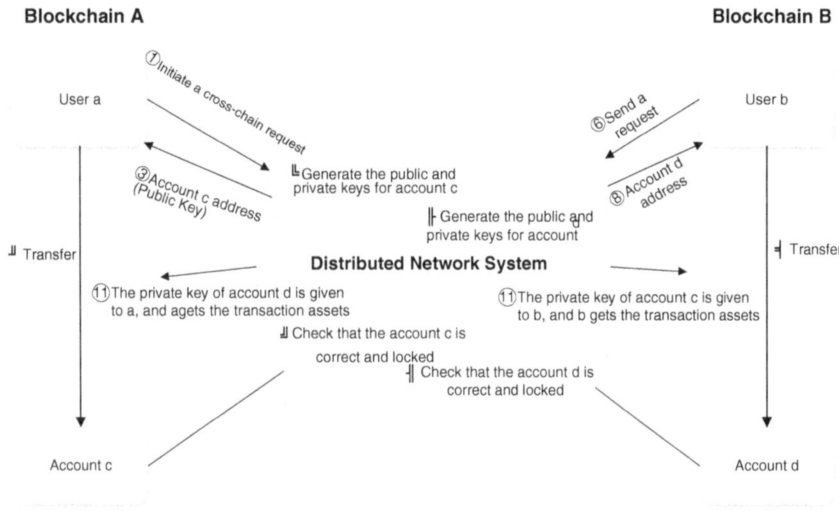

Figure 6.11 The cross-chain process for distributed private key control.

CPS. As CPS mainly defines system structures, communication protocols, data formats, workflow processes, and other standard specifications, this technology is currently in its nascent stage and is often utilized alongside relay technology. Whether it can emerge as a prominent cross-chain solution depends on the industry's acceptance level toward the protocol standard.

The six major mainstream cross-chain technologies will connect different blockchain micro-ecosystems, which are built on the concept of sovereignty and are designed by organizations or communities according to specific scenario requirements to achieve specific purposes and value propositions. In the future, sovereign blockchain ecosystems can interact and cooperate through cross-chain technology to jointly promote the development of a sovereign Internet.

6.4.3 Co-Governed Community of Shared Future in Cyberspace

The digital age has ushered in an era of unprecedented interconnectivity, with the rise of blockchain technology being one of its most transformative developments. Blockchain networks, with their ability to offer secure, transparent, and immutable records, have proliferated rapidly across various sectors, from finance to supply chain management to sovereign data governance.

However, this explosive growth has brought with it a significant challenge: the need for effective and efficient interconnectivity among a multitude of blockchain networks. The concept of a "Co-Governed Community of Shared Future in

Cyberspace" speaks to this necessity, envisioning a cyberspace where multiple blockchains can communicate seamlessly and reliably, fostering a collaborative digital environment.

6.4.3.1 The Challenge of Interconnectivity

The sheer number of blockchain networks in existence poses a daunting task for achieving full interconnectivity. If we were to attempt direct cross-chain communication between each pair, as one might first imagine, the number of required communication nodes would be $n(n-1)/2$, where n represents the number of blockchains. This approach scales poorly, with a complexity of $O(n^2)$, rendering it impractical for large-scale implementations. Such complexity not only poses technical difficulties but also raises concerns about the robustness, security, and efficiency of the entire system.

6.4.3.2 A Central Relay Chain as the Solution

To overcome these challenges, a central relay chain presents a more viable solution. This design simplifies the connectivity model by positioning a single relay chain at the heart of the network. Other blockchains then only need to establish a connection with this central chain, significantly reducing the number of required communication nodes to $2(n-1)$ and bringing the complexity down to $O(n)$. This makes the system scalable and feasible for widespread adoption.

6.4.3.3 The Role of MIS in Cross-Chain Solutions

MIS, with its hierarchical structure and performance capabilities, emerges as an ideal candidate for the central relay chain in this grand vision of interconnected blockchain networks. Governed by multiple parties, including authoritative organizations and various national governments, MIS offers the kind of reliability and compliance that is crucial for widespread trust and adoption.

The multilateral governance of MIS ensures that cross-chain data transmission is not only secure but also adheres to the necessary regulatory standards, facilitating cooperation across different jurisdictions. This is essential in a world where digital transactions often span multiple countries, each with its own legal and regulatory framework.

6.4.3.4 Performance and Efficiency

From a performance perspective, MIS's efficient hierarchical design allows it to handle the demands of cross-chain operations among a large number of networks. It acts as a robust backbone, capable of routing and verifying transactions with high speed and reliability. This efficiency is paramount, as the relay chain will invariably face a high volume of cross-chain data traffic.

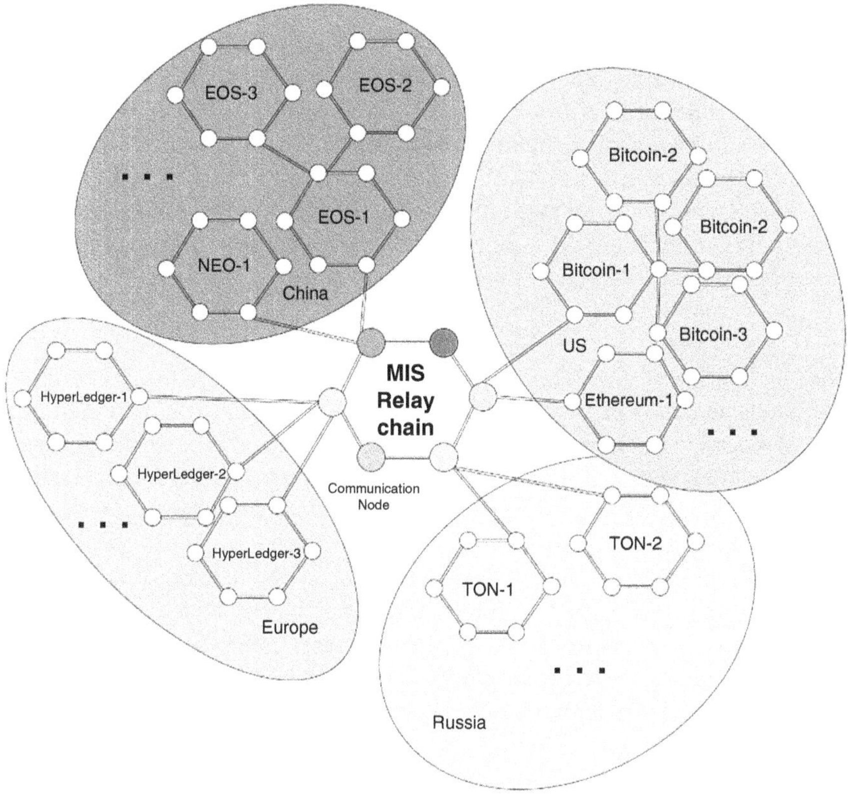

Figure 6.12 MIS as a relay chain.

6.4.3.5 Implementation of MIS as a Relay Chain

As depicted in Figure 6.12, MIS takes on the role of a relay chain by establishing a communication node for each supported blockchain network. Blockchain networks then connect to the MIS network's communication node, thus enabling cross-chain operations.

For instance, consider a scenario where China wants to engage in bulk commodity trade with Europe, requiring the exchange of a goods certificate between China's sovereign chain and Europe's sovereign chain. Here's how the process would work:

Step 1: A cross-chain transaction initiates from the China chain to the Europe chain.

Step 2: The MIS communication node of the China chain sends a message to the MIS chain's China communication node, following the established cross-chain protocol.

Step 3: The message is verified through the transport layer, ensuring its authenticity and integrity.

Step 4: The application layer fields are then sent internally to the Europe communication node within MIS.

Step 5: The Europe communication node on the MIS chain constructs a new transport layer message.

Step 6: This message is sent to the MIS communication node on the Europe chain.

Step 7: After verification, the cross-chain transaction is deemed complete, and the goods certificate is successfully transferred.

6.4.3.6 The Shared Sovereign Internet and a Co-Governed Cyberspace

The implementation of MIS as the central relay chain enables the creation of a shared sovereign Internet, where sovereign blockchains can interact without compromising their autonomy or security. This fosters a co-governed environment in cyberspace, where different nations and organizations can collaborate while still maintaining control over their digital assets and data.

Moreover, the MIS framework can be expanded to include not just sovereign blockchains but also corporate, public, and private blockchains, creating a truly interconnected network that spans different sectors and industries. This democratization of data exchange could spur innovation, streamline international trade, and enhance global governance mechanisms.

6.4.3.7 The Future of Co-Governed Cyberspace

The vision of a Co-Governed Community of Shared Future in Cyberspace is not without its challenges. Issues such as cross-chain security, data privacy, and regulatory compliance must be meticulously addressed. However, the potential benefits are immense.

We could see a future where digital identities are portable across borders, where supply chains are fully transparent and efficient, and where financial transactions are seamless and inclusive. This would represent a significant step toward a more connected, cooperative, and harmonious global society. The MIS as a relay chain is more than a technical solution; it's a foundation for building a collaborative and resilient digital infrastructure that can adapt to the evolving needs of societies and economies worldwide.

In this envisioned future, the MIS relay chain would serve as a facilitator for numerous applications:

International trade: By simplifying the process of transferring digital assets and credentials across borders, the MIS could reduce the friction in international trade, making it faster and more cost-effective.

Global supply chains: With a reliable and transparent relay chain, global supply chains could become more resilient against disruptions. Tracking the provenance and status of goods could be done in real-time, allowing for better planning and response to any irregularities.

Financial services: Cross-chain transactions facilitated by the MIS could revolutionize financial services by enabling more seamless currency exchanges, remittances, and multi-currency wallets, potentially increasing financial inclusion worldwide.

Sovereign data governance: Sovereign chains connected through the MIS could securely share and verify citizen data when necessary, such as for visa applications or international education credentials, while maintaining data sovereignty.

Smart contracts: Complex smart contracts that span multiple blockchains could be executed more effectively, enabling new types of decentralized applications and services.

6.4.3.8 Ensuring Security and Privacy in a Co-Governed Cyberspace

Security and privacy are paramount concerns in the Co-Governed Community of Shared Future in Cyberspace. As the MIS relay chain becomes a critical piece of infrastructure, it would need to incorporate advanced cryptographic techniques and robust consensus mechanisms to prevent any form of tampering or unauthorized access.

Privacy would also be a major focus, with the implementation of privacy-preserving technologies such as zero-knowledge proofs enabling the verification of transactions without revealing sensitive information. The design of the MIS would need to balance transparency with the need to protect individual and corporate data.

6.4.3.9 Regulatory Compliance and Standardization

For the MIS to be truly effective, it must operate within an agreed-upon framework of standards and regulations. This requires international collaboration to establish cross-chain communication protocols that are secure, transparent, and compliant with global regulations.

Standardization efforts would need to cover various aspects, including:

Interoperability protocols: Defining how blockchains communicate, including message formats and verification processes.

Security standards: Ensuring that all participating chains meet high-security standards to maintain the integrity of the network.

Data governance: Developing rules for data sharing and privacy that comply with international laws, such as GDPR.

Operational guidelines: Establishing procedures for the maintenance, upgrade, and scaling of the MIS infrastructure.

6.4.3.10 The Role of Multilateral Governance

The governance of the MIS relay chain is inherently multilateral. It involves the collaboration of diverse stakeholders, including governments, private sector entities, and nongovernmental organizations. This governance structure must be transparent and democratic to build trust and ensure that the infrastructure operates in the best interest of all parties involved.

A governing council or consortium could be established to oversee the MIS, with representatives from different regions and sectors. This body would be responsible for making decisions on upgrades, dispute resolution, and the integration of new blockchains into the network.

The concept of a Co-Governed Community of Shared Future in Cyberspace is ambitious, yet it represents the next logical step in the evolution of blockchain technology. By enabling scalable and efficient cross-chain communication through a central relay chain like the MIS, we can unlock the full potential of blockchain networks and build a more interconnected and cooperative digital world.

The success of this vision will depend on the collective effort of the international community to address technical, security, privacy, and regulatory challenges. It will require foresight, collaboration, and a commitment to shared values and objectives. If achieved, the result will be a cyberspace where innovation thrives, economies are more integrated, and societies are more connected than ever before.

The journey toward a Co-Governed Community of Shared Future in Cyberspace is just beginning, and the MIS relay chain could very well be the cornerstone that enables this new era of digital collaboration.

6.5 Chapter Summary

This chapter delves into a novel network management technology for multiple types of identifiers that combines blockchain technology. The motivation behind this stems from the security vulnerabilities associated with the centralization of the existing DNS, thereby necessitating the implementation of a decentralized system called MIS for co-governance and autonomy. The core architecture is based on a basic single-chain MIS, with scalability for large networks achieved through a hierarchical strategy similar to multi-chain approaches. The key functions include identity management and access control, registration, update, revocation, resolution, and inter-translation of identifiers. Additionally, cross-chain transfers are supported to provide an open, co-governed, and shared Internet solution.

Discussion Questions

6.1 What are the advantages of the four-tier architecture of basic MIS?

A: The foundational MIS's quad-level structure enhances scalability substantially. Inter-tier connections are deliberately designed with loose coupling, ensuring that modifications within one tier have minimal impact on the others' discrete functionalities. Moreover, it emphasizes robust security protocols for data storage; resource data is encrypted and access is confined to users who meet predetermined policies. The system's consensus mechanism is both efficient and streamlined, bolstering read/write operations via indexing and minimizing blockchain data load through the implementation of RS encoding and strategic timeline management.

6.2 What are the characteristics of the consensus mechanism in basic MIS?

A: Basic MIS designs a consensus tier that is built upon the efficient PPoV consensus algorithm. This tier includes three node rights – bookkeeping, voting, and aggregating. The bookkeeper proposes transactions, while the voter reviews them and the aggregator controls vote results. Moreover, basic MIS enhances the PPoV algorithm by using BLS signatures instead of ECDSA, reducing block header size through signature aggregation. Furthermore, to effectively handle different types of data within basic MIS, two additional strategies are introduced – RS code and timeline strategy. These strategies enable direct caching without encoding for hot data and partial caching with encoding for warm data. On the other hand, cold data is solely encoded without being cached at all. By implementing these strategies, redundancy is significantly reduced while ensuring optimal read/write performance.

6.3 What functions does MIS have?

A: MIS implements a comprehensive DNS alternative system, facilitating the management and resolution of multiple identifiers. Its primary functionalities encompass identifier registration, update, revocation, and resolution. It also supports cross-identifier space resolution through inter-translation of identifiers, enabling users to access related resource data by resolving various types of identifiers. Meanwhile, MIS is compatible with the legacy DNS by forwarding query requests to get DNS responses. With these functions, MIS can act as a large-scale relay chain for global cross-chain transmission.

References

Back, A., Corallo, M., Dashjr, L., Friedenbach, M., Maxwell, G., Miller, A., Poelstra, A., Timón, J. and Wuille, P., 2014. Enabling blockchain innovations with pegged sidechains. https://kevinriggen.com/files/sidechains.pdf, 72, pp. 201–224.

Block Collider Team, 2018. Block Collider Whitepaper. https://s3.amazonaws.com/blockcollider/blockcollider_wp.pdf.

BlockStream (2023), Elements. https://elementsproject.org.

Boneh, D., Lynn, B. and Shacham, H., 2001, November. Short signatures from the Weil pairing. In International Conference on the Theory and Application of Cryptology and Information Security (pp. 514–532). Berlin, Heidelberg: Springer Berlin Heidelberg.

Brown, R.G., 2018. The corda platform: An introduction. Retrieved, 27, p. 2018.

Burdges, J., Cevallos, A., Czaban, P., Habermeier, R., Hosseini, S., Lama, F., Alper, H.K., Luo, X., Shirazi, F., Stewart, A. and Wood, G., 2020. Overview of polkadot and its design considerations. arXiv preprint arXiv:2005.13456.

Campbell, M. and Konstantopoulos, G., 2018. Plasma cash initial release-plasmabacked nfts now available on loom network sidechains. https://medium.com/loom-network/plasma-cash-initial-release-plasma-backed-nfts-now-available-on-loom-network-sidechains-37976d0cfccd.

Ethereum and Consensys (2016). BTC Relay: A bridge between the Bitcoin blockchain & Ethereum smart contracts. http://btcrelay.org.

Hopwood, D., Bowe, S., Hornby, T. and Wilcox, N., 2016. Zcash protocol specification. GitHub: San Francisco, CA, USA, 4(220), p. 32.

Kalodner, H.A., Carlsten, M., Ellenbogen, P.M., Bonneau, J. and Narayanan, A., 2015, June. An empirical study of namecoin and lessons for decentralized namespace design. In WEIS (Vol. 1, No. 1, pp. 1–23).

Kwon, J. and Buchman, E., 2019. Cosmos whitepaper. A Netw. Distrib. Ledgers, 27.

Lee, S.S., Murashkin, A., Derka, M. and Gorzny, J., 2023, May. Sok: Not quite water under the bridge: Review of cross-chain bridge hacks. In 2023 IEEE International Conference on Blockchain and Cryptocurrency (ICBC) (pp. 1–14). IEEE.

Lerner, S.D., 2015. Rsk. *RootStock Core Team, White Paper.*

Lisk Foundation, 2023. Blockchain interoperability. https://lisk.com/documentation/intro/blockchain-interoperability.html.

Lu, J., Yang, B., Liang, Z., Zhang, Y., Demmon, S., Swartz, E. and Lu, L., 2017. Wanchain: Building super financial markets for the new digital economy (p. 34). Technical report.

Nakamoto, S., 2008. Bitcoin: A peer-to-peer electronic cash system. Decentralized business review.

OneLedger. Public Blockchain White Paper v2.0. https://blog.oneledger.io/hubfs/Website/Whitepaper/oneledger-whitepaper.en.pdf.

Ou, W., Huang, S., Zheng, J., Zhang, Q., Zeng, G. and Han, W., 2022. An overview on cross-chain: Mechanism, platforms, challenges and advances. *Computer Networks*, 218, p. 109378.

Poon, J. and Dryja, T., 2016. The bitcoin lightning network: Scalable off-chain instant payments.

Spoke, M. and NE Team, 2017. Aion: Enabling the decentralized internet. AION, White Paper.

Syed, T.A., Alzahrani, A., Jan, S., Siddiqui, M.S., Nadeem, A. and Alghamdi, T., 2019. A comparative analysis of blockchain architecture and its applications: Problems and recommendations. *IEEE access*, 7, pp. 176838–176869.

Wang, H., Li, H., Smahi, A., Zhao, F., Yao, Y., Chan, C.C., Wang, S., Yang, W. and Li, S.Y.R., 2023. MIS: A multi-identifier management and resolution system in the metaverse. *ACM Transactions on Multimedia Computing, Communications and Applications*, 20, pp. 1–25.

Wicker, S.B. and Bhargava, V.K. eds., 1999. *Reed-Solomon codes and their applications*. John Wiley & Sons.

Xie, T., Zhang, J., Cheng, Z., Zhang, F., Zhang, Y., Jia, Y., Boneh, D. and Song, D., 2022, November. zkbridge: Trustless cross-chain bridges made practical. In Proceedings of the 2022 ACM SIGSAC Conference on Computer and Communications Security (pp. 3003–3017).

Yang, G., Zang, C., Chen, J., Guo, D. and Zhang, J., 2022. Distributed fusion cross-chain model and architecture. *IET Blockchain*, 2(2), pp. 29–43.

7

Integrating Consortium Blockchain and Mimic Security in Distributed Storage System

This chapter provides a comprehensive engineering implementation of a mimic distributed secure storage system integrating blockchain technology. First, we will introduce the current development status of the combination of blockchain and storage systems, and explain the original intention of designing a mimic distributed secure storage system. Next, we will introduce the endogenously secure mimic distributed object storage system that effectively mitigates attacks based on unknown vulnerabilities and backdoors to ensure data security across additional storage devices. Finally, our focus lies on exploring the application of blockchain in the storage field through a blockchain logging system based on the Parallel Proof of Vote (PPoV) consensus algorithm.

7.1 Background Introduction and Requirement Analysis

In distributed systems, resource sharing is the foundation and distributed storage systems form the bottom layer of many distributed applications. Distributed storage systems allow processes distributed on different servers to share data in a safe and reliable manner. Different from centralized systems, distributed systems need to deal with the synchronization problems caused by shared data and solve the consistency and reliability problems of copy and cache on every individual node. In a distributed storage system, inter-process communication and network communication services need to have long-term performance, high availability, fault isolation and mistrust tolerance.

Traditional network storage is limited by performance, capacity, software and hardware costs when faced with storing PB-level, ZB-level, or higher data, and scalability has become a serious bottleneck. Large-scale distributed storage system has become an effective system for storing massive data due to its high throughput,

Principles and Applications of Blockchain Systems: How to Overcome the CAP Trilemma in Consortium Blockchain, First Edition. Hui Li and Han Wang.

Published 2025 by John Wiley & Sons, Inc.

high availability, high scalability, and low hardware cost, and has been widely deployed and used. The current mainstream distributed storage systems in the industry include Google File System (GFS) (Ghemawat, Gobioff, and Leung 2003, pp. 29–43), Microsoft's Azure (Brunetti 2011, p. 9), Amazon's Dynamo (DeCandia et al. 2007, pp. 205–220), Apache's Hadoop Distributed File System (HDFS) (Shvachko et al. 2010, pp. 1–10) and Ceph (Weil et al. 2006, pp. 307–320), an open-source storage platform that complies with Portable Operating System Interface for UNIX (POSIX) standards. Among them, HDFS is an open-source implementation of GFS and is widely used as backend infrastructure in many large enterprises, such as Yahoo, Amazon, Facebook, and eBay.

The gradual rise of blockchain technology in recent years has shown its huge advantages in building decentralized networks. Blockchain technology provides all participating nodes in a trustless network with a global operation view of a log that is almost impossible to tamper with, ensuring that all nodes can independently obtain and verify all global transaction records. At the same time, this method eliminates central maintenance costs, improves the overall operating efficiency of the system, and further optimizes resource allocation methods. Therefore, many storage fields, such as cloud storage systems, distributed storage systems, databases, etc., have begun to try to integrate blockchain technology into storage systems to improve system security (Sharma, Jindal, and Borah 2021, p. 102970; Ge et al. 2022, pp. 1092–1104; Hong et al. 2023, pp. 1685–1698; Lai, Liu, and Lo 2023, pp. 1–28). Centralized intermediate functions serve as the performance bottleneck of distributed storage architecture, limiting the scalability of the system and accompanied by problems such as the possibility of users' private information being eavesdropped and leaked. Distributed storage systems combined with blockchain technology can achieve decentralized management of transactions and data, ensuring metadata security and the consistency and reliability of application data.

The Inter Planetary File System (IPFS) (Benet 2014) is a mature distributed file system implemented based on blockchain, which provides a high-throughput, content-addressed block storage model that can save nearly 60% of the network bandwidth and supports permanent data storage and historical version review. On the other hand, BigChainDB (McConaghy et al. 2016, pp. 53–72) fills the gap in the decentralized ecology. It is a decentralized database combined with blockchain technology, which ensures decentralized control and immutability of transactions. It has the performance of millions of write operations per second, storage of petabytes of data, and subsecond response times.

The application scenarios for distributed storage technology merged with blockchain are extensive. For instance, it facilitates the implementation of decentralized network transmission protocols, reducing reliance on the backbone network for Internet applications. It also provides management services for digital assets to both enterprises and individuals, lowering the costs and risks associated with management while addressing the issue of opaque historical records. However, it still struggles to avoid attacks such as double-spending, selfish mining, and 51% attacks, which can forge and tamper with the blockchain ledger. They also lack defense against attacks based on unknown vulnerabilities and backdoors. Therefore, the future direction of distributed storage technology merged with blockchain should focus on constructing a decentralized and inherently secure storage ecosystem. This involves researching consensus algorithms with reduced communication costs and superior robustness, exploring decentralized identity management, key management, and access control technologies, as well as investigating high-performance log management technologies that ensure data immutability and process transparency. These efforts aim to achieve multilateral co-government. To counter unknown vulnerabilities and backdoor attacks specifically: implementing a data reading/writing process capable of detecting such attacks; employing resource scheduling strategies that randomly perturb attack behavior; establishing defense mechanisms for promptly eliminating problematic data storage media through effective cleaning procedures.

The mimic storage system introduced in this chapter is a decentralized and endogenously secure distributed storage system developed by the Peking University Lab of China Environment for Network Innovations (CENI). It aims to ensure the security and reliability of data. The mimic storage system not only serves as an auxiliary storage solution for the blockchain but also implements a blockchain logging system. The subsequent sections will also provide detailed explanations of the principles and implementation of the blockchain logging system.

The first thing that needs to be introduced is the meaning of mimicry. Mimic Phenomenon (MP) refers to an ecological adaptation phenomenon in which an organism can imitate another organism or environment in characteristics such as color, texture, and shape, thereby benefiting one or both parties. According to the classification of defensive behavior, it can be included in the category of adaptive defense based on endogenous mechanisms, which can also be called Mimic Guise (MG). If this camouflage is not only limited to color, texture, and shape but can also imitate the camouflage of another creature or environment in behavior and form, we call it Mimic Defense (MD) (Zheng et al. 2022, pp. 422–435).

Inspired by biomimicry in nature, Prof. Jiangxing Wu from the Chinese Academy of Engineering has introduced this adaptive defense mechanism into cyberspace (Wu 2022a, p. 156301). This method proves effective in addressing the cybersecurity challenge of being vulnerable to attacks in cyberspace, particularly when facing major threats like unknown vulnerabilities, backdoors, viruses, and trojans. It overcomes several limitations of traditional security methods in dealing with uncertain threats. The Cyberspace Mimic Defense (CMD) theory emerged as the times required.

The current state of cybersecurity is characterized by a susceptibility to attacks and challenges in defense (Wu 2022b, pp. 179–185). This situation can be attributed to two fundamental factors:

1) There exist unknown and unidentified threats in the current cyberspace. Such threats are usually based on vulnerabilities in the software and hardware components of information systems, or deliberate implantation of software and hardware backdoors in the industrial chain in the era of globalization to implement human attacks. With the current level of science and technology and cognitive abilities of mankind, it is still impossible to make a scientific determination that a given complex information system has no loopholes and no backdoors from a theoretical level, nor can it completely avoid design defects or completely eliminate backdoors from an engineering level. This makes attacks based on unknown vulnerabilities, backdoors or virus Trojans have become the biggest security threat in cyberspace.
2) The current defensive systems in cyberspace are precise defense based on the perception of threat characteristics. Based on known risks or assumptions of unknown risks, it requires prior knowledge support regarding the source, characteristics, methods, and behaviors of attacks. In defensive mechanisms, it falls under acquired immunity, usually necessitating encryption or authentication functionalities as baseline defenses. Obviously, there are vulnerabilities in defensive systems and mechanisms when dealing with unknown attacks based on unknown vulnerabilities, backdoors or viruses, and Trojans. Especially in an ecological environment where the credibility of system software and hardware components cannot be guaranteed, there are almost no real-time and efficient responses to uncertain threats other than "remedial measures," and there is no absolute guarantee that encryption authentication links or functions will not be deliberately bypassed or short-circuited. In addition, the static, similar, and deterministic nature of the existing information system architecture also provides attackers with many conveniences such as target identification, defensive behavior detection, attack technology testing and improvement, and attack effect evaluation. At the same time, most information systems adopt a resource-sharing operating mechanism in a single processing space. As long as an intruder can enter this space, he or she may achieve the desired operation through the resource-sharing mechanism. This is also one of the important basic conditions for many network attack theories, including the "side channel" attack principle currently employed to breach the "physically isolated network." Therefore, key issues such as the certainty of the information system architecture and mechanism, the vulnerability of the passive defensive system, and the lack of active immunity mechanisms together constitute the largest security black hole in cyberspace.

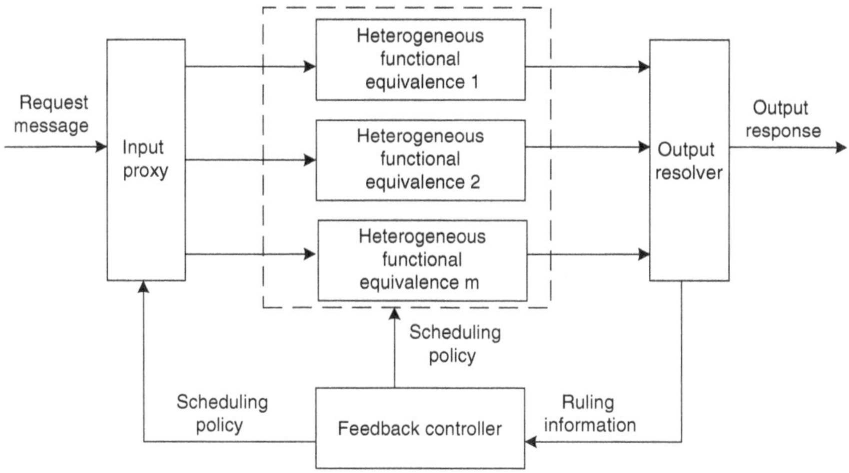

Figure 7.1 Mimic defense architecture.

As shown in Figure 7.1, the MD architecture includes core components such as input proxy, heterogeneous functional equivalents, output resolver, and feedback controller. The input proxy of the system forwards input to heterogeneous functional equivalents within the current service pool. The output vectors of these heterogeneous functional equivalents are submitted to an output resolver for voting, resulting in the system output. We collectively refer to the input proxy and the output resolver as Mimic Bracket (MB). CMD's unique endogenous defense mechanism based on generalized robust control architecture technology excels in five aspects: First, it has the capability to convert targeted man-made and deterministic attack actions against individual vulnerability backdoors within the MBs into the mimic world. Second, attack events with uncertain effects can be transformed into reliability issues with controllable probabilities within MBs. Third, the strategy scheduling based on mimic judgment and the multidimensional dynamic reconstruction negative feedback mechanism can exhibit an uncertainty effect from the attacker's perspective. Fourth, with the help of the logical expression mechanism of relatively correct axioms, uncertain threats can be perceived without relying on attacker information or behavioral characteristics. Fifth, it can transform or normalize nontraditional security threats into classical reliability and robust control problems, enabling appropriate handling of such challenges.

Currently, prototypes and products of routers, Web servers, and distributed storage systems with MD attributes have been successively launched, accompanied by rigorous testing. The findings demonstrate that MD technology indeed reduces the probability of unknown vulnerabilities and backdoor exposure, and can greatly improve the system security. Despite the increasing complexity of network environments, distributed storage systems can alleviate the pressure brought by the growing amount of massive data; however, the security of the storage system still faces a great test.

In order to further improve the security of the system, it is of great significance to collect and manage logs in the mimic storage system. The mimic distributed storage system includes multiple functional modules and multiple server nodes, such as system management configuration, functionally equivalent executors, and input and output agent modules. In order to improve the efficiency of system managers, a log management module is designed to promptly detect abnormal situations that the system may suffer. The log management module is mainly responsible for collecting logs scattered on various servers. Through centralized log management, system managers can avoid inefficiently logging in to the production server to view log records. When a system is maliciously attacked, it is usually accompanied by malicious tampering or even malicious deletion of log data, making it difficult to conduct effective electronic evidence collection of related security incidents. It is also difficult for system administrators to trace intrusions and repair vulnerabilities in the system in a timely manner. The mimic distributed storage system uses the log management module to protect log data and prevent log records from being destroyed intentionally or unintentionally.

The log records in the mimic distributed storage system primarily encompass system logs and user access logs. System logs record the startup and shutdown of services and nodes, resource usage and fault information of the virtual storage system, which are crucial for monitoring the operating status and security. User access logs serve to record user login and logout activities and track user behavior. They can help analyze user behavior characteristics and detect abnormal situations in a timely manner. Typical log content includes objects such as service type, log level, operation time, source/target objects involved in operations, and operation details.

In response to the basic needs of the log management module of the mimic distributed storage system, the logging system collects the log data of each functional module and server node, enabling centralized log management while enhancing the efficiency of system management. At the same time, this protects the security of the log data and prevents it from being maliciously modified or even deletion. Additionally, it provides functions such as log auditing, electronic evidence collection, and tracing intrusion behaviors. The basic functional points of the logging system are listed below:

1) *Flexible log collection function*: The mimic distributed storage system is built upon a dynamic redundant heterogeneous model, comprising multiple functional modules and server nodes. To mitigate the occurrence of similar defects,

diverse technology stacks are employed in the mimic storage executor. Therefore, the system needs to have flexible log collection capabilities that can accommodate various types of log sources.

2) *Secure persistent storage function*: Logging is of utmost importance for mimic storage systems. Administrators can analyze potential system scenarios based on log data, trace intrusion behaviors, and promptly address vulnerabilities. In addition, the system provides log auditing and electronic voucher functions for security events when necessary, necessitating robust measures to prevent intentional or unintentional tampering or deletion of log records.
3) *High available distributed architecture design*: Due to the importance of logging, the log management module should not have a single point of failure. Considering future business growth, this system needs to support horizontal expansion. Each system module must provide external services in cluster mode, and no single point of risk is allowed.
4) *Log query and analysis*: For the convenience of users in querying and analyzing the system-generated log data, the system should possess convenient functionalities such as querying by block height, retrieving data for a specified block height, searching log data for specific error codes, and querying log data within specified time frames.

At present, most of the log data in the industry are persistently stored in traditional databases. Single-machine or distributed databases are selected based on the magnitude of the log data, such as MySQL and Hadoop Database (HBase) based on the Structured Query Language (SQL). In the application scenarios of big data on the Internet, the industry also stores log data in distributed file systems such as HDFS in text format. Subsequently, they employ distributed computing technologies for data mining and personalized recommendations, among other tasks. Blockchain improves the security of traditional storage systems through smart contracts and other methods. The blockchain records completed transaction data in all nodes and does not support deletion and update operations. The consensus algorithm prevents single points of evil and ensures the security and availability of data. However, the blockchain has the defects of high write latency and low throughput. There are also differences in query methods between blockchain and distributed databases. The query function of distributed database requires the work of multiple nodes. When there are too many read, write, and query operations, its performance will decline rapidly. Conversely, each node within a blockchain stores complete data independently enabling independent execution of query operations. Log data is a very important part of the mimic distributed storage system. It records user access and system operating status. System administrators analyze abnormal behaviors based on log data, and system configuration managers initiate adaptive defense functions based on abnormal behaviors. In order to prevent attackers from modifying or even deleting system log data during intrusion attempts, making it difficult to track system defects and vulnerabilities, log data is persistently stored in the blockchain. The chain data structure and cryptography technology are used in the blockchain to ensure that the data cannot be tampered with, and its point-to-point multicopy method also improves the security of the data.

Currently, the industry has developed a variety of distributed logging system, such as Apache's Chukwa (Boulon et al. 2008, pp. 1–5) and LogDevice developed by Facebook. Chukwa developed by Apache is an open-source data collection system for monitoring large distributed systems. It is built on top of Hadoop's HDFS and map/reduce framework, inherits Hadoop's scalability and robustness, and can handle terabytes of data. Facebook's LogDevice log storage system is a decentralized distributed system that can handle high-concurrency transactions in large-scale clusters while meeting the requirements of high availability, continuous writing, and returning data in record order. ELK Stack is a set of tools developed by Elastic to collect, format, index, analyze, and visualize data. It includes three open-source projects: Elasticsearch, Logstash, and Kibana. Elasticsearch is a search and analytics engine, Logstash is a server-side data processing pipeline that pulls data from multiple sources simultaneously, transforms it, and sends it into Elasticsearch, and Kibana allows users to consume charts and graphs from Elasticsearch Visualize data. Bilibili's billions logging system is built on the basis of the Elastic Stack. Its effective fragmentation and management mechanism reduces the memory consumption of the system, reduces the number of disk IOs, and improves the retrieval speed when the amount of data is large.

These traditional logging systems primarily focus on efficient designs for log collection, query, and analysis, but pay less attention to the design of log storage. They usually use existing distributed storage systems like HDFS for data storage. However, despite enhancing system fault tolerance through redundancy, they fail to address the presence of malicious nodes within the cluster. Attacks on critical nodes such as the name node in HDFS can lead to system collapse or even data deletion. Blockchain is a special distributed storage system. The consensus algorithm that controls the operation of the blockchain system exhibits Byzantine fault tolerance, that is, it has a certain tolerance for the existence of malicious nodes. Building a logging system through blockchain technology would significantly enhance its security.

Next, we will discuss the mimic distributed object storage system (Yu et al. 2021, pp. 109–120) developed by the Peking University Lab of CENI. This system is designed based on blockchain technology and MD theory. It has the characteristics of decentralization and endogenous security, while also integrating a self-developed blockchain logging system with tamper-proof properties.

7.2 Mimic Distributed Secure Storage System

With the advent of big data, cloud computing, and the Internet of Things, the Internet has seen a continuous increase in vast amounts of unstructured data such as images, audio, and videos. Distributed object storage systems have emerged as the mainstream solution for cloud storage. As the number of distributed applications grows, data security within these systems has become a focal point. Traditional defense mechanisms for distributed object storage systems involve patching discovered system vulnerabilities or modifying corresponding structures and upgrades. However, these approaches are reactive and struggle to address unknown security threats. Building upon the theory of MD, an inherently secure mimic distributed storage system is introduced and continuously developed and improved. Dynamic redundancy and heterogeneous functions are applied within the architecture of this distributed object storage system to increase attack costs while significantly enhancing the security and availability of data. This section will describe the design and implementation of the mimic distributed object storage system from three aspects: system principle, system architecture, and core functions. It will also analyze how the system ensures the security and reliability of data.

7.2.1 System Principle

The principles of system implementation will be introduced in this section, covering three main aspects: the technologies used, the system's model design, and its encompassed features.

7.2.1.1 Related Technologies

The following introduces the important design concepts and technologies used in the mimic distributed object storage system:

1) *Mimic defense*: MD is an active defense behavior. Since its idea has been applied in the cyberspace security field, it is often referred to as cyberspace MD. Proposed by Prof. Jiangxing Wu of the Chinese Academy of Engineering, this theory aims to prevent severe system threats caused by "unknown vulnerabilities" through imitation of the "mimic phenomenon" observed in the biological world.
2) *Dynamic heterogeneous redundancy (DHR)*: DHR is the principle method for MD. It is based on the Dissimilar Redundancy Structure (DRS) in the reliability field and introduces multidimensional dynamic redundancy. It combines the high reliability offered by DRS with the strong security provided by mimicry. Consequently, it has been widely applied to router, web, storage, and other

fields. Specifically, the foundation of DHR architecture is heterogeneity. The greater the difference in attributes between the executor sets, the less likely to have the same loopholes and the stronger the defense capabilities. Through the combination of redundancy and heterogeneity, attackers who rely on a specific environment and platform cannot easily break the system. Furthermore, the dynamic transformation mechanism adds dynamics based on redundancy and heterogeneity. When one or more heterogeneous executors are breached, after receiving the warning message, the dynamic transformation mechanism will regenerate new heterogeneous executors to replace the currently attacked heterogeneous executors. This renders previous attacks ineffective due to their inability to reproduce information within the altered environment, effectively erasing all progress made by attackers.

3) *Erasure coding*: EC is a data redundancy mechanism in distributed systems. It has been widely studied and applied in data processing and other fields due to its high storage utilization and strong data availability (Balaji et al. 2018, pp. 1–45). A (k, n)-threshold erasure code splits the original data into k parts, then generates n slices using a complex encoding algorithm, and finally stores them in different nodes. The original data can be recovered by using any m $(m \geq k)$ slices. When $m = k$, this erasure code is a Maximum Distance Separable (MDS) code (Li and Li 2013, pp. 259–272), which has the property of optimal storage utilization. In particular, the Reed–Solomon code is the most widely studied coding scheme that satisfies the characteristics of MDS in history. It has been successfully employed in actual large-scale distributed storage systems such as Ceph and HDFS.

7.2.1.2 Mimic Distributed Object Storage Model

Based on the MD concept and EC technology, an object storage architecture generally consists of three parts: client, object storage device, and metadata server. Among them, the client provides users with simple and easy-to-use storage service platforms and interacts with metadata servers and object storage devices. The metadata server is responsible for the storage and management of object metadata and provides functions such as object location service and permission access control for clients. The object storage device is the core which manages persistent objects by providing an object access interface for clients to complete data reading and writing.

The mimic distributed object storage model adds multiple erasure codes, dynamic random transformations, and other functions, and uses multiple redundancies and active defense mechanisms to increase the redundancy and the uncertainty of data storage, to respond to attacks, and to improve the system security.

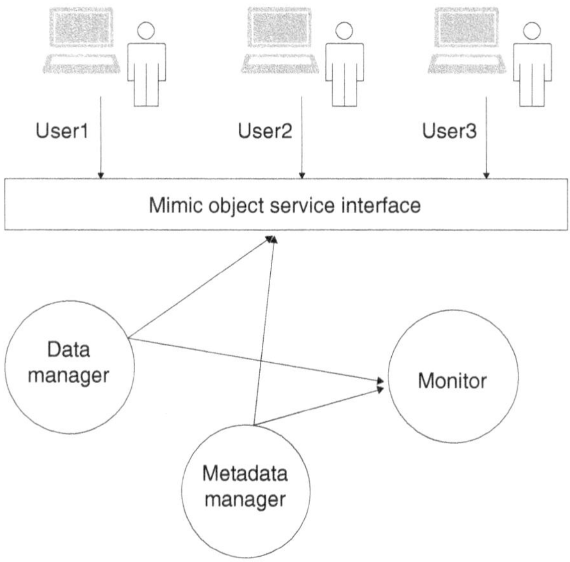

Figure 7.2 Mimic distributed object storage model.

In the actual system design, data management and metadata management are commonly separated. Additionally, a monitor is incorporated into the system, enabling dynamic configuration of both data management nodes and metadata management nodes. The system offers users a mimic object service interface to realize redundancy and heterogeneity. The system model is shown in Figure 7.2.

7.2.1.3 Storage Model Characteristics

The distributed object storage system with mimic features has the following characteristics:

1) *Redundancy*: The system's data redundancy strategy combines erasure codes and multiple copies. The former focuses on object data to improve hardware utilization and data reliability, while the latter pertains to object metadata.
2) *Heterogeneity*: At the software level, diverse erasure codes are employed to encode stored data. At the hardware level, data nodes and metadata nodes use hardware devices with different architectures, operating system platforms and versions to increase the heterogeneity of the system and prevent rapid attacks on a single vulnerability.
3) *Dynamic configuration*: The system realizes the dynamics of MD mainly through the monitor module. The monitor module is responsible for monitoring data nodes and metadata nodes, updating their statuses according to

attacker traces, and actively taking them offline when necessary while issuing data migration instructions. After the node is successfully offline, the administrator needs to repair the node to eliminate security risks. Nodes in a safe state can be online at any time and added to the running system. In addition, when using erasure code for data encoding, dynamic adjustments are made to the parameters, thereby enhancing system uncertainty and further bolstering its security.

4) *Low storage cost*: Compared with the multicopy strategy, erasure code has the characteristics of smaller memory usage, higher fault tolerance, and smaller repair bandwidth. The system adopts multiple erasure codes as the realization of redundancy and heterogeneity, which has high space utilization and strong fault tolerance. Uploaded files are encoded by erasure code, and data is stored in units of parity chunks. This facilitates the fine-grained deduplication of data that further improves the space utilization rate.
5) *Tamper-proof logs*: The log information is stored in the blockchain to ensure its integrity and prevent any unauthorized modifications. And the system can make corresponding strategies based on the log audit results to improve security performance.

7.2.2 System Architecture

The architecture of the mimic distributed object storage system is shown in Figure 7.3. It is mainly divided into three parts: mimic interface service module, metadata service module, and data service module. Each service module is

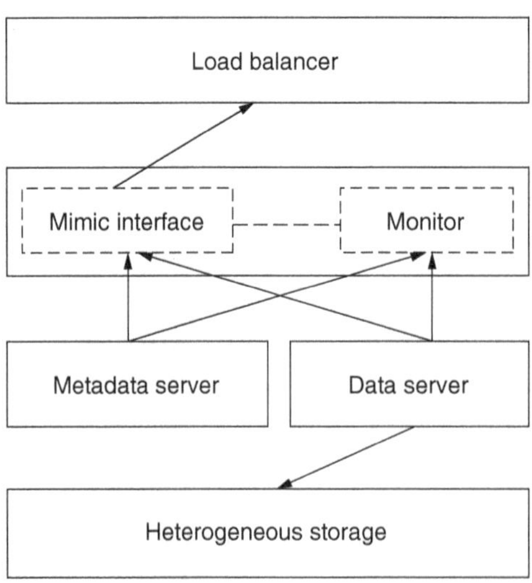

Figure 7.3 Architecture of the mimic distributed object storage system.

composed of multiple service nodes, supporting horizontal expansion, and fundamentally solving the problem of data capacity. Both the metadata service module and data service module are completely transparent to users.

7.2.2.1 Mimic Interface Service

Nodes of the mimic interface service module have three states: executor, monitor, and candidate. All these states support multinode deployment. The executor provides Representational State Transfer (RESTful) Hypertext Transfer Protocol Secure (HTTPS) interface services and is responsible for processing client requests forwarded by the load balancer module. The monitor is responsible for monitoring the status information of the metadata service and data service nodes and detecting attacks or data loss. All data nodes in the system are distributed to monitors, with each monitor managing a specific set of nodes uniquely assigned to it. A monitor is responsible for preserving the states of both its own managed data nodes and those managed by other monitors. When a new monitor adds or an existing one exits, the topology of data nodes managed by monitors in the system is dynamically updated.

The presence of at least one candidate is essential for each monitor, as it ensures the continuity of services in case of unavailability. In such scenarios, a candidate can seamlessly transition into a new monitor and effectively maintain service provision, thereby guaranteeing high availability.

The mimic interface service perceives data nodes and metadata nodes through heartbeat information. The consistent hash is adapted to locate and route data information and metadata information through two hash rings, respectively. The data transmission between the mimic interface service, metadata service, and data service is through the HTTPS protocol to ensure security.

7.2.2.2 Metadata Service

The metadata service module is a crucial component responsible for managing the metadata information of a file, including the creation time, permission information, and correction code information. Comprising multiple metadata services, each of which is an independent program, it supports horizontal expansion. The metadata service stores metadata in an Elasticsearch cluster, leveraging the Elasticsearch database to manage structured metadata. Both the metadata service and the Elasticsearch cluster operate independently of each other. The metadata service offers a RESTful HTTPS interface while also sending heartbeat information to inform other nodes of its existence.

7.2.2.3 Data Service

The data service module is a vital component responsible for data storage. It comprises several data services that support horizontal expansion, enabling each service to function as an independent program. Additionally, the module can mount various storage clusters such as IPFS, Ceph's File System (CephFS), thereby ensuring heterogeneity and replaceability. In the context of the mimic distributed object storage system, the data service stores file data utilizing the local file system. However, instead of preserving the entire file, it stores the parity chunk information of the file after erasure coding. Through erasure coding, each chunk serves as a unit within the data service for storing file data. Subsequently, the metadata information in the metadata service stores the location information of each chunk. The data service provides a REST-style HTTPS interface, and every data service sends heartbeat information to alert other nodes of its existence.

7.2.3 Core Functions

This section introduces the design and implementation of some core functionalities in the mimic distributed object storage system, including data positioning, data migration, and data recovery.

7.2.3.1 Data Positioning

In distributed systems, consistent hashing (Karger et al. 1997, pp. 654–663) solves the problem of data distribution and routing in the dynamic network topology. With the assistance of consistent hashing, systems can optimize data location operations.

Two hash circles are used in the mimic distributed object storage system to manage data information and metadata information. Upon object upload, the system encodes the object, storing all generated chunks in the data nodes. Simultaneously, the metadata information of the object is stored within the metadata nodes, in triplicate.

When a client sends an object upload request, the load balancer module distributes the request to the interface service module, and the executor is responsible for processing the request. The system selects three erasure codes through a dynamic selection algorithm, encodes the uploaded object, and stores the encoded parity chunk to the corresponding data node via data location. Subsequently, the metadata information of the object is stored in the corresponding metadata node, again in triplicate. Finally, the result of the object upload request is returned to the client. The process of uploading an object is illustrated in Figure 7.4.

Data positioning is divided into two parts: data and metadata. (1) Data. The system stores both the parity chunks encoded by the erasure code and the data chunks to the data nodes respectively. During storage, each chunk undergoes a series of operations. First, the hash value of each chunk is computed. Next, the smallest data node larger than the computed hash value is identified. Finally, the chunk is stored on the selected data node. (2) Metadata. The system stores the metadata in three metadata nodes. During storage, the system computes a hash value based

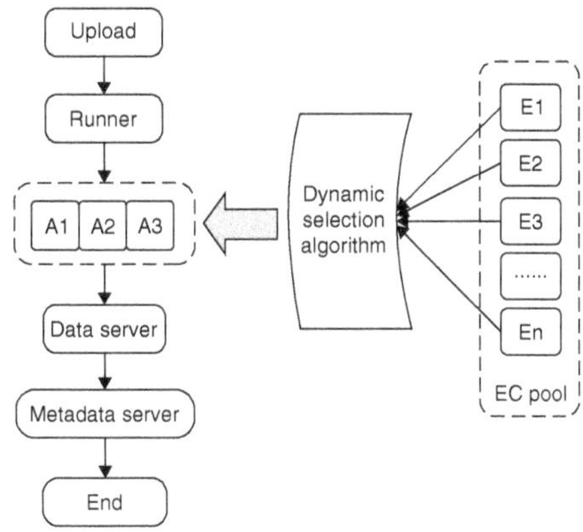

Figure 7.4 The process of uploading an object in the mimic distributed object storage system.

on the object ID and maps it to the hash ring using a pseudorandom algorithm. Three metadata nodes are then selected on the hash circle for storing the corresponding metadata information.

When receiving the object download request, the load balancer module distributes the request to the interface service module. The executor is responsible for processing the request. First, the system calculates the hash value according to object ID, maps the hash value to the hash ring of metadata through a pseudorandom algorithm, and obtains the metadata information from the first metadata node. Subsequently, it retrieves hash values of all parity chunks based on this metadata information and maps them onto the hash ring. The target node is selected as the smallest data node greater than each respective hash value, from which parity chunk information is obtained. Three pieces of object information are then decoded using corresponding erasure code and parameter information before being returned to the client following multivalue judgment principles.

7.2.3.2 Data Migration

Data migration is often a necessary operation when a data node engages in online and offline operations.

In offline scenarios, data migration is required when a data node's security is reduced due to multiple attacks, or when a data node becomes unavailable due to hardware or other reasons. The offline operation takes certain measures on the data node, but ensures no loss of data. During the migration process, it is essential to locate the next clockwise data node on the hash ring from the current node. Subsequently, all the data from the current node is migrated to the designated next node.

In online scenarios, data migration is required when a new data node is added to the system. The process involves mapping the node to the hash ring, and then migrating part of the data from the target node to the newly added node. Specifically, the mapping point is taken as the starting point, and the first node found in a clockwise direction is designated as the target node. When the target node is identified, the data from the node where the mapping point falls on the hash ring is migrated to the newly added node.

In conclusion, when data nodes perform online and offline operations, data migration is necessary to ensure the system operates seamlessly. By following the proper procedures, data can be migrated efficiently and without loss, thereby minimizing any disruptions that may arise during online or offline operations.

7.2.3.3 Data Recovery

The system employs erasure coding technology to enhance reliability. In the event of data loss, as long as the number of missing chunks does not exceed the parameter n set in the (k, n) erasure code being used, recovery is possible. The system employs two distinct strategies to recover the lost data. Specifically, when an object is downloaded, and a data chunk is found to be missing, the system utilizes the erasure code to recover the data and stores the retrieved data chunk back into the data node. Additionally, the system constantly monitors objects to determine if data loss or tampering has occurred. In such cases, the system recovers the lost data using the erasure code and stores it back into the data node.

7.3 Logging System in Mimic Storage Based on Consortium Blockchain

Conventionally distributed logging systems typically rely on distributed databases or file systems to store log data. Despite advancements in large-scale distributed storage technology, which now provides petabyte-level data storage processing capabilities, dominant distributed logging systems still face security vulnerabilities that make data susceptible to tampering. In recent years, blockchain technology has emerged as a rapidly evolving distributed storage solution, offering decentralization, tamper-resistant data integrity, and reduced reliance on trust. Consequently, integrating blockchain technology into logging systems presents an opportunity to enhance their security. As a core technology within the realm of blockchain, the consensus algorithm plays a critical role in ensuring data consistency across different nodes, thereby enabling Byzantine fault tolerance. However, most consensus algorithms are serialized, and the system's throughput performance declines significantly as the number of nodes increases. To address this challenge and enhance the scalability of the blockchain system, the proposed solution leverages the PPoV consensus algorithm by enabling multiple bookkeepers to generate blocks simultaneously.

The logging system must be capable of addressing complex application scenarios that encompass diverse operating systems and application software, leading to the generation of logs in multiple formats. Consequently, it should prioritize the collection and storage of logs generated by various software, as opposed to constructing a unified log recording module. A distributed logging system requires the following features:

1) *Robustness*: In the event of a small number of nodes crashing, the system is still able to operate normally. Furthermore, when a crashed node recovers and rejoins the network, its data will be synchronized to the latest state.
2) *Scalability*: The system allows for new nodes to freely join and leave the logging system, and new nodes can automatically synchronize to the latest state upon joining.
3) *Consistency*: The data state of the majority of normal nodes remains consistent within a specific delay error range.
4) *High throughput*: The logging system exhibits a high data processing throughput.

The aforementioned features are essential elements that the logging system must possess in order to handle complex log processing requirements while ensuring the security and reliability of the data.

7.3.1 System Architecture

To enhance the security of log data in the mimic storage system, blockchain technology is utilized to construct a mimic storage logging system. The architecture of integrating blockchain into the logging system is depicted in Figure 7.5, encompassing a log collection unit, a log storage unit, and a log query and analysis unit. The mimic distributed storage system comprises multiple log sources such as I/O agents, various heterogeneous executors, and clustered configuration management modules. The log collection unit is tasked with gathering log data from diverse modules, filtering out invalid log data, transforming log formats, and subsequently selecting server nodes at random for publication of log data. In order to prevent server nodes from being overwhelmed by simultaneous requests, load balancing is implemented during publication of log data. The log query and analysis unit are responsible for retrieving log records from the blockchain and supports query operations based on blockchain height, block logs, time range, and error code. The blockchain server network serves as the core component of the mimic storage logging system, with each node communicating with one another to establish a decentralized network, collectively providing externally available log storage

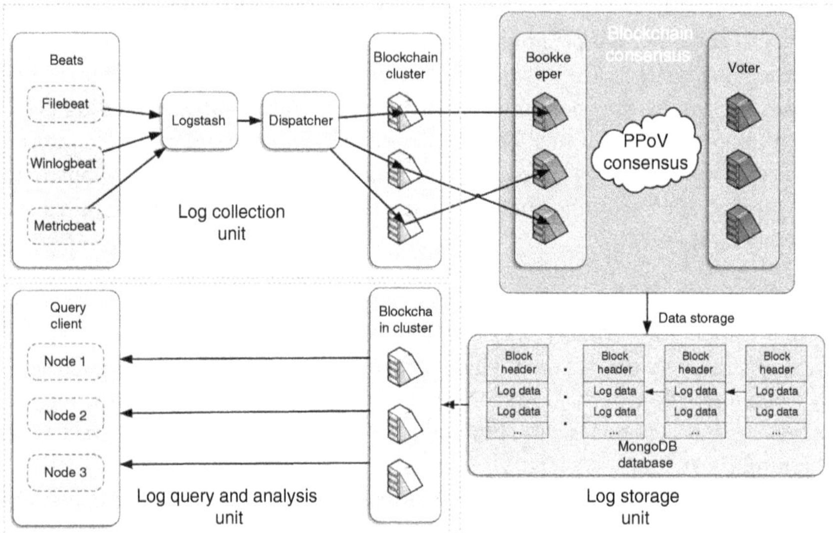

Figure 7.5 The architecture of the blockchain-based logging system.

functions. To enhance the efficiency, scalability, and security of the blockchain-based logging system, PPoV is adopted as its consensus protocol.

In contrast to conventional storage logging systems, blockchain does not immediately store transaction data in the database upon receipt from the log collection unit. Instead, bookkeepers maintain logs in a memory pool of transactions. Only when a bookkeeper enters the Prepare phase will it pack a certain amount of transactions from the memory pool into a block for consensus and storage. Consequently, the latency of data storage in the blockchain system is higher than that of general conventional storage systems. Due to this reason, the log collection unit only needs to ensure the transmission of log data to the blockchain server cluster without waiting for the completion of data storage.

In order to handle the diversity of log formats generated by different application software and systems, the logging systems typically standardize various log data formats and convert them into a unified standard format, as illustrated in Table 7.1. The design of the blockchain-based logging system considers the compatibility of multiple log formats and the ability to support expansion, making it easy to expand storage capacity and adopt new query methods after the addition of new log formats without major adjustments. Consequently, the system adopts JavaScript Object Notation (JSON) as the fundamental format for log storage and MongoDB (Bradshaw, Brazil, and Chodorow 2019) as the underlying database for storing log data with flexible query features.

Table 7.1 Standard log format field types.

Name	Value type	Description
Level	String	Priority of log
Time	Double	Generation time of log
Message	String	Content of log
Type	Int	Type of log
IP	String	IP address of log source
Port	Int	Port number of log source
System	String	System information
Application	String	Application-specific information
None	None	Field to be added

7.3.2 Core Functions

The core functions of the mimic storage logging system based on the consortium blockchain can be categorized into two main categories: log collection and dispatch, as well as log storage. The former involves the gathering and organization of log data, while the latter comprises multiple modules responsible for block communication, synchronization, and log storage. The specific details are outlined as follows:

7.3.2.1 Log Collection and Dispatch

The log collection unit is primarily responsible for collecting log data. This logging system utilizes an open-source log collection tool in conjunction with a self-developed log dispatcher, taking advantage of several mature and reliable log collection tools available on the market that are capable of collecting various types of data. In the Elastic application stack, the Beats tool series serves as a set of data collectors supporting multiple data types, such as file collection, system and service metrics collection, and network data collection. Simultaneously, the Logstash tool in the Elastic application stack filters the data collected by Beats and then dispatches the data to each blockchain node through the log dispatcher designed in this system.

Similar to Beats and Logstash, log dispatcher is also a lightweight application. It utilizes multithreaded asynchronous message processing to concurrently receive log data sent from Beats or Logstash and writes the log data into an in-memory buffer. The log processing section comprises a main thread that continuously runs in a loop and a fixed number of log processing threads. The main thread reads log data from the memory buffer and processes it through the log processing thread. The primary task of the processing thread is to convert the log data into JSON format, apply hash function computation to each log, and cache the data through the Hash Table. Furthermore, the main thread is responsible for retrieving a portion of the cached log data, adding it to the tail of the log message queue, and then dispatching log data from the head of this queue to each blockchain node.

The network layer of log dispatcher is based on the Phxaxos network library and follows the node discovery in blockchain to obtain the address of each blockchain node and the communication status between nodes. The log dispatch process utilizes batch dispatch to ensure the load balancing of each node, where a dynamic allocation of logs based on the network communication load is performed. Nodes with better network communication conditions are dispatched more log data, while nodes with poorer conditions receive less log data.

7.3.2.2 Design of Blockchain-Based Log Storage

Blockchain-based log storage is the most fundamental and intricate function, coordinated by multiple modules and subfunctions. The specific implementation details are categorized into the following parts.

7.3.2.2.1 Overall Architecture

The consensus algorithm serves as the fundamental component of the blockchain, relying on a variety of elements including network and database modules for its implementation. These foundational modules collectively constitute the blockchain infrastructure of this logging system, as depicted in Figure 7.6.

The introduction of each module is as follows:

1) *Network module*: The network module, as a fundamental component of the blockchain, plays a pivotal role in communication. It offers two methods for message transmission: one is directed toward a specific node by its IP and port, while the other involves broadcasting to all nodes within the network. Moreover, the network module incorporates node discovery methods to identify new joining nodes and remove offline nodes from the active node list.
2) *Database module*: This module is designed based on MongoDB to store block data, and offers an interface for general data queries.
3) *Account management module*: This module is responsible for maintaining the on-chain records of various accounts, including voters, candidates, bookkeepers, and local node account information.
4) *Message management module*: This module defines a standardized message format and provides methods for generating various types of messages.

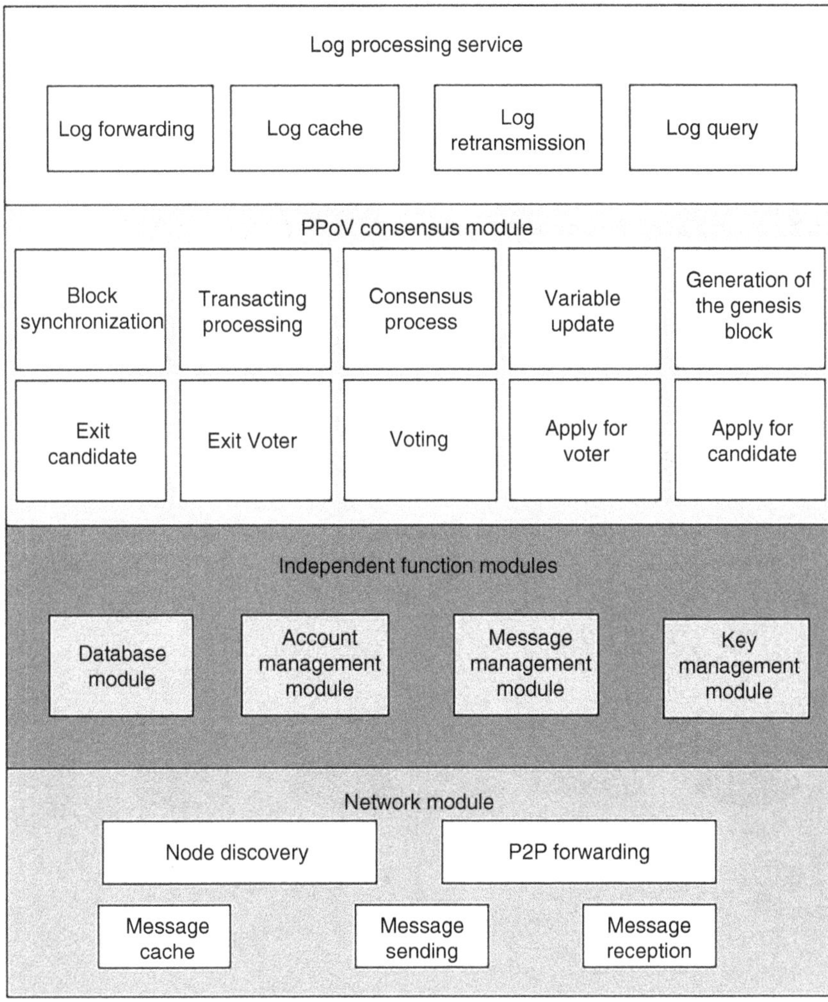

Figure 7.6 Functional modules of the blockchain-based logging system.

5) *Key management module*: This module provides key management functions, including random key generation, loading existing keys, data signing and verification, as well as data hashing.
6) *PPoV consensus module*: This module implements the PPoV consensus algorithm and some auxiliary functions to meet specific application requirements such as block synchronization, genesis block generation, and ordinary block generation.

7) *Log processing service*: This service, based on the implementation of the PPoV blockchain, offers log receiving, processing, and query services. It can receive and store log data on the blockchain and supports querying and analyzing the stored log data.

7.3.2.2.2 Design of Asynchronous Communication Model

Blockchain-based log storage is designed based on an asynchronous communication mode. A blockchain program fundamentally operates as a data-driven state machine, where each node changes its state through communication with other nodes. As depicted in Figure 7.7, the state of the entire system can be segmented by the blockchain's height, and the generation process of each block group constitutes a cycle. Overall, the state of the blockchain system exhibits characteristics of infiniteness, orderliness, and periodicity.

The system state of each node is determined by the height of its local blockchain. Due to the asynchronous communication used in the blockchain system, the arrival time of messages at different nodes is inconsistent, making it impossible to guarantee consistent states across all nodes simultaneously. Additionally, since

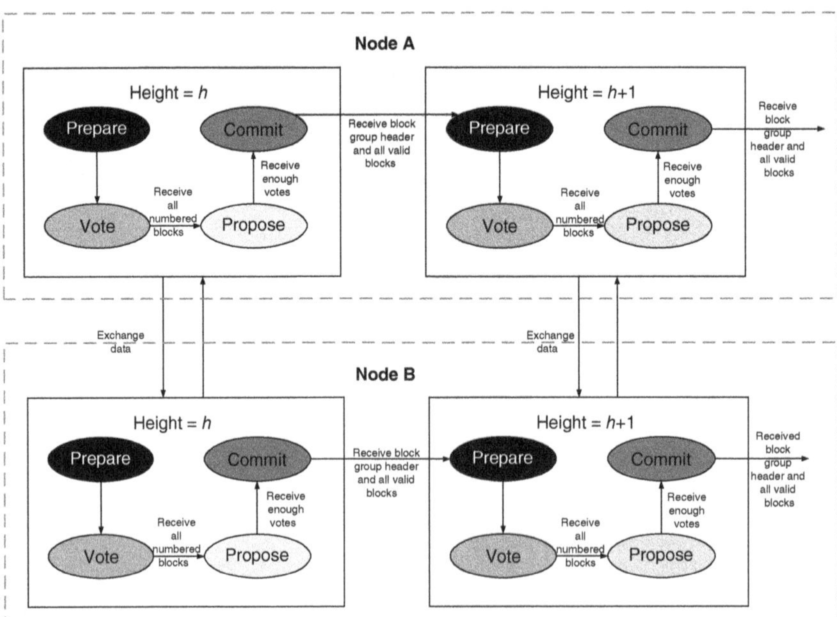

Figure 7.7 The working principle of data-driven state.

node operations are data-driven, receiving inconsistent messages may lead to abnormal operations or errors being returned to the message-sending node.

To address the issue of state inconsistency in asynchronous blockchains, this system proposes a solution that involves each node executing two threads: a main thread responsible for iterating through executing operations in each state, and a message processing thread dedicated to handling received messages. The core of the proposed solution lies in out-of-order receiving and sequential processing. Upon receiving a message, the message processing thread verifies its status, discarding invalid messages while storing valid ones in the message buffer. During each loop execution, the main thread checks for messages in the buffer that meet the required status; if found, it processes them accordingly; otherwise, it skips buffered message processing. Additionally, blockchain states primarily depend on height as a parameter. This means that nodes transition only from states with lower heights to those with higher heights. When a node receives a message from another node, it compares their respective blockchain heights with that of the received message. If the received message's state is lower than its own height state, it is discarded; if it is greater than or equal to its own height state, it is temporarily stored for subsequent processing.

The system effectively implements the functions of each module in the context of asynchronous communication, ensuring message processing correctness and enhancing efficiency. Consequently, it successfully tackles the challenge of state inconsistency in blockchain systems.

7.3.2.2.3 Main Logic Design

The system divides the operation process of the blockchain program into four phases: node discovery, blockchain loading, block group synchronization, and genesis or ordinary block generation. As illustrated in Figure 7.8, during the node discovery phase, the primary task is to communicate with other nodes in the network and exchange IP addresses to obtain node information and prepare for subsequent communication. In the blockchain loading phase, the node retrieves locally stored blockchain data and loads it into memory. The key focus of the block group synchronization phase is to request block group data from other nodes in the network and update the local blockchain data and memory state to achieve consistency with other nodes. Following successful completion of block group synchronization, the node must check the blockchain's height. If the height is less than 0, it indicates that no genesis block has been generated, and the system enters the genesis block generation phase. Otherwise, it enters the ordinary block generation phase, commencing the processing and recording of new transactions and blocks.

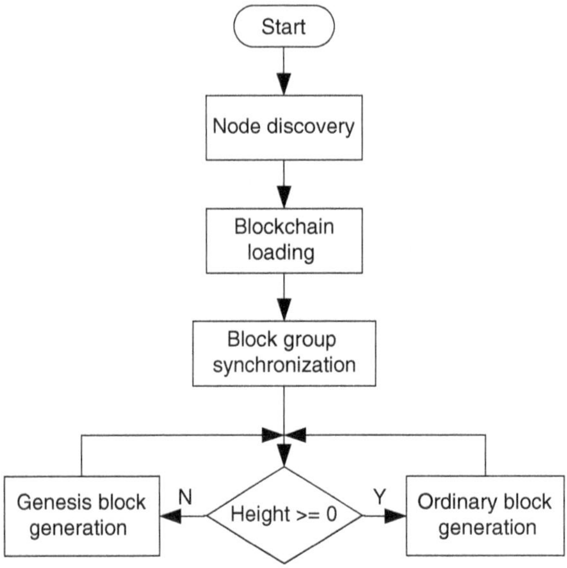

Figure 7.8 Main logic of blockchain operation process.

7.3.2.2.4 Block Group Synchronization

Block group synchronization, referred to as block synchronization hereafter, is a crucial function of blockchain. When a new node joins the blockchain network, it must acquire data from other nodes in the network until the local blockchain data is updated to the latest state. Similarly, when a node network recovers from failure or restarts after an outage, it also requires data from other nodes to update the local blockchain to the most recent state. Currently, mainstream block synchronization methods are primarily categorized into two types: active and passive. Active synchronization involves nodes actively requesting data from other nodes, while passive synchronization entails receiving new block group data generated by the network nodes in the block group buffer and awaiting the main thread to perform the commit operation.

The block synchronization algorithm employed by this system integrates active and passive synchronization. Specifically, while actively requesting a block group, the node adds the newly published block group it receives to the block group buffer. Once the requested block group has been updated, the node will process other received block groups from the block group buffer and update them accordingly. This approach enables nodes to effectively synchronize blocks by combining active acquisition of data with passive reception of new blocks, thereby ensuring up-to-date local blockchain maintenance.

Active synchronization first requests the height of each node from the blockchain network. Once the height request is completed, it enters the block group synchronization phase and continuously requests block groups with higher heights than the local blockchain from other nodes until the target height is reached. The corresponding pseudocode is displayed in Algorithm 7.1.

Algorithm 7.1 ActiveSynchronization

```
Input:node_set
Output:Go to normal state
    max_height←-1;
    for each node N in node_set do
       h←RequestHeight(N);
       if h>max_height then
          max_height←h;
       end if
     end for
     height←getLocalBlockChainHeight();
     while heightdo
       RequestBlockGroup(height+1);
     end while
     state←Normal.
```

However, a potential issue arises with using only active synchronization. Consider a scenario where one node initiates block synchronization while other nodes in the network continue to generate new block groups. Suppose that at time t, node A synchronizes and the maximum blockchain height across all nodes is $H(t)$, with no network communication delay. Then A requests $H' = H(t)$ from the whole network. Since active synchronization takes time Ts, and the time to generate a block group is fixed to Tg, if condition

$$(n-1)^{*}Tg < t < t + Ts < n^{*}Tg, n \text{ is any positive integer} \tag{7.1}$$

holds true, after synchronization no new block group will be generated in the network; thus, ensuring that blockchain height remains unchanged, that is, $H(t + Ts) = H(t)$. Consequently, the blockchain will be synchronized to the latest block group and work normally. Equation (7.1) necessitates $Ts < Tg$, thereby imposing a lower bound on Tg that that significantly impacts block generation speed and data throughput. More seriously, because t is random, even if Tg surpasses Ts by a considerable margin, there remains a possibility of failing to achieve synchronization with the latest block group. Such a case can be partly addressed by requesting the network height again after active synchronization completion and synchronizing newly generated block groups. Therefore, this system introduces passive synchronization as an ultimate solution. New block groups received during active synchronization are stored in a buffer for subsequent retrieval in sequential order after synchronization completion, ensuring local blockchain data is synchronized with the latest state.

7.3.2.2.5 Design of Transaction Pool

Upon receiving transaction data, the bookkeeper is responsible for deduplicating and storing it in the transaction pool. During block generation, the transaction data is retrieved from the pool to generate a transaction list. However, utilizing an array as a container for storing transactions results in a time complexity of $O(N)$ when reading from the pool and storing in the list. Furthermore, the removal of packed transactions from the transaction pool after extraction also yields a time complexity of $O(N)$.

To enhance the efficiency of creating transaction lists and deleting transactions, the system divides the transaction pool into multiple unit transaction pools. JSON is employed as the fundamental format for communication and block construction. So, the transaction list is stored in the block in the form of a JSON array. To prevent unnecessary time consumption due to JSON data parsing, each unit transaction pool also uses a JSON array as its storage container, as depicted in Figure 7.9.

Typically, deduplicate checking involves comparing the hash value of each transaction. However, performing a hash operation on each transaction in the transaction pool when a new transaction is added would significantly increase

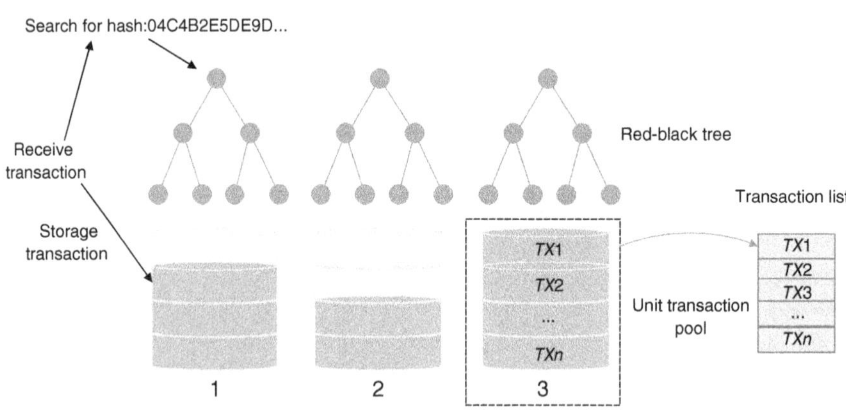

Figure 7.9 The structure of transaction pool.

time consumption. To achieve rapid deduplicate checking, the transaction pool initializes a separate hash set for each unit transaction pool to maintain the hash values of transactions. This set uses a red-black tree implementation, resulting in a time complexity of $O(log\ N)$ to search for a certain hash value.

During the generation of the transaction list, as the number of transactions in a unit transaction pool cannot exceed the maximum transaction storage capacity of a block, a unit transaction pool can be directly utilized as a transaction list while emptying the packed transaction list. Consequently, this optimization strategy achieves constant time complexity $O(1)$ for both creating and deleting a transaction list, effectively enhancing bookkeeper's processing efficiency.

7.4 Chapter Summary

With the rapid advancement of next-generation information technologies, data volume is experiencing exponential growth. The emergence of such vast amounts of data not only accelerates the rapid evolution of storage technology but also imposes stringent requirements for consistency, reliability, and security in storage systems. Traditional approaches to disaster recovery, virus eradication, and vulnerability repair are reactive measures that pose challenges when defending against attacks, especially unknown security threats. The mimic distributed secure storage system incorporates a multitude of dynamic heterogeneous redundant technologies to ensure safe, efficient, and uninterrupted operation, effectively resisting various network attacks including known vulnerabilities and unknown threats. Simultaneously, the system leverages consortium blockchain to protect logs, ensuring maximal data integrity while strengthening access control and privacy protection, as well as enhancing system resilience against failures.

Discussion Questions

7.1 Briefly describe the architecture of the mimic distributed secure storage system.

A: The system is mainly divided into three parts: mimic interface service module, metadata service module, and data service module. Each service module is composed of multiple service nodes, facilitating horizontal scalability and effectively addressing data capacity issues. In particular, both the metadata and data service modules operate transparently to users.

7.2 Briefly describe the characteristics of mimic storage.

A: Mimic storage leverages erasure coding and multiple replicas to achieve data redundancy, ensuring low storage costs through high space utilization and robust fault tolerance. Specifically, it employs multiple erasure codes for object data and a multireplica redundancy strategy for object metadata. Additionally, it exhibits heterogeneity at both the software and hardware levels by utilizing different hardware devices and multiple erasure codes. In the actual system implementation, a monitor module is used to facilitate dynamic configuration by tracking node activity and issuing data migration instructions. Moreover, the system dynamically adjusts parameters during the data encoding process to enhance security. Furthermore, log information is stored on blockchain to ensure tamper resistance and integrity.

7.3 Briefly describe the advantages of applying consortium blockchain to a logging system.

A: By incorporating consortium blockchain technology into the logging system in mimic storage, the integrity of log data can be guaranteed, and tampering can be prevented, effectively thwarting unauthorized modification. Specifically, consortium blockchain offers several advantages. First, it enables a precise definition of participants and access rights, thereby providing better control over who can access, retrieve, add, or modify log records. This enhances data security significantly. Second, consortium blockchain aids in more effectively managing data privacy by securely sharing critical audit information while ensuring privacy. Additionally, the decentralized nature of blockchain not only enhances fault tolerance but also mitigates the potential risk associated with a single point of failure. Ultimately, the customizability and scalability of consortium blockchain allow for flexible adjustments based on actual needs to accommodate different storage systems and business requirements.

References

Balaji, S.B., Krishnan, M.N., Vajha, M., Ramkumar, V., Sasidharan, B. and Kumar, P.V., 2018. Erasure coding for distributed storage: An overview. *Science China Information Sciences*, 61, pp. 1–45.

Benet, J., 2014. Ipfs-content addressed, versioned, p2p file system. arXiv preprint arXiv:1407.3561.

Boulon, J., Konwinski, A., Qi, R., Rabkin, A., Yang, E. and Yang, M., 2008, October. Chukwa, a large-scale monitoring system. In Proceedings of CCA (Vol. 8, pp. 1–5).

Bradshaw, S., Brazil, E. and Chodorow, K., 2019. *MongoDB: The definitive guide: powerful and scalable data storage.* O'Reilly Media.

Brunetti, R., 2011. *Windows Azure step by step.* Microsoft Press.

DeCandia, G., Hastorun, D., Jampani, M., Kakulapati, G., Lakshman, A., Pilchin, A., Sivasubramanian, S., Vosshall, P. and Vogels, W., 2007. Dynamo: Amazon's highly available key-value store. *ACM SIGOPS Operating Systems Review*, 41(6), pp. 205–220.

Ge, Z., Loghin, D., Ooi, B.C., Ruan, P. and Wang, T., 2022. Hybrid blockchain database systems: Design and performance. *Proceedings of the VLDB Endowment*, 15(5), pp. 1092–1104.

Ghemawat, S., Gobioff, H. and Leung, S.T., 2003, October. The Google file system. In Proceedings of the Nineteenth ACM Symposium on Operating systems principles (pp. 29–43).

Hong, Z., Guo, S., Zhou, E., Chen, W., Huang, H. and Zomaya, A., 2023. GriDB: Scaling blockchain database via sharding and off-chain cross-SHARD Mechanism. *Proceedings of the VLDB Endowment*, 16(7), pp. 1685–1698.

Karger, D., Lehman, E., Leighton, T., Levine, M., Lewin, D. and Panigrahy, R., 1997, May. Relieving hot spots on the World Wide Web. In Proceedings of the 29th Annual ACM Symposium on the Theory of Computing (pp. 654–663).

Lai, Z., Liu, C. and Lo, E., 2023. When private blockchain meets deterministic database. *Proceedings of the ACM on Management of Data*, 1(1), pp. 1–28.

Li, J. and Li, B., 2013. Erasure coding for cloud storage systems: A survey. *Tsinghua Science and Technology*, 18(3), pp. 259–272.

McConaghy, T., Marques, R., Müller, A., De Jonghe, D., McConaghy, T., McMullen, G., Henderson, R., Bellemare, S. and Granzotto, A., 2016. Bigchaindb: a scalable blockchain database. White paper, BigChainDB, pp. 53–72.

Sharma, P., Jindal, R. and Borah, M.D., 2021. Blockchain-based decentralized architecture for cloud storage system. *Journal of Information Security and Applications*, 62, p. 102970.

Shvachko, K., Kuang, H., Radia, S. and Chansler, R., 2010, May. The hadoop distributed file system. In 2010 IEEE 26th Symposium on Mass Storage Systems and Technologies (MSST) (pp. 1–10). IEEE.

Weil, S.A., Brandt, S.A., Miller, E.L., Long, D.D. and Maltzahn, C., 2006, November. Ceph: A scalable, high-performance distributed file system. In Proceedings of the 7th Symposium on Operating Systems Design and Implementation (pp. 307–320).

Wu, J., 2022a. Development paradigms of cyberspace endogenous safety and security. *Science China Information Sciences*, 65(5), p. 156301.

Wu, J., 2022b. Cyberspace endogenous safety and security. *Engineering*, 15, pp. 179–185.

Yu, H., Li, H., Yang, X. and Ma, H., 2021. On distributed object storage architecture based on mimic defense. *China Communications*, 18(8), pp. 109–120.

Zheng, Y., Li, Z., Xu, X. and Zhao, Q., 2022. Dynamic defenses in cyber security: Techniques, methods and challenges. *Digital Communications and Networks*, 8(4), pp. 422–435.

8

Quantum Blockchain and Its Potential Applications

In the current era of digitalization, the focus has shifted toward the security and efficiency of communication. Despite significant progress in information transmission and storage with traditional communication technology, it still faces numerous challenges, particularly in the realms of data security and privacy protection. In response to this, quantum blockchain technology came into being. By integrating the fundamental principles of quantum mechanics with blockchain technology, quantum blockchain offers a novel approach that is not only more secure and efficient but also sets a new standard for communication security, thereby significantly enhancing the speed and accuracy of information transmission while elevating information security to unprecedented levels.

8.1 Quantum Computing and Communication Theory

With the rapid advancement of quantum computing technology, we find ourselves entering a new era driven by the principles of quantum mechanics. Quantum computing serves as a groundbreaking computational paradigm, introducing unparalleled power and speed. Diverse communication theories and technologies rooted in quantum computing offer a more secure and efficient method of information transmission, overcoming various limitations and deficiencies present in classical communication systems. This section will delve into the quantum properties, the essentials of quantum computing, and its close relationship with the field of communication. By exploring how these two domains intersect, our aim is to establish a solid foundation for future technological developments, that will bring innovative changes to modern communication technologies.

Principles and Applications of Blockchain Systems: How to Overcome the CAP Trilemma in Consortium Blockchain, First Edition. Hui Li and Han Wang.

Published 2025 by John Wiley & Sons, Inc.

8.1.1 Quantum Physical Concepts and Qubit Properties

In physics, the term "quantum" refers to the smallest and indivisible unit involved in a fundamental interaction. When a physical quantity undergoes quantization, it means it has a minimum unit. In the case of light, this smallest unit is known as the photon. Within the framework of classical mechanics, quantum exhibits a range of seemingly counterintuitive properties, and here are four physical phenomena illustrating these characteristics.

Phenomenon 1: When a photon is emitted and passes through two slits in the same plane, with its projection mapped onto a screen, the expected outcome is two bright lines, each corresponding to a slit. However, interference streaks appear on the receiving screen instead. This suggests that each light particle seems to traverse both slits simultaneously, interfering with itself – an observation contradictory to the pure particle model.

Phenomenon 2: To determine the slit through which a single photon travels, researchers introduced a detector to observe the photon's behavior. Surprisingly, when observed, the interference fringes on the receiving screen vanished, replaced by two distinct light spots, each corresponding to a slit. When the observation ceased, the interference fringes reappeared. Regardless of the detector's position – whether behind the slit or observing the photon after it passed through – the same phenomenon occurred. This result implies that the observation influences the behavior of photons, irrespective of the observation's location.

Phenomenon 3: The states of two entangled quantum particles are closely interconnected. Consider two entangled electrons with entangled spin states. When the spin state of one electron is measured, the result immediately determines the spin state of the other electron, regardless of the distance between them. For instance, measuring an electron and determining an "up" spin means the other electron, no matter how far away, has a "down" spin without further measurement.

Phenomenon 4: Consider an electron trapped in a "potential well," akin to being confined between two impenetrable barriers. According to classical physics, if the electron lacks sufficient energy to overcome the wall, it remains trapped inside indefinitely. However, in quantum physics, the electron can seemingly appear on the other side of the wall suddenly, even without gaining adequate energy.

The aforementioned phenomena indicate substantial disparities between quantum physics and classical physics, collectively revealing key characteristics of the quantum world.

1) *Superposition*: In the quantum world, a particle can exist in a superposition of multiple states. This means that, before measurement, the particle doesn't have a fixed state but exists in various possible states with certain probabilities.

2) *Measurement collapse*: In quantum physics, the measurement process itself affects the system being measured. When a quantum particle in a superposition state is measured, it collapses into a specific state. The specific mechanism and reasons behind this collapse process remain one of the central focuses in modern physics.
3) *Quantum interference*: Quantum particles can experience interference effects through specific pathways. Interference arises due to the wave-like nature of quantum particles, causing reinforcement of their probability amplitudes in certain places and cancellation in others.
4) *Quantum entanglement*: Two or more quantum particles can exist in a highly correlated entangled state. When the states of two particles are entangled, measuring one particle instantaneously determines the state of the other, and this property is independent of the distance between them.
5) *Quantum tunneling*: A quantum particle has a finite probability of passing through an energy barrier, even if the particle's energy is lower than that of the barrier.

The characteristics of the quantum world not only hold profound significance in fundamental physics but also offer a fresh perspective for information processing. When attempting to apply these quantum features to computing, it leads to the research field of quantum computing. In quantum computing, classical bits 0 and 1 are replaced by quantum bits (qubits). A qubit encompasses both 0 and 1 states, but unlike classical bits, it can exist as a combination of these two states, as illustrated in Figure 8.1.

In contrast to the classical bits 0 and 1, the fundamental states of a qubit are typically represented as $|0\rangle$ or $|1\rangle$. This combination of vertical lines and angle brackets is known as Dirac notation. Any arbitrary superposition state of a qubit can be expressed as:

$$|\psi\rangle = \alpha|0\rangle + \beta|1\rangle. \tag{8.1}$$

The terms α and β, referred to as probability amplitudes, have magnitudes squared that represent the probabilities of measuring the corresponding states.

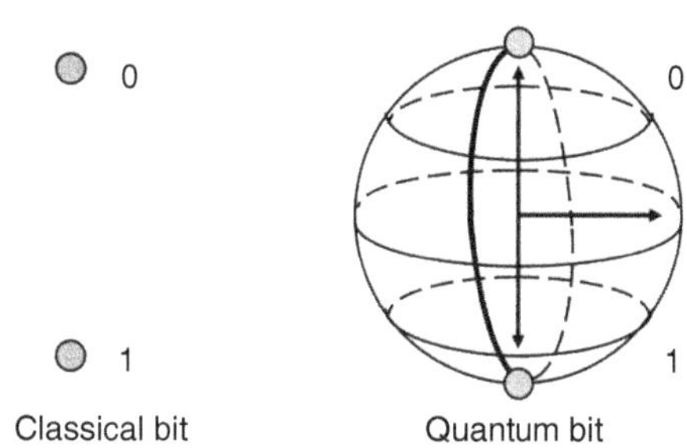

Figure 8.1 Comparison between classical bits and qubits. *Source:* Swan, Santos, and Witte (2020)/World Scientific Publishing Co Pte Ltd.

In other words, the probability of being in the $|0\rangle$ state is $|\alpha|^2$, and the probability of being in the $|1\rangle$ state is $|\beta|^2$. Since the sum of probabilities must be 1, it follows that $|\alpha|^2 + |\beta|^2 = 1$. While α and β can be complex numbers, in many cases, treating them as real numbers is also feasible (Bernhardt 2019). To better represent this superposition state, vectors are used to describe $|0\rangle$ and $|1\rangle$:

$$|0\rangle = \begin{bmatrix} 1 \\ 0 \end{bmatrix}, \quad |1\rangle = \begin{bmatrix} 0 \\ 1 \end{bmatrix}. \tag{8.2}$$

Therefore, the superposition state can be represented as Equation (8.3), indicating that the state of a qubit is a vector in a two-dimensional complex vector space. The states $|0\rangle$ and $|1\rangle$ are referred to as computational basis states, forming a set of orthogonal bases for this vector space. Also, since $|\alpha|^2 + |\beta|^2 = 1$, from a geometric perspective, the state of a qubit is a unit vector in the two-dimensional complex vector space.

$$|\psi\rangle = \alpha|0\rangle + \beta|1\rangle = \begin{bmatrix} \alpha \\ \beta \end{bmatrix}. \tag{8.3}$$

The abstract mathematical form can be challenging to grasp. Introducing the experiment conducted by Otto Stern and Walther Gerlach on silver atoms' spin will help illustrate the physical significance of qubits. According to the atomic planetary model, there is an unpaired electron in the outermost orbit of a silver atom, and as the electron moves, it generates a magnetic field. Because electrons in the inner orbits exist in pairs with opposite spin directions, the magnetic fields they produce cancel each other out. However, the magnetic field produced by the unpaired electron in the outermost orbit doesn't have an opposite electron to cancel it out. Therefore, viewing a silver atom as a small magnet is appropriate.

As illustrated in Figure 8.2, Stern and Gerlach designed an experimental apparatus with a constant magnetic field directed in a fixed direction. Silver atoms passing through this apparatus experience deflection due to the force applied. From the perspective of classical mechanics, considering that the magnetic field formed by the electron spin of a silver atom is constant, the degree of atomic deflection corresponds to the direction of the atomic magnetic axis. The direction of the magnetic axis is determined by the direction of the electron spin. Therefore, this apparatus can be used to determine the direction of electron spin. When measured in the vertical direction and considering only rotation in a two-dimensional plane, if the magnetic axis is completely horizontal, the atom will not deflect. However, if the magnetic axis is completely vertical, the atom will experience maximum deflection. Expressing the direction of electron spin in terms of the spin's North (N) or South (S) pole, with the upward direction considered 0°, Figure 8.3 corresponds respectively to the spin N in direction 0° and the spin S in direction 0°.

Assuming the classical viewpoint is correct, when a large number of atoms are transmitted through the apparatus, one would expect to observe a continuous line on the screen from top to bottom. However, the experimental results show that this

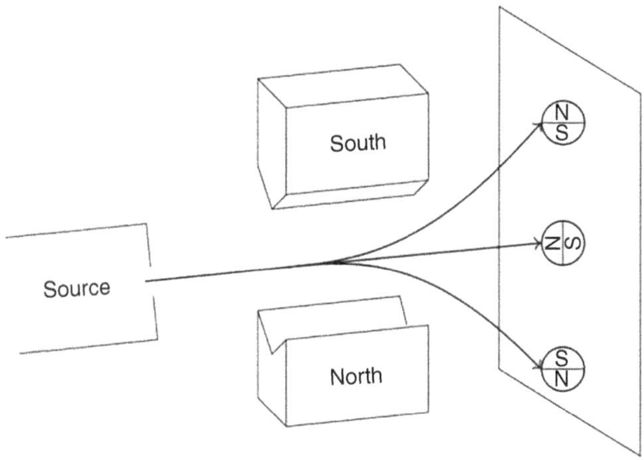

Figure 8.2 Stern-Gerlach apparatus.

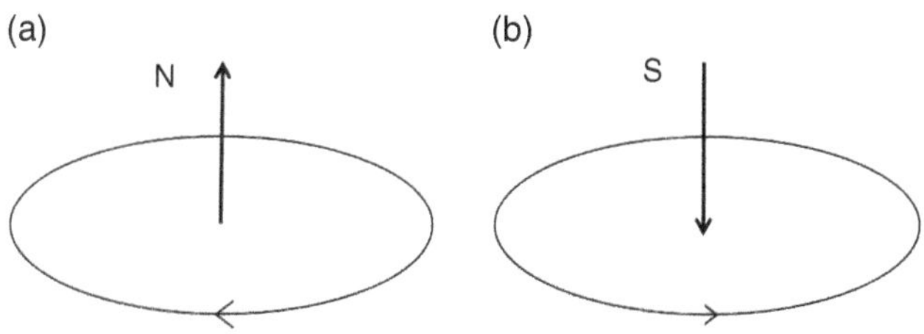

Figure 8.3 Electron spin direction and its expression. (a) Spin N in direction 0°. (b) Spin S in direction 0°.

Figure 8.4 The deflection schematic of silver atoms in the Stern-Gerlach experimental apparatus.

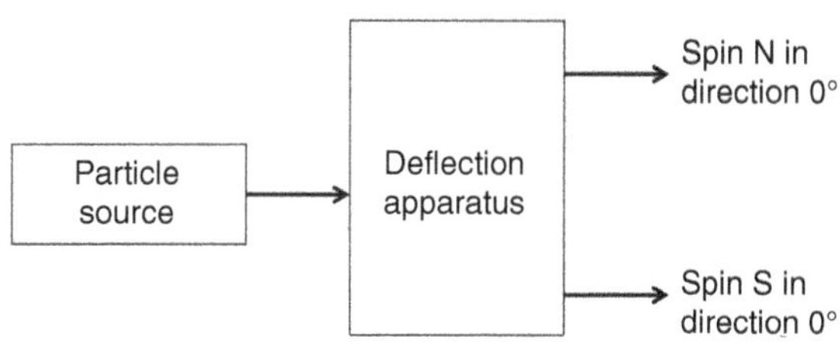

line does not appear; instead, only two points are visible on the screen – one at the top and the other at the bottom. All the atoms behave like vertically aligned slender magnetic bars, with their magnetic axes having no direction other than vertical. As illustrated in Figure 8.4, all electrons either have a spin N in direction 0° or a spin S in direction 0°.

Taking the experiment further: place two additional apparatus behind the first one, with one positioned appropriately to capture atoms deflected upward in the

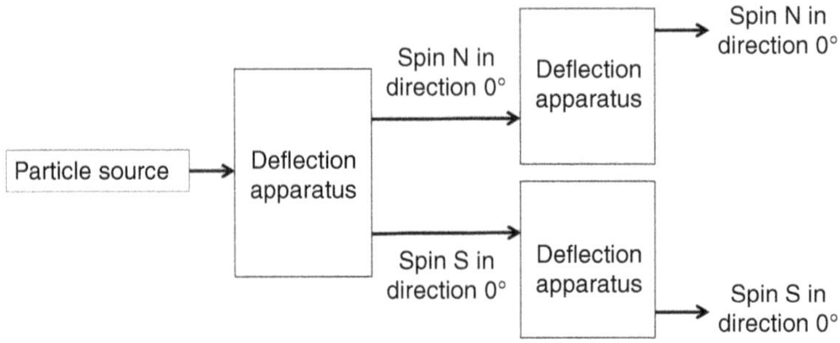

Figure 8.5 Schematic of the repetition of the Stern-Gerlach apparatus experiment with deflected silver atoms.

first apparatus and the other to capture atoms deflected downward. Repeat the same experiment. The measurement results are as shown in Figure 8.5: if the spin N of the electron is measured in the 0° direction for the first time, the spin N of the same electron will still be in the 0° direction for the second measurement. Similarly, if the initial measurement shows the spin S of the electron in the 0° direction, the spin S of the same electron will still be in the 0° direction for the second measurement.

If the front apparatus remains stationary and the two apparatuses behind it are rotated 90° to the horizontal, measuring the electron's spin direction first in the vertical direction and then in the horizontal direction, the following results will occur: for atoms deflected upward by the first detector, when they pass through the second detector, about half of the electrons have spin N in the 90° direction, while the other half have spin S in the 90° direction. In other words, the sequence of north and south spins is entirely random in the 90° direction. The same results apply to atoms deflected downward by the first detector, with approximately half of the electrons having spin N in the 90° direction and the other half having spin S in the 90° direction. The sequences of N and S are also completely random.

Conducting the consecutive three measurements as illustrated in Figure 8.6, first measured in the vertical direction, then in the horizontal direction, and finally measuring again in the vertical direction, while only observing electrons that initially had spin N in the 0° direction for the first measurement and spin N in the 90° direction for the second measurement. In the third measurement, exactly half of the electrons have spin N in the 0° direction, while the other half have spin S in the 0° direction. This result is consistent with the second measurement, indicating that the sequences of N and S are entirely random. This outcome suggests that when measured again in the vertical direction, the electron's spin direction is independent of its initial spin direction.

In quantum mechanics, the foundational model is described by a vector space, and the dimension of this vector space is determined by the number of possible

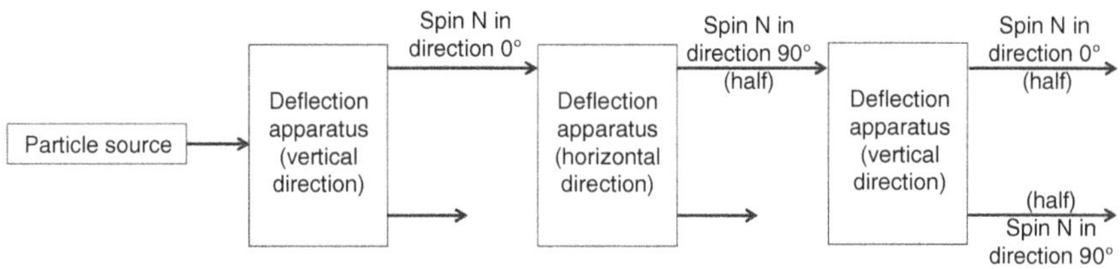

Figure 8.6 Schematic of three consecutive Stern-Gerlach apparatus experiments with deflected silver atoms.

measurement outcomes. For electron spin, regardless of the measurement direction, spin measurements always yield only two potential outcomes. Therefore, a two-dimensional complex vector space can be used to describe it. Since the experiment is conducted only within the same plane, representation can be achieved using a two-dimensional real vector space. Similar to the earlier discussion on $|0\rangle$ and $|1\rangle$, a choice of orthogonal basis must be made before describing the direction of electron spin. Different measurement directions correspond to distinct bases.

Establishing the ordered standard orthogonal basis for measuring spin in the vertical direction is given by $(|N\rangle, |S\rangle)$. The first basis vector corresponds to the electron having a spin N in the 0° direction, while the second basis vector corresponds to a spin S in the 0° direction.

$$|N\rangle = \begin{bmatrix} 1 \\ 0 \end{bmatrix}, \quad |S\rangle = \begin{bmatrix} 0 \\ 1 \end{bmatrix}. \tag{8.4}$$

Establishing the ordered standard orthogonal basis for measuring spin in the horizontal direction is given by $(|E\rangle, |W\rangle)$. The first basis vector corresponds to the electron having a spin N in the 90° direction, while the second basis vector corresponds to a spin S in the 90° direction.

$$|E\rangle = \begin{bmatrix} \frac{1}{\sqrt{2}} \\ \frac{-1}{\sqrt{2}} \end{bmatrix}, |W\rangle = \begin{bmatrix} \frac{1}{\sqrt{2}} \\ \frac{1}{\sqrt{2}} \end{bmatrix}. \tag{8.5}$$

When measuring the spin of an electron in the vertical direction, the initial state of the incoming electron's spin is not known and can be denoted as $c_1 | N\rangle + c_2 | S\rangle$. After the measurement, only two outcomes will occur: either an upward deflection, resulting in the state becoming $|N\rangle$, or a downward deflection, leading to the state becoming $|S\rangle$.

Repeating the spin measurement in the vertical direction. Assuming the first apparatus causes the atom to deflect upward, the corresponding state of the electron must be $0 \mid N\rangle + 1 \mid S\rangle$. Upon a subsequent measurement, the probability of remaining in the state $|N\rangle$ is $1^2 = 1$, and the probability of transitioning to the state $|S\rangle$ is $0^2 = 0$. This implies that it will stay in the state $|N\rangle$, and the atom will deflect upward once again. Similarly, if the atom deflects downward initially, the corresponding electron will be in the state $0 \mid N\rangle + 1 \mid S\rangle$. Regardless of how many times it is measured in the vertical direction, it will remain in this state.

In accordance with the second step of the experiment, measurements are initially conducted in the vertical direction, followed by measurements in the horizontal direction. Assuming that after the initial measurement, the electron has a spin N in the 0° direction, that is, the state is $|N\rangle$. Before performing the horizontal measurement, it is necessary to express this vector as a linear combination of the corresponding basis. This entails determining values x_1 and x_2 that satisfy the equation $|N\rangle = x_1 \mid E\rangle + x_2 \mid W\rangle$, which is equivalent to solving the system of equations:

$$\begin{cases} \frac{1}{\sqrt{2}}x_1 + \frac{1}{\sqrt{2}}x_2 = 1, \\ \frac{-1}{\sqrt{2}}x_1 + \frac{1}{\sqrt{2}}x_2 = 0. \end{cases} \tag{8.6}$$

By respectively solving for the values of x_1 and x_2, we can obtain:

$$|N\rangle = \frac{1}{\sqrt{2}}|E\rangle + \frac{1}{\sqrt{2}}|W\rangle. \tag{8.7}$$

In other words, when measuring in the horizontal direction, there is a probability $\left(\frac{1}{\sqrt{2}}\right)^2 = \frac{1}{2}$ that the electron's state transitions to $|E\rangle$ and a probability $\left(\frac{1}{\sqrt{2}}\right)^2 = \frac{1}{2}$ that it transitions to $|W\rangle$. This indicates that the probabilities of the electron having a spin N and S in the 90° direction are equal, both being $\frac{1}{2}$.

For the third measurement, the same logic applies, and we can obtain:

$$|E\rangle = \frac{1}{\sqrt{2}}|N\rangle - \frac{1}{\sqrt{2}}|S\rangle. \tag{8.8}$$

This indicates that when measuring again in the vertical direction, there is a probability $\left(\frac{1}{\sqrt{2}}\right)^2 = \frac{1}{2}$ that the electron's state transitions to $|N\rangle$ and a probability $\left(-\frac{1}{\sqrt{2}}\right)^2 = \frac{1}{2}$ that it transitions to$|S\rangle$.

The above example aids in understanding the qubit state and its representation. However, while this form is concise, it has limited expressiveness. Since physically observable quantum states are unaffected by global phases, the global phase can be ignored, and only relative phases are considered (Wilde 2011). Here, the global phase refers to a common phase factor that does not alter the probability distribution, while the relative phase refers to the phase difference between two coefficients. Therefore, by fixing the global phase α and considering only the relative phase β, it is possible to rewrite it as Equation (8.9), where α, β, and φ are all real numbers.

$$|\psi\rangle = \alpha|0\rangle + e^{i\varphi}\beta|1\rangle. \tag{8.9}$$

Considering the constraint $|\alpha|^2 + |\beta|^2 = 1$, it is advantageous to express this form using trigonometric functions and replace α and β with a single variable θ:

$$\alpha = cos\,\frac{\theta}{2},\quad \beta = sin\,\frac{\theta}{2}. \tag{8.10}$$

Therefore, Equation (8.9) can be further rewritten as:

$$|\psi\rangle = cos\,\frac{\theta}{2}|0\rangle + e^{i\varphi}\,sin\,\frac{\theta}{2}|1\rangle, \tag{8.11}$$

where φ and θ define a point on the unit sphere in three dimensions, as illustrated in Figure 8.7. This sphere is referred to as the Bloch sphere, and it effectively maps the two-dimensional complex vector space to a three-dimensional real vector space. This mapping provides an enhanced intuitive comprehension of the behavior and properties of qubits, serving as an effective means to visualize the state of a

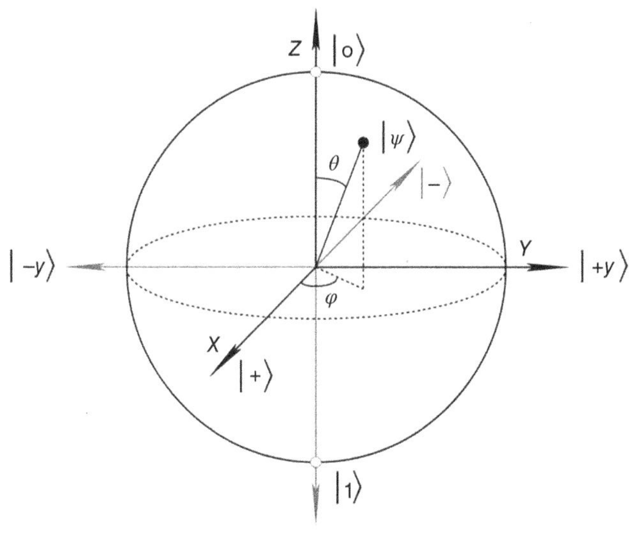

Figure 8.7 Schematic of the Bloch sphere.

single qubit. However, this visualization approach has limitations when it comes to imagining multiple qubits, as it becomes challenging to straightforwardly extend it to multiple qubits.

Multiple qubits are commonly described using tensor products. Consider two qubits, each employing a different set of standard orthogonal bases, one utilizing $(|a_0\rangle, |a_1\rangle)$, and the other utilizing $(|b_0\rangle, |b_1\rangle)$. The state of the first qubit is represented as $|v\rangle = c_0 | a_0\rangle + c_1 | a_1\rangle$, and the second qubit is represented as $|w\rangle = d_0 | b_0\rangle + d_1 | b_1\rangle$. The tensor product of the two is denoted as $|v\rangle \otimes | w\rangle$. For the sake of convenience, the notation $\otimes$ can be omitted, and this expression can be abbreviated as $|v\rangle | w\rangle$, or simply written as $|vw\rangle$. Expanding it in algebraic form:

$$|vw\rangle = c_0d_0|a_0b_0\rangle + c_0d_1|a_0b_1\rangle + c_1d_0|a_1b_0\rangle + c_1d_1|a_1b_1\rangle. \tag{8.12}$$

For simplicity, we use single letters to represent these probability amplitudes:

$$r = c_0d_0, \quad s = c_0d_1, \quad t = c_1d_0, \quad u = c_1d_1. \tag{8.13}$$

Then Equation (8.12) can be rewritten as:

$$r|a_0\rangle|b_0\rangle + s|a_0\rangle|b_1\rangle + t|a_1\rangle|b_0\rangle + u|a_1\rangle|b_1\rangle. \tag{8.14}$$

As previously mentioned, the sum of probabilities equals 1, thus implying that $r^2 + s^2 + t^2 + u^2 = 1$. In Equation (8.12), the two qubits are considered independent, meaning they are nonentangled. For nonentangled qubits, both ru and st are equal to $c_0c_1d_0d_1$, so $ru = st$.

If we also use Equation (8.14) to describe the states of two qubits, ensuring $r^2 + s^2 + t^2 + u^2 = 1$. Then, for entangled qubits, the following theorem holds: If $ru \neq st$, the two qubits are entangled.

Illustrating this theorem with a concrete example, consider a scenario where two qubits are:

$$\frac{1}{2}|a_0\rangle|b_0\rangle + \frac{1}{2}|a_0\rangle|b_1\rangle + \frac{1}{\sqrt{2}}|a_1\rangle|b_0\rangle + 0|a_1\rangle|b_1\rangle. \tag{8.15}$$

Assuming the measurement of the first qubit, the tensor product expression can be rewritten in the following form:

$$\frac{1}{\sqrt{2}}| a_0\rangle\left(\frac{1}{\sqrt{2}}| b_0\rangle + \frac{1}{\sqrt{2}}|b_1\rangle\right) + \frac{1}{\sqrt{2}}|a_1\rangle(1|b_0\rangle + 0|b_1\rangle). \tag{8.16}$$

According to Equation (8.16), it can be inferred that by measuring the first qubit initially, the probability of observing either 0 or 1 is $\frac{1}{2}$. Assuming the measurement result is 0, the tensor product becomes an unentangled state:

$$|a_0\rangle\left(\frac{1}{\sqrt{2}}|b_0\rangle + \frac{1}{\sqrt{2}}|b_1\rangle\right). \tag{8.17}$$

The second qubit then becomes:

$$\frac{1}{\sqrt{2}}|b_0\rangle + \frac{1}{\sqrt{2}}|b_1\rangle. \tag{8.18}$$

Similarly, if the measurement result is 1, the second qubit transforms into $1 \mid b_0\rangle + 0 \mid b_1\rangle$, that is $|b_0\rangle$.

This example demonstrates that for entangled qubits, when measuring one qubit, the other qubit immediately transitions to one of two states, depending on the measurement outcome of the measured qubit. It's important to note that qubits correspond to the states of particles, such as the spin direction of an electron. Therefore, entangled qubits refer to the entanglement of the state vectors of the particles, not the particles themselves.

For two qubits, the dimensionality of their states should be four-dimensional. Further generalizing, in a quantum system composed of m qubits, each qubit contributes two dimensions, and the total dimensionality of the system is 2^m. Using n to represent 2^m, this state can be defined as:

$$|\psi\rangle = [c_1, c_2, ..., c_n]^T. \tag{8.19}$$

This is a column vector of size $n \times 1$, called a ket. Using the symbol $*$ to represent complex conjugation, correspondingly, a row vector of size $1 \times n$, called a bra, can be defined as:

$$\langle\psi| = [c_1^*, c_2^*, ..., c_n^*]. \tag{8.20}$$

We define an inner product on the vector space as a function that takes as input two vectors from the vector space and produces a complex number as output. For $|u\rangle$ and $|v\rangle$ in the vector space, we denote their inner product by $\langle u \mid v\rangle$. The inner product must satisfy:

1) *Conjugate symmetry:* $\langle u \mid v\rangle = (\langle v \mid u\rangle)^*$;
2) *Linearity in the second argument:* $\langle u \mid v + w\rangle = \langle u \mid v\rangle + \langle u \mid w\rangle$;
3) *Positive definiteness:* $\langle u \mid u\rangle \geq 0$ with equality only for $u = 0$.

For a vector space composed of k-tuples of complex numbers, its natural inner product is defined as:

$$\langle u|v\rangle = \sum_{j=1}^{k} u_j^* v_j = [u_1^*, u_2^*, ..., u_k^*][v_1, v_2, ..., v_k]^T, \tag{8.21}$$

where $\langle u| = [u_1, u_2, ..., u_k]$, $|v\rangle = [v_1, v_2, ..., v_k]^T$. For the finite-dimensional case, a Hilbert space $\mathcal{H}$ is simply a vector space with an inner product.

This section uses the example of electron spin to explain qubits and their mathematical expressions. However, in reality, electron spin is not the only physical system that can be used to represent qubits; the concept of qubits can be realized through various physical systems. In addition to electron spin, other common implementations include the polarization of photons, quantum states of superconducting circuits, ion states in ion traps, and certain atomic internal energy levels.

Quantum mechanics describes phenomena at the microscopic level mentioned above. Unlike classical mechanics, where physical entities can be precisely measured, the theory of quantum mechanics is inherently probabilistic, meaning that predictions can only be made probabilistically for measurement outcomes. Mathematically, quantum mechanics is described by Hilbert space $\mathcal{H}$and its operators. The evolution of a quantum system is entirely characterized by the time evolution of its state, defined as a unit vector in Hilbert space. Let $|\psi(t)\rangle$ be the state of quantum system at time t, which is also referred to as a wave function. The state $|\psi(t_1)\rangle$ and $|\psi(t_2)\rangle$ at t_1 and t_2 are connected through Equation (8.22).

$$|\psi(t_2)\rangle = \boldsymbol{U}(t_1, t_2)|\psi(t_1)\rangle, \tag{8.22}$$

where $\boldsymbol{U}(t_1, t_2)$ is a unitary operator depending only time t_1 and t_2. In fact, there exists a self-adjoint operator $\boldsymbol{H}$, which is known as the Hamiltonian of the quantum system, such that

$$\boldsymbol{U}(t_1, t_2) = exp[-i\boldsymbol{H}(t_2 - t_1)]. \tag{8.23}$$

With Hamiltonian $\boldsymbol{H}$, we may describe the continuous time evolution of $|\psi(t)\rangle$ by the Schrödinger equation:

$$i\frac{\partial \mid \psi(t)\rangle}{\partial t} = \boldsymbol{H}|\psi(t)\rangle, \quad i = \sqrt{-1}. \tag{8.24}$$

Alternatively, a quantum system can be described by a density operator (or density matrix). A density operator $\boldsymbol{\rho}$ is an operator on $\boldsymbol{H}$ which (1) is self-adjoint, $\boldsymbol{\rho} = \boldsymbol{\rho}^*$; (2) is semi-positive definite; (3) has unit trace, $\mathrm{Tr}(\boldsymbol{\rho}) = 1$.

Following the convention in quantum information science, we reserve notation $\boldsymbol{\rho}$ for state, density operator or density matrix. A state is often classified as a pure state or an ensemble of pure states. A pure state is a unit vector $|\psi\rangle$ in $\boldsymbol{H}$, which corresponds to a density operator $\boldsymbol{\rho} = \mid \psi\rangle\langle\psi|$, and an ensemble of pure states corresponds to the case that the quantum system is in one of states $|\psi_j\rangle, j = 1, \ldots, J$, with probability p_j being in state $|\psi_j\rangle$, and the corresponding density operator

$$\rho = \sum_{j=1}^{J} p_j \mid \psi_j\rangle\langle\psi_j \mid . \tag{8.25}$$

8.1.2 Quantum Gates and Quantum Circuits

After delving into the understanding of qubits and their representations, the next step is to comprehend how to manipulate these qubits. This introduces the concept of quantum gates, which play a pivotal role in exerting control over qubits.

In classical computing, logical operations such as AND, OR, and NOT are commonly used as functions. For example, the AND operation is a function that takes two inputs and produces one output, while the NOT operation is a function with one input and one output. A specific type of function known as a Boolean function takes a series of truth values (1 or 0) as input and returns a truth or false value for each input combination. Within Boolean functions, it is possible to generate any function defined by a truth table using only AND and NOT. Furthermore, there is a binary operation called NAND (NOT AND), which can logically represent any Boolean function. In other words, any Boolean operation can be replaced by an equivalent function using only NAND, making it functionally complete.

It was realized that if logic could be represented algebraically, machines could be designed to perform logical computations. The renowned scholar Claude Shannon demonstrated that all Boolean algebra can be executed using electrical switches, forming the fundamental idea behind all modern computer circuit designs. Combinations of switches corresponding to binary operators are called gates, with common gates including AND, OR, and NOT. Due to its functional completeness, the NAND gate is a universal gate. By connecting these gates together to form circuits, essential functions such as computation and storage in computer systems are achieved.

Quantum gates and circuits are a natural extension of classical gates and circuits and provide an alternative perspective on mathematical language. Quantum gates operate on qubits and perform computations. From a mathematical perspective, quantum gates perform various operations on vectors. Considering these operations as mathematical functions, it becomes evident that quantum gates can be represented by matrices.

1) *Gate I:* The gate I is defined by the identity matrix $\begin{bmatrix} 1 & 0 \\ 0 & 1 \end{bmatrix}$. As an identity operation, it does not alter the qubit.
2) *Gate Z*: The gate Z is defined by the matrix $\begin{bmatrix} 1 & 0 \\ 0 & -1 \end{bmatrix}$. It will keep the probability amplitudes of $|0\rangle$ unchanged while altering the sign of the probability amplitude for $|1\rangle$.
3) *Gate X*: The gate X is defined by the matrix $\begin{bmatrix} 0 & 1 \\ 1 & 0 \end{bmatrix}$. It will cause a flip in the probability amplitudes of $|0\rangle$ and $|1\rangle$.
4) *Gate Y*: The gate Y is defined by the matrix $\begin{bmatrix} 0 & -i \\ i & 0 \end{bmatrix}$. It not only flips $|0\rangle$ and $|1\rangle$ but also applies a rotation in three-dimensional space.

The above four gates only operate on a single qubit. These four quantum gates are named after Wolfgang Pauli, thus referred to as Pauli transformations.

5) *Hadamard gate*: The Hadamard gate is defined by the matrix $\frac{1}{\sqrt{2}}\begin{bmatrix} 1 & 1 \\ 1 & -1 \end{bmatrix}$. It can transform standard basis vectors into superposition state, and it also operates solely on a single qubit: $H(|0\rangle) = \frac{1}{\sqrt{2}}(|0\rangle + |1\rangle)$, $H(|1\rangle) = \frac{1}{\sqrt{2}}(|0\rangle - |1\rangle)$.
6) *Controlled-NOT(CNOT)gate*: The CNOT gate is a type of gate that operates on two qubits, and it can flip the probability amplitudes of $|10\rangle$ and $|11\rangle$:$CNOT(r|00\rangle + s|01\rangle + t|10\rangle + u|11\rangle) = r|00\rangle + s|01\rangle + t|11\rangle + u|10\rangle$. Therefore, it has the capability to entangle two nonentangled qubits. The CNOT gate is defined by the matrix:

$$CNOT = \begin{bmatrix} 1 & 0 & 0 & 0 \\ 0 & 1 & 0 & 0 \\ 0 & 0 & 0 & 1 \\ 0 & 0 & 1 & 0 \end{bmatrix}. \tag{8.26}$$

7) *Swap gate*: The Swap gate is also a type of gate that operates on two qubits, used to swap the states of two qubits. For example, for two qubits initially in states $|0\rangle$ and $|1\rangle$, respectively, the Swap gate will result in the first qubit being in state $|1\rangle$ and the second qubit being in state $|0\rangle$. The Swap gate is defined by the matrix:

$$Swap = \begin{bmatrix} 1 & 0 & 0 & 0 \\ 0 & 0 & 1 & 0 \\ 0 & 1 & 0 & 0 \\ 0 & 0 & 0 & 1 \end{bmatrix}. \tag{8.27}$$

The Hadamard gate, the CNOT gate, and the Swap gate are commonly used quantum gates in quantum algorithms and quantum communication, typically represented by specific diagrams, as shown in Figures 8.8–8.10.

The quantum gates exhibit the following four distinctive properties:

1) In classical computation, there are only a finite number of Boolean functions for a given number of inputs. When the number of inputs is 1, there are only two Boolean functions; when the number of inputs is 2, there are four Boolean functions; and for n inputs, there are 2^n possible Boolean functions, i.e., 2^n classical gates. The situation is radically different for quantum gates, where there are infinitely many single-qubit gates, each corresponding to any orthogonal matrix.

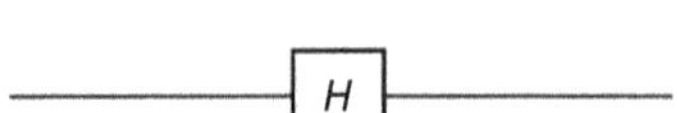

Figure 8.8 The Hadamard gate.

2) If only a finite number of gates are used and connected in a finite way, a finite number of circuits will be obtained. Therefore, there is no situation where a finite number of gates can generate an infinite number of circuits. Additionally, there is no finite set of quantum gates that can generate any other quantum circuit. Although universal quantum gates are nonexistent, it has been demonstrated that there exists a finite set of gates that can approximate all possible circuits.
3) Since quantum gates correspond to matrices, quantum gates are linear and reversible. For a single qubit gate, the corresponding matrix should exhibit unitarity $UU^{\dagger} = I$, where $U^{\dagger}$ is the conjugate transpose of the matrix U.
4) Classical gates can perform replication operations, but it is impractical in quantum gates. Any quantum gate cannot achieve the replication of an arbitrary qubit.

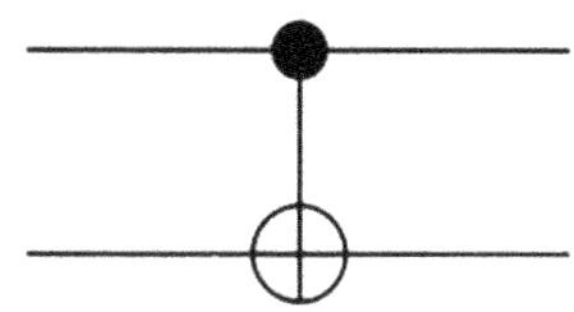

Figure 8.9 The CNOT gate.

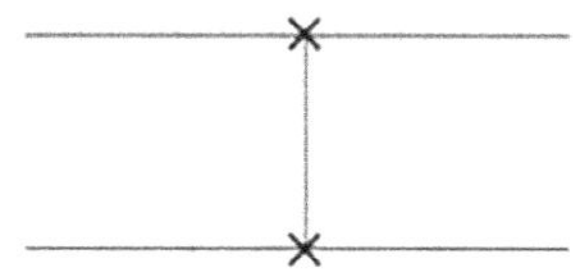

Figure 8.10 The Swap gate.

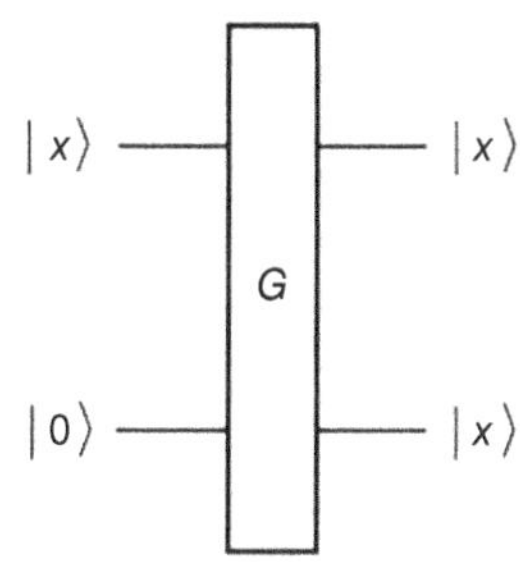

Figure 8.11 A hypothetical quantum cloning gate.

The term "cloning" is commonly used to describe the process of copying in the quantum realm. Figure 8.11 depicts a hypothetical quantum cloning gate G, where $|0\rangle$ is an ancillary bit, and $|x\rangle$ is the qubit to be cloned. The question of whether cloning is achievable is equivalent to whether gate G exists. Use a proof by contradiction: assuming the existence of gate G, then demonstrating two logically consistent but mutually contradictory outcomes. Eventually, this leads to the conclusion that the initial assumption of the existence of the G gate is incorrect. The detailed proof is presented below.

If gate G exists, the cloning property implies the following three conclusions:

a) $G(|00\rangle) = |00\rangle$;

b) $G(|10\rangle) = |11\rangle$;

c) $$G\left(\left(\frac{1}{\sqrt{2}}(|0\rangle + |1\rangle)\right)|0\rangle\right) = \left(\frac{1}{\sqrt{2}}(|0\rangle + |1\rangle)\right)\left(\frac{1}{\sqrt{2}}(|0\rangle + |1\rangle)\right)$$
$$= \frac{1}{2}(|00\rangle + |01\rangle + |10\rangle + |11\rangle).$$

Since the gate G, like all matrix operations, must be linear, conclusions (a) and (b) lead to the inference:

$$G\left(\frac{1}{\sqrt{2}}\,|\,00\rangle + \frac{1}{\sqrt{2}}\,|\,10\rangle\right) = \frac{1}{\sqrt{2}}\,|\,00\rangle + \frac{1}{\sqrt{2}}\,|\,11\rangle. \tag{8.28}$$

However,

$$\frac{1}{\sqrt{2}}\,|\,00\rangle + \frac{1}{\sqrt{2}}\,|\,11\rangle \neq \frac{1}{2}(|\,00\rangle + |\,01\rangle + |\,10\rangle + |\,11\rangle). \tag{8.29}$$

This result contradicts conclusion (c). Therefore, gate G does not exist, and it is impossible to construct a quantum gate that can clone an arbitrary qubit. In this example, the choice of $|0\rangle$ as the ancillary bit is arbitrary, and the same proof can be applied regardless of the specific value chosen for the ancillary bit. This conclusion is known as the no-cloning theorem. The no-cloning theorem has profound implications in the quantum world, serving as the foundation for many quantum technologies and a crucial premise for the security of quantum communication.

Quantum circuits are collections of quantum gates interconnected through input and output lines without loops. In theory, there should be countless types of quantum circuits. This section introduces three commonly used ones, which find wide applications in quantum communication, quantum entanglement, and other fields.

8.1.2.1 Bell Circuit

The Bell circuit is a commonly used quantum circuit that connects Hadamard gates with CNOT gates, as shown in Figure 8.12.

For a pair of qubits $|00\rangle$, when the first qubit $|0\rangle$ becomes $\frac{1}{\sqrt{2}}(|\,0\rangle + \,|\,1\rangle)$ after passing through the Hadamard gate, both qubits consequently become $\frac{1}{\sqrt{2}}(|\,00\rangle + \,|\,10\rangle)$. When they pass through the CNOT gate, they transform into $\frac{1}{\sqrt{2}}(|\,00\rangle + \,|\,11\rangle)$. Similarly, the other three pairs of standard bases can be computed to yield the corresponding outputs, as shown in Table 8.1.

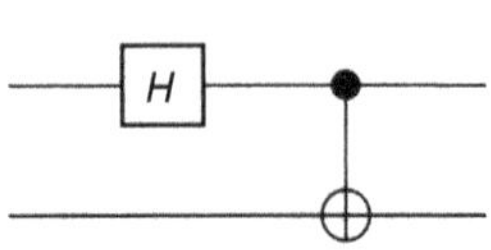

Figure 8.12 The Bell circuit.

8.1.2.2 Reverse Bell Circuit

As both the Hadamard gate and the CNOT gate can transform their outputs back to the inputs, a reverse Bell circuit, as depicted in Figure 8.13, can be defined. This circuit transforms the Bell states back to the standard basis. The corresponding truth table is shown in Table 8.2.

Table 8.1 Truth table for the Bell circuit.

Input	Output
$\|00\rangle$	$\frac{1}{\sqrt{2}}(\|00\rangle + \|11\rangle)$
$\|01\rangle$	$\frac{1}{\sqrt{2}}(\|01\rangle + \|10\rangle)$
$\|10\rangle$	$\frac{1}{\sqrt{2}}(\|00\rangle - \|11\rangle)$
$\|11\rangle$	$\frac{1}{\sqrt{2}}(\|01\rangle - \|10\rangle)$

8.1.2.3 GHZ Circuit

The Greenberger-Horne-Zeilinger state (GHZ state) is an entangled state that involves three or more qubits. When three or more particles enter an entangled state, it is referred to as a multipartite entangled state. Figure 8.14 depicts a simple GHZ circuit. GHZ states play a crucial role in quantum cryptography and various quantum algorithms.

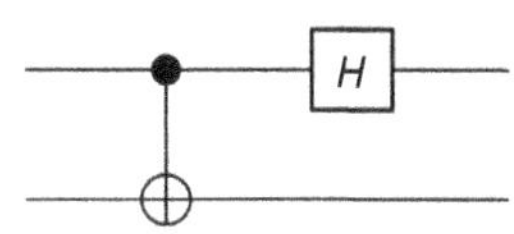

Figure 8.13 The reverse Bell circuit.

8.1.2.4 W State Circuit

The W state circuit is another way to achieve entanglement of multiple particles. The special property of the W state is that if one qubit is lost, the remaining qubits can still maintain their entanglement. This implies that the W state is relatively

Table 8.2 Truth table for the reverse Bell circuit.

Input	Output
$\frac{1}{\sqrt{2}}(\|00\rangle + \|11\rangle)$	$\|00\rangle$
$\frac{1}{\sqrt{2}}(\|01\rangle + \|10\rangle)$	$\|01\rangle$
$\frac{1}{\sqrt{2}}(\|00\rangle - \|11\rangle)$	$\|10\rangle$
$\frac{1}{\sqrt{2}}(\|01\rangle - \|10\rangle)$	$\|11\rangle$

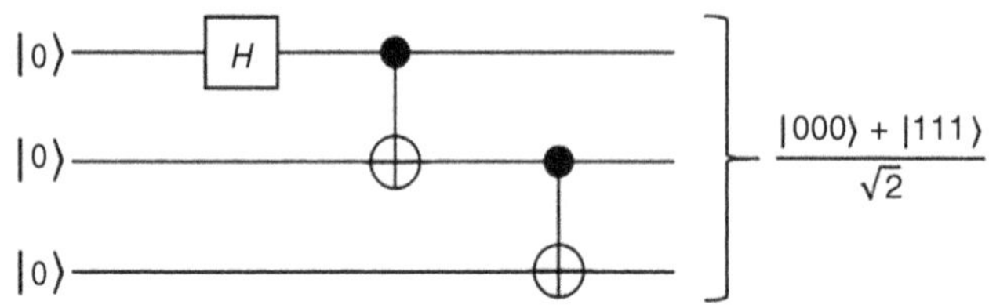

Figure 8.14 A GHZ circuit consisting of three qubits.

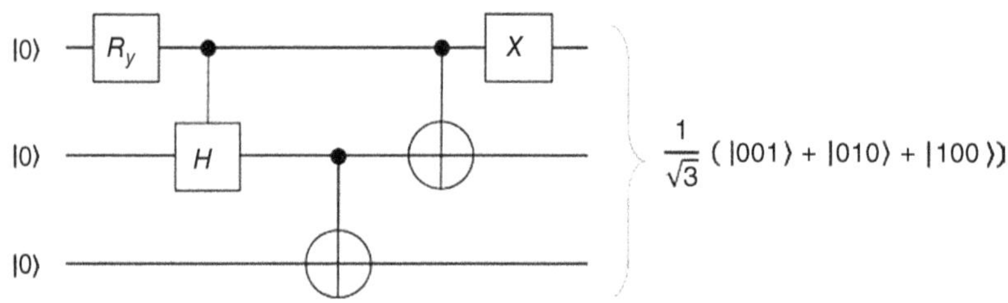

Figure 8.15 A W state circuit consisting of three qubits.

robust against partial measurements or partial damage, which is of significant importance in quantum communication and error correction. Figure 8.15 depicts a simple W state circuit.

Classical gates and circuits are used in classical computation, just as quantum gates and circuits are employed in quantum computation. Quantum algorithms often exhibit significant advantages in terms of execution speed compared to classical algorithms. The fundamental reason for this acceleration can be attributed to the capability of quantum algorithms to place the input state in a superposition of all potential inputs and process these superposition states in parallel. However, quantum parallelism does not imply running the algorithm simultaneously on all possible inputs; it signifies that each possible input has a certain probability of occurring. Therefore, compared to classical algorithms, quantum algorithms can leverage this superposition property to more efficiently execute algorithms on multiple inputs. Famous quantum algorithms include the Deutsch-Jozsa black-box solution algorithm, Shor's discrete log problem and factorization algorithm, and Grover's search algorithm.

David Deutsch is one of the founders of quantum computing. In 1985, he published a landmark paper describing quantum Turing machines and quantum computation (Deutsch 1985, pp. 97–117). This paper also includes the first algorithm showcasing the superiority of quantum algorithms over classical one – the Deutsch algorithm. The algorithm involves a core concept known as query complexity. This concept describes how many times an algorithm needs to query a specific function (often referred to as an oracle) to solve a given problem.

The algorithm describes a unary function with inputs of 0 or 1 and outputs of 0 or 1. There are four such functions: f_0, f_1, f_2, and f_3. Where $f_0(0) = f_0(1) = 0$; $f_1(0) = 0$, $f_1(1) = 1$; $f_2(0) = 1$, $f_2(1) = 0$; $f_3(0) = f_3(1) = 1$. f_0 and f_3 are called the constant function, as they output the same value for both inputs. f_1 and f_2 are called the balanced function, as they output 0 for half of their inputs and 1 for the other half. The question posed by Deutsch is: Given a randomly selected function from these four functions, how many oracle queries are needed to determine whether the function is constant or balanced?

In classical computation, to answer this question, one must substitute both 0 and 1 into the function, requiring two queries. However, the use of quantum gates and circuits can reduce the number of queries. To achieve this, construct a gate corresponding to these four functions, as shown in Figure 8.16, where i can take the values 0, 1, 2, or 3.

Operating on two qubits, where the top qubit $|x\rangle$ serves as the only true input, this operation generates outputs for both qubits. However, the first output $|x\rangle$ merely duplicates the original input information, offering no new data. As for the second output $|y \oplus f_i(x)\rangle$, its result depends on the second input $|y\rangle$: it is either the function value of the top input or the negation of that function value. Combining the quantum gates with the function, Deutsch designed the circuit depicted in Figure 8.17. The small gauge symbol at the right end of the top wire indicates the measurement of that qubit.

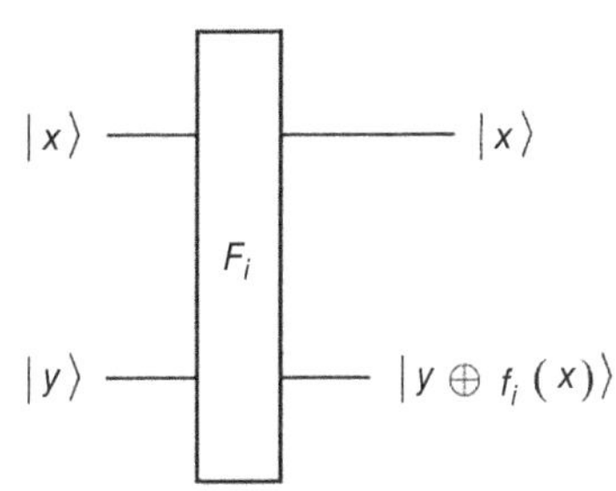

Figure 8.16 The quantum gates corresponding to the four functions.

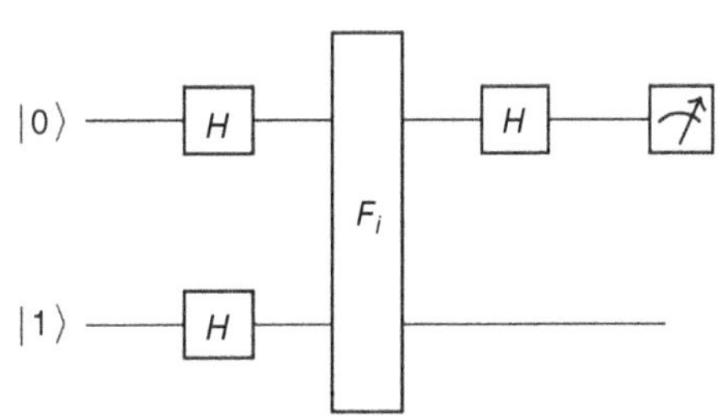

Figure 8.17 The circuit of the Deutsch algorithm.

The qubits $|0\rangle \otimes |1\rangle$ are input. They go through the Hadamard gates, which puts them in the state:

$$\frac{1}{2}(|00\rangle - |01\rangle + |10\rangle - |11\rangle). \tag{8.30}$$

These then go through the F_i gate. The state becomes:

$$\frac{1}{2}(|0\rangle\otimes|f_i(0)\rangle - |0\rangle\otimes|1\oplus f_i(0)\rangle + \\ |1\rangle\otimes|f_i(1)\rangle - |1\rangle\otimes|1\oplus f_i(1)\rangle). \tag{8.31}$$

Since $|f_i(0)\rangle - |1\oplus f_i(0)\rangle$ is equal to either $|0\rangle - |1\rangle$ or $|1\rangle - |0\rangle$, we obtain Equations (8.32) and (8.33).

$$|f_i(0)\rangle - |1\oplus f_i(0)\rangle = (-1)^{f_i(0)}(|0\rangle - |1\rangle), \tag{8.32}$$

$$|f_i(1)\rangle - |1\oplus f_i(1)\rangle = (-1)^{f_i(1)}(|0\rangle - |1\rangle). \tag{8.33}$$

Therefore, the quantum state that goes through the F_i gate can be rewritten as:

$$\frac{1}{\sqrt{2}}\left((-1)^{f_i(0)}|0\rangle + (-1)^{f_i(1)}|1\rangle\right)\otimes\frac{1}{\sqrt{2}}(|0\rangle - |1\rangle). \tag{8.34}$$

That is, the two qubits are not entangled, and the top qubit has state:

$$\frac{1}{\sqrt{2}}\left((-1)^{f_i(0)}|0\rangle + (-1)^{f_i(1)}|1\rangle\right). \tag{8.35}$$

Based on this, each of the four possibilities for f_i can be calculated. The next step in the circuit is to pass the qubit through a Hadamard gate. After the Hadamard gate, measurement is performed: If $i = 0$, the qubit is $|0\rangle$. If $i = 1$, the qubit is $|1\rangle$. If $i = 2$, the qubit is $-|1\rangle$. If $i = 3$, the qubit is $-|0\rangle$.

When measuring the qubit on the standard basis, if i equals 0 or 3, the result will be 0; and if i equals 2 or 3, the result will be 1. Since f_0 and f_3 are constant functions and f_1 and f_2 are balanced functions, by observing whether the measurement yields 0 or 1, it becomes possible to ascertain whether the original function is constant or balanced with just one query to the oracle. Therefore, for Deutsch's problem, there is a slight speedup when using a quantum algorithm.

The Deutsch algorithm illustrates the unique advantages of quantum computation compared to classical computation, laying the foundation for research in quantum theory and broader studies in quantum computing. However, the practical application of the Deutsch algorithm is limited. In contrast, the Shor algorithm (Shor 1994, pp. 124–134) is a quantum algorithm with extensive practical applications. The core objective of the Shor algorithm involves factoring large integers into their prime factors, a task that typically requires exponential time on classical computers but can be solved in polynomial time on quantum

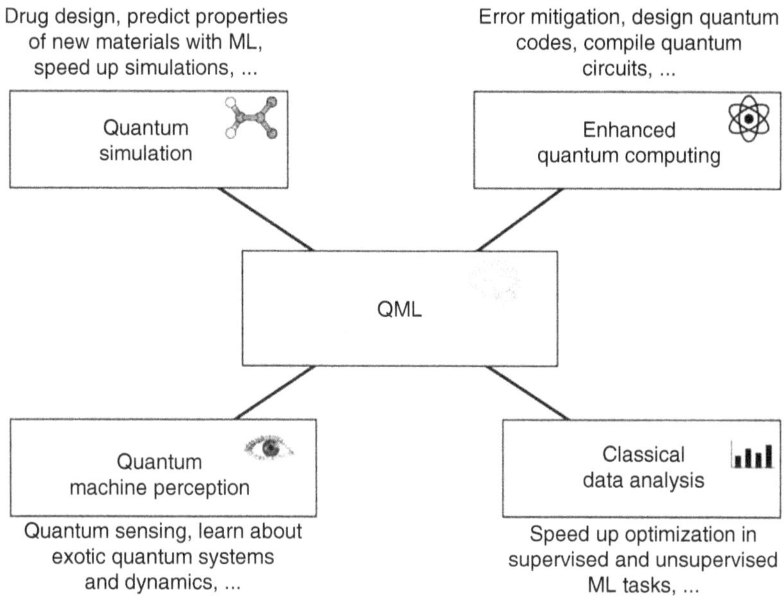

Figure 8.18 Applications of QML. *Source:* Cerezo et al. (2022, pp. 567–576)/With permission of Springer Nature.

computers. This feature endows the Shor algorithm with revolutionary potential in the fields of cryptography, secure communication, and data encryption.

Quantum algorithms represent the forefront of quantum computing, leveraging the parallelism of qubits to solve a range of problems in a remarkable manner. These algorithms hold potential applications in fields such as information security, database search, combinatorial optimization, and materials science. Particularly when confronted with large-scale data and complex problems, the significance of quantum computing becomes indispensable. For example, machine learning, a domain that deals with large-scale data and intricate issues, has seen the emergence of a new interdisciplinary field known as Quantum Machine Learning (QML) by integrating machine learning theory with quantum computing, as depicted in Figure 8.18. The development and application of QML indicate that quantum algorithms offer innovative possibilities for tackling problems that traditional computers find challenging, ushering in a new era of computational capabilities.

8.1.3 Quantum Memory and Quantum Computers

Classical computing relies on classical computers and storage devices, while quantum computing requires quantum counterparts. Following the classical computing paradigm, a quantum memory should be a component of a quantum computer. In theory, to achieve a large-scale, fault-tolerant quantum computer, a method for storing quantum information is indeed needed for error correction during the computation. However, in current quantum computing experiments, qubits are typically used directly, rather than being retrieved from a quantum memory. This is because current quantum computers are still in the early stages, and many experiments have not yet required long-term storage of quantum information. Therefore, current quantum computers are, in practice, a type of computational devices rather than classical computers in the traditional sense.

8.1.3.1 Quantum Memory

Referring to the concept of classical memory, quantum memory is a device capable of preserving quantum states. Before delving into the structure and principles of quantum memory, it is essential to revisit its origin, namely the slow light experiments. The principle of the constancy of the speed of light posits that the speed of light is always a fixed value in a vacuum. However, in certain mediums, the speed of light can actually be lower or higher than this constant. This phenomenon of slow and superluminal speeds is achieved in mediums exhibiting normal and anomalous dispersion, respectively. In essence, a light pulse can be considered a combination of multiple frequency components. Due to the dispersive nature of the medium, these different-frequency lights propagate at varying speeds within it. As light propagates through such medium, the phase relationships of these frequency components change, altering the shape of the pulse and resulting in either slow light or superluminal effects. Furthermore, if absorbed by the medium and converted into the coherent state of atom instead, this state can later be transformed back into a light pulse again, thus realizing the storage and retrieval functions of light.

The initial optical memory was designed for storing classical pulsed light. However, researchers later shifted their focus toward exploring the storage of single photons carrying quantum information, with applications in multi-photon synchronization, quantum computing, and long-distance quantum communication. This shift in focus has led to an abundance of experimental and theoretical studies on optical or quantum memory. The primary approaches in this field include Electromagnetically Induced Transparency (EIT) quantum storage, the Duan-Lukin-Cirac-Zoller (DLCZ) storage scheme, Faraday interaction, reversible inhomogeneous broadening, and Atomic Frequency Comb (AFC). The core of these approaches involves the interaction between light and material, as well as the interference or evolution and restoration of the internal states or phase relationships within the material. The following provides a brief overview of these methods.

EIT is a phenomenon associated with quantum physics that allows light to propagate through an absorbing medium without loss. This phenomenon is achieved by using two beams of light: one is a strong control beam, and the other is a weak probe beam. Normally, the medium would absorb the probe beam; however, when the control beam simultaneously interacts with the medium, it alters its quantum

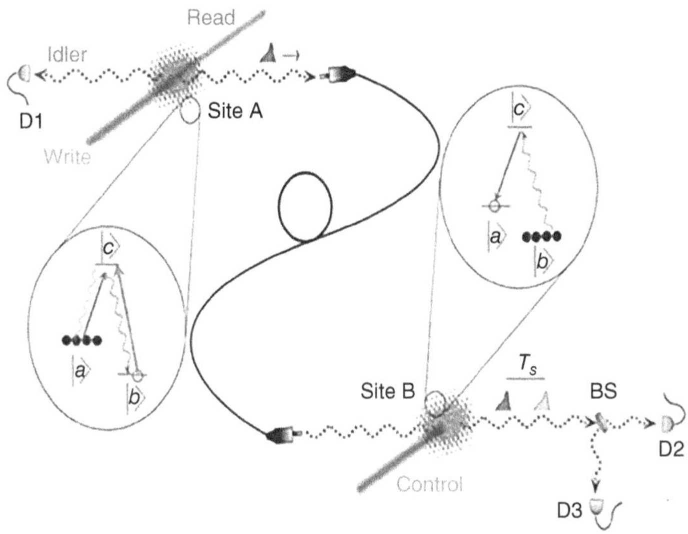

Figure 8.19 Generation, transmission, storage, and retrieval of single photons in an electromagnetic field.

state, making it transparent and allowing the probe beam to pass through without being absorbed. EIT quantum storage (Chanelière et al. 2005, pp. 833–836) is a method that leverages this phenomenon to store optical information. As illustrated in Figure 8.19, in EIT storage, the probe light is temporarily converted into the atomic excited state in the medium. When the control light is turned off, the information is locked in the atomic system. When retrieving the information, the control light is applied again, and the stored information is converted back into light and released from the medium. This storage method has multiple potential advantages, such as high efficiency, long coherence time, and low noise. Therefore, it is widely considered a crucial component of future quantum information processing and communication systems.

DLCZ storage scheme (Duan et al. 2001, pp. 413–418), proposed by L. M. Duan, M. D. Lukin, J. I. Cirac, and P. Zoller in 2001, is centered around establishing entanglement between two spatially separated atomic ensembles. An atomic ensemble refers to a system composed of a large number of interacting atoms that collectively respond to the excitation of light, forming a collective quantum state.

The specific process of the scheme is as follows. As shown in Figure 8.20, weak laser pulses illuminate two atomic ensembles separately, and each ensemble has the potential to emit a signal photon. However, due to the low probability of each atomic ensemble emitting a signal photon, typically, only one of L or R emits a photon. When a photon is detected from either L or R, it is impossible to

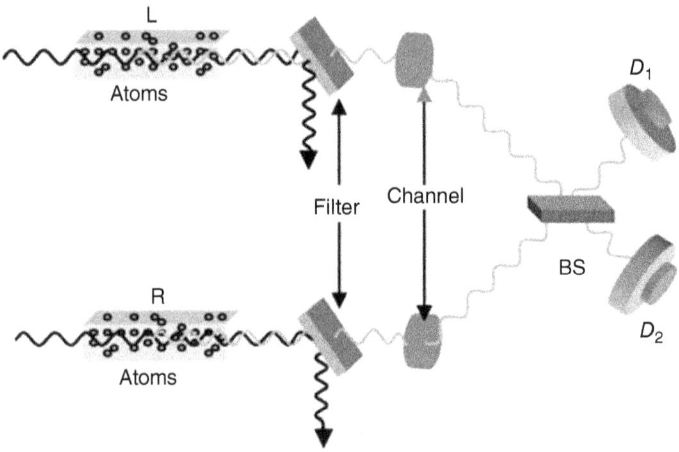

Figure 8.20 Principle of entanglement establishment between two atomic ensembles in the DLCZ scheme.

distinguish from which atomic ensemble the photon originated. This uncertainty leads to the generation of quantum entanglement between the collective excitation states of the two atomic ensembles. Signal photons are detected using a Beam Splitter (BS) and a pair of photon detectors. Since the path information of the photons is erased at the BS, if a photon is detected by the detectors, this measurement result will project the collective excitation states of the two atomic ensembles onto an entangled state. Once entanglement is confirmed, the collective excitation state in the atomic ensemble can serve as a quantum memory to store information. When needed, it can be transformed into a new photon through specific operations. This photon contains the quantum information of the original signal photon and can be used for further quantum communication processes.

The advantages of the DLCZ scheme lie in its avoidance of precise control over each individual atom but instead relying on the collective effects of atomic ensembles. This significantly reduces the experimental complexity and enhances the feasibility of the scheme. Additionally, atomic ensembles typically have a longer coherence time, which is advantageous for maintaining the integrity of quantum information. In the field of quantum information transfer, the DLCZ storage scheme is considered a crucial milestone as it provides a practical framework for realizing quantum Internet and large-scale quantum communication systems.

The quantum storage scheme (Julsgaard et al. 2004, pp. 482–486) based on the Faraday interaction is primarily built upon the Faraday effect, which describes the phenomenon where the polarization plane of light undergoes rotation in the presence of a magnetic field. This effect enables the interaction between the atomic states in a material and the polarization state of incident light, facilitating the quantum information conversion between light and material. The core idea of this scheme is to utilize an external magnetic field to control the atomic states within the material, thereby altering their interaction with light. Specifically, the incident light first interacts with the material in a magnetic field, resulting in rotation of its polarization state due to the Faraday effect. This new polarization state reflects the interaction process between light and the atoms in the material and can be read out again, forming the output light pulse. In the storage and retrieval process, precise control of the parameters of the atoms in the material and the external magnetic field is required. During the storage phase, the direction and intensity of the magnetic field are adjusted to maximize the Faraday rotation effect. In the retrieval phase, the magnetic field conditions are altered, allowing the atoms in the material to re-emit the previously stored polarization state of light. The experimental setup for storage is illustrated in Figure 8.21. The advantage of this quantum storage scheme based on Faraday interaction lies in its ability to operate at room temperature without requiring a highly condensed atomic state, making it notably practical in certain specific application domains.

The Controlled Reversible Inhomogeneous Broadening (CRIB) quantum storage scheme (Alexander et al. 2006, p. 043602) utilizes the intrinsic inhomogeneous frequency width of materials to store photons. Broadening refers to the distribution range of a particular characteristic in energy or frequency and can result in a

Figure 8.21 Experimental setup for quantum storage based on the Faraday effect. *Source:* Julsgaard et al. (2004) / with permission of Springer Nature.

range of levels or responses rather than strict single values. In a medium with inhomogeneous broadening, light of different frequencies is absorbed at different positions, forming a so-called frequency grid. To generate inhomogeneous broadening, a common method is to apply a nonuniform potential using an external electric or magnetic field, causing shifts in the atomic or molecular energy levels in the material. During the storage phase, by adjusting this potential for precise control, photons are stored in different parts of the material. In the reading phase, the process of reversing the inhomogeneous broadening causes the photons to be re-emitted at specific times and positions. The CRIB storage scheme has high efficiency and a long storage time. However, achieving efficient storage and retrieval requires precise control of the conditions of inhomogeneous broadening, which may pose significant challenges in experiments.

The AFC quantum storage scheme (Afzelius et al. 2009, p. 052329) is a technology based on the specific energy level structure in solid-state materials. It is designed to address the issue of inhomogeneous broadening in solid-state systems. Solid-state materials are processed optically or by other methods to create a comb-like structure in their absorption spectrum. This means that only light at specific frequencies is absorbed, while other frequencies pass through the medium without absorption. As shown in Figure 8.22, when a pulse interacts with the specific frequency comb, it is absorbed by each tooth and then re-emitted after a certain time delay. This time delay is determined by the structure of the frequency comb, especially the frequency difference between adjacent teeth. By appropriately selecting

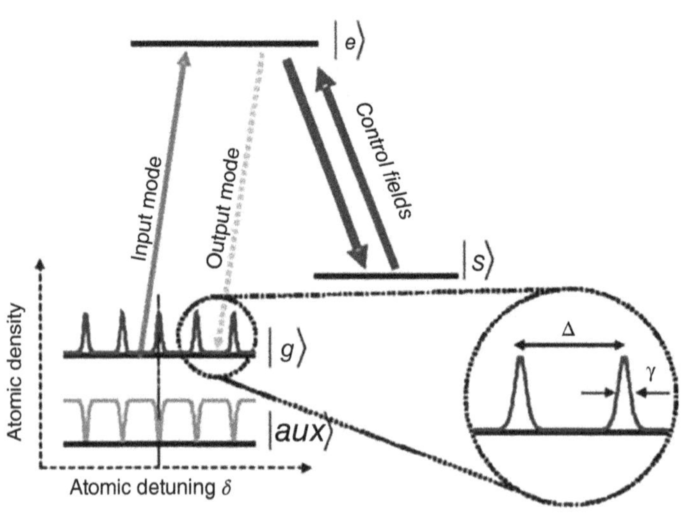

Figure 8.22 Schematic of AFC quantum storage.

or preparing this frequency comb, efficient storage and on-demand release of light pulses can be achieved. Additionally, due to its intrinsic frequency structure, the AFC scheme can simultaneously store light with multiple frequencies or time patterns. It is currently primarily applied to solid-state crystals doped with rare-earth ions, which have the appropriate energy-level structure to form the required frequency comb.

Over the past two decades, through continuous and unremitting efforts and exploration, storage technology has evolved from cold atomic storage to hot atomic storage, from narrowband storage to broadband storage, and has successfully transitioned from classical optical storage to quantum storage. The storage efficiency and lifespan of quantum storage devices are now approaching practical levels. Current research, in addition to further developing the aforementioned storage schemes, is actively exploring new storage approaches. For example, the team led by Mohammad Mirhosseini proposed converting electric quantum states into sound for quantum information storage (Bozkurt et al. 2023, pp. 1–7). The phenomenon of Collective Induced Transparency (CIT) discovered by the California Institute of Technology team is believed to enable information storage in the ensemble of strongly coupled atoms (Lei et al. 2023, pp. 1–6.), contributing to the development of more efficient quantum storage devices.

Quantum storage technology reveals how to precisely store and manipulate quantum information at the microscopic scale. This fine control and storage of information, in fact, pave the way for broader applications in the field of quantum technology. For instance, quantum storage offers possibilities for quantum entanglement and quantum Internet, as well as opens avenues for exploring deeper physical phenomena such as multipartite entanglement within storage devices, interference between light and atomic spins, and precision measurements. The low noise and unique quantum properties of quantum storage may also contribute to new perspectives in fundamental physics research. However, current quantum storage devices still face challenges, including the requirements for high efficiency, low noise, long lifespan, and room temperature operation, which have not all been simultaneously satisfied. Achieving truly practical quantum storage devices will require further efforts in the future.

8.1.3.2 Quantum Computers

According to the current stage of research, the development of quantum computers can naturally be divided into three phases.

The first phase involves the achievement of quantum computer prototypes, representing the early stage of quantum computing. The primary focus is on establishing small-scale quantum systems to validate fundamental quantum principles and operations. During this phase, the number of qubits is limited, and prototypes may be significantly affected by noise. These early prototypes are mainly used for research purposes rather than practical computing tasks.

The second phase is the era of quantum computational advantage, also known as the quantum supremacy phase. This phase represents a milestone event: a quantum computer surpasses the capabilities of state-of-the-art classical computers in a specific task. This does not imply that quantum computers outperform classical computers in all tasks but rather in certain specific and often artificially designed ones. The computational complexity of these tasks has been rigorously mathematically demonstrated to exhibit exponential or super-exponential growth on classical computers, while on quantum computers, it grows polynomially, showcasing the quantum advantage. In this phase, the number of qubits typically ranges from 50 to 100, but error correction techniques are not employed to ensure quantum coherence. As a result, quantum computers in this phase are referred to as specialized quantum computers, capable of addressing problems within their coherence time.

The final phase is the successful development of a fully functional and powerful quantum computer called universal quantum computer, marking the era when quantum technology truly integrates into mainstream computing. This signifies the ultimate goal of quantum computer advancement, that is, capable of solving any computable problem and finding widespread applications across various domains. The realization of a universal quantum computer requires meeting two basic conditions: first, achieving a qubit count on the order of tens of thousands to millions; second, implementing error correction techniques that meet practical standards.

The field of quantum computing research is extensive, with various technological approaches attempting to provide solutions for constructing efficient and stable quantum computers. Currently, multiple research paths are pursued in academia, including ion trap quantum computing, superconducting quantum computing, photonic quantum computing, neutral atom quantum computing, among others. While these technologies have different implementation methods, they all aim to address the core technical challenges in quantum computing.

8.1.3.2.1 Ion Trap Quantum Computing

Ion trap technology is a major technical approach in quantum computing with several decades of research history. The core of ion trap computing lies in using electromagnetic fields to capture and isolate individual or multiple ions. In this technology, ions are suspended in space, isolated from the external environment. This isolation helps reduce interactions with the external environment, thereby enhancing the coherence time of qubits. Each captured ion can be utilized as a qubit, with the internal energy levels of the ion, such as its ground state and excited state, serving as the 0 and 1 of the qubit. Transition between these two energy levels can be achieved through appropriate laser manipulation.

In an ion trap, laser interactions with specific ions can be used to implement single-qubit operations. However, when it comes to operations involving multiple qubits, the complexity increases. A common approach is to leverage collective vibrational modes between ions, also known as the motion of ions. Through specific sequences of laser pulses, the quantum state of one ion can be coupled to the collective motion of the entire ion chain, providing the possibility of implementing logical gate operations between two ions.

Ion trap technology has several distinct advantages. First, it offers exceptional precision in single-ion operations compared to other technologies. Second, as ions are trapped in a vacuum, their interaction with the external environment is significantly reduced, ensuring a relatively long coherence time for quantum information. Moreover, entanglement of multiple qubits, complex quantum algorithms, and other advanced quantum operations have been demonstrated in ion trap systems. However, this methodology also faces challenges. As the number of ions to be handled increases, precise control and operation become more difficult, directly affecting the scalability of the quantum system. Additionally, compared to other technologies, the operation speed of ion trap computing is relatively slow.

In the early stages of quantum computing research, the National Institute of Standards and Technology in the United States made several breakthroughs in ion trap technology. Dave Wineland's team used an ion trap to construct the first CNOT gate (Monroe et al. 1997, p. R2489), contributing significantly to the field, and he was awarded the Nobel Prize in Physics in 2012. Furthermore, companies like IonQ, Honeywell, and China's Yaozheng Quantum claim significant breakthroughs in their ion trap quantum computers. Figure 8.23 shows the ion trap quantum computer prototype manufactured by Yaozheng Quantum. In 2022, the team led by Thomas Monz in Austria successfully implemented a set of

Figure 8.23 Ion trap quantum computer prototype. *Source:* Photo by Hefei Yaozheng Quantum Technology Co., Ltd.

operations for universal computation on two logical qubits using a 16-ion trap quantum computer (Postler et al. 2022, pp. 675–680), marking the first instance of universal computation on fault-tolerant qubits.

8.1.3.2.2 Superconducting Quantum Computing

The foundation of superconducting quantum computing lies in leveraging microscopic quantum effects in superconducting circuits, where Josephson junctions play a crucial role. Josephson junctions consist of two superconducting materials separated by an insulating layer, allowing quantum pairing of electrons to pass through. This unique structure can form two distinct quantum states corresponding to the 0 and 1 states of a qubit, and transitions between these states can be achieved through external microwave pulses.

In superconducting quantum computing, single-qubit operations can be realized by applying microwave pulses to the superconducting qubits. The implementation of multi-qubit logic gates is more complex and involves considering the interactions between superconducting qubits. For example, adjusting the coupling strength between adjacent qubits allows the realization of multi-qubit logic gates such as the CNOT gate.

Superconducting quantum computing offers several attractive advantages, with the most notable being the integrability and fast operation speed. Researchers can integrate a large number of superconducting qubits on a relatively small chip using existing microelectronics technology. Compared to other quantum computing technologies, superconducting qubits operate at very high speeds, making them particularly suitable for quantum algorithms requiring significant computational power. However, superconducting quantum computing suffers from short quantum coherence time due to the sensitivity of superconducting qubits to external disturbances, such as thermal noise and microwave radiation, which can lead to the loss of quantum information. Therefore, extending the coherence time of superconducting qubits and implementing efficient quantum error correction are critical challenges in current research.

Several companies have made significant contributions to the field of superconducting quantum computing, with Google undoubtedly leading the way. In October 2019, Google published a milestone paper in Nature (Arute et al. 2019, pp. 505–510), presenting their superconducting quantum computer, Sycamore, with a 53-qubit superconducting chip as shown in Figure 8.24. They claimed to achieve quantum computational supremacy by completing a quantum circuit sampling task in 200 seconds. In December 2022, Google reported successfully simulating a two-dimensional holographic wormhole using Sycamore (Jafferis et al. 2022, pp. 51–55). The term "holographic" here refers to a simplified approach to related physical problems involving quantum mechanics and gravity.

Figure 8.24 The 53-qubit superconducting quantum chip introduced by Google. *Source:* Arute et al., (2019) / Springer Nature.

While the practical significance of this work is still debated, it underscores the vast potential of superconducting quantum computing technology.

8.1.3.2.3 Photonic Quantum Computing

The core of photonic quantum computing lies in photons, the fundamental particles of light. Properties of the photons, such as polarization, orbital angular momentum, or spatiotemporal modes, can be used as qubits to store and transmit information. Implementing photonic quantum computing typically requires specific photonic logic gates. These gates are based on linear optical elements like BSs, phase modulators, polarization rotators, and nonlinear optical effects. While pure linear optical systems cannot implement all quantum logic gates, combining single-photon sources, detectors, and nonlinear elements allows for the construction of a universal quantum computing model.

The primary advantage of photonic quantum computing is its ability to operate at room temperature without the need for complex cooling systems. Additionally, photon systems offer extremely fast information transfer, particularly beneficial for quantum communication and quantum network applications. Photonic quantum computing can also be integrated with existing optical fiber communication technologies, providing the potential for establishing large-scale quantum networks. However, the main challenges faced by photonic quantum computing include achieving efficient single-photon sources and high-performance single-photon detectors. Moreover, nonlinear optical effects typically require high-intensity light fields, posing a challenge at the single-photon level. However, these challenges are gradually being addressed by leveraging new physical systems such as quantum dots, atomic clouds, or solid-state defects.

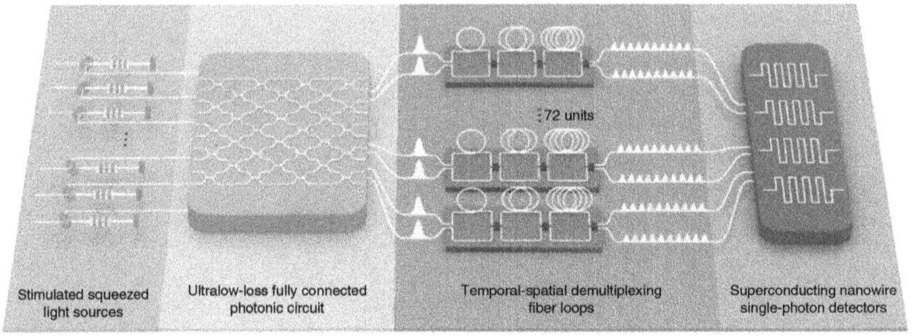

Figure 8.25 The principle of experimental apparatus in Jiuzhang 3.0.

Research on photonic quantum computing has been ongoing for several decades, involving numerous research organizations worldwide. In 2020, the team led by Jian-Wei Pan and Chao-Yang Lu at the University of Science and Technology of China successfully built a prototype of a quantum computer named "Jiuzhang," consisting of 76 photons (Zhong et al. 2020, pp. 1460–1463). During the solution of a Gaussian boson sampling problem with 50 million samples, Jiuzhang demonstrated quantum computational superiority by completing the task in just 200 seconds. In October 2023, the team achieved another milestone by constructing the "Jiuzhang 3.0," a quantum computing prototype with 255 photons (Deng et al. 2023, p. 150601). The principle of this device is illustrated in Figure 8.25.

8.1.3.2.4 Neutral Atom Quantum Computing

The fundamental principle of neutral atom quantum computing lies in the quantum states of internal electrons in neutral atoms, typically the ground state of hyperfine structure. These states can be used as qubits. Through precise laser manipulation, quantum entanglement can be created and operated between atoms. Additionally, employing cooling and laser techniques among atoms allows for their confinement in an optical lattice or array, enabling accurate pairwise interactions.

Neutral atom quantum computing has several advantages. First, as atoms are natural quantum systems, they possess inherent standardization and repeatability. Second, the interaction between neutral atoms and the external environment is relatively weak, helping to reduce decoherence effects. However, this also poses many challenges, such as how to precisely manipulate a large number of neutral atoms and how to achieve large-scale quantum entanglement.

In recent decades, the field of neutral atom quantum computing has seen many breakthroughs. For example, in 2022, Hannes Bernien and his team created a dual-element neutral atom array composed of rubidium and cesium atoms, allowing individual control of each atom and achieving the first neutral atom system consisting of 512 qubits (Singh et al. 2022, p. 011040). However, compared to other technological approaches, neutral atom quantum computing is still in a rapidly evolving stage. With continuous advancements in various technologies in this field, neutral atom quantum computing is expected to move toward more practical applications, bringing innovation to future quantum information technology.

In fact, there are still many other technological pathways for quantum computing, each possessing the potential to build a quantum computer. These include harnessing special particles in topological quantum computing from the field of topological physics, utilizing quantum methods based on point defects in specific solid-state materials, and employing quantum techniques involving small quantum dots in semiconductors. To sum up, each quantum computing technology has its unique advantages and challenges. The choice of which technology to use depends on specific application needs, technological maturity, and economic efficiency. However, regardless of the selection, the key remains in improving the quality of qubits, increasing interactions between qubits, and developing effective error correction strategies. As various technological pathways continue to advance, the era of a universal quantum computer is on the horizon.

8.1.4 Quantum Key Distribution and Quantum Communication

Secure sending, transmission, and reception have always been the goal of information transfer while various quantum properties provide precisely the security sought for information. Classical information security typically relies on the encryption-decryption method: communicating parties establish one or more keys through a protocol, where the sender encrypts the original information using its key, sends the encrypted information to the receiver, and upon receiving the encrypted information, the receiver decrypts it using a corresponding key to recover the original information. The security of this method relies on keys; thus, ensuring key security guarantees information security. Quantum Key Distribution (QKD) is a class of key generation protocols that leverage the no-cloning theorem to guarantee absolute key security. The security in this context has been rigorously proven mathematically. The communication process using QKD is illustrated in Figure 8.26: first, generate and exchange a quantum key based on the QKD protocol, and then use this quantum key for communication over a classical channel.

In addition, quantum technology can serve not only to secure information under classical transmission methods but also to be employed for information transmission itself. Superdense coding and quantum teleportation represent two significant applications of quantum communication. Superdense coding enables the transmission of information equivalent to two classical bits using only one qubit. Quantum teleportation, on the other hand, allows the transfer of qubit information without physically transmitting the qubit itself.

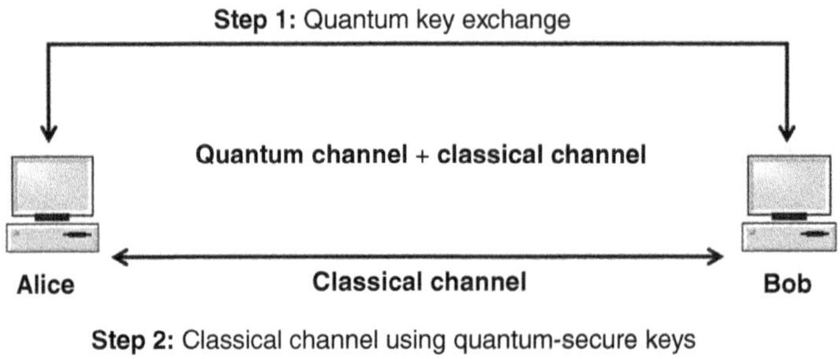

Figure 8.26 The communication process utilizing QKD.

8.1.4.1 Quantum Key Distribution

In the field of QKD, there are various implementation methods, and the BB84 protocol (Bennett and Brassard 2014, pp. 7–11) is particularly noteworthy. This protocol is not only the first QKD protocol in history but also the most well-known one to date. Its name is derived from the originators and the year of proposal – Bennett and Brassard in 1984. The BB84 protocol utilizes the principles of quantum mechanics, specifically the superposition and entanglement states of quantum particles, to ensure the secure exchange of keys. This concise and efficient method laid the foundation for the development of quantum encryption technology and inspired many other QKD protocols that followed.

The BB84 protocol uses two sets of standard orthogonal bases: the linear vertical polarization basis V: $\begin{bmatrix}1\\0\end{bmatrix}\begin{bmatrix}0\\1\end{bmatrix}$ and the linear diagonal polarization basis H: $\begin{bmatrix}\frac{1}{\sqrt{2}}\\ \frac{-1}{\sqrt{2}}\end{bmatrix}\begin{bmatrix}\frac{1}{\sqrt{2}}\\ \frac{1}{\sqrt{2}}\end{bmatrix}$, where classical bit 0 corresponds to the first vector and classical bit 1 corresponds to the second vector.

Alice, Bob, and Eve are three frequently occurring roles in the field of cryptography: Alice wants to send a ciphertext to Bob, while Eve attempts to eavesdrop. In the BB84 protocol, the communicating parties, namely Alice and Bob, select a classical bit string as the key with equal probability. For each bit, Alice randomly chooses one from two sets of bases. She then sends the qubit composed of the corresponding basis vectors to Bob, and records which set of bases was used for each bit. If the string to be sent is a key of length $8n$, she will obtain a string of length $8n$, which is the sum of the bases. Note that the number $8n$ is only for the convenience of subsequent expressions.

Bob also randomly and with equal probability chooses from two bases. He then measures the qubit using the chosen basis and, like Alice, he records which set of bases he chose. At the end of the transmission, he also possesses two strings of length $8n$. One is composed of the measured 0s and 1s, and the other is composed of the selected *V*s and *H*s.

After the transfer of qubits, they need to use classical channels to compare their strings of *V*s and *H*s. Since Alice and Bob randomly choose bases, there is a 50% chance they select the same basis and a fifty percent chance they choose different bases. If Bob and Alice choose the same basis, Bob will undoubtedly receive the bit sent by Alice, and the corresponding bit will be retained. However, if they opt for different bases, Bob will correctly obtain the bit half of the time and incorrectly the other half. In other words, he cannot determine the accuracy of this portion of the information, leading to its complete discarding. The result of this part is that they all possess binary strings of the same length, approximately $4n$.

Next is to check if Eve is eavesdropping. Due to the no-cloning theorem, Eve can also only randomly choose one set of bases for measurement, and then send the measurement results to Bob. This means that when Alice and Bob choose the same basis, half of the time Eve also chooses the same, and half of the time Eve chooses differently. In this half of the erroneous choices, Eve again has half of the time obtained incorrect bits. That is, approximately n bits sent by Eve to Bob are incorrect.

Therefore, Alice and Bob only need to compare half of the bits they obtained when choosing the same basis, about $2n$ bits. If they are entirely identical, it proves that Eve has not eavesdropped, and they can choose the remaining $2n$ bits as the key, while the bits involved in the comparison cannot be used as the key due to being transmitted over an insecure channel. Conversely, if there are around n non-matching bits in the comparison, it proves that Eve is eavesdropping, and they need to find another way to ensure communication security.

In addition to BB84, there are many other QKD protocols, most of which are improvements and developments of the BB84 protocol. These protocols have their own characteristics; some are more suitable for short distances, some can be applied to long distances, some have higher equipment requirements, and others are relatively easier to implement. The choice of which protocol to use typically depends on implementation complexity, security requirements, and communication distance. With the advancement of technologies, new QKD protocols and variants continue to be proposed to address evolving technological and security challenges.

8.1.4.2 Superdense Coding

The initial setup for superdense coding is that Alice and Bob each have a particle, and they are in an entangled state:

$$\frac{1}{\sqrt{2}}|00\rangle + \frac{1}{\sqrt{2}}|11\rangle. \tag{8.36}$$

Alice intends to transmit a message to Bob containing two classical bits, specifically one of the combinations: 00, 01, 10, or 11. This technique necessitates Alice to perform corresponding operations based on the information she wants to send. She will employ quantum gates to manipulate her qubits, causing the entangled quantum state to transform into a Bell state. For instance, if Alice wishes to transmit 01, she would utilize the gate X, which will cause a flip in the probability amplitudes of $|0\rangle$ and $|1\rangle$, and the state of the two qubits becomes:

$$\frac{1}{\sqrt{2}}|10\rangle + \frac{1}{\sqrt{2}}|01\rangle. \tag{8.37}$$

The relationship between Alice's intended message and the changes to the state of two qubits is shown in Table 8.3, which precisely corresponds to the truth table of the Bell circuit. After the transformation, Alice transfers her qubit to Bob. Bob then processes the two qubits using the inverse Bell circuit, converting them into an unentangled state. By measuring the unentangled state of the two qubits, Bob can obtain the information Alice originally wanted to transmit. This process involves the transfer of only one qubit but successfully conveys the information of two classical bits.

8.1.4.3 Quantum Teleportation

The initial setup for quantum teleportation and superdense coding is the same. Alice and Bob each have a particle, and these two particles share an entangled state. Additionally, Alice has one more particle $|\psi\rangle = a \mid 0\rangle + b \mid 1\rangle$, but she doesn't know the value of the probability amplitudes a and b of this quantum state. Therefore, the initial state of the three qubits is:

$$(a|0\rangle + b|1\rangle) \otimes \left(\frac{1}{\sqrt{2}}|00\rangle + \frac{1}{\sqrt{2}}|11\rangle\right). \tag{8.38}$$

Table 8.3 The relationship between Alice's intended message and the changes to the state of two qubits.

Alice's intended message	State of the two qubits
00	$\frac{1}{\sqrt{2}}(\mid 00\rangle + \mid 11\rangle)$
01	$\frac{1}{\sqrt{2}}(\mid 01\rangle + \mid 10\rangle)$
10	$\frac{1}{\sqrt{2}}(\mid 00\rangle - \mid 11\rangle)$
11	$\frac{1}{\sqrt{2}}(\mid 01\rangle - \mid 10\rangle)$

The outcome of the quantum teleportation is that Alice and Bob, through some method, alter the particle in Bob's possession to be in the state $a \mid 0\rangle + b \mid 1\rangle$. The process can be inferred based on the result: at the end, Bob will have a particle in a nonentangled state, while at the beginning, Bob and Alice's particles were in an entangled state. To disentangle, a measurement must be made. Clearly, this measurement cannot be conducted by Bob. If Bob were to measure, he would obtain a particle in state $|0\rangle$ or $|1\rangle$, not the desired $a \mid 0\rangle + b \mid 1\rangle$. Therefore, it must be Alice who performs the measurement. Furthermore, in order for Alice's additional particle to transmit information, a correlation between her two particles is necessary, indicating the need for them to be entangled. To accomplish these goals, the two qubits controlled by Alice must be put through a reverse Bell circuit.

Since Alice is manipulating her qubits, in order to distinguish between the actions of Alice and Bob, the state of three qubits is denoted as follows:

$$\frac{a}{\sqrt{2}}|00\rangle \otimes |0\rangle + \frac{a}{\sqrt{2}}|01\rangle \otimes |1\rangle + \frac{b}{\sqrt{2}}|10\rangle \otimes |0\rangle + \frac{b}{\sqrt{2}}|11\rangle \otimes |1\rangle. \tag{8.39}$$

Alice put her two qubits through a reverse Bell circuit:

$$\begin{aligned}&\frac{1}{2}\mid 00\rangle \otimes (a|0\rangle + b|1\rangle) + \frac{1}{2}|01\rangle \otimes (a|1\rangle + b|0\rangle)\\&\quad + \frac{1}{2}\mid 10\rangle \otimes (a|0\rangle - b|1\rangle) + \frac{1}{2}|11\rangle \otimes (a|1\rangle - b|0\rangle).\end{aligned} \tag{8.40}$$

Alice now measures her two qubits on a standard basis. She will get one of $|00\rangle$, $|01\rangle$, $|10\rangle$ and $|11\rangle$, each with probability 1/4. Each measurement she performs causes Bob's particle to transition to the corresponding state. Subsequently, Alice transmits her measurement results to Bob, enabling him to know the state of the qubit in his possession. The information of these two bits can be transmitted through a classical channel. Finally, Bob employs the appropriate quantum gates based on the state of the particle he possesses, which makes Bob's qubit end in state $a \mid 0\rangle + b \mid 1\rangle$.

It should be noted that at any moment during the process, only one qubit is in a certain state $a \mid 0\rangle + b \mid 1\rangle$. At the beginning, Alice's qubit is in this state. In the end, Bob's qubit is in this state. Therefore, this process does not violate the no-cloning theorem, since at any given time, only one person's qubit is in this state.

Furthermore, during the process of quantum teleportation, when Alice passes her two qubits through the corresponding circuit, Bob's qubit instantly transitions to one of the four states. However, at this point, he has not gained any information; he must wait for Alice to send him two classical bits before he can determine which state corresponds to the original state of Alice's qubit. In other words, the information is not transmitted from Alice to Bob in an instant.

Quantum teleportation and superdense coding are sometimes considered inverse operations. In superdense coding, Alice sends one qubit to transmit information for two classical bits to Bob. Conversely, in quantum teleportation, Alice sends information for one qubit to Bob using two classical bits. For superdense coding, Alice uses quantum gates for encoding, and Bob uses the reverse Bell circuit for decoding. On the other hand, for quantum teleportation, Alice uses the reverse Bell circuit for encoding, and Bob uses quantum gates for decoding.

Currently, quantum teleportation technology primarily employs entangled photons, allowing implementation at relatively long distances. The first experiment on quantum teleportation was conducted by the Zeilinger team in Austria in 1997 (Bouwmeester et al. 1997, pp. 575–579). This groundbreaking research garnered widespread international attention, injecting new vitality into global quantum information studies. Subsequently, quantum transmission research has advanced worldwide. In 2012, Jian-Wei Pan's team achieved quantum teleportation and QKD over hundreds of kilometers in the Qinghai Lake region (Yin et al. 2012, pp. 185–188), laying a solid foundation for the development of long-distance quantum communication. In 2017, China's "Micius" quantum satellite successfully realized quantum teleportation from space to the ground (Lu et al. 2022, p. 035001), marking another significant advancement in the field of quantum communication and demonstrating its immense potential for future space applications. In 2022, Hermans' team achieved nonadjacent node quantum teleportation in a three-node network (Liu et al. 2023, p. 210801). In 2023, the team led by Jian-Wei Pan achieved over a thousand kilometers of fiber-based dual-field QKD (Hermans et al. 2022, pp. 663–668). These studies and experiments will undoubtedly propel the advancement of quantum transmission toward realizing a quantum Internet.

8.2 Quantum Blockchain – Solving Trilemma of Distributed Systems

This section introduces the key aspects of quantum blockchain technology. First, we explore the vulnerability of traditional blockchain technology in the face of quantum computing threats and how to implement blockchain schemes based on QKD. In addition, we introduce the Quantum Proof of Vote (Q-PoV) consensus scheme, which uses quantum properties to achieve anonymous voting and addresses the security and privacy issues in traditional voting schemes. Finally, we introduce how the unique advantages of quantum technology, such as quantum entanglement and parallelism, provide new possibilities to break through the theoretical limitations of traditional distributed systems.

8.2.1 Quantum Blockchain Solution

Traditional blockchain technology has received a lot of attention for its decentralized, transparent, and immutable characteristics. However, with the rapid development of quantum computing technology, traditional encryption technology gradually shows its vulnerability. Quantum algorithms can quickly solve the mathematical problems that traditional digital signature and encryption algorithms rely on, which poses a threat to the security of the traditional blockchain system (Fedorov et al. 2018, pp. 465–467). In order to protect the security of the blockchain system, new schemes that can resist quantum computing attacks are needed. The quantum blockchain scheme based on QKD then comes into being, which provides a new guarantee for the key security of the blockchain.

The rapid development of quantum computing technology exposes the vulnerability of traditional digital signature and encryption algorithms. However, in the quantum blockchain scheme based on QKD, the establishment of private keys no longer depends on these algorithms, but instead leverages the laws of quantum physics, which fundamentally solves the problem that traditional encryption algorithms may be compromised by quantum computing. The QKD-based quantum blockchain scheme emphasizes the consistency and integrity of information. Through the QKD, all parties in the blockchain network can authenticate each other's identity, thus ensuring the credibility of information transmission. There exist many variants of QKD-based quantum blockchain schemes. Here we introduce an implementation scheme proposed by Kiktenko et al. (2018, p. 035004), whose core idea is to combine two key technologies: Byzantine fault-tolerant state machine replication and QKD. In this scheme, the key distribution is conducted through the quantum channel to ensure the security of information transmission.

The generation of a substantial amount of shared secret data during each QKD communication session enables its utilization for subsequent session authentication. Therefore, a small amount of "seed" secret key that the parties share before their first QKD session ensures their secure authentication for all future communication (Tysowski et al. 2018, p. 024001). In this way, QKD can be used in place of classical digital signatures. The identity authentication based on hash tag and QKD can simultaneously protect the identity security of the message sender and the security of communication. The specific process is as follows:

Step 1: Generate the private key: Alice and Bob generate a shared key K_{aut} through QKD.

Step 2: Transmit the message and generate the hash tag: When Alice wants to send a message M_i to Bob, she first uses K_{aut} to generate its hash tag $h(M_i)$, and then sends the message M_i and the hash tag $h(M_i)$ to Bob.

Step 3: Receive the message and verify the hash tag: After receiving M_i and $h(M_i)$, Bob recalculates the hash tag $h'(M_i)$ of M_i using K_{aut} and compares $h(M_i)$ with $h'(M_i)$. If the hash tags coincide, Bob can be certain that the message has arrived from Alice.

Different from the traditional blockchain scheme, the generation of blocks in the quantum blockchain scheme is no longer conducted by a single miner. Instead, the

Byzantine fault-tolerant state machine replication is used to realize the consensus mechanism in the form of broadcast, which ensures that the system can maintain consistency in the presence of a certain number of malicious or faulty nodes. At the same time, all nodes have an equal say in the process of block generation and are not controlled or influenced by centralized miners, which highlights the fairness and decentralization characteristics of blockchain.

The specific implementation process of the broadcast protocol is as follows: At the beginning, each node holds a specific private value, which represents the state or information of the node. The nodes transmit these secret values to each other through the established two-way authentication channel. In multiple rounds of communication, the nodes transmit the secret values received by each other and the information of other nodes in an interactive way to form an interactive consensus vector V^{cons}. This vector satisfies the following properties: (1) all honest nodes obtain the same consensus vector V^{cons}; (2) the i-th component of V^{cons} equals V_i for all honest nodes. Through the above interaction, Byzantine fault-tolerant state machine replication ensures that all honest nodes can form a consistent consensus vector V^{cons} even if there are $m < n/3$ malicious or faulty nodes out of n nodes.

The proposed scheme has been realized in an urban environment in Moscow, and the main parameters of the implemented blockchain for four nodes network are listed in Table 8.4. Its block generation process is shown in Figure 8.27: When a block is generated in a 4-node quantum blockchain, the same copy of the transaction needs to be sent to all other nodes. Transactions of nodes A, B, and C are denoted as txn_A, txn_B, and txn_C, respectively, while node D tries to transmit

Table 8.4 Main parameters of the implemented quantum-secured blockchain.

Parameter	Value
Number of nodes in the network	$n = 4$
Upper bound on the number of faulty nodes	$m = 1$
Number of rounds in the broadcast protocol	2
Duration of broadcast protocol	<10s
Time between block generation events	5 min
Authentication hash length	40 bit
Quantum key consumption in the initial broadcast of a transaction	40 bit
Quantum key consumption in the broadcast protocol	80 bit
Average quantum key consumption required for a transaction rate of 10 per minute	<7 bit • s^{-1}

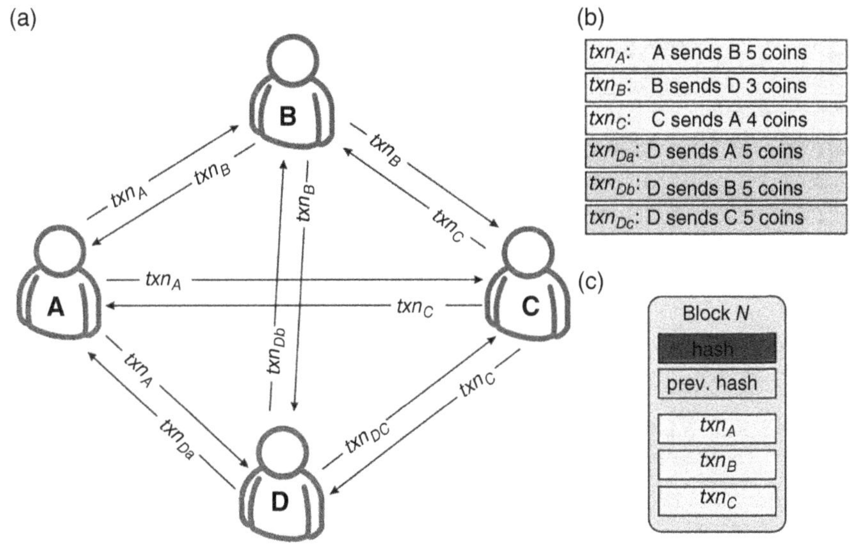

Figure 8.27 Generation of a block in a quantum-secure blockchain. (a) Each node who wishes to implement a transaction sends identical copies of that transaction to all other nodes. (b) Transaction contents. (c) The nodes implement the broadcast protocol to reconcile the unconfirmed transactions and form the block.

different versions of the same transaction txn_{Da}, txn_{Db}, and txn_{Dc} to different parties, which is discovered and excluded by other nodes.

8.2.2 Quantum Proof of Vote Consensus

In the context of the current information age, electronic voting has been widely used in the field of election and consensus decision-making as an efficient and convenient voting method. It also plays an important role in the PoV consensus scheme, such as electing representative nodes and achieving a consensus mechanism. However, traditional voting schemes are vulnerable to man-in-the-middle attacks, data tampering and information leakage, indicating the need for further improvement in the security and anonymity of the PoV consensus process.

In view of the shortcomings of traditional electronic voting in terms of security and anonymity, the Peking University Lab for China Environment for Network Innovations (CENI) proposed a Q-PoV consensus. This consensus is based on the self-tallying quantum anonymous voting scheme (Wang et al. 2016, p. 022333), and it enhances the consensus process of PoV. Utilizing the unique nature of quantum to achieve anonymous voting helps prevent the disclosure of voting information and ensures that the voting results are not tampered with.

8.2.2.1 Quantum Fourier Transform and Two Quantum Entangled States

The core idea of the classic Fourier transform is to decompose a signal into a series of sine and cosine components of different frequencies. This transformation facilitates the analysis of the frequency components of the signal, thereby better understanding the properties of the signal. The Discrete Fourier Transform (DFT) is the application of Fourier transform on discrete signals. It converts a finite-length discrete signal into the frequency domain and represents it as a discrete set of frequencies. DFT converts a sequence of length $x_0, x_1, \ldots, x_{m-1}$ into another sequence $y_0, y_1, \ldots, y_{m-1}$. The definition of any value y_k in the output sequence is:

$$y_k = \frac{1}{\sqrt{m}} \sum_{j=0}^{m-1} e^{\frac{2\pi ijk}{m}} x_j. \tag{8.41}$$

where i represents the imaginary unit that satisfies $i^2 = -1$, $x_0, x_1, \ldots, x_{m-1}$ correspond to the sampling points in the time domain for the discrete signal, j is the index of sequence $x_0, x_1, \ldots, x_{m-1}$, k is the index of the output sequence $y_0, y_1, \ldots, y_{m-1}$. Here $j, k \in \{0, 1, \ldots, m-1\}$.

Quantum Fourier Transform (QFT) is a transformation similar in form to DFT. For a quantum system in m levels, QFT transforms any arbitrary basis $|j\rangle$ on a set of orthonormal basis $|0\rangle, |1\rangle \cdots |m-1\rangle$ into:

$$|j\rangle \overset{QFT}{\rightarrow} \frac{1}{\sqrt{m}} \sum_{j=0}^{m-1} e^{\frac{2\pi ijk}{m}} |k\rangle. \tag{8.42}$$

where j represents the index of the input quantum state, representing the initial state of the quantum system, i.e., the initial basis of the quantum state. k represents the index of the output quantum state in another set of standard orthogonal bases. Here $j, k \in \{0, 1, \ldots, m-1\}$.

The QFT operation of any quantum state $|\psi\rangle$ of in the orthonormal basis $|0\rangle, |1\rangle \cdots |m-1\rangle$ can be written as:

$$|\psi\rangle_C = \sum_{j=0}^{m-1} x_j |j\rangle \overset{QFT}{\rightarrow} |\psi\rangle_F = \sum_{j=0}^{m-1} y_k |k\rangle. \tag{8.43}$$

The QFT operation is equivalent to performing a DFT operation on the probability amplitudes x_j of the standard orthonormal basis $|0\rangle, |1\rangle \cdots |m-1\rangle$ to obtain a new set of probability amplitudes y_k, satisfying $\sum_{j=0}^{m-1} x_j^2 = \sum_{k=0}^{m-1} y_k^2 = 1$. In order to distinguish two different bases before and after the QFT operation, the basis before transformation can be called the computational basis, and the basis after transformation can be called the Fourier basis. We use subscripts C to indicate the computational basis and use subscripts F to indicate the Fourier basis. For example, $|\psi\rangle_C$ is the state in the computational basis, $|\psi\rangle_F$ is the state on the Fourier basis.

Using computational basis, Fourier basis and the conversion between them, two special quantum entangled states $|X_n\rangle$ and $|S_n\rangle$ can be designed.

The definition of $|X_n\rangle$ is the GHZ state of n qubits in the Fourier basis in a quantum system in m levels:

$$| X_n\rangle_F = \frac{1}{\sqrt{m}} \sum_{j'=0}^{m-1} | j'\rangle_{0,F} \, | j'\rangle_{1,F} \cdots | j'\rangle_{n-1,F}, \tag{8.44}$$

where $|j'\rangle_{i,F}$ represents the state of the ith qubit on the Fourier basis. It can be seen from Equation (8.45) that if any qubit in the entangled state $|X_n\rangle_F$ is measured on the Fourier basis, all qubits will collapse into the same state, that is, the measurement result of each particle is the same.

Use $\mathcal{F}$ to represent the QFT operation, we have:

$$| j'\rangle_F = \mathcal{F} \, | j\rangle_C = \frac{1}{\sqrt{m}} \sum_{k=0}^{m-1} e^{\frac{2\pi i}{m} jk} \, | k\rangle_C. \tag{8.45}$$

Change the state $|X_n\rangle_F$ on the Fourier basis in Equation (8.45) to the state $|X_n\rangle_C$ on the computational basis:

$$| X_n\rangle_C = \frac{1}{\sqrt{m}} \sum_{j=0}^{m-1} \mathcal{F} \, | j\rangle_{0,C} \otimes \mathcal{F} | j\rangle_{1,C} \otimes \cdots \otimes \mathcal{F} | j\rangle_{n-1,C}. \tag{8.46}$$

Putting the QFT operation into Equation (8.46), we have:

$$| X_n\rangle_C = \frac{1}{\sqrt{m}} \sum_{j=0}^{m-1} \left[\left(\frac{1}{\sqrt{m}} \sum_{k=0}^{m-1} e^{\frac{2\pi i}{m} jk} | k\rangle_{0,C} \right) \otimes \cdots \otimes \left(\frac{1}{\sqrt{m}} \sum_{k=0}^{m-1} e^{\frac{2\pi i}{m} jk} | k\rangle_{n-1,C} \right) \right]. \tag{8.47}$$

Further simplification of the above formula can be obtained:

$$|X_n\rangle_C = \frac{1}{\sqrt{m}} \sum_{j=0}^{m-1} m^{-\frac{n}{2}} \sum_{k_0, k_1, \cdots, k_{n-1}} e^{2\pi i \frac{j}{m}(k_0 + k_1 + \cdots + k_{n-1})} \, | k_0\rangle_C \otimes \cdots \otimes |k_{n-1}\rangle_C. \tag{8.48}$$

Exchange the order of summation in Equation (8.48):

$$|X_n\rangle_C = m^{-\frac{n+1}{2}} \sum_{k_0, k_1, \cdots, k_{n-1}} \left(\sum_{j=0}^{m-1} e^{2\pi i \frac{j}{m}(k_0 + k_1 + \cdots + k_{n-1})} \right) | k_0\rangle_C \otimes \cdots \otimes | k_{n-1}\rangle_C. \tag{8.49}$$

Considering $e^{2\pi i} = 1$, if and only if $\sum_{i=0}^{n-1} k_i \bmod m = 0$, $\frac{j}{m}(k_0 + k_1 + \cdots + k_{n-1})$ is an integer and $e^{2\pi i \frac{j}{m}(k_0 + k_1 + \cdots + k_{n-1})} = 1$, that is $\sum_{j=0}^{m-1} e^{2\pi i \frac{j}{m}(k_0 + k_1 + \cdots + k_{n-1})} = m$.

If $\sum_{i=0}^{n-1} k_i \bmod m \neq 0$, $\sum_{j=0}^{m-1} e^{2\pi i \frac{j}{m}(k_0 + k_1 + \cdots + k_{n-1})} = 0$. Therefore, Equation (8.49) can be rewritten as:

$$| X_n\rangle_C = \frac{1}{\sqrt{m^{n-1}}} \sum_{\sum_{i=0}^{n-1} k_i \bmod m = 0} | k_0\rangle_C | k_1\rangle_C \cdots | k_{n-1}\rangle_C. \tag{8.50}$$

Equation (8.50) shows that when the entangled state $|X_n\rangle_C$ is measured in the computational basis, the sum over all the n measurement outcomes modulo m is equal to zero. The coefficient $1/\sqrt{m^{n-1}}$ is the probability amplitude, indicating that there are m^{n-1} possible existence forms of $|k_0\rangle_C | k_1\rangle_C \cdots | k_{n-1}\rangle_C$.

According to the properties of quantum entangled states $|X_n\rangle$ in the computational basis and the Fourier basis, the following theorem can be summarized:

Theorem 8.1 If a n-particle m-level quantum state is in the form of $|X_n\rangle$, there are: (1) When measured on the computational basis, the sum over all the n measurement outcomes modulo m is equal to zero; (2) When measured on the Fourier basis, the measurement outcomes are all the same.

The definition of $|S_n\rangle$ is the entangled state of n qubits in the computational basis in a quantum system in m levels:

$$| S_n\rangle_C = \frac{1}{\sqrt{n!}} \sum_{S \in P_n^n} (-1)^{\tau(S)} | s_0\rangle_C | s_1\rangle_C \cdots | s_{n-1}\rangle_C, \tag{8.51}$$

where $|s_i\rangle_C$ represents the state of the ith particle in the computational basis, P_n^n represents the set of all permutations of $\{0, 1, \ldots, n-1\}$, S is a permutation in the form $S = \{s_0, s_1, \ldots, s_{n-1}\}$ and $\tau(S)$ is defined as the number of transpositions of pairs of elements of S that must be composed to place the elements in canonical order $012 \cdots n-1$. The coefficient $1/\sqrt{n!}$ is the probability amplitude, indicating that the total number of permutations of $\{0, 1, \ldots, n-1\}$ is $n!$. Following are a few simple examples of $|S_n\rangle_C$:

$$|S_2\rangle_C = \frac{1}{\sqrt{2}}(| 01\rangle - | 10\rangle), \tag{8.52}$$

$$|S_3\rangle_C = \frac{1}{\sqrt{6}}(| 012\rangle - | 021\rangle - | 102\rangle + | 120\rangle + | 201\rangle - | 210\rangle), \tag{8.53}$$

$$|S_4\rangle_C = \frac{1}{\sqrt{24}}(| 0123\rangle - | 0132\rangle - | 0213\rangle + | 0231\rangle + \cdots + | 3210\rangle). \tag{8.54}$$

Equation (8.51) and the above three examples show that the measurements of $|S_n\rangle$ in the computational basis can form a disordered arrangement of $\{0, 1, \ldots, n-1\}$. In addition, $|S_n\rangle$ also has a special property that it is n-lateral rotationally invariant (Wang et al. 2016, p. 022333), which means the measurements of $|S_n\rangle$

in any basis is a disordered arrangement of $\{0, 1, \ldots, n-1\}$, that is, the measurements of all particles are different in any basis.

These properties of $|S_n\rangle$ can be summarized as the following theorem:

Theorem 8.2 If a n-particle n-level quantum state is in the form of $|S_n\rangle$, whenever the state is measured in the computational basis or the Fourier basis, the permutation of the outcomes of n particles is a random element of the set P_n^n.

In the field of quantum computing, the use of the Fourier transform is instrumental because it allows for the description and analysis of complex quantum systems in a simpler and more manageable way, thereby simplifying the process of problem-solving and aiding in a deeper understanding of the essence of quantum systems. Therefore, quantum computing relies on the Fourier transform as a powerful tool to explore and understand quantum phenomena more comprehensively and effectively.

The special properties of two quantum multiparticle entangled states $|X_n\rangle$ and $|S_n\rangle$ contribute to achieving anonymous data statistics. These states have been utilized in various quantum schemes, including anonymous voting (Dolev, Pitowsky, and Tamir 2006) and ranking (Huang et al. 2014, p. 032325). Inspired by these schemes, we propose the Q-PoV consensus based on $|X_n\rangle$ and $|S_n\rangle$, ensuring the correctness, anonymity and immutability of the consensus process.

8.2.2.2 Design of Q-PoV Consensus

All parameters used in the Q-PoV consensus are shown in Table 8.5.

In PoV consensus, the bookkeeper and the voters jointly carry out the consensus process. After transactions are packaged as a pre-block by the duty bookkeeper, it is transmitted to all voters to check the pre-block header and transaction information, and then the voter expresses the validation result "pass" or "fail" in the form of a vote. After more than half of the voters have passed the verification, the duty bookkeeper supplements the pre-block and officially publishes it to the network. Overall, PoV has achieved efficient consortium chain consensus with low communication complexity, improving the response speed of blockchain networks, and achieving higher partition tolerance.

Q-PoV consensus follows the consensus process of classical PoV, achieving anonymous voting and counting based on two classes of quantum multiparticle entangled states, $|X_n\rangle$ and $|S_n\rangle$. The overall consensus process is briefly described as follows: First, the duty bookkeeper distributes $|X_n\rangle$ to all voting nodes and performs the security tests. Each voting node uses the received valid particles to construct multiple anonymous "ballot boxes." Then, the duty bookkeeper distributes $|S_n\rangle$ to all voting nodes in a similar manner, with the valid particles used to construct random ballot indexes, determining the ballot box each voting node

Table 8.5 Parameters used in the Q-PoV consensus.

Symbol	Definition	Annotation
m	Level of the quantum system	The number of orthogonal computational bases, equal to the number of voting options.
n	Number of particles	The number of particles in a quantum entangled state, equal to the number of voting nodes.
x	Subscript	Row index in a matrix.
k	Subscript	Sequence number of voting nodes.
l	Subscript	Subscript for row index x.
V	Voting node	The participants in the consensus process, where V_k represents the k-th voting node.
L	Duty bookkeeper	The node that assists in the consensus process.
p	Particle	Constituent elements of $\|X_n\rangle$.
t	Particle	Constituent elements of $\|S_n\rangle$.
S	Particle set	The set of particles p, the column of a particle matrix composed of p.
T	Particle set	The set of particles t, the column of a particle matrix composed of t.
δ	Security strength	The number of row indexes selected by each voting node in a security test.
r	Ballot matrix	—
d	Ballot index	—
P_n	Set of all permutations of $\{0, 1, ..., n-1\}$	—
R	Ballot matrix statistic	—
N	Number of votes	—

ultimately uses. Finally, each voting node modifies the ballot box according to its ballot index, and the duty bookkeeper conducts vote counting.

The overall communication process of the voting protocol is shown in Figure 8.28, which includes three steps:

1) The duty bookkeeper L distributes the quantum state $|X_n\rangle$ to voting nodes V_0, V_1, ..., V_{n-1}, and the voting nodes construct the initial ballot matrix r;
2) The duty bookkeeper L distributes the quantum state $|S_n\rangle$ to voting nodes V_0, V_1, ..., V_{n-1}, and the voting nodes construct the ballot index d;
3) All the voting nodes publish the revised ballot matrix r', and the duty bookkeeper L conducts vote counting.

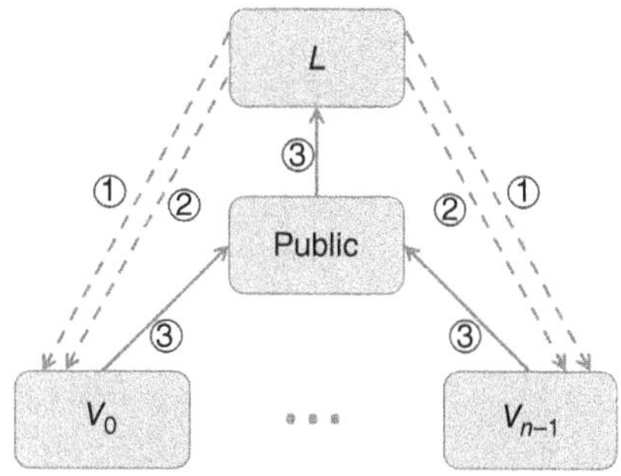

Figure 8.28 Communication process of Q-PoV.

Step 1: Distribution of Secret Ballot Boxes
First, the duty bookkeeper L prepares $n + n\delta_0$ copies of quantum state $\|X_n\rangle$, where δ_0 is the security strength parameter. The x-th copy of $\|X_n\rangle$ consists of n particles, $p_{x,0}$, $p_{x,1}$, ..., $p_{x,n-1}$, then all particles form a particle matrix $P_{(n+n\delta_0)\times n}$ with $n + n\delta_0$ rows and n columns. Subsequently, the duty bookkeeper L distributes all the columns of this matrix to the corresponding voters, where the k-th column $S_k = \left\{p_{0,k}, p_{1,k}, \ldots, p_{n+n\delta_0-1,k}\right\}^T$ is distributed to V_k. Here, $p_{x,k}$ denotes the particle in row x and column k of the particle matrix, $0 \leq x \leq n + n\delta_0 - 1$, $0 \leq k \leq n - 1$. Subsequently, each voter performs a security test to ensure that the distributed quantum states are intact, where the order does not matter. Suppose that starting from voter V_0, V_0 randomly picks out δ_0 particles as the test particles, and chooses from computational or the Fourier basis with uniform distribution for each test state. Then the row index of test particles $\{x_0, x_1, \ldots, x_{\delta_0-1}\}$ and the selected measurement basis are published, where $x_0, x_1, \ldots, x_{\delta_0-1} \in \{0, 1, \ldots, n + n\delta_0 - 1\}$. After receiving this public information, all other voters are required to measure their test particles with the same row index and measurement basis. The measurement result of a test particle in row x_l and column k is denoted by $r_{x_l,k}$. The properties of $\|X_n\rangle$ are used to check whether the quantum state is intact. If V_0 chooses the computational basis, it needs to check whether $\sum_{l=0}^{n-1} r_{x_l,k} \bmod m = 0$ holds true. If V_0 chooses the Fourier basis, it must verify whether $r_{x_l,0}, r_{x_l,1}, \ldots, r_{x_l,n-1}$ are identical. The failure of the above condition indicates a test failure, requiring V_0 to notify other nodes to abort the protocol. Conversely, the satisfaction of either condition signifies a test success, in which case the same testing procedure is executed by the subsequent voter.

Repeat the same procedure until the test performed by each voter is passed or abort the protocol in some intermediate process.

After each security test, δ_0 test particles are discarded. After all the voters have passed the security test, each voter retains only n valid particles, and uses the computational basis to measure its particles to obtain n measurement values. We use a matrix $r_{n \times n}$ with n rows and n columns to denote the measurement results of all voters. The k-th column of matrix r corresponds to the measurement results of particles held by V_k, which also represents the ballot of the voter V_k. Through subsequent renewal of the matrix, the voters can anonymously convey voting information. So, we refer to matrix r as the ballot matrix.

Step 2: Distribution of Secret Ballot Indexes

Similar to the distribution of $|X_n\rangle$, the duty bookkeeper L prepares $1 + n\delta_1$ copies of the quantum state $|S_n\rangle$. The x-th copy of $|S_n\rangle$ consists of n particles, $t_{x,0}$, $t_{x,1}$, ..., $t_{x,n-1}$. Then all particles form a particle matrix $t_{(1+n\delta_1) \times n}$ with $1 + n\delta_1$ rows and n columns. Then the distribution node sends the column $T_k = \{t_{0,k}, t_{1,k}, \ldots, t_{n\delta_1,k}\}^T$ to the voter V_k, where $t_{x,k}$ denotes the particle in the x-th row and k-th column, $0 \le x \le n\delta_1, 0 \le k \le n-1$. A security test is then conducted to ensure the integrity of $|S_n\rangle$. δ_1 particles are randomly selected as test particles, and calculation basis or Fourier basis is also randomly selected as the measurement basis to measure the test particles according to the published row index. Then the duty bookkeeper L checks whether the measurement results of each test particle satisfy $\{d_{x_l,0}, d_{x_l,1}, \ldots, d_{x_l,n-1}\} \in P_n$ according to properties of quantum state $|S_n\rangle$, where x_l is the row index selected for the l-th round of security test, and $d_{x_l,k} \in \{0, 1, \ldots, m-1\}$ denotes the measurement results of the particles in the x_l-th row and k-th column. The above process is repeated until all voters have passed the test.

After the security tests pass, all voters discard the test particles. Each voter subsequently has only one valid particle left and measures the particle on a computational basis. Suppose that the valid particles are $t_{0,0}$, $t_{0,1}$, ..., $t_{0,n-1}$, the measurement result $d_{0,k}$ corresponds to an index used to denote the ballot box selection of the voter V_k. The rotation invariance of $|S_n\rangle$ ensures the anonymity of voting.

Step 3: Vote Casting

After steps 1 and 2, suppose that each voter V_k now has n ballot numbers, $r_{0,k}$, $r_{1,k}$, ..., $r_{n-1,k}$, and one index number, $d_{0,k}$. Suppose the voting option of the voter V_k is v_k, $r'_{x,k}$ denotes the modified $r_{x,k}$, voter V_k votes to $v_k \in \{0, 1, ..., m-1\}$ by adding v_k to $r_{x,k}$:

$$r'_{x,k} = \begin{cases} r_{x,k} + v_k \bmod m, \text{ if } x = d_{0,k} \\ r_{x,k}, \text{ if } x \neq d_{0,k} \end{cases}. \tag{8.55}$$

All voters publish their updated votes (Broadbent and Tapp 2007, pp. 410–426) to obtain the final ballot matrix r'. By summing r' by row, the number of votes received by the l-th voting item can be calculated as follows:

$$R_x = \sum_{k=0}^{n-1} r'_{x,k} \bmod m, \tag{8.56}$$

$$N_l = \sum_{R_x = l} 1, \tag{8.57}$$

where R_x denotes the summation result of the x-th row of the updated ballot matrix r' and N_l is used to count the number of occurrences of $R_x = l$. We use 0 to denote the block verification passes, and 1 to denote the verification fails. When $N_0 > n/2$, indicating that more than half of the voters pass, the block verification of this round of voting is completed. Then the duty bookkeeper writes the voting results into the block header and issues the official block to the whole network. When more than half of the voters have received the official block, this round of consensus is completed the next round of consensus process is carried out.

8.2.2.3 Q-PoV Workflow Example

We introduce a simple example to illustrate the workflow of Q-PoV consensus. Suppose the number of voters $n = 4$, the number of voting candidates $m = 2$ which include the block verification passes or fails. For simplicity, we assume that no eavesdropping or attack occurs. Therefore, we ignore the security testing steps and assume successful distribution. The ballot matrix r is assumed to be:

$$r = \begin{pmatrix} 0 & 1 & 0 & 1 \\ 1 & 1 & 0 & 0 \\ 1 & 0 & 0 & 1 \\ 0 & 0 & 1 & 1 \end{pmatrix} \tag{8.58}$$

After distribution of $|S_n\rangle$, it is assumed that the index sequence is $d = \{0, 1, 3, 2\}$, and the voting sequence of all voters is $v = \{0, 0, 1, 0\}$, denoting V_0, V_1 and V_3 pass the verification. The process of voting statistics is shown in Table 8.6. The final voting

Table 8.6 A simple example of Q-PoV consensus.

	V_0	V_1	V_2	V_3	R
$r'_{0,k}$	0+0	1	0	1	0
$r'_{1,k}$	1	1+0	0	0	0
$r'_{2,k}$	1	0	0	1+0	0
$r'_{3,k}$	0	0	1+1	1	1

result sequence is $R = \{0, 0, 0, 1\}$, $N_0 = \sum_{R_x = 0} 1 = 3 > n/2$, and the block verification in this round of consensus is completed.

Q-PoV retains the advantages of PoV while enhancing integrity and security in the voting process by introducing quantum resources. Specifically, in the same vein as the PoV-series consensus, Q-PoV eliminates the need for Proof-of-Work relying on computing power, ensuring high block generation efficiency. It can operate normally as long as there are more than half of the normal working voters and one honest bookkeeper in the network. In addition, the Q-PoV consensus makes flexible utilization of the special properties of quantum multiparticle entangled states. On the one hand, $|X_n\rangle$ is used to realize correct statistics of voting results; on the other hand, the unordered ballot index sequence is distributed to ensure the anonymity of the ballot box selection based on the rotation invariance of $|S_n\rangle$. Moreover, each round of quantum distribution is accompanied by the security test to ensure the integrity of the distributed quantum states. Combining the above three means, Q-PoV ultimately achieved correct, anonymous and immutable consensus in a quantum blockchain.

8.2.3 FLP and CAP Theorems in Quantum Blockchain

In today's digital age, distributed systems and blockchain technology have become integral components. The design and implementation of these systems often involve distributed consensus, where multiple nodes agree on a certain value or decision in the network. Traditional distributed theory is constrained by FLP theorem (Fischer, Lynch, and Paterson 1985, pp. 374–382) and Consistency, Availability, Partition Tolerance (CAP) theorem (Brewer 2000, pp. 343477–343502). However, with the rapid development of quantum technology, we need to re-examine conventional theories pertaining to distributed systems. The properties of quantum computing, such as quantum entanglement and parallelism offer unparalleled advantages in overcoming the limitations of traditional distributed theory.

8.2.3.1 Quantum Technology and FLP Theorem

The FLP theorem states that in an asynchronous distributed system, a consensus decision cannot be reached in a finite time if there are likely to be faulty nodes. However, the introduction of quantum technology poses a challenge to this theorem.

A representative work is the quantum distributed consensus protocol proposed by Helm (Helm 2008, p. 445), which takes advantage of the principle of quantum entanglement by distributing entangled qubits to each node, and utilizes the measured collapse effect to achieve fault-tolerant distributed consensus.

In this protocol, each node receives and measures a qubit and makes a decision based on the measurement results. The key is that once one node measures its qubit, the quantum state of all the other nodes will instantly collapse to the same value because of quantum entanglement, thus achieving consistency. This consensus approach does not require complex two-way communication and agreement protocols, which sharply contrasts with traditional distributed computing methods.

In addition, the protocol demonstrates resistance to network delays and Byzantine failures. Even in the presence of malicious nodes or communication delays between nodes, the protocol ensures that consensus can be reached, which is an advantage brought about by the unique nature of quantum entanglement and collapse phenomena. If a qubit arrives later on one node, the other nodes will continue to function normally, and the late qubits will still contain the agreed value. The correlation of qubits ensures that measurement will not affect the consensus, which means that no matter what Byzantine failure occurs, a consistent consensus will eventually be reached in a finite time.

With cutting-edge technologies such as quantum and metaverse booming, we can boldly predict that future quantum devices will become prevalent in personal use. This vision will dismantle the existing barriers between consortium and public blockchains and open up entirely new possibilities for decentralization. With the increased computing power of individual users, it is expected to reduce the dependence on large nodes and professional computing resources, making decentralization widely achievable. Therefore, consensus mechanisms limited in traditional scenarios, such as voting-based consensus algorithms, will find straightforward applications in public blockchains. The popularization of quantum technology may not only induce changes in the theoretical framework of distributed systems but also significantly impact the practical operation and participant roles within these systems.

8.2.3.2 Quantum Technology and CAP Theorem

When we examine the impact of quantum technology on the CAP theorem, we inevitably delve into the core principles of distributed systems. Traditional distributed system theory asserts that partitioning may occur in distributed systems, where nodes in the network cannot communicate with each other properly. In this scenario, it is impossible to balance the consistency of the partition content with the proper functioning of the distributed system. Consequently, a trade-off between consistency, availability, and partition tolerance is inevitable. However, the introduction of quantum technology has created conditions to overcome this limitation.

Traditional asymmetric encrypted communications rely on complex mathematical problems to protect the content of communications, but these algorithms may no longer ensure sufficient security in the face of quantum computing attacks, which can solve these problems in a reasonable amount of time. In addition, data transmission in traditional communications may be subject to eavesdropping or tampering. In contrast, quantum communication systems take advantage of the nature of quantum entanglement to enhance security, making communication secure. Any attempt to eavesdrop or disrupt communications will leave traces at the quantum level, meaning an attacker cannot interfere with communications without being detected, providing security in the partitioned systems.

The distinctive advantages of quantum technology in information transmission provide security at the information-theoretic level for communication, which triggers a rethink of the CAP theorem. One foundation of the CAP theorem is that partitioning is inevitable. However, when communication is secured at the information-theoretic level, this premise needs to be revisited. The introduction of quantum technology will bring great changes to information transmission and enhance security for communication, so it will no longer necessarily entail a trade-off between consistency and availability. Therefore, with the advent of the quantum era, the pressure brought by the CAP trilemma will be reduced in both consortium and public blockchain scenarios, which will also provide great flexibility and plasticity for the design and implementation.

In general, with the rapid development of quantum technology, the traditional distributed theory is facing unprecedented challenges. It is reasonable to anticipate that the introduction of quantum technologies in the near future will not only bring new perspectives to distributed systems but will also fundamentally change the blockchain field. The traditional distributed theory, including the FLP theorem and the CAP theorem, requires reassessment to align with the new paradigm brought by quantum technology. This revolutionary change will not only open up fresh opportunities, but also new challenges. Therefore, there is an urgent need to establish novel theories and algorithms tailored to the quantum era to fully exploit the unique potential of quantum technology and improve the efficiency, reliability and security of distributed systems.

8.3 Scalable Quantum Computer Network

In the technological surge of the 21st century, quantum computing is regarded as the harbinger of the next computing revolution. However, despite the formidable power of individual quantum computers, their true potential lies in their ability to be interconnected with one another. The quantum computer network opens up an entirely new paradigm of computation, which could fundamentally alter the ways we process information, solve problems, and explore the unknown. It has the potential to achieve ultra-fast information transmission and processing while offering unprecedented levels of security. As research progresses and technologies mature, this field is gradually transitioning from theoretical concepts to practical applications.

8.3.1 Quantum Internet

Reflecting on the technological developments of the 1980s, the emergence of the Internet was hailed as a technological revolution that changed the world. It significantly facilitated the dissemination of information, connecting the globe into a seamless network. Today, another imminent revolution is quietly emerging – quantum Internet, also known as quantum information network.

The quantum Internet establishes a communication network bridging quantum and classical technologies. As illustrated in Figure 8.29, the quantum Internet is not a replacement for the classical Internet; instead, it constitutes a quantum-interconnected network where quantum and classical technologies coexist. Quantum Internet typically refers to its quantum component. Unlike classical networks, the quantum Internet utilizes entanglement, quantum teleportation and other quantum communication technologies to achieve secure information exchange that surpasses classical limitations. It not only enhances speed and efficiency but also presents unprecedented possibilities in terms of security and novel application scenarios. From the fundamental principles of physics, quantum Internet challenges traditional understandings of information transmission and

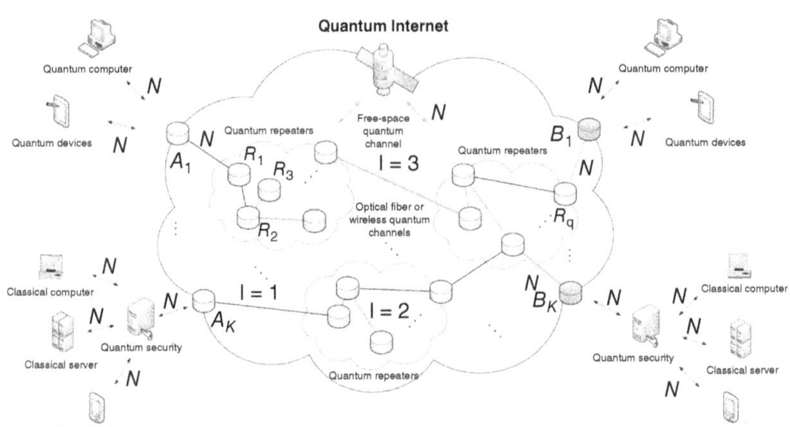

Figure 8.29 The structure of a quantum Internet. *Source:* Gyongyosi and Imre (2022, pp. 52–63) / with permission of ACM (The Association for Computing Machinery).

encryption. It heralds a new chapter in future communication. The network is expected to provide revolutionary capabilities for secure communication, distributed quantum computing and advanced quantum sensing.

Similar to the classical Internet, the physical devices in the quantum Internet also form the foundation of connectivity. The quantum Internet consists of three fundamental quantum physical components – transmission channels, quantum end nodes, and quantum repeaters. Quantum end nodes encompass various quantum processors within the network, ranging from small nodes capable of simple state preparation and measurement to high-performance large-scale quantum computers. Transmission channels are responsible for connecting these quantum nodes. However, losses incurred during channel transmission impose limitations on the distance over which qubits can be effectively transmitted. To overcome this challenge, the implementation of quantum repeaters becomes indispensable for extending transmission distances efficiently. Theoretically speaking, leveraging these repeaters ensures reliable qubit transfer across any given distance.

Quantum repeaters have two core functions: entanglement swapping and entanglement purification. Figure 8.30 illustrates the principle of entanglement swapping in quantum repeaters: first, entanglement is generated separately between the repeater and nodes on the left and right. Then, the repeater transfers the qubit entangled with the left node to the right node, successfully creating entanglement over distances where direct transmission is not feasible. Entanglement purification, also known as entanglement distillation, involves error correction during the transmission process, generating high-quality entangled states from low-quality ones to enhance the degree of entanglement between qubits.

The communication process using a quantum repeater is divided into three steps. First, entanglement is established between adjacent nodes, including both quantum end nodes and repeaters. Subsequently, entanglement swapping occurs within the quantum repeater, entangling the qubits between quantum end nodes. The third step is the process of entanglement purification.

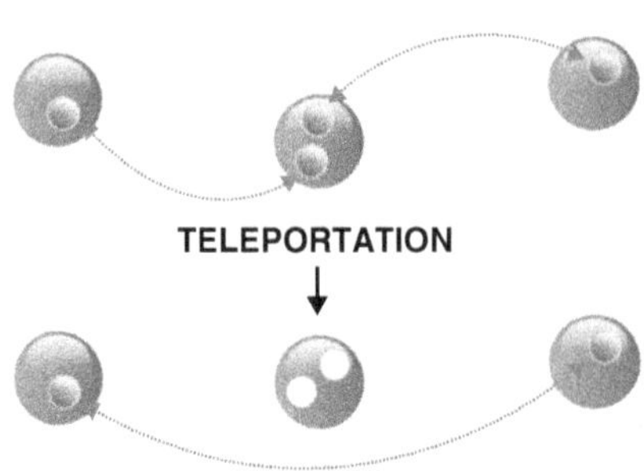

Figure 8.30 Principle of entanglement swapping in quantum repeater.

The development of quantum repeaters can be categorized into three generations based on different entanglement purification methods (Singh et al. 2021, pp. 2218–2247), as illustrated in Table 8.7. In the first generation of quantum repeaters, bidirectional classical communication is required for verifying the generation and purification of entanglement. This process faces performance bottlenecks as communication distance increases. Therefore, the second generation of quantum repeaters employs quantum error correction codes to achieve entanglement purification, eliminating the need for receiving purification confirmation. This allows qubits to immediately engage in the next entanglement without waiting. However, the second-generation quantum repeaters still require bidirectional signal transmission to reduce loss errors. In the third generation of quantum repeaters, bidirectional signal transmission is replaced by unidirectional signal transmission using loss-resistant encoding. Quantum information is encoded in

Table 8.7 Three generations of quantum repeaters.

	First-generation QR	**Second-generation QR**	**Third-generation QR**
Loss error	HEG (two-way signaling)	HEG (two-way signaling)	QEC (one-way signaling)
Operation error	HEP (two-way signaling)	QEC (one-way signaling)	QEC (one-way signaling)
Procedure	1) Create entangled pairs over L_0 beween adjacent stations 2) At k-th level, connect two pairs over L_k and extend to $L_{K+1} = 2L_K$, followed by HEP 3) After n nesting levels, obtain high fidelity pair over $L_{tot} = 2^n L_0$	1) Prepare encoded states $\|0\rangle_L$ and $\|+\rangle_L$ 2) Use teleportation-based nonlocal CNOT gates to create encoded Bell pairs between adjacent stations 3) Connect intermediate stations to create long distance encoded Bell pair	1) Encode information with a block of qubits that are sent through a lossy channel 2) Use QEC to correct both loss and operation errors 3) Relay the encoded information to the next station; and repeat steps 2 and 3
Characteristic time scale	Max($L_{tot}/c, t_0$)	Max($L_0/c, t_0$)	t_0
Cost coefficient (C')	Poly(L_{tot})	PolyLog(L_{tot})	PolyLog(L_{tot})

Source: Wei et al. (2022) / John Wiley & Sons.

material qubits, then transferred to photons and transmitted through the communication channel. At the receiving end, the photon's state is once again converted back into material qubits for error correction. This scheme is referred to as fully fault-tolerance, indicating its high resilience in error handling. These developments in quantum repeaters are crucial for realizing a quantum Internet.

In addition to the fundamental physical devices, a quantum Internet requires corresponding network architecture and protocols. Due to the unique properties of quantum mechanics, especially the no-cloning theorem and quantum measurement collapse, mapping existing classical network frameworks directly onto quantum devices for quantum Internet implementation is impractical. For instance, routing choices in quantum communication may cause damage to quantum information, necessitating entirely new routing algorithms to ensure the integrity of entanglement. Therefore, implementing a quantum Internet requires the reconstruction of appropriate network models and protocols. Wehner et al. drawing inspiration from the TCP/IP model, proposed a layered model for a quantum network (Dahlberg et al. 2019, pp. 159–173), as depicted in Table 8.8. It divides the network into five layers: the physical layer, the link layer, the network layer, the transport layer, and the application layer.

In this model, the physical layer is responsible for attempting to generate entanglement between two nodes within well-defined time slots. The device triggering entanglement attempts at a given moment and responsible for this in the physical layer is called an automated node. The physical layer presents no decision in generating entanglement. Conversely, it relies on a specific protocol, referred to as Midpoint Heralding Protocol (MHP), that coordinates the automated nodes. The MHP dictates that the physical layer polls the link layer to determine whether entanglement needs to be generated within a given time slot. If affirmative, an activation signal is triggered, and the physical layer provides the results of the entanglement generation attempts through specific heralding signals.

The second layer, the link layer, is responsible for utilizing the Quantum Entanglement Generation Protocol (QEGP) to produce entanglement. The QEGP

Table 8.8 Functional allocation in a quantum network stack.

Application	
Transport	Qubit transmission
Network	Long distance entanglement
Link	Robust entanglement generation
Physical	Attempt entanglement generation

specifies that the link layer receives entanglement requests containing multiple parameters from higher layers and issues corresponding instructions to the lower-layer protocols. These parameters include remote node information, the number of entangled pairs, request type, minimum fidelity and so on. Through these specific parameters, QEGP performs fidelity assessments and schedules entanglement requests to ensure robust generation of entanglement at the link layer. Additionally, the link layer can request the physical layer to perform other operations, such as initialization or qubit measurements, through specific commands.

The third layer, the network layer, is responsible for generating long-distance entanglement using the functionalities of the link layer, which can be achieved through entanglement swapping. The network layer also includes an entanglement manager to track entanglement resources within the network.

Last, the fourth layer, the transport layer, uses methods such as quantum teleportation based on the requests from the application layer to transmit qubits.

The network model proposed by Wehner is not a fully mature or uniquely viable solution. In fact, there are currently various conceptualizations regarding quantum Internet models or protocols. Figure 8.31 illustrates three relatively comprehensive model proposals for quantum Internet, each with its own distinctions. However, to a certain extent, these proposals draw inspiration from classical network models and share many unresolved issues related to network protocols, layer division, and functional allocation.

Compared to the high maturity of the classical Internet, the quantum Internet is still in its early stages of evolution, currently undergoing initial research and development. However, it holds tremendous potential and expectations. An article by Stephanie Wehner's team published in Science (Wehner, Elkouss, and Hanson 2018, p. eaam9288) outlines the future development roadmap of the quantum Internet, dividing its evolution into six stages, as illustrated in Figure 8.32: trusted repeater network, preparation and measurement network, entanglement generation network, quantum memory network, few qubit fault-tolerant network and quantum computing network.

The first stage, the trusted repeater network, serves as a transitional phase and is the current state of development. It significantly differs from subsequent stages as it does not support end-to-end qubit transmission. Despite its functional limitations, the trusted repeater network provides the technical foundation and developmental direction for the future quantum Internet, acting as a crucial stepping stone. Specifically, it typically consists of at least two end nodes and a series of short-distance links connecting nearby repeaters. The connections between these repeaters rely on QKD to exchange encryption keys. Through these paired keys, end nodes can generate their own keys contingent on the trustworthiness of all repeaters. These trust-based repeaters may potentially be upgraded to true quantum repeaters in the future.

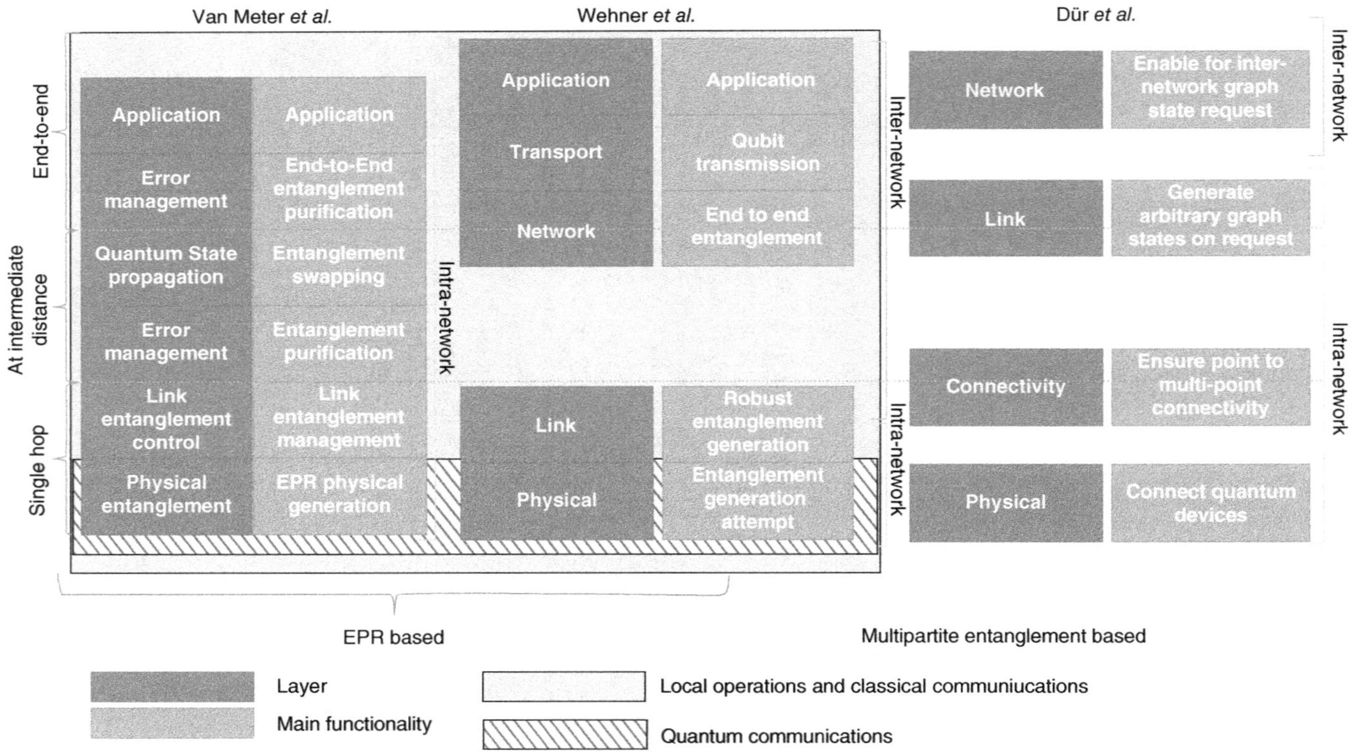

Figure 8.31 Joint representation of three quantum Internet layered models. *Source:* Illiano et al. (2022) / with permission of ELSEVIER.

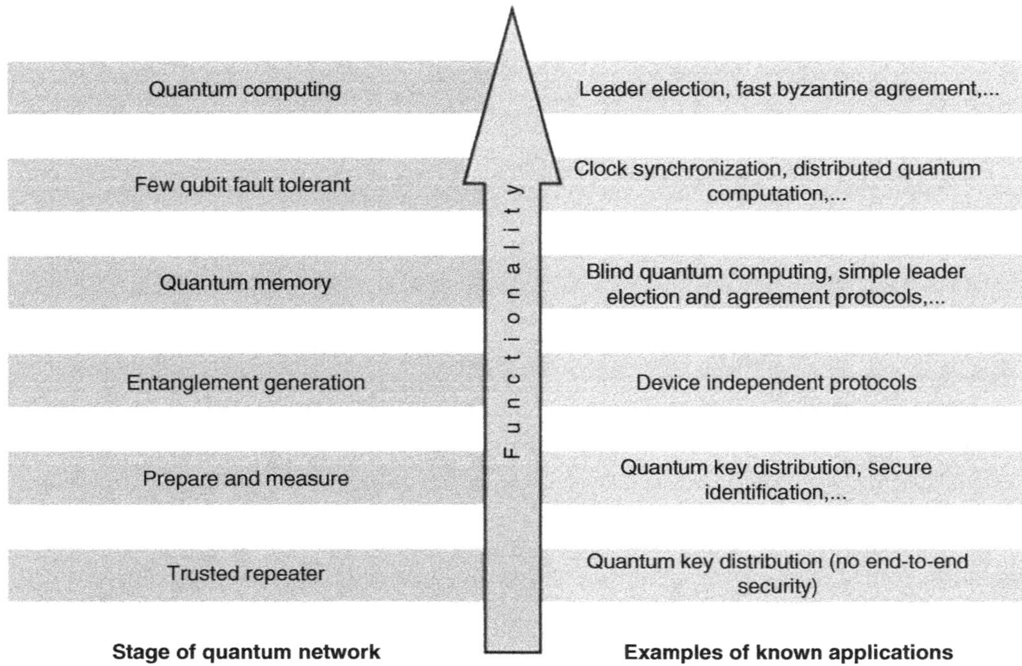

Figure 8.32 Six stages of quantum Internet development and their corresponding applications.

The second stage, the preparation and measurement network, marks the first that offers end-to-end quantum functionality. In this stage, QKD between two end nodes is possible without trusting any intermediary nodes or devices. Beyond QKD, it supports various other quantum protocols, allowing the sender to prepare and transmit complex quantum states to different nodes in the network. While this stage enables quantum information transmission, the receiver may selectively measure or ignore certain incoming qubits during the transmission process. Furthermore, due to technological and quantum constraints, information may be lost or require retransmission.

The third stage, the entanglement generation network, has a special emphasis on the end-to-end generation of quantum entanglement and facilitates immediate local measurements without the need for quantum storage. A notable feature of this stage is its ability to generate entanglement in a deterministic or heralded fashion. Deterministic entanglement generation refers to a process with close to a 100% success rate. Heralding is a slightly weaker form of deterministic entanglement generation in which it provides an independent signal to indicate the successful generation of entanglement. This stage also includes networks that allow the generation of multipartite entangled states although it is not a necessary condition to enter this stage. And it does not require end nodes to possess quantum storage capabilities. The entanglement generation network is a crucial step toward advanced functionalities, serving as the foundation for many quantum communication protocols.

In the fourth stage, the quantum memory network, end nodes in the network acquire quantum memory capabilities and achieve global quantum control. With these capabilities, the network can execute more complex quantum protocols, such as those addressing tasks in distributed systems, which often require temporary memory of quantum states during quantum or classical communication processes. Furthermore, this stage signifies the network's ability to perform entanglement distillation and generate multipartite entangled states through local storage and control. It's important to note that the quantum memory network does not demand a certain level of precision for executed operations, and quantum operations in this stage may not have reached a fully fault-tolerant level. However, it has sufficient capacity to handle quantum information and perform specific quantum network tasks.

The fifth stage, the few qubit fault-tolerant network, primarily focuses on the fault tolerance of local quantum operations. While many known quantum Internet protocols may not require fault tolerance, incorporating fault-tolerant local operations enables the execution of more complex local quantum computations. Theoretically, it can extend storage time indefinitely for protocols involving any number of communication rounds. The term "few qubit" in this stage implies that the available qubit quantity is still small enough for end nodes to be efficiently simulated on classical computers. However, this does not mean the entire network can be efficiently simulated, as classical computing usually cannot replicate the effects of quantum entanglement.

The last stage, the quantum computing network, comprises quantum computers capable of freely engaging in quantum communication. In this stage, the quantum Internet gains a new capability: finding answers to computational problems that classical computers cannot efficiently solve. It is not merely an enhancement of the previous stages but enters an entirely new realm of computation. When quantum computers can freely and arbitrarily exchange quantum information, their collaboration results in an exceptionally powerful computing network. This network has the ability to handle complex tasks beyond the scope of classical computers. Each quantum computer can be viewed as a super node in the network, capable of executing advanced local quantum algorithms while sharing, exchanging, and integrating information with other quantum computers to perform larger-scale collaborative tasks. For instance, two quantum computers can jointly solve a problem through quantum entanglement and communication, achieving computation speeds faster than their independent operation. Importantly, due to the nature of quantum computing, this stage opens up new possibilities globally by supporting innovative algorithms, communication protocols, and security standards. It not only signifies a significant technological leap but also anticipates innovative breakthroughs in various cutting-edge scientific, engineering, and business applications.

The classification of quantum Internet development is based on the achievable functionalities and technical requirements at each stage. Other methods for categorizing the future of the quantum Internet based on key enabling technology requirements and expected application scenarios are also feasible. In fact, these classifications are merely visionary concepts for the future quantum Internet and regardless of the classification method, the quantum Internet is currently in its infancy, with ongoing research primarily focused on exploration. Technological pathways in areas such as quantum entanglement manipulation, quantum state storage and conversion, quantum repeaters, and transmission have not yet converged, and clear solutions are yet to emerge. Therefore, the likelihood of these major breakthroughs in crucial control factors for the practical application on a large scale in the short term remains relatively low.

Faced with the challenges and opportunities of the quantum Internet, governments and businesses worldwide are diligently advancing technological development and investing substantial funds and resources. In 2018, the European Union announced its ambitious plan to invest over 1 billion euros in the "Quantum Flagship Program" for quantum technology research over the next decade. Simultaneously, the US government's funding allocation for this purpose is substantial, reaching up to 850 million dollars in 2023 alone. Not to be left behind, the UK has declared a commitment of 2.5 billion pounds in its quantum technology strategy over the next decade, with an expected additional 1 billion pounds in private investment. China has also invested significant human and material resources in relevant research. Major corporations, including Google, IBM, and Microsoft, are intensifying their investments as well. Given these efforts and investments, there is reason to believe that in the near future, the quantum Internet will gradually become integrated into the lives of ordinary people.

8.3.2 Quantum Multi-Identifier Network Architecture with Quantum Identifier

While the visionary concept of the quantum Internet is still in its early exploratory phase, as the landscape of reality continues to evolve, there is a pressing need for the various capabilities of the quantum Internet to meet the ever-changing demands. Consequently, a natural inclination emerges toward integrating quantum communication with existing Internet frameworks as a transitional step from the current networks to the quantum Internet.

Currently, various network frameworks exist encompassing both traditional and novel approaches. Among these frameworks, the Multi-Identifier Network (MIN) stands out as the sole framework demonstrating impeccable compatibility with quantum transmission. Introducing quantum identifiers into the MIN system and establishing Quantum Multi-Identifier Network (Q-MIN) (Li et al. 2023) add a new dimension to the network. Building upon the robust architecture of MIN, Q-MIN expands the range of identifier types while maintaining the physical components of existing quantum communication networks intact. This expansion enhances the applicability of quantum communication networks, rendering communication more flexible, versatile, and secure.

Due to the evolutionary nature of the MIN system from classical network systems, and the inherent differences in physical transmission between classical communication and quantum communication, dual-channel support is required. Additionally, the deployment requires the combined use of classical and quantum physical hardware, along with the integration of MIN system and quantum communication system software to meet the requirements of Q-MIN. Specific conditions include:

Hardware condition 1: Hardware devices supporting quantum preparation and detection.
Software condition 1: Software system devices capable of managing and controlling Hardware Condition 1.
Hardware condition 2: Classical communication devices supporting MIN.
Software condition 2: Software systems for MIN, including the Multi-Identifier System (MIS) and the Multi-Identifier Router (MIR).

Software-and-hardware condition: Based on the aforementioned four conditions, it is imperative to ensure seamless communication between the quantum system software and MIN's software systems, while ensuring their proper functionality in accordance with specified requirements.

These conditions ensure that each router in Q-MIN supports the resolution, storage, and forwarding of content received from a previous router along any given path, thereby achieving the joint routing of quantum and real information.

In MIN, MIR is required to communicate with MIS for verifying the source of each packet and detecting tampering or forgery. MIS also necessitates synchronization with each other to promptly update various essential information. Similarly, in Q-MIN, device deployment includes bidirectional communication between Quantum Multi-Identifier Routers (Q-MIRs), between Q-MIR and classical MIR, between classical MIRs, between Quantum Multi-Identifier Systems (Q-MISs), between Q-MIS and two types of MIRs, and finally, between different terminal network devices and two types of MIRs.

According to the above description, Q-MIN supports progressive deployment on existing MIN, and secure quantum communication does not interfere with general MIN communication. The device deployment is illustrated in Figure 8.33.

The MIN packet is based on the TLV encoding scheme, as shown in Figure 8.34, including three parts: Type, Length, and Value. The TLV encoding scheme exhibits strong scalability as it allows for the arbitrary addition of fill content, and different TLV blocks can be combined and overlaid to form a more comprehensive expression of information. Q-MIN enhances MIN primarily in the Identifier area and Signature area.

The Identifier area of MIN must include one or more network identifiers, which the MIR can utilize to process network packets. In the case of Q-MIN, this functionality is employed by incorporating a new type of quantum basis identifier into the Identifier area through Q-MIS. The specific type and length of the identifier can be determined based on actual network conditions, with a randomly selected value falling within the prescribed length limit.

Similarly, in MIN, the Signature area typically encompasses one or more digital signatures that generally cover the Identifier area and Read-only area. Each signature also contains two TLV blocks: metadata information and the resulting outcome. In the context of Q-MIN, this characteristic is leveraged by signing the Identifier area and the Read-only area separately before integrating all the TLV blocks of signatures to form the Signature area in the MIN packet.

For the Mutable area in MIN packet, Q-MIN makes no modifications. The improvements made to the Identifier area and Signature area align with the basic principles of applying new types of identifiers, as well as router storage and forwarding in MIN. Therefore, Q-MIS and Q-MIR can read and identify these modifications.

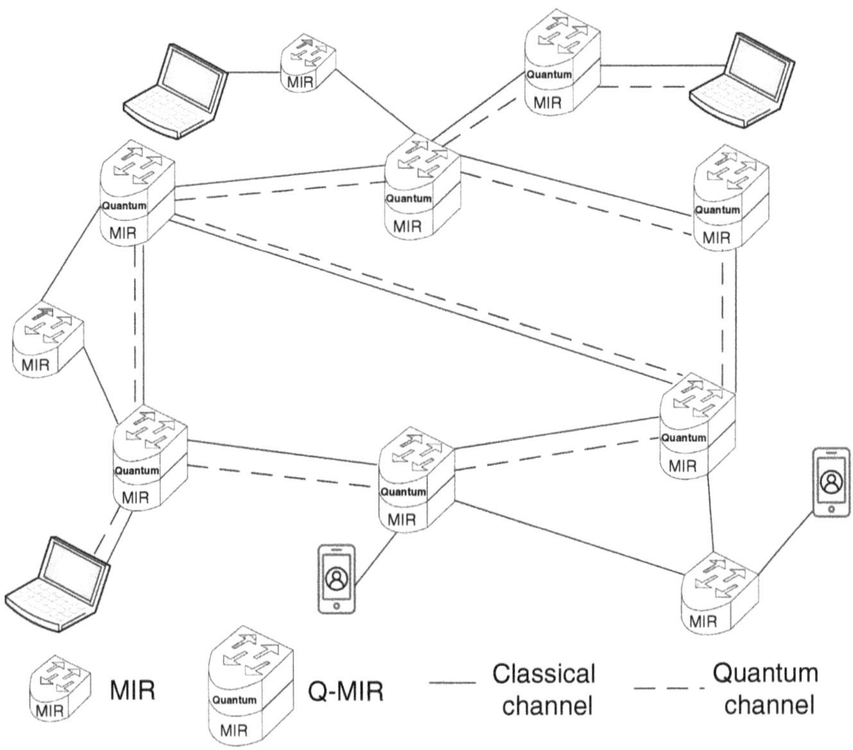

Figure 8.33 Example of overlapping deployment of classical MIN and Q-MIN.

Q-MIN is essentially an extension of MIN in the quantum domain, so it only modifies and innovates the classical communication part. For the quantum transmission part, Q-MIN exclusively employs the corresponding methods. This section will use the BB84 protocol as an example to illustrate one approach through which MIN can be extended in the quantum domain.

Quantum states have properties of uncertainty and unclonability, and the accurate content expressed by a quantum state can only be obtained when the preparation basis and measurement basis are consistent. Based on this property, Q-MIN defines a quantum identifier as the accurate content expressed by the combination of quantum states and bases, which is the key formed in the BB84 protocol. In addition, since communication parties need to transmit the basis sequence through a classical channel and verify for eavesdropping before forming the quantum key, Q-MIN incorporates the basis sequence as an alternative identifier in cases where quantum identifiers have not yet been established.

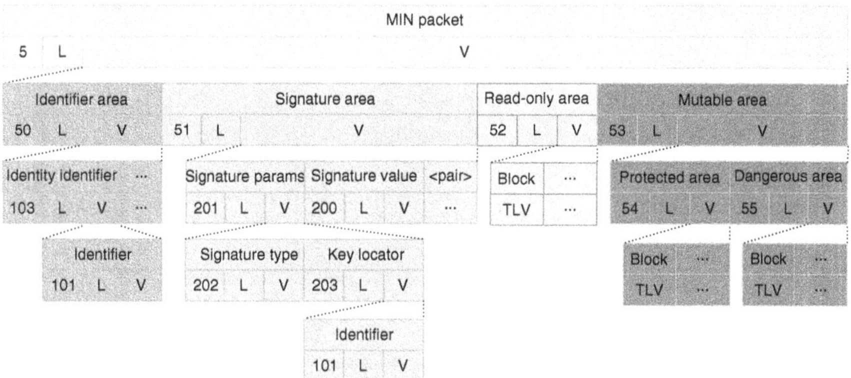

Figure 8.34 General format of MIN packet.

Due to the incompatibility between the transmission of quantum states and classical information, a dual-channel approach is employed for this purpose. To address timing concerns, a 'stop-and-wait' strategy is adopted during the dual-channel transmission process. Initially, the sender transmits the MIN packet through the classical channel, followed by preparation and transmission of the quantum state after receiving acknowledgment from the receiver.

When using quantum identifiers for network communication, each Q-MIR that the communication passes through must perform the process of reading quantum basis identifier information, generating quantum identifiers, and regenerating quantum states and quantum basis sequences. Therefore, each Q-MIR needs to regenerate the corresponding quantum sequences and quantum basis sequences. It is important to note that since the BB84 protocol does not involve entangled quantum, it permits measurement of the qubits and subsequent generation of new quantum states based on these measurement results. Furthermore, this process only encompasses replication of quantum information without violating the no-cloning theorem.

According to the requirements and characteristics of Q-MIN, a complete transmission process is illustrated in Figure 8.35.

Step 1: (Optional) A new user submits an application to Q-MIS for registering their quantum identifiers, encompassing the quantum basis identifier and quantum identifier, and acquires the corresponding identifier information.

Step 2: The sender generates a MIN packet and transmits it to the receiver. The sender first randomly generates a quantum basis sequence as the quantum basis identifier and includes it in the Identifier area of the MIN packet while keeping

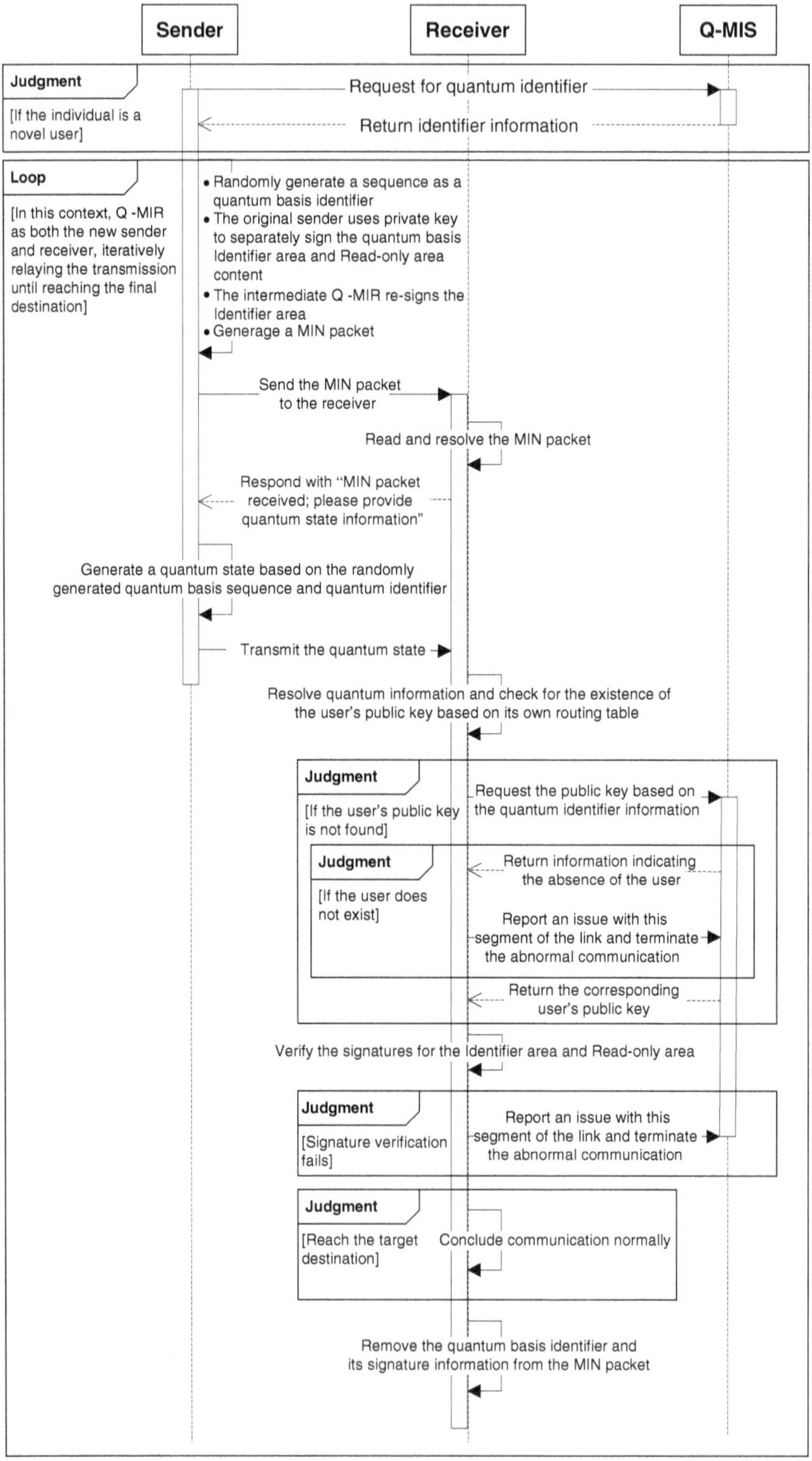

Figure 8.35 Communication process of a pure quantum identifier in Q-MIN.

a record. Additionally, the original sender signs both contents of the quantum basis and Read-only area with its private key separately. The intermediate routers re-sign the modified Identifier area, and all signatures are also added to the Signature area of the MIN packet. Once completed, the sender transmits the MIN packet to its intended receiver.

Step 3: Upon receiving the MIN packet, the receiver determines from the Type value in the Identifier area that this MIN packet needs to resolve a complete quantum identifier, but lacks the quantum state information. Therefore, the receiver controls the quantum receiving device to enter the receiving state and responds to the sender with "MIN packet received; please provide quantum state information."

Step 4: The sender, based on its quantum identifier and the currently stored quantum basis sequence, uses the quantum device to generate the corresponding quantum state and sends it to the receiver.

Step 5: The receiver, based on the quantum basis information in the received MIN packet, decodes the true information of the quantum identifier according to the BB84 protocol. Next,

Step 5.1: Checks if the original sender's public key exists,

Step 5.1.1: If not, the current receiver requests Q-MIS to download the identity and public key information of the original sender.

Step 5.1.1.1: Upon successful retrieval, proceed to Step 5.2.

Step 5.1.1.2: If unable to retrieve, proceed to Step 5.3.

Step 5.1.2: If it exists, proceed to Step 5.2.

Step 5.2: With the current public key, verify the signature. If the verification passes, proceed to Step 6. If the verification fails, proceed to Step 5.3.

Step 5.3: Accurately report the encountered communication error to Q-MIS for processing and terminate the ongoing communication.

Step 6: After successful verification of the signatures in the Identifier area and Read-only area,

Step 6.1: The current receiver determines whether it can provide the required content or serve as the destination.

Step 6.1.1: If affirmative, communication ends, and the router processes the relevant services and contents.

Step 6.1.2: If negative, this receiver becomes the new sender, removes the quantum basis identifier and signature of the previous sender from the MIN packet, and repeats Step 2–6 until the complete information reaches the destination receiver.

Similar to contemporary networks, throughout the entire process described above, each Q-MIR in the path, except for the original sender and the final receiver, has a dual role as both sender and receiver, relaying the communication until completion. In terms of security, considering channel interference and eavesdropping, once an issue arises in communication, any communication issues that arise can be promptly identified by a receiver in Step 5 and reported to Q-MIS for handling by relevant administrators.

However, Q-MIN requires simultaneous operation of dual channels, which is much more challenging to monitor compared to a single channel. By using a "stop-and-wait" mode, eavesdroppers face difficulties in obtaining complete information from both channels simultaneously. Moreover, quantum states are highly susceptible to interference. If eavesdropping occurs and the quantum state is disrupted, Q-MIR can immediately notify administrators to inspect the line's security issues. Furthermore, considering eavesdroppers forging information without relevant user identity information, Q-MIR can promptly detect this information and notify administrators for handling and inspection. Therefore, to further enhance security, emphasis is placed on securing information in the Read-only area. To achieve the one-time pad requirement, the QKD protocol can be used again during communication for key negotiation to encrypt content within this area. The communication process is shown in Figure 8.36.

Step 1: The sender initiates the quantum-based MIN communication by transmitting a MIN packet to the receiver, resembling the previous MIN packet structure but with an empty Value in the Read-only area. Upon detecting this quantum-based communication, the receiver acknowledges receipt and requests the quantum state.

Step 2: The sender generates the corresponding quantum state based on its quantum identifier and sends it to the receiver.

Step 3: After successfully receiving the quantum state, the receiver obtains the complete quantum identifier and proceeds with signature verification to ensure its authenticity. Subsequently, an examination is conducted to verify that the Read-only area is devoid of content. Immediately thereafter, the receiver engages in encrypted communication with the sender.

Step 4: Following the mutual verification of the key employed by both parties through the dual channel, the sender transmits information encrypted with quantum keys to the receiver, encompassing all content within the Read-only area.

Step 5: Upon receiving all the information, the receiver, now acting as a sender, continues to relay the process by maintaining the established route through storage and forwarding.

The aforementioned approach enables the security measures to fully satisfy the requirements of one-time pad for secure communication in information theory. It facilitates secure communication by leveraging quantum identifier and novel Q-MIN technology.

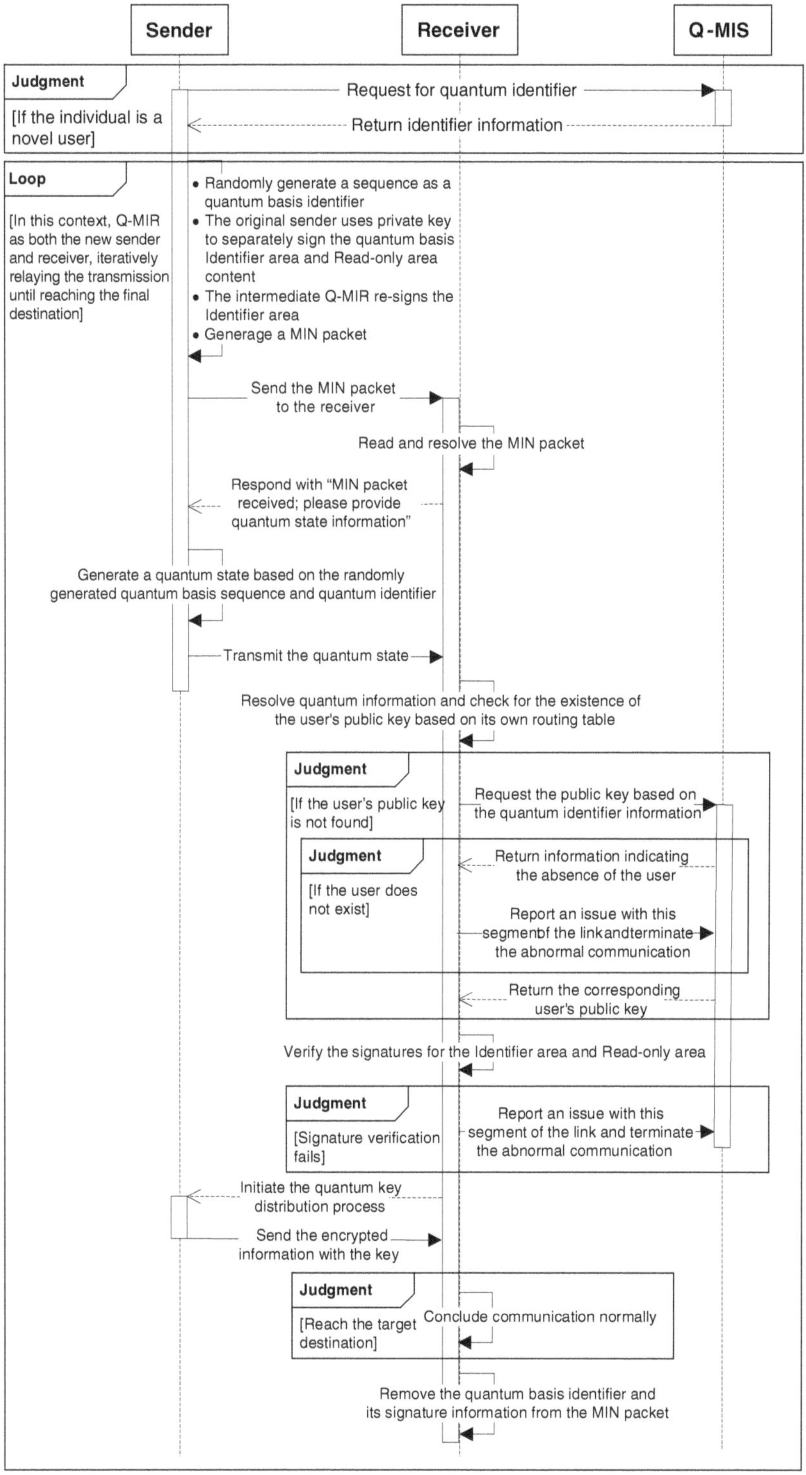

Figure 8.36 Communication of a quantum identifier in Q-MIN with one-time pad.

8.3.3 Quantum Multi-Identifier System and Router

The architecture of classical MIN can be broadly divided into the management plane and the data plane. The data plane's functions are carried out by MIR, which partially supports the resolution of various network identifiers such as identity, content, and service. It also enables efficient and scalable routing, addressing, and forwarding based on heterogeneous identifiers. The management plane's functions are handled by MIS, which supports the generation and management of various identifiers. Consensus algorithms are employed by supervisory nodes in the management plane to verify identifier data. Upon consensus being reached, ownership and operation information is recorded on the blockchain to achieve both tamper-proofing and traceability.

The fundamental similarity between Q-MIS and the original MIS lies in their provision of distributed identifier registration, identity information binding, as well as identifier management and resolution services for users and devices in the network. However, to accommodate a new identifier type like the quantum identifier, support from MIS is required. On the other hand, in MIS, each network entity corresponds to a record that contains its authentic information along with specific details about various identifiers it possesses. Consequently, for an entity necessitating a quantum identifier, an application involving the mapping of the quantum identifier to the real user must be submitted to Q-MIS prior to initiating communication.

Q-MIR is essentially a combination of MIR and the quantum repeater. The quantum repeater reads quantum basis identifier information, generates and resolves quantum identifiers, and regenerates quantum states and quantum basis sequences. The MIR component communicates with MIS or Q-MIS, along with other MIR or Q-MIR, providing routing and addressing services for the quantum repeater based on received information. When transmitting classical information, Q-MIR operates identically to MIR.

In fact, the specific form of Q-MIN supporting quantum identifiers has not been determined. The proposed possibilities earlier are just one possibility, and the meaning of Q-MIN may further expand with the development of quantum technology in the future. Correspondingly, the functionalities of Q-MIS and Q-MIR will also undergo updates and iterations.

In summary, Q-MIN integrates the future network MIN with existing quantum communication, harnessing the unique characteristics of quantum no-cloning and uncertainty to significantly enhance network security. Moreover, it achieves improved availability of quantum communication without additional physical devices or costs, enabling flexible routing and expanding its applicability. Furthermore, it explores scalable and practical solutions for large-scale quantum communication in the future. By integrating Q-MIN into the existing software and hardware infrastructure while leveraging the advantages of current network communication solutions, substantial savings in software and hardware costs are achieved. This integration enriches the application ecosystem within the future Internet, playing a pivotal role in its continuous evolution and fostering integrated development with quantum communication.

8.3.4 Future Prospect of Quantum Technology

With the continuous progress of science and technology, quantum technology in the field of networks has transitioned from the theoretical stage to the practical application stage. This cutting-edge technology based on the microscopic world of particles is opening new chapters in digital communication and network security. As we delve into and gradually master this technology, it can be anticipated that quantum technology will contribute to achieving security across all layers of communication networks.

Classical transmission channels have inherent issues such as replicability, easy storage, and undetectable eavesdropping. While these problems can be partially addressed through various high-level protocols, fundamental issues at the physical layer persist. First, data can be effortlessly duplicated at this layer, providing eavesdroppers with the opportunity to repeatedly attempt to copy and decode transmitted data without fear of detection. This characteristic also facilitates man-in-the-middle attacks, where an attacker can intercept, copy, modify, and resend data packets without the knowledge of the sender and receiver. Second, the ease of storage implies that even if current technology cannot crack a particular encryption protocol, malicious actors can store the data for an extended period, waiting for technological advances that might break it. This "store to crack later" strategy poses a significant threat to data containing long-term valid or sensitive information. Thirdly, undetectable eavesdropping presents a challenge or impossibility in perceiving intrusions when classical signals are intercepted or monitored by unauthorized entities. This stealth advantage enjoyed by malicious eavesdroppers further complicates network security maintenance efforts. While many efforts in network security have been focused on upper-layer protocols and encryption technologies, however, these measures merely patch vulnerabilities at the physical layer without fundamentally addressing the underlying problem.

Quantum communication overcomes not only the major drawbacks of the physical layer in classical networks but also provides an entirely new and unconditionally secure means of communication by leveraging the unique properties of quantum mechanics. According to the fundamental principles of quantum mechanics, a quantum system changes when measured. This implies that any attempt by a malicious eavesdropper to intercept and measure the transmitted qubits will inevitably disturb the system's state, thereby alerting the communicating parties to the intrusion. Not only that, quantum communication offers unconditional security that does not rely on computational complexity or unbroken encryption algorithms but is based on the fundamental laws of quantum physics. For example, using QKD technology ensures security even when faced with an attacker possessing unlimited computational resources. Even if a key is exposed at some point, keys shared through QKD protocols remain secure, as each execution of a QKD protocol generates an entirely new and independent key.

Current quantum communication requires integration with traditional Internet frameworks, meaning that current quantum technology provides protection for classical transmission systems. However, as quantum computing, quantum storage, and quantum communication technologies further develop and become more widespread, the future may witness the emergence of an increasingly independent quantum Internet framework. Quantum technology will further enhance the security of information transmission.

However, quantum technology not only provides a robust shield for information transmission but also poses a destructive threat to the current security foundations of information transmission. Quantum computers have the capability to break certain public-key cryptographic systems that are currently considered secure, such as RSA and Elliptic Curve Cryptography (ECC), in polynomial time. Thus, the development of quantum technology threatens to completely undermine the foundation of traditional public-key cryptography. In response to this imminent danger, researchers have begun developing new encryption technologies known as post-quantum cryptography or quantum-resistant cryptography. These new encryption schemes are designed to remain secure even in the face of quantum computers. Compared to traditional cryptographic algorithms, some post-quantum cryptographic algorithms may require larger keys, more computational resources, or greater communication overhead, necessitating careful consideration when choosing and deploying these algorithms.

8.4 Chapter Summary

Security has consistently been a significant concern in the field of communication, and the combination of quantum technology and blockchain presents an effective solution to address this issue. This chapter begins by introducing the relevant concepts of quantum technology and discussing its applications in information security and transmission, such as QKD protocols and quantum teleportation. By integrating quantum technology with blockchain, the chapter explores the advantages and application scenarios of quantum blockchain, which make the limitations of the FLP theorem and CAP theorem require reassessment. Finally, an overview of the current development of the quantum Internet is provided, encompassing prospects for its future advancements as well as integration of existing network systems with quantum communication. Although applications of quantum technology are still relatively limited, it is certain that in the future, quantum technology will bring unprecedented breakthroughs in information security.

Discussion Questions

8.1 Briefly describe the BB84 protocol.

A: The BB84 protocol is a type of QKD protocol. In BB84, two sets of standard orthogonal bases are used. Both communicating parties randomly choose one of these bases. Alice uses quantum transmission to send qubits to Bob and classical communication to send the basis she selected. Bob compares the bases chosen by both parties and only uses the bit information corresponding to matching bases. They then transmit half of the bits through a classical channel. If this portion of bits is entirely the same, it can be used as the key. If about half of the bits are different, it indicates potential eavesdropping.

8.2 How does quantum technology impact the CAP theorem?

A: The CAP theorem posits that in a distributed system, partitions may occur, meaning nodes in the network are unable to communicate normally. This fundamental premise can lead to inconsistency among partitions. However, by distributing entangled qubits and utilizing the measurement collapse effect, consistency can be ensured even in the event of network partitions. Furthermore, in quantum communication systems, any attempt to eavesdrop or interfere with communication leaves traces at the quantum level, making it impossible for attackers to interfere unnoticed. Therefore, when both consistency and communication security can be guaranteed at the quantum level, the traditional CAP theorem needs to be reconsidered.

8.3 Briefly explain the differences between Q-MIS and MIS, as well as Q-MIR and MIR.

A: Q-MIS is an extension of MIS rather than a fundamentally different system. To support the inclusion of new identifiers, MIS needs to provide relevant service support, including distributed identifier registration, identity information binding, and management and resolution services for network users and devices. Consequently, Q-MIS enhances its services by mapping network entities requiring quantum identifiers to submit quantum identifiers and linking them to real users. On the other hand, Q-MIR combines MIR with the quantum repeater. The quantum repeater is responsible for reading quantum basis identifier information, generating and resolving quantum identifiers, as well as regenerating quantum states and sequences for redistribution. MIR is responsible for information exchange with Q-MIS and other Q-MIRs while providing routing and addressing services for quantum repeaters based on corresponding information. It should be noted that when transmitting classical information, Q-MIR functions identically to MIR.

References

Afzelius, M., Simon, C., De Riedmatten, H. and Gisin, N., 2009. Multimode quantum memory based on atomic frequency combs. *Physical Review A*, 79(5), p. 052329.

Alexander, A.L., Longdell, J.J., Sellars, M.J. and Manson, N.B., 2006. Photon echoes produced by switching electric fields. *Physical Review Letters*, 96(4), p. 043602.

Arute, F., Arya, K., Babbush, R., Bacon, D., Bardin, J.C., Barends, R., Biswas, R., Boixo, S., Brandao, F.G., Buell, D.A. and Burkett, B., 2019. Quantum supremacy using a programmable superconducting processor. *Nature*, 574(7779), pp. 505–510.

Bennett, C.H. and Brassard, G., 2014. Quantum cryptography: Public key distribution and coin tossing. *Theoretical Computer Science*, 560, pp. 7–11.

Bernhardt, C., 2019. *Quantum computing for everyone*. Mit Press.

Bouwmeester, D., Pan, J.W., Mattle, K., Eibl, M., Weinfurter, H. and Zeilinger, A., 1997. Experimental quantum teleportation. *Nature*, 390(6660), pp. 575–579.

Bozkurt, A., Zhao, H., Joshi, C., LeDuc, H.G., Day, P.K. and Mirhosseini, M., 2023. A quantum electromechanical interface for long-lived phonons. *Nature Physics*, pp. 1–7.

Brewer, E.A., 2000, July. Towards robust distributed systems. In PODC (Vol. 7, No. 10.1145, pp. 343477–343502).

Broadbent, A. and Tapp, A., 2007. Information-theoretic security without an honest majority. In Advances in Cryptology–ASIACRYPT 2007: 13th International Conference on the Theory and Application of Cryptology and Information Security, Kuching, Malaysia, December 2–6, 2007. Proceedings 13 (pp. 410–426). Springer Berlin Heidelberg.

Cerezo, M., Verdon, G., Huang, H.Y., Cincio, L. and Coles, P.J., 2022. Challenges and opportunities in quantum machine learning. *Nature Computational Science*, 2(9), pp. 567–576.

Chanelière, T., Matsukevich, D.N., Jenkins, S.D., Lan, S.Y., Kennedy, T.A.B. and Kuzmich, A., 2005. Storage and retrieval of single photons transmitted between remote quantum memories. *Nature*, 438(7069), pp. 833–836.

Dahlberg, A., Skrzypczyk, M., Coopmans, T., Wubben, L., Rozpędek, F., Pompili, M., Stolk, A., Pawełczak, P., Knegjens, R., de Oliveira Filho, J. and Hanson, R., 2019. A link layer protocol for quantum networks. In Proceedings of the ACM Special Interest Group on Data Communication (pp. 159–173).

Deng, Y.H., Gu, Y.C., Liu, H.L., Gong, S.Q., Su, H., Zhang, Z.J., Tang, H.Y., Jia, M.H., Xu, J.M., Chen, M.C. and Zhong, H.S., 2023. Gaussian boson sampling with pseudo-photon-number resolving detectors and quantum computational advantage. *Physical Review Letters*, 131, p. 150601.

Deutsch, D., 1985. Quantum theory, the Church–Turing principle and the universal quantum computer. *Proceedings of the Royal Society of London. Series A, Mathematical and Physical Sciences*, 400(1818), pp. 97–117.

Dolev, S., Pitowsky, I. and Tamir, B., 2006. A quantum secret ballot. arXiv preprint quant-ph/0602087.

Duan, L.M., Lukin, M.D., Cirac, J.I. and Zoller, P., 2001. Long-distance quantum communication with atomic ensembles and linear optics. *Nature*, 414(6862), pp. 413–418.

Fedorov, A.K., Kiktenko, E.O. and Lvovsky, A.I., 2018. Quantum computers put blockchain security at risk. *Nature* 563, pp. 465–467.

Fischer, M.J., Lynch, N.A. and Paterson, M.S., 1985. Impossibility of distributed consensus with one faulty process. *Journal of the ACM*, 32(2), pp. 374–382.

Gyongyosi, L. and Imre, S., 2022. Advances in the quantum Internet. *Communications of the ACM*, 65(8), pp. 52–63.

Helm, L.K., 2008, August. Quantum distributed consensus. In PODC (p. 445).

Hermans, S.L.N., Pompili, M., Beukers, H.K.C., Baier, S., Borregaard, J. and Hanson, R., 2022. Qubit teleportation between non-neighbouring nodes in a quantum network. *Nature*, 605(7911), pp. 663–668.

Huang, W., Wen, Q.Y., Liu, B., Su, Q., Qin, S.J. and Gao, F., 2014. Quantum anonymous ranking. *Physical Review A*, 89(3), p. 032325.

Illiano, J., Caleffi, M., Manzalini, A. and Cacciapuoti, A.S., 2022. Quantum Internet protocol stack: A comprehensive survey. *Computer Networks*, 213, p. 109092.

Jafferis, D., Zlokapa, A., Lykken, J.D., Kolchmeyer, D.K., Davis, S.I., Lauk, N., Neven, H. and Spiropulu, M., 2022. Traversable wormhole dynamics on a quantum processor. *Nature*, 612(7938), pp. 51–55.

Julsgaard, B., Sherson, J., Cirac, J.I., Fiurášek, J. and Polzik, E.S., 2004. Experimental demonstration of quantum memory for light. *Nature*, 432(7016), pp. 482–486.

Kiktenko, E.O., Pozhar, N.O., Anufriev, M.N., Trushechkin, A.S., Yunusov, R.R., Kurochkin, Y.V., Lvovsky, A.I. and Fedorov, A.K., 2018. Quantum-secured blockchain. *Quantum Science and Technology*, 3(3), p. 035004.

Lei, M., Fukumori, R., Rochman, J., Zhu, B., Endres, M., Choi, J. and Faraon, A., 2023. Many-body cavity quantum electrodynamics with driven inhomogeneous emitters. *Nature*, pp. 1–6.

Li, H., Meng, X.Z., Lin, L.H., Wang, F., Yao, Y., Wang, X.P., Wang, B., Zhang, H.Y., Hou, H.X., Ma, H.J. and Zhang Z., 2023. A High-Security Communication System with Quantum Identifier Routing and Addressing in the Network Layer. Chinese Patent No. CN116527248A.

Liu, Y., Zhang, W.J., Jiang, C., Chen, J.P., Zhang, C., Pan, W.X., Ma, D., Dong, H., Xiong, J.M., Zhang, C.J. and Li, H., 2023. Experimental twin-field quantum key distribution over 1000 km fiber distance. *Physical Review Letters*, 130(21), p. 210801.

Lu, C.Y., Cao, Y., Peng, C.Z. and Pan, J.W., 2022. Micius quantum experiments in space. *Reviews of Modern Physics*, 94(3), p. 035001.

Monroe, C., Leibfried, D., King, B.E., Meekhof, D.M., Itano, W.M. and Wineland, D.J., 1997. Simplified quantum logic with trapped ions. *Physical Review A*, 55(4), p. R2489.

Postler, L., Heuβen, S., Pogorelov, I., Rispler, M., Feldker, T., Meth, M., Marciniak, C. D., Stricker, R., Ringbauer, M., Blatt, R. and Schindler, P., 2022. Demonstration of fault-tolerant universal quantum gate operations. *Nature*, 605(7911), pp. 675–680.

Shor, P.W., 1994, November. Algorithms for quantum computation: Discrete logarithms and factoring. In Proceedings 35th Annual Symposium on Foundations of Computer Science (pp. 124–134). IEEE.

Singh, A., Dev, K., Siljak, H., Joshi, H.D. and Magarini, M., 2021. Quantum Internet – applications, functionalities, enabling technologies, challenges, and research directions. *IEEE Communications Surveys & Tutorials*, 23(4), pp. 2218–2247.

Singh, K., Anand, S., Pocklington, A., Kemp, J.T. and Bernien, H., 2022. Dual-element, two-dimensional atom array with continuous-mode operation. *Physical Review X*, 12(1), p. 011040.

Swan, M., Santos, R. and Witte, F., 2020. Quantum computing. In IEEE Internet Computing, PP(99):1-1.

Tysowski, P.K., Ling, X., Lütkenhaus, N. and Mosca, M., 2018. The engineering of a scalable multi-site communications system utilizing quantum key distribution (QKD). *Quantum Science and Technology*, 3(2), p. 024001.

Wang, Q., Yu, C., Gao, F., Qi, H. and Wen, Q., 2016. Self-tallying quantum anonymous voting. *Physical Review A*, 94(2), p. 022333.

Wehner, S., Elkouss, D. and Hanson, R., 2018. Quantum Internet: A vision for the road ahead. *Science*, 362(6412), p. eaam9288.

Wei, S.H., Jing, B., Zhang, X.Y., Liao, J.Y., Yuan, C.Z., Fan, B.Y., Lyu, C., Zhou, D.L., Wang, Y., Deng, G.W. and Song, H.Z., 2022. Towards real-world quantum networks: A review. *Laser & Photonics Reviews*, 16(3), p. 2100219.

Wilde, M.M., 2011. From classical to quantum Shannon theory. arXiv preprint arXiv:1106.1445.

Yin, J., Ren, J.G., Lu, H., Cao, Y., Yong, H.L., Wu, Y.P., Liu, C., Liao, S.K., Zhou, F., Jiang, Y. and Cai, X.D., 2012. Quantum teleportation and entanglement distribution over 100-kilometre free-space channels. *Nature*, 488(7410), pp. 185–188.

Zhong, H.S., Wang, H., Deng, Y.H., Chen, M.C., Peng, L.C., Luo, Y.H., Qin, J., Wu, D., Ding, X., Hu, Y. and Hu, P., 2020. Quantum computational advantage using photons. *Science*, 370(6523), pp. 1460–1463.

9

Practical Application of Large-Scale Blockchain

This chapter provides an introduction to the practical application of large-scale consortium blockchains. It covers various aspects of developing a consortium blockchain network, including constructing an optimized network topology for distributed nodes, deploying a Peer-to-Peer (P2P) broadcast protocol, establishing a necessary blockchain infrastructure, and detecting smart contracts. It also briefly introduces the Solidity programming language, which is utilized for smart contract development. By studying these materials, readers will acquire the knowledge necessary to construct robust and secure consortium blockchain networks, develop proficiency in establishing efficient consortium blockchain infrastructure, and write smart contracts that have undergone rigorous security testing.

9.1 Construction of Network Topology

This section commences at the physical layer, delving into the configuration and testing of the network topology for consortium blockchain nodes.

Here, we will elucidate the utilization of Docker (Merkel 2014, p. 2; Boettiger 2015, pp.71–79) and Weave (Weaveworks n.d.) tools to construct the network topology, as depicted in Figure 9.1, across four servers. On server 0, there are four network nodes labeled 00, 01, 02, and 03, while the other three servers feature identical node configurations. The figure showcases the connections between nodes through lines, with green lines representing intra-server connections and blue lines representing inter-server connections.

To facilitate the introduction, we will assume the following for convenience: the IP addresses of the four servers, denoted as 0, 1, 2, and 3, are 172.111.1.159, 172.111.1.160, 172.111.1.161, and 172.111.1.162, respectively. Additionally, it is assumed that all servers are running the Ubuntu 16.04 64-bit operating system. Readers can easily follow the provided steps for their computer operations.

Principles and Applications of Blockchain Systems: How to Overcome the CAP Trilemma in Consortium Blockchain, First Edition. Hui Li and Han Wang.

Published 2025 by John Wiley & Sons, Inc.

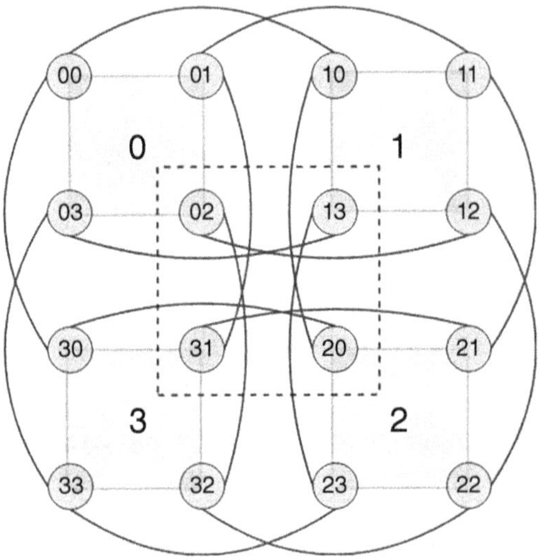

Figure 9.1 The network topology of consortium blockchain nodes.

Step 1: Allocate an address to each node and partition the network segment as depicted in Figures 9.2, 9.3, and Table 9.1.

Step 2: Each server hosts four Docker containers. Let us focus on the server with the IP address 172.111.1.159:

```
docker run -itd -name fut159-1 ubuntu /bin/bash
docker run -itd -name fut159-2 ubuntu /bin/bash
docker run -itd -name fut159-3 ubuntu /bin/bash
docker run -itd -name fut159-4 ubuntu /bin/bash
```

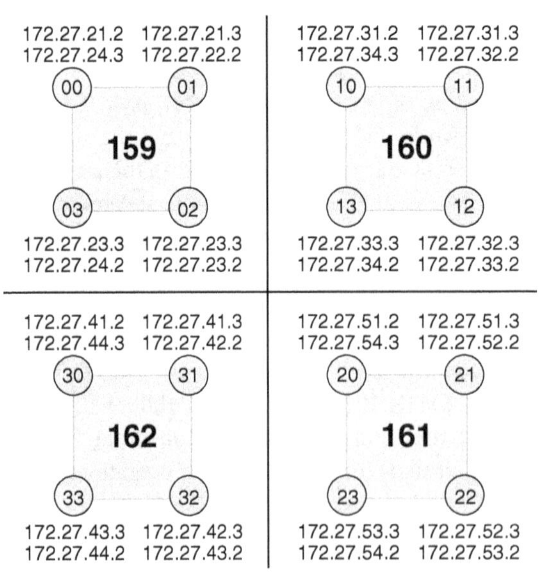

Figure 9.2 Configuration of internal addresses for four hosts.

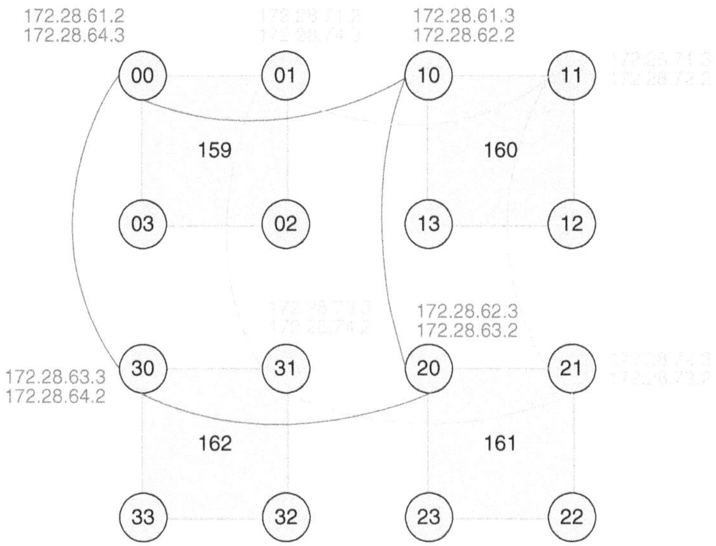

Figure 9.3 Configuration of cross-host addresses.

Likewise, on the 172.111.1.160 server, run four Docker containers named fut160-1, fut160-2, fut160-3, and fut160-4.

On the 172.111.1.161 server, run four Docker containers named fut161-1, fut161-2, fut161-3, and fut161-4.

On the 172.111.1.162 server, run four Docker containers named fut162-1, fut162-2, fut162-3, and fut162-4.

Step 3: Utilize the "weave" networking tool to establish connectivity between containers across different hosts. Let us take the 172.11.1.159 server as an example to perform the weave interworking operation:

```
weave connect 172.111.1.160
weave connect 172.111.1.161
weave connect 172.111.1.162
```

Similarly, perform weave interworking on the other three servers.

After completing the weave interworking, proceed with configuring the IP for each server. Let us use the operation on the 172.111.1.159 server as an example. Start by querying the container ID on the server using the following command:

```
docker ps
```

Table 9.1 Address configuration of each node on four servers.

Server	Docker	IP	Server	Docker	IP
159	1	172.27.21.2	161	1	172.27.51.2
		172.27.24.3			172.27.54.3
		172.28.61.2			172.28.62.3
		172.28.64.3			172.28.63.2
	2	172.27.21.3		2	172.27.51.3
		172.27.22.2			172.27.52.2
		172.28.71.2			172.28.72.3
		172.28.74.3			172.28.73.2
	3	172.27.22.3		3	172.27.52.3
		172.27.23.2			172.27.53.2
		172.28.81.2			172.28.82.3
		172.28.84.3			172.28.83.2
	4	172.27.23.3		4	172.27.53.3
		172.27.24.2			172.27.54.2
		172.28.91.2			172.28.92.3
		172.28.94.3			172.28.93.2
160	1	172.27.31.2	162	1	172.27.41.2
		172.27.34.3			172.27.44.3
		172.28.61.3			172.28.63.3
		172.28.62.2			172.28.64.2
	2	172.21.31.3		2	172.27.41.3
		172.27.32.2			172.27.42.2
		172.28.71.3			172.28.73.3
		172.28.72.2			172.28.74.2
	3	172.27.32.3		3	172.27.42.3
		172.27.33.2			172.27.43.2
		172.28.81.3			172.28.83.3
		172.28.82.2			172.28.84.2
	4	172.27.33.3		4	172.27.43.3
		172.27.34.2			172.27.44.2
		172.28.91.3			172.28.93.3
		172.28.92.2			172.28.94.2

CONTAINER ID	IMAGE	COMMAND	CREATED	STATUS	PORTS	NAMES
84af9d238c9e	forppov:1.0	"/bin/bash"	6 minutes ago	Up 6 minutes		fut159-4
9b0fc94a87d0	forppov:1.0	"/bin/bash"	6 minutes ago	Up 6 minutes		fut159-3
87b83fd51201	forppov:1.0	"/bin/bash"	6 minutes ago	Up 6 minutes		fut159-2
0b344833ed5a	forppov:1.0	"/bin/bash"	6 minutes ago	Up 6 minutes		fut159-1

Figure 9.4 Result of querying Docker id.

After obtaining the CONTAINER ID of each container on the server as depicted in Figure 9.4, configure the server's IP as follows:

```
weave attach 172.27.21.2/24 0b344833ed5a
weave attach 172.27.24.3/24 0b344833ed5a
weave attach 172.28.61.2/24 0b344833ed5a
weave attach 172.28.64.3/24 0b344833ed5a
weave attach 172.27.21.3/24 87b83fd51201
weave attach 172.27.22.2/24 87b83fd51201
weave attach 172.28.71.2/24 87b83fd51201
weave attach 172.28.74.3/24 87b83fd51281
weave attach 172.27.22.3/24 9b0fc94a87d0
weave attach 172.27.23.2/24 9b0fc94a87d0
weave attach 172.28.81.2/24 9b0fc94a87d0
weave attach 172.28.84.3/24 9b0fc94a87d0
weave attach 172.27.23.3/24 84af9d238c9e
weave attach 172.27.24.2/24 84af9d238c9e
weave attach 172.28.91.2/24 84af9d238c9e
weave attach 172.28.94.3/24 84af9d238c9e
```

The remaining three servers are configured in a similar manner.

Once the IP addresses for all four servers are configured, a ping connectivity test is conducted, as depicted in Figure 9.5. During the test, it is observed that hosts within the same network segment can be successfully pinged, as well as hosts across different hosts within the same network segment. However, pinging hosts in different network segments does not yield successful results.

Step 4: To enable cross-segment communication, the Open Shortest Path First (OSPF) (Moy 1998) service is enabled on each node of every server. To initiate the OSPF service, you must enable packet forwarding using the following command:

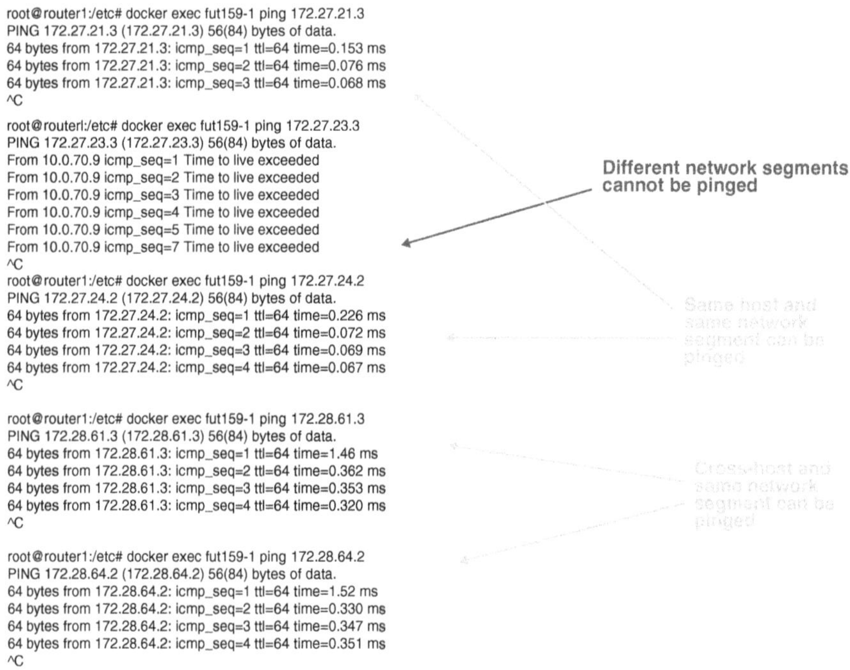

Figure 9.5 Once the configuration is complete, perform a ping connectivity test.

```
echo 1 > /proc/sys/net/ipv4/ip_forward
```

The server device can be transformed into a router capable of enabling OSPF services through the utilization of Quagga (Jakma and Lamparter 2014, pp. 42–48), an open-source routing software suite. Install Quagga, along with its default components, zebra and ospfd, by executing the following command:

```
sudo apt-get install quagga
```

To configure zebra, create a zebra.conf file at /etc/quagga by executing the following command:

```
sudo vim /etc/quagga/zebra.conf
```

In the zebra.conf file, include the following four sentences, ensuring that the hostname is unique for each server:

```
hostname RouterA
password zebra
enable password zebra
log stdout
```

Once the zebra configuration is finalized, utilize the following command to launch zebra in the foreground. This allows for monitoring the running state of zebra, ensuring its smooth operation. To run zebra in the background, utilize the -d parameter.

```
sudo zebra
```

If encountering the error message "ZEBRA: Can't create pid lock file /run/quagga/zebra.pid (No such file or directory), exiting," you can resolve it by executing the following command. Afterward, restart zebra, and you will see the message "ZEBRA: Zebra 1.2.4 starting: vty@2601."

```
sudo mkdir /run/quagga/
sudo chmod 777 /run/quagga/
```

Lastly, configure ospfd by creating a new ospfd.conf configuration file at /etc/quagga using the following command:

```
sudo vim /etc/quagga/ospfd.conf
```

In the ospfd.conf file, include the following configuration:

```
hostname RouterA
password zebra
enable password zebra
router ospf
ospf router-id 192.168.2.10
network 192.168.1.0/24 area 0
network 192.168.2.0/24 area 0
debug ospf event
log stdout
```

Once the ospfd configuration is finalized, initiate ospfd in the foreground by executing the following command:

```
sudo ospfd
```

The message "OSPF: OSPFd 1.2.4 starting: vty@2604" confirms the successful startup of OSPF. At this stage, the physical network topology of the consortium blockchain nodes is complete.

9.2 P2P Broadcast Protocol

The P2P broadcast protocol described in this section is the Matching-Gossip protocol, adapting to the hypercube-based physical topology. You can find the source code in https://github.com/MIN-Group/matching-gossip.git. This section details the deployment of the Matching-Gossip protocol to offer readers greater insights into how it works and is used in the network layer of consortium blockchains.

9.2.1 Environment Setup

This section provides guidance on preparing the deployment environment. A step-by-step process is outlined for readers to reproducibly implement the environment. Those well-versed in Linux systems may optionally consider manual environment construction as in Section 9.2.1.1. It is advised that most readers leverage the preconfigured Docker container in Section 9.2.1.2 to efficiently establish the necessary surroundings.

9.2.1.1 Manual Environment Setup

The platform used is the Ubuntu 18.04 system. First, install necessary tools, the Golang language environment, and Python libraries. Refer to the third paragraph of the provided Dockerfile for detailed commands to "Installing various tools," as shown below. Note that root privileges are required for these commands; non-root users may need to prefix each with "sudo."

```
apt-get update && apt-get upgrade && wget https://golang.
google.cn/dl/go1.21.3.linux-amd64.tar.gz && tar -C /usr/
local -xzf go1.21.3.linux-amd64.tar.gz && apt-get -y
install expect && apt-get -y install python3-pip && pip3
install -i https://pypi.tuna.tsinghua.edu.cn/simple flask
```

Next, set the environment variables. Open the /etc/profile file using an editor like Vim. Press "i" to enter insert mode and add the variables as shown in Figure 9.6. Note that the MASTER and SLAVE values must be replaced with your own master and slave server IP addresses. Replace WORKDIR with the absolute

Figure 9.6 Diagram of environment variable settings.

path to run.sh in the downloaded source code. Also replace USER and PASSWD with your SSH username and password for server login.

```
vim /etc/profile
```

Then run the topology script to generate the configuration files. As shown below, execute the command from the top-level source directory.

```
mkdir config && rm -rf mgossip/config && rm -rf gossip/
config && python3 topology.py && cp -r config mgossip && cp
-r config gossip
```

This completes manual construction of the deployment environment.

9.2.1.2 Using Docker Containers for Simplified Setup

It should be noted that manually building the environment in the previous section can introduce various issues due to differences in platforms, versions, and file system variations between readers. To address this, we provide pre-configured Docker containers that can easily be deployed. Readers simply need to pull the pre-packaged container image from the cloud and launch it.

First, install Docker. The command is as follows.

```
sudo apt-get install docker.io
```

Then pull the Docker container image from the cloud. This may take some time.

```
sudo docker pull mingroup/mgossip:v1.0
```

Start two containers functioning as the master and slave servers.

```
sudo docker run -it -name mgossip-master mingroup/mgossip:
v1.0
sudo docker run -it -name mgossip-slave mingroup/mgossip:
v1.0
```

The two commands will start two containers and provide access via the Command Line Interface (CLI). You may need to modify environment variables, as Docker assigns default IP addresses starting from 172.17.0.2. For these containers, the master's IP is 172.17.0.2 and slave is 172.17.0.3. If additional containers exist, MASTER and SLAVE variables should match the actual IPs. To enable SSH on the slave, enter the following command in its CLI.

```
service ssh restart
```

To ensure smooth execution of the protocol, the master server must be able to access the slave server via SSH. Running the following command on the master server will cache the slave's SSH key. This prevents the master from asking to confirm the key during subsequent evaluations over SSH. Enter "yes" when prompted on the command line.

```
cd $WORKDIR && scp root@$SLAVE:/Gossip/slave.py slave.py
```

9.2.2 Operation and Evaluation

Regardless of the method used to set up the environment, at this stage, the reader needs to open two terminals – one for the master server and one for the slave server. This allows the subsequent steps to be carried out.

In terms of running evaluations, the reader has two options.

The first one is to run the run.sh script to perform a single evaluation. You may need to use a command to grant executable permission to run.sh beforehand.

```
sudo chmod 777 run.sh
```

Next, the run.sh can be executed to run evaluations with different configurations by modifying command line parameters. For example, a Matching-Gossip evaluation on a two-dimensional hypercube topology. The relevant commands below run on the master and slave servers. Each run.sh command contains ten parameters: Gossip protocol version, config file address, first node number, last node number, server flag, start available port number, end available port number, GossipNodes, limitTime, and number of occupied ports. The protocol version "Gossip" indicates a classic Gossip evaluation, while "MGossip" is for Matching-Gossip. The first node number i and last node number j mean the server will run nodes i to j. These nodes read the config sequentially. The server flag denotes the role – 1 for master, 0 for slave. Sufficient available ports are required to avoid errors from occupied ports. Additional run.sh command details can be found in the readme.md file.

```
bash run.sh mgossip config/hybercube-2.ini 1 2 1 30000
30500 2 200000000 2
bash run.sh mgossip config/hybercube-2.ini 3 4 0 30000
30500 2 200000000 2
```

We also provide a way to run evaluations in batches. Readers first need to run the slave.py program on the slave server. Then, they should modify parameters in master.py as needed, such as the number of repeated runs for a single evaluation (the default is 20). After making changes, they run the master.py program.

No matter which way readers run the evaluation, they will obtain the original metric data after each evaluation run. As shown in Figure 9.7, the first three lines

```
node convergence rate: 1.00
convergence time: 1064069719 ns
total packet the network send: 575
infected nodes every gossip epoch: [3, 1]
convergence_rate_every_epoch: [0.75, 1.0]
```

Figure 9.7 Original metric data diagram.

provide the convergence rate, convergence time, and network load for a single evaluation, respectively.

After repeated evaluations, the reader can run clean_data.py to sort through the previous data. Run the following command, where the data_dir command line parameter specifies the directory containing the original metric data. From here, the reader can analyze the output data.

```
python3 clean_data.py -data_dir data
```

This section provides a guide to evaluation to help readers understand the Matching-Gossip protocol. By introducing the environment setup, evaluation operation and process, we aim to reduce the difficulty for readers in implementing evaluations.

9.3 Solidity Language

In the preceding section, we established the physical topology of the consortium blockchain, paving the way for the subsequent blockchain development. Similar to traditional computing systems, developers face challenges when attempting to write executable machine code directly. Hence, a high-level programming language is indispensable as a development tool to enhance efficiency in the development process.

Solidity is a robust and object-oriented high-level language used for implementing smart contracts. During the design phase, Solidity syntax closely resembles JavaScript, enabling developers to swiftly adapt to it. While Solidity is a prominent choice, there are other languages specifically tailored for smart contracts, including Serpent, Vyper, Mutan, and more. Certain smart contract platforms, such as Hyperledger Fabric (Androulaki et al. 2018, pp. 1–15), offer the flexibility to write smart contracts in languages like Golang. However, Solidity stands out as a mature and widely adopted language for smart contracts, making it the primary focus of this section.

Unlike conventional programming languages, Solidity was initially developed specifically for writing smart contracts on the Ethereum platform. As a result, certain aspects of its syntax are intricately linked to the functionality of Ethereum. Consequently, Solidity introduces specialized types (such as address, event, etc.) and unique keywords (such as payable, now, etc.) to accommodate the requirements of Ethereum smart contracts. Furthermore, Solidity necessitates incorporating the characteristics of Ethereum smart contracts to define the specific storage locations of variables during the coding process. These distinct features will be explored in greater detail in subsequent sections. For an encompassing comprehension of the Solidity language, we recommend the following resources:

Github: https://github.com/ethereum/solidity
Online compiler: http://remix.ethereum.org/
Documentation: https://docs.soliditylang.org/en/v0.8.23/

9.3.1 Getting Started Example

This section will elucidate the fundamental structure of Solidity through a Hello World program. Readers can follow the steps outlined below to commence their journey with Solidity.

9.3.1.1 Open the Online Compiler

Remix (http://remix.ethereum.org/) serves as the official online compiler for Ethereum's Solidity and Vyper languages. It's important to note that the interface of Remix may undergo changes due to regular version updates. As of the time of writing, the current version is depicted in Figure 9.8.

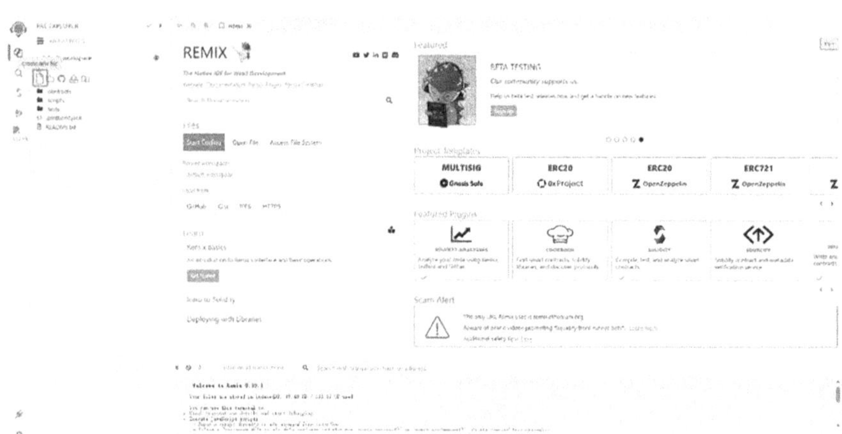

Figure 9.8 Remix online compiler.

9.3.1.2 Solidity Program

Execute the "Create New File" command to generate a fresh contract source file named HelloWorld.sol. Then, input the provided code into the editor that appears for the newly created file.

```
pragma solidity 0.6.0;

contract HelloWorld {

    string public myString;
    uint public myNumber;

    constructor() public {
 myString = "Hello, World!";
    }

    function plus(uint a, uint b) public {
        myNumber = a + b;
    }
}
```

At the beginning of this contract, the Solidity language version is specified to inform the compiler about the intended language compatibility. Additionally, you have the option to define a version range for Solidity, import additional .sol files, and perform other relevant configurations.

Within the specific contract definition, the contract name is initially declared as HelloWorld, similar to the concept of a class in object-oriented programming languages. In the body of the contract, two storage variables are defined: myString, a string variable, and myNumber, an integer variable. The constructor, denoted as constructor(), is responsible for initializing the contract. In this case, when the contract is deployed, the value "Hello, World!" will be assigned to myString. Furthermore, the plus function adds the two arguments, a and b, and assigns the result to myNumber.

Considering space limitations, only a brief overview of the example contract is provided here. The syntax is further covered in the rest of the chapter, or you can refer to the documentation for detailed information.

9.3.1.3 Compile

Once you have entered the code, add the SOLIDITY COMPILE icon in the Plugin manager, which is the Solidity compiler, and switch to the compilation interface. Following that, proceed to click on "Compile HelloWorld. sol" in the editor to initiate the contract compilation.

Figure 9.9 Remix online contract compilation.

Figure 9.10 The environment used for deploying contracts.

During this step, the editor will perform a formal check and compile the Solidity source code into EVM Bytecode. This EVM Bytecode can be deployed to the Ethereum blockchain or any other smart contract platform with an EVM environment. Additionally, the compilation process generates the corresponding Ethereum virtual machine bytecode and Application Binary Interface (ABI). To view these details, simply click on "Compilation Details" located in the bottom-left corner of the interface, as depicted in Figure 9.9.

9.3.1.4 Deploy

After the compilation process, locate the DEPLOY & RUN TRANSACTIONS icon on the left side of the interface to proceed with testing the deployment of the contract, as illustrated in Figure 9.10.

In Figure 9.10, the test environment "Remix VM (Merge)" represents an EVM environment simulated using JavaScript within the browser. To deploy the compiled HelloWorld contract to the simulation environment, simply click on the Deploy button.

9.3.1.5 Test

Once the deployment is finished, click on the arrow symbol situated to the left of the HelloWorld contract in Deployed Contracts within the DEPLOY & RUN TRANSACTIONS interface. This will expand the contract's functions, allowing you to conduct invoking tests.

As depicted in Figure 9.11, click the variables myNumber and myString individually to observe the current state of the contract. Presently, myNumber holds the value 0, while myString is assigned the value "Hello World." The aforementioned functions are, in fact, two read-only methods pertaining to the contract's state. When the variables are declared as public in the Solidity source file, the compiler automatically generates default read-only functions for both variables during the compilation phase.

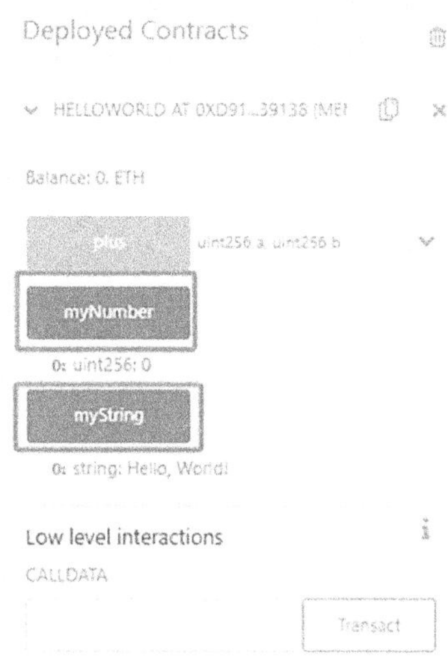

Figure 9.11 Contract function testing 1.

In Figure 9.12, the plus function is invoked. Input the parameters a and b for the plus function as "1" and "2," respectively. Proceed to click on the plus button to execute the function invoking. Upon the successful completion of the transaction, verify the updated value of myNumber. You will observe that myNumber has been modified to reflect the sum of a and b.

Remix's online Ethereum virtual machine environment simulates the transaction information invoked to the smart contract and presents it in the console. Readers can access the transaction details of a specific transaction, which include the origin address, contract address, Gas consumption value, contract functions, and parameters. This allows readers to examine and analyze various aspects of the transaction in detail.

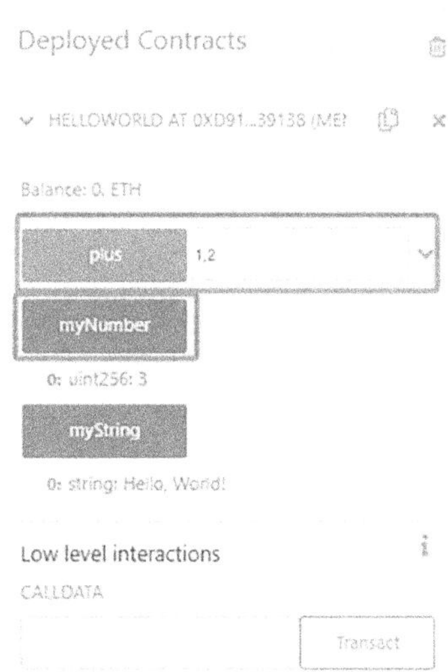

Figure 9.12 Contract function testing 2.

Note: The Remix online compiler provides the capability to simulate not only the Ethereum virtual machine in the browser but also to interface with specific Ethereum blockchain nodes. In this section, the presentation and experiments are conducted within the virtual Ethereum virtual machine environment, with a focus on the syntax, compilation, and execution of smart contracts.

9.3.2 Basic Syntax

This section presents the fundamental syntax in Solidity as outlined below.

9.3.2.1 Common Types

a) **Booleans**

It is declared with *bool* and, as in traditional programming languages, can be either true or false.

b) **Integers**

The *int* keyword is used to declare signed integer variables, while the *uint* keyword is used for unsigned integer variables. When declaring an integer variable, it is possible to specify the number of bits it occupies. For instance, *int*8 represents an 8-bit signed integer variable, and the number of bits can range from 8, 16, all the way up to 256. If the number of bits is not specified, the compiler defaults to the maximum number of bits during compilation, resulting in *int* being compiled as *int*256. Developers need to pay attention to the number of bits in an integer as it can introduce potential vulnerabilities related to integer overflow.

c) **Address**

The *address* keyword is used for declaration and represents the Ethereum account's address type, which has the same length as the Ethereum account. This type stores a 20-byte value. However, an address type variable also includes multiple member variables, enabling operations such as retrieving account balances, transferring funds between accounts, and invoking functions through these member variables. The specifics are outlined below.

balance: Retrieve the balance of a specific address. Usage: *<address > . balance* (*uint*256).

transfer: Initiate a transfer of funds to the specified address. If the transfer fails, an exception is thrown. Usage: *<address > . transfer*(*uint*256 *amount*).

send: Send funds to the designated address. If the send operation fails, it returns false. Usage: *<address > . send*(*uint*256 *amount*).

call/callcode/delegatecall: Issue contract invoke messages to the specified address. Usage:*<address > . call*(...).

d) **Fixed-Size Byte Arrays**
It is declared by *byte + array length*, such as *byte*1, *byte*2, ..., *byte*32.

e) **Dynamically Sized Byte Arrays**
It is declared by *bytes* or *string*.

f) **Arrays**
It is declared by *type* + [ ]. And it can be manipulated using the push method to add elements or by accessing the length property to determine the size of the array.

g) **Mappings**
It is declared by *mapping(key type = > value type)*. However, it is important to note that key types cannot be mappings, dynamically sized arrays, contracts, enums, or structs. In the Ethereum state tree, where the mapping is stored, the actual value of the key is not stored directly. Instead, the keccak256 hash of the key is stored, allowing for efficient querying of the corresponding value while reducing storage requirements. Unlike arrays, mappings do not have a length property since they are not indexed sequentially.

h) **Structs**
Primitive variables can be combined into a single structure using the *struct* keyword. When declaring a variable, you can specify its visibility as either public or private. This determines whether the variable can be accessed by external calls to the contract. Additionally, you have the option to specify the storage location of the variable as either storage or memory. This determines whether the variable is stored in the contract's storage or in memory during execution. It is important to note that different storage locations for the same variable will result in different Gas costs. Typically, each variable has a default location, and the compiler will prompt the developer to change it if necessary.

Presented below is a concrete example for better illustration. To proceed, it is recommended to follow the steps outlined in Section 9.2.1 to access the Remix online compiler. Once the compiler is accessible, enter the provided code:

```
pragma solidity 0.6.0;
contract Test1 {
 struct myStruct {
   bool myBool;
   uint myUint;
   address myAddress;
   string myString;
 }
 myStruct[] public myArray;
 mapping(uint => string) public myMapping;
 constructor() public {
```

```
    myStruct memory myElement = myStruct(true, 1, msg.
sender, "Hello");
    myArray.push(myElement);
    myMapping[10086]="World";
  }
}
```

Within the aforementioned smart contract, several elements are declared, including a struct, an array of structs, and an integer-to-string mapping. These variables are declared as public to facilitate easy testing and viewing of their values. In the constructor function of the smart contract, various operations are performed sequentially, such as initializing array elements, adding array elements, and adding mapping elements.

Deploy the contract and then test the *myArray* and *myMapping* functions to retrieve the respective values of the array and mapping following the execution of the constructor.

9.3.2.2 Function Types

In Solidity, functions are declared as follows:

```
function (<parameter types>) {public|private|internal|
external}
[pure|constant|view|payable] [returns()]
```

The function type descriptions enclosed in square brackets [] are optional. Table 9.2 presents the various function types available in Solidity.

The aforementioned design of function types aims to enhance the security of smart contract development while considering development efficiency. Readers can write their own contract functions and tests.

9.3.2.3 Special Variables

The Ethereum virtual machine offers opcodes that allow access to certain blockchain information. In Solidity, corresponding special variables and functions are also predefined. Here are some notable ones:

block. blockhash(blockNumber): Retrieve the hash of a specific block, with nearly 256 block hashes available.

block. coinbase: Return the address of the miner for the block in which the contract is being executed.

block. difficulty: Provide the mining difficulty of the block in which the contract is being executed.

block. gaslimit: Return the Gas limit of the block in which the contract is being executed.

Table 9.2 Function types in Solidity.

Type	Description
Public	It is accessible both internally and externally to the contract. It can be invoked by individuals or contracts outside the contract.
Private	It is only visible within the contract itself. Other contracts or external entities cannot access or invoke private functions.
Internal	It is visible to the internals, specifically within the current Solidity source file. Other contracts in the same source file can access internal functions.
External	It is visible to the outside but can only be accessed through the "contract. function" syntax. External functions cannot be invoked internally within the contract.
Pure	Functions with this modifier do not have access to read or modify the contract's state.
Constant	Similar to pure functions, constant functions do not allow state modifications.
View	Like constant functions, view functions are read-only and do not modify the contract's state.
Payable	It allows functions to receive Ether. Note that when invoking a contract, attempting to transfer Ether to a function without the "payable" modifier will result in failure.

block. number: Provide the height or number of the block at which the contract is being executed.

block. timestamp: Return the timestamp of the block at which the contract is being executed.

gasleft(): Retrieve the remaining Gas available for the contract to execute, calculated as gasLimit minus the current gasUsed.

msg. data: Represent the calldata of the contract message. Multiple invokings or messages can occur within a transaction.

msg. gas: Provide the remaining available Gas for the contract message.

msg. sender: Represent the sender of the contract message.

msg. sig: Represent the first four bytes of the calldata, serving as the function identifier. Functions with the same name and argument types will have the same identifier after compilation.

msg. value: Represent the value in wei of the Ether sent with the contract message.

now: Equivalent to *block. timestamp*, provide the current timestamp.

tx. gasprice: Indicate the Gas price of the contract transaction.

tx. origin: Represent the origin of the contract transaction.

this: Refer to the current contract and can be explicitly converted to an address type.

selfdestruct(*address*): Delete the contract code and transfer the remaining balance to a specified address.

suicide(*address*): Similar to *selfdestruct*(), delete the contract code and transfer the remaining balance to a specified address.

Readers can conduct experiments with the return values of individual variables using the Remix compiler. In addition to the commonly used special variables mentioned earlier, there are several other special variables and functions available, including time units, ABI encoding, cryptographic functions, and more. It is recommended to consult the documentation for further information and guidance on utilizing these features when necessary.

9.3.2.4 Event Logs

In Ethereum, the contract's state data is stored in the state tree, and the execution results are also written to the state. However, relying solely on the state tree for state recording can be inefficient when the upper application needs to access specific contract states during its execution (e.g., the ID of a purchased product). It would require comparing previous state changes or traversing the incremental array of state records, which can be costly. To address this, Ethereum uses event logs for recording. Unlike the state tree, the event tree is a unidirectional output that cannot be read by the contract itself. However, it provides an efficient means for the upper application to query and observe the operation and status of the contract. Events allow the upper application to track the occurrence and content of specific actions within a contract. This enables a concise and low-consumption way for the upper application to observe contract activities. To demonstrate this, readers can follow the steps outlined in Section 9.2.1 to access the Remix online compiler and input the provided contract code:

```
pragma solidity 0.6.0;

contract Test2 {

 uint myUint;

 event numnberIsSet(uint);

 function set(uint num) public {
   myUint = num;
   emit numberIsSet(num);
 }
}
```

This contract code introduces a variable called *myUint* and defines an event called *numberIsSet*, which accepts an *uint* as an argument. Within the *set*() function, we *emit* the event. However, instead of writing it directly to the state tree, we write it to the receipt of the Ethereum virtual machine. During execution, the Ethereum node collects these receipts, generates a receipt tree, calculates the root of the receipt tree, and records it in the block.

When executing *set*(100) in the Remix virtual Ethereum environment, an output will be displayed on the console. The transaction receipt includes various fields, with the *logs* field containing the recorded *numberIsSet* event along with the parameter value of 100. In the underlying implementation, the *numberIsSet* event and its argument types are hash-encoded as *topic*. Similar to function signatures, events with the same name have the same *topic* value. During block processing, all transaction receipts are used to compute a Bloom filter, which is then stored as the value of *logsBloom* in the block. The Bloom filter, while unable to definitively confirm the presence of a value in a set, can effectively indicate its absence. This characteristic significantly reduces query costs for the upper application. As a result, when the upper application observes the contract, it simply needs to request the *logsBloom* value of the block from the Ethereum node. By analyzing the *logsBloom* value, the upper-level application determines whether the event of a specific contract in a block has not occurred. In case it hasn't, the application waits for the next block. If it may or may not have occurred, the upper-level application requests the existence and content of the event receipt from the node.

In summary, both the event log and the state tree serve as storage options that can be utilized by smart contracts. However, there are notable distinctions between them. The event log is unidirectional and unreadable, resulting in reduced Gas costs for its operations. On the other hand, the state and receipt are not entirely stored within the block itself. Instead, they are modified by transactions on the blockchain. The values of the tree root and bloom filter, which represent the state and receipt respectively, are recorded in the block.

9.3.2.5 Error Handling

Similar to traditional computer programs, Ethereum smart contracts may encounter exceptions or errors defined by developers during their operation. For example, a transaction may be initiated by an address that lacks the necessary permission to call a particular function. As a result, transactions within the contract's execution need to be processed. Unlike the *try – catch* mechanism found in traditional computer programs, Solidity, the programming language used for Ethereum smart contracts, does not currently provide built-in exception catching. In Ethereum smart contracts, when an exception occurs, typically all the states modified by the transaction are rolled back and rendered invalid. However, Solidity offers low-level invocation functions such as *call*, *delegatecall*, and *callcode*. These functions return *false* in the event of an exception, allowing for the state modifications made outside the subcall to remain intact, without being rolled back. In the underlying implementation of Ethereum's pre-program, the state rollback is achieved by recording the state root. In other words, when an exception occurs, Ethereum reverts to the state root prior to the execution of the transaction, and no logging is performed.

To illustrate, readers can follow the steps in Section 9.2.1 to open the Remix online compiler and enter the following contract code:

```
pragma solidity 0.6.0;

contract Test3 {

 uint public myUint;

 constructor() public {
   myUint = 10;
 }

 function set() public {
   myUint = 20;
   require(myUint<5);
   myUint = 30
 }
}
```

The mentioned contract showcases the setting of the variable *myUint* and assigns a value to it within the function to observe the variable's change. In the *set*() function, there is a requirement statement *require*(*myUint* < 5) that checks the value of *myUint*. If it is less than 5, an exception is thrown. After calling *set*(), the *myUint* variable will always have the value of 10, not 20 or 30. This characteristic of Ethereum contracts resembles the concept of atomicity in databases. It implies that during a contract call, all transactions must execute successfully, or all executions will fail. This aspect contributes to ensuring the security of users when executing the contract, particularly in scenarios involving asset swaps.

Including require, Solidity provides the following special functions for error handling:

assert(condition): If the condition parameter is false, it results in the current transaction having no effect and consuming the remaining Gas allocated to the transaction.

require(condition, [message]): If the condition parameter is false, the state change is reverted, and if a message parameter is included, an error message is generated.

revent([message]): Terminate the run and undo the state change, and if a message parameter is included, an error message is generated.

9.4 Establishment of Blockchain Infrastructure

Due the decentralization and tamper-resistance of blockchains, Decentralized Applications (DApps) built on smart contracts hold significant potential. Considering their definitions and architectures may vary, this section primarily focuses on introducing a typical development approach for DApps.

9.4.1 Establishment of a Private Blockchain

To begin with, it is necessary to establish the blockchain environment by setting up a single-node Ethereum private blockchain network. It is assumed that the reader possesses an experimental resource package. The initial step is to unpack it and place the "geth.exe" and "genesis.json" files in the same directory. Use the command line tool to navigate to the directory and execute the following command:

```
geth -datadir mydata init genesis.json
```

In this command, the *geth* command specifies the data location for the blockchain, which is set as the *mydata* folder within the directory. It also initializes the genesis block using the "genesis. json" file.

To execute the Ethereum node, input the following command:

```
geth -datadir mydata -networkid 666 -rpc -rpccorsdomain
"*" -allow-insecure-unlock console
```

Similar to the previous command, the *datadir* configuration specifies the storage location of data in the *mydata* folder. The *networkid* configuration sets the blockchain network ID as 666 to prevent conflicts with other nodes on the Internet, although readers can choose any other number as well. The *rpc* configuration enables the Remote Procedure Call (RPC) interface of the Ethereum node, allowing cross-domain calls from a browser to any address through the *rpccorsdomain* setting. It also permits unlocking accounts through HTTP. Lastly, the *console* command opens the console, which allows user input and facilitates experimentation.

In fact, the console acts as a JavaScript console connected to the nodes and includes the web3.js library. It can be utilized to query information about Ethereum nodes, such as:

```
web3.eth.blockNumber
web3.eth.getBlock('latest')
```

The two aforementioned commands retrieve the current height and content of the latest block. This section solely covers experiment-related operations, and for a comprehensive understanding of the Go-ethereum and Web3.js interface specifications, it is recommended to refer to the official documentation.

In the current node, there is no wallet address. To create a new account, execute the following command:

```
personal.newAccount("");
```

In the above command, the parameter in parentheses represents the password, which is currently set as an empty string for the convenience of subsequent experiments. Once a new account is created, a private key will be generated and saved in the data directory. The console will display the public key address of the newly created account. To confirm the account details, readers can enter the following command:

```
web3.eth.accounts
web3.eth.getBalance(web3.eth.accounts[0])
```

The aforementioned command retrieves the address and balance of the account stored in the node. From the console output, it can be observed that the balance of Ether in the new account is currently zero.

To deploy the contract, it is necessary to add balance to the account. This can be done manually by starting mining and executing the following command:

```
miner.start(); admin.sleepBlocks(1); miner.stop();
```

When executing the above commands in a single line, the geth client will perform the following actions: Start mining and await block generation; End mining, and the Coinbase address used for mining will default to the first of the local accounts, which is the new account mentioned above. During the initial mining process, the geth client will generate the Directed Acyclic Graph (DAG) required for mining, based on the machine configuration. However, in rare cases, it is possible that no blocks are mined. If this occurs, you can resolve the issue by deleting the data directory *mydata* and restarting from the *init* command. In the case of multicore CPU, it is also possible to mine more than one block due to the low mining difficulty.

Once the mining process is complete, readers can use the following command to check the block number and account balance again:

```
web3.eth blockNumber
web3.eth.getBalance(web3.eth.accounts[0])
```

At this point, the console output will indicate that the block height and the account's Ether balance (in wei) have increased, indicating that the mining process has been successful.

Please note that although the geth client has a developer mode (– – *dev* configuration), it may not provide a comprehensive understanding of transaction confirmation, mining, and other processes. It is recommended to build a private Ethereum chain that requires manual mining for a more practical understanding.

To interconnect multiple Ethereum nodes, readers can repeat the previous steps to create a new data directory and open a new node client. In the new node, use the *admin. nodeInfo. enode* command to obtain the enode identity address of the node. Then, in the original node, use the *admin. addPeer(enode)* command to connect it to the new node. Finally, monitor the status of each node using appropriate commands, which will not be elaborated upon here.

9.4.2 Deployment and Testing of Smart Contracts

Section 9.2 provides instructions on writing and testing Ethereum smart contracts within a browser environment. Section 9.3.1 demonstrates running the Golang version of the Ethereum client and establishing a test environment for a private blockchain. In this section, the focus is on deploying the smart contract to the previously created Ethereum private blockchain.

1) Open the Remix online compiler, create a new contract named Share.sol, and enter the following code:

```
pragma solidity 0.6.0;
contract Share {
  struct oneShare {
   address sender;
   string text;
  }
  oneShare[] public allShare;
  event Added(uint);

  functon NewShare(string memory something) public {
   allShare.push(oneShare(msg.sender, something));
   emit Added(allShare.length-1);
  }
  function getLength() public view returns (uint) {
   return.allShare.length;
  }
}
```

The above contract includes a struct array called *allShare*, which stores the user address and shared information. The event *Added* is triggered to output the index of the shared information. The function *NewShare* is responsible for recording information into the array and generating an event, while the function *getLength* returns the length of the array.

Once finished typing, review and compile the contract.

2) In the "Deploy & run transactions" function of the Remix compiler, select "Web3 Provider" from the Environment drop-down menu. Upon the appearance of a pop-up dialog, click on the "OK" button. As mentioned in Section 9.3.1, the default RPC port is set to 8545, thus no modification is required at this step.

   After establishing a connection with the node, it is imperative to unlock the local node's account in order to enable RPC invocation. To accomplish this, execute the following command within the node console:

```
personal.unlockAccount(eth.accounts[0], "", 3600);
```

   The aforementioned command unlocks the account for a duration of 3600 seconds using an empty string.

3) In Remix compiler, click the Deploy button to send and deploy the transaction.

   The outputs displayed in both the Remix console and the node console indicate that the transaction has been successfully sent, yet it remains in an unpackaged state. At this stage, execute the following command in the node console to examine the packaged transactions.

```
eth.pendingTransactions
```

The mining command should be executed again in the node console to ensure the transaction is properly packaged.

```
miner.start(); admin.sleepBlocks(1); miner.stop();
```

Once the mining process is completed, the contract is deployed on the blockchain. Readers can check Remix and the node console for obtaining output information. Let us proceed with testing the functionality of the contract by expanding it in Remix and invoking *NewShare('Hello, World!')*. This will initiate a transaction that calls upon the contract.

After sending the transaction and before packaging it into a block, invoke the *getLength* function in the Remix compiler and inspect the packaged transaction in the node console. It will be evident that there is no alteration in the contract's state prior to including the called contract transaction within a block.

Execute the following command again to generate blocks.

```
miner.start(); admin.sleepBlocks(1); miner.stop();
```

Once the block is packaged, the contract status can be observed in Remix, and the corresponding transaction information is displayed both in Remix and the node console, indicating a successful invocation of the contract function.

In the development of DApps, after deploying the smart contract on the blockchain, it is essential to construct a graphical user interface (GUI) for user interaction. Notably, numerous popular DApps employ a combination of lightweight wallets and third-party nodes. This approach eliminates the need for users to operate their own Ethereum nodes; they only require possession of their wallet's private key and can utilize the DApp through a browser-based light wallet (or a browser extension like MetaMask). Although this significantly lowers the barrier to adopting blockchain applications, it also introduces certain centralization concerns due to users' lack of personal blockchain node operation.

9.5 Smart Contract Security Detection

In the preceding section, we demonstrated the deployment process of a basic smart contract. Due to their management of high-value tokens and possession of immutability and other characteristics, smart contracts have encountered numerous security threats in recent years. Consequently, extensive research on smart contract security has emerged, with particular emphasis on detecting vulnerabilities within these contracts. Several prominent projects focused on identifying smart contract vulnerabilities include Smartcheck (Tikhomirov et al. 2018, pp. 9–16), Oyente (Luu et al. 2016, pp. 254–269), MAIAN (Nikolić et al. 2018, pp. 653–663), Manticore (Mossberg et al. 2019, pp. 1186–1189), and Mythril (Mueller 2018, p. 54).

This section mainly introduces Smartcheck in consideration of its remarkable efficiency. Smartcheck is a static analysis tool designed for Ethereum smart contracts, which performs syntax and lexical analysis on the contract source code. It utilizes a parser combined with Solidity syntax to generate an intermediate representation in the form of a parse tree. Security attributes are then matched against this representation through queries. By fully translating the target source code into an intermediate representation and enabling matching of all elements, Smartcheck achieves comprehensive code coverage. Leveraging static program analysis technology, it exhibits high detection accuracy in identifying various vulnerabilities.

```
管理员: Windows PowerShell
(node:764) Warning: Accessing non-existent property 'which' of module exports inside circular dependency
E:\test\Cr2.sol
jar:file:/C:/Users/71980/AppData/Roaming/npm/node_modules/@smartdec/smartcheck/jdeploy-bundle/smartcheck-2.0-jar-with-de
pendencies.jar!/solidity-rules.xmlline 3:18 mismatched input '=' expecting '=>'
line 3:27 extraneous input ')' expecting {'solidity', 'experimental', 'from', 'constructor', 'block', 'coinbase', 'diffi
culty', 'gaslimit', 'number', 'timestamp', 'blockhash', 'msg', 'data', 'gas', 'sender', 'sig', 'value', 'now', 'this', '
tx', 'origin', 'gasprice', 'public', 'internal', 'external', 'private', 'constant', 'length', 'balance', 'emit', '_', 'r
evert', Identifier}
ruleId: SOLIDITY_CALL_WITHOUT_DATA
patternId: om991k
severity: 2
line: 5
column: 20
content: call.value(balances[msg.sender])()

ruleId: SOLIDITY_UPGRADE_TO_050
patternId: 83k1no
severity: 1
line: 5
column: 20
content: call.value(balances[msg.sender])()

ruleId: SOLIDITY_VISIBILITY
patternId: b51ce0
severity: 1
line: 3
column: 0
content: mapping(address=><missing ';'>
```

Figure 9.13 Example usage of the Smartcheck tool.

The following will present the procedural steps for utilizing Smartcheck.

Step 1: Install Smartcheck by utilizing the NPM package and execute the subsequent command with administrative privileges.

```
npm install @smartdec/smartcheck -g
```

Step 2: Start the analysis. Execute the subsequent command:

```
smartcheck -p
```

The -p parameter is used to specify the solidity contract file to be analyzed, while the optional -r parameter allows for specifying the Smartcheck analysis rules. By default, it utilizes the built-in rules files.

The output will be displayed as shown in Figure 9.13 if the above two steps are executed successfully.

9.6 Chapter Summary

This chapter presents a comprehensive guide to comprehending and implementing a large-scale consortium blockchain. Starting from the physical layer, it covers various aspects such as the network topology establishment, P2P protocol implementation, system construction, smart contract deployment, and security detection. Consequently, it enables the development of efficient and secure consortium blockchain applications that cater to diverse industries and fields.

Discussion Questions

9.1 Please briefly describe the performance metrics in the P2P broadcast protocol.

A: The key metrics are convergence time and network load. Convergence time is the duration from when a message first starts propagating to when it is fully disseminated across the distributed system. Network load refers to the number of network packets sent by each node during this propagation process.

9.2 Please briefly describe the similarities and differences between event log and state tree in Solidity.

A: Both event log and state tree serve as storage spaces for smart contracts' outputs. However, the event log is a unidirectional output that cannot be read, resulting in its operation being priced at a lower Gas cost. Similarly, the state and receipt themselves are not entirely recorded in the block but undergo changes through blockchain transactions, with only the root value and Bloom filter value being recorded in the block.

9.3 Please describe the steps to develop a DApp.

A: The first step involves establishing the blockchain environment, followed by deploying the smart contract onto the established blockchain, and ultimately constructing a user-friendly graphical interface, such as web interaction, to facilitate invoking the smart contract.

References

Androulaki, E., Barger, A., Bortnikov, V., Cachin, C., Christidis, K., De Caro, A., Enyeart, D., Ferris, C., Laventman, G., Manevich, Y. and Muralidharan, S., 2018, April. Hyperledger fabric: A distributed operating system for permissioned blockchains. In Proceedings of the Thirteenth EuroSys Conference (pp. 1–15).

Boettiger, C., 2015. An introduction to Docker for reproducible research. *ACM SIGOPS Operating Systems Review*, 49(1), pp. 71–79.

Jakma, P. and Lamparter, D. (2014) Introduction to the quagga routing suite. *IEEE Network*, 28(2), pp. 42–48.

Luu, L., Chu, D.H., Olickel, H., Saxena, P. and Hobor, A., 2016, October. Making smart contracts smarter. In Proceedings of the 2016 ACM SIGSAC Conference on Computer and Communications Security (pp. 254–269).

Merkel, D., 2014. Docker: Lightweight linux containers for consistent development and deployment. *Linux Journal*, 239(2), p. 2.

Mossberg, M., Manzano, F., Hennenfent, E., Groce, A., Grieco, G., Feist, J., Brunson, T. and Dinaburg, A., 2019, November. Manticore: A user-friendly symbolic execution framework for binaries and smart contracts. In 2019 34th IEEE/ACM International Conference on Automated Software Engineering (ASE) (pp. 1186–1189). IEEE.

Moy, J.T., 1998. *OSPF: Anatomy of an Internet routing protocol.* Addison-Wesley Professional.

Mueller, B., 2018. Smashing ethereum smart contracts for fun and real profit. *HITB SECCONF Amsterdam*, 9, p. 54.

Nikolić, I., Kolluri, A., Sergey, I., Saxena, P. and Hobor, A., 2018, December. Finding the greedy, prodigal, and suicidal contracts at scale. In Proceedings of the 34th Annual Computer Security Applications Conference (pp. 653–663).

Tikhomirov, S., Voskresenskaya, E., Ivanitskiy, I., Takhaviev, R., Marchenko, E. and Alexandrov, Y., 2018, May. Smartcheck: Static analysis of ethereum smart contracts. In Proceedings of the 1st International Workshop on Emerging Trends in Software Engineering for Blockchain (pp. 9–16).

Weaveworks, n.d. Introducing weave net. https://www.weave.works/docs/net/latest/overview/

Index

Principles and Applications of Blockchain Systems: How to Overcome the CAP Trilemma in Consortium Blockchain, First Edition. Hui Li and Han Wang.

Published 2025 by John Wiley & Sons, Inc.

o

p

q

www.ingramcontent.com/pod-product-compliance
Lightning Source LLC
Jackson TN
JSHW011918310125
78069JS00001B/87
9781394237227